Gun Digest® PRESENTS



# GUNSMITHING THE 1911

## THE BENCH MANUAL

BY
PATRICK
SWEENEY

CAUTION: Technical data presented here, particularly technical data on handloading and on firearms adjustment and alteration, inevitably reflects individual experience with particular equipment and components under specific circumstances the reader cannot duplicate exactly. Such data presentations therefore should be used for guidance only and with caution. Caribou Media accepts no responsibility for results obtained using these data.

Published by

Gun Digest® Books, an imprint of Caribou Media Group, LLC
Gun Digest Media
5583 W. Waterford Ln., Suite D
Appleton, WI 54913
gundigest.com

To order books or other products visit us online at gundigeststore.com
For questions email customer service at info@gundigest.com

ISBN-13: 978-1-959265-13-9

Edited by Corey Graff
Cover Design by Gene Coo
Interior Design by Jon Stein

Printed in the United States of America

10 9 8 7 6 5 4 3 2

# DEDICATION

I dedicate this book to all those who have used the 1911 to maintain our freedom and security—men and women in the military and law enforcement, and those citizens who have used one in defense of self or others.

I'd also like to thank the gunsmiths who have been so kind in answering questions, sending photos, and generally just being nice guys when it came to giving up some of their time to help. Ned Christiansen, Jess Christiansen, Stan Chen, Jason Burton, and Irv Stone III of Bar-Sto have all been veritable gushers of info. Thanks guys.

And, of course, Felicia. And our three poodles. Yes, we're back up to three.

Last but not least, you the reader. Without your continued interest, I'd be doing something else. I don't know what, but it probably wouldn't be as much fun.

# TABLE OF CONTENTS

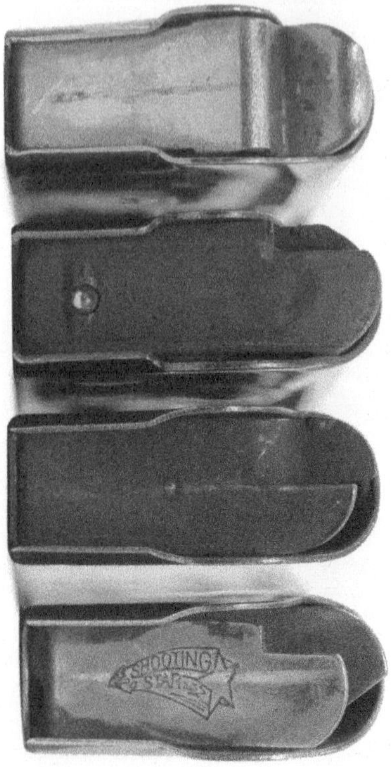

38 SUPER



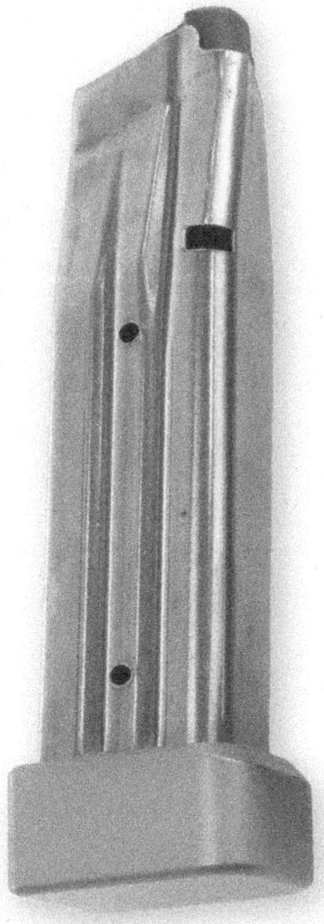

# INTRODUCTION

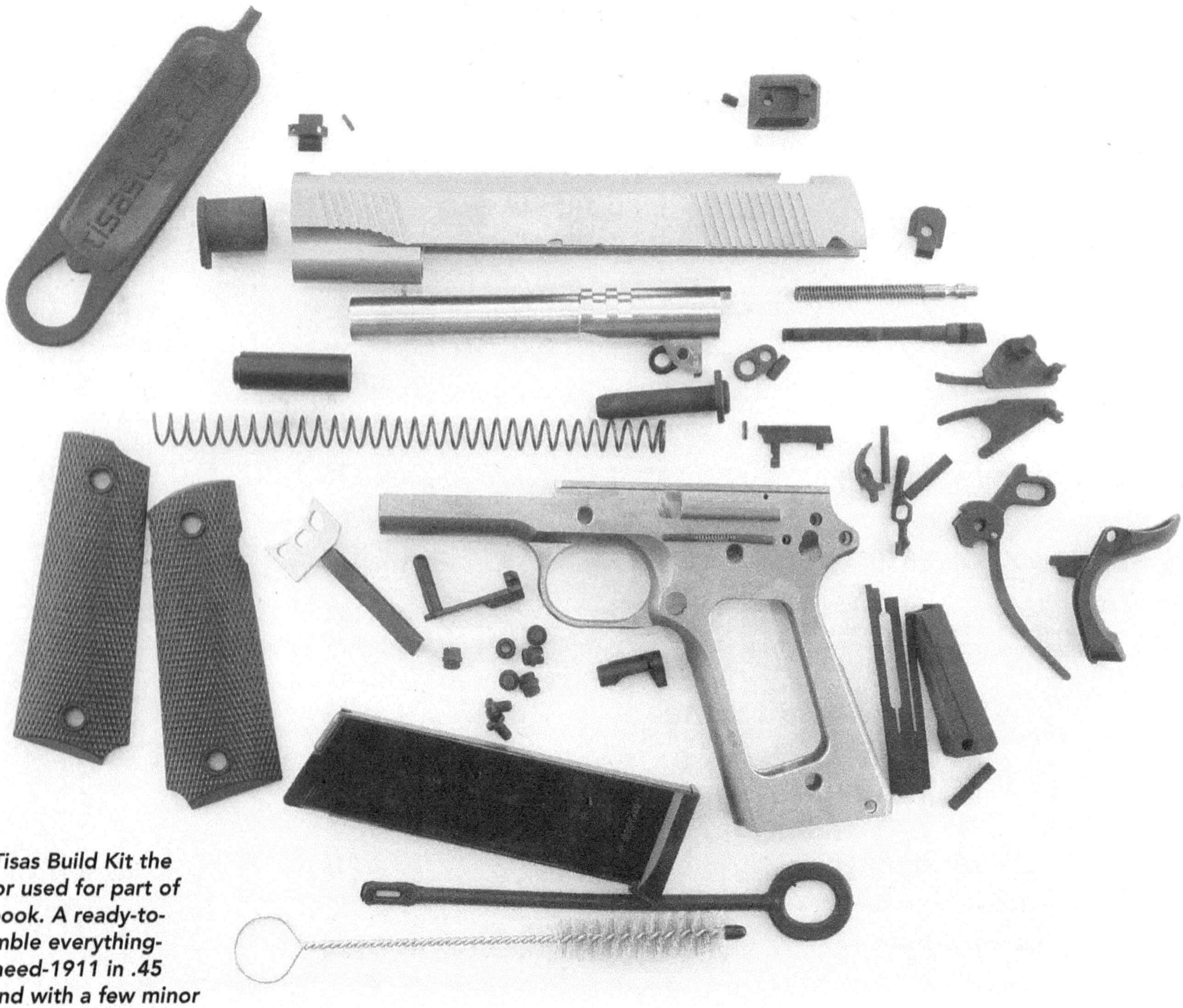

*The Tisas Build Kit the author used for part of the book. A ready-to-assemble everything-you-need-1911 in .45 kit, and with a few minor fitting details, it all went together with no fuss.*

## WELCOME TO THE CLUB.

Why a book about gunsmithing the 1911? Simple: Time. Many new gun owners have purchased a handgun for defense, competition, sport or "just because." But most have only ever seen a 1911 in video games or at the counter of the local gun shop when they bought their pistol—most likely a plastic-framed, striker-fired, hi-cap pistol. It has now been more than an entire generation since the 1911 was ascendant, the exemplar to which all other pistols were compared. Once-common 1911 knowledge is now known pretty much just in the heads of the old-timers. Rather than let it fade to be rediscovered (a painful, expensive, and time-consuming process), I wanted to document it here. Well, as much as can be jotted down in one volume that isn't a doctoral thesis. Other books are deeply technical, but this isn't one. I'm looking to give you, the new or relatively new 1911 owner, a roadmap for improving, maintaining, and upgrading your pistol when needed. Many intermediate 1911 shooters will benefit as well.

*Today's out-of-the-box 1911 can shoot as well as some of the custom-built ones of the early era of IPSC. This Savage (yes, Savage!) shot these 25-yard groups.*

A cursory online search will leave you awash in 1911 memes. That's probably because most of them are true. Look at it this way: developed in the first decade of the 20th century and adopted in (oh, is it *that* obvious?) 1911, the pistol we're covering here is made in an essentially unchanged form to this day. Yes, better alloys, tighter dimensions, and extra features adorn contemporary models. Still, someone who spent a weekend with the new Army pistol in 1912 could easily use one produced today. They'd be amazed at two-handed shooting and the speed at which we can shoot these days, and reloads, oh man, reloads. But it would all be clear, obvious and accessible. That person, even if they were a mechanical genius of the time and adapted to the then-new-fangled automobiles of 1912, could not even get into a vehicle today, let alone start it and drive off in it.

The 1911 has a reputation for being hard-recoiling, unreliable, and inaccurate. All bunk, although some would have had a small kernel of truth back in the Neolithic era. Yes, the .45 does recoil, but don't tell the top female shooters that because they are managing .45 or 40s at Major, even though some are barely five feet tall. Complain about recoil at your peril. There was a time when the 1911 might have been considered unreliable, but that time has passed. Now, the best (and even the merely good) are as reliable out of the box as any industrial product. Regarding accuracy, the era of CNC manufacturing has made everything more precise. Heck, today's low-cost bolt-action hunting rifle shoots as well or better than the tuned sniper rifles of a generation ago. Today's 1911 is a superior product to those of yesteryear.

And it is also highly valued. Let's take a first-year production Glock and put it on the counter at the local gun shop as a test: Ho-hum, another Glock. Now, take a WWII-production USGI 1911A1 and put it on the counter. Even the Glock owner will drift over and try to look casual while drooling. Let me put it this way: in 2054, no one will open the door to a barn someplace in the countryside and get excited: "Oh joy, a 2004 Honda Civic." (Or: Kia, Subaru, Hyundai, etc.) But open a barn today and discover a 1971 Chevy Camaro ... Ford Mustang ... or Plymouth Roadrunner. Oh my, the cries of glee.

So, welcome to *Gunsmithing the 1911: The Bench Manual*—a guide and tutorial on selecting, maintaining, upgrading, and assessing your 1911 and analyzing any shortcomings. This is a light gunsmithing book but not a detailed step-by-step guide. Once you have read this book, you still won't be able to hang out your pistolsmithing shingle. Even having read this book and worked on your 1911s, you probably won't be up to running a custom shop dedicated to the type. Heck, owning a whole bookshelf full of home DIY electrical system books isn't enough to prep you for the certification test to be a licensed electrician; why expect one book on 1911s to do so?

*Recoil? When a woman who is just over five feet tall handles a 1911 loaded to Major, you have to be careful when complaining about recoil.*

But what you will have is all the info you will need to look over, buy, test, upgrade, diagnose and maintain your 1911, and keep it running for decades to come.

OK, fair warning: if you want to buy a box o' parts and assemble the 1911 of your dreams from it, you will likely need more than this book. Starting from that point is *not* like building an AR-15. While many 1911 parts will be "assemble and run," others are not. The AR-15 has the mil-spec standards, and while there are variances, most rifle and accessory makers have hewed as closely as they can to the standards. The Glock fans here will jump in and say, "Look, the 1911 needs a pistolsmith to keep it running, and the Glock doesn't. Score for perfection." Well, yes and no.

You can own a vanilla-plain 1911 or a top-end custom one, and you are still a 1911 owner. It used to be an exclusive club, but that has changed despite the 9mm pistol ownership surge. One thing that attracts people to the 1911 is the option to improve or enhance it, like this slide serration work Jason Burton has done. Try that with a Glock. Photo: Jason Burton

Glocks have been built now (and we'll be doing a fair amount of "comparison to other guns" in this book) for over half a century. For the first 30+ years of that, there were no Glock clones. There were but one or two factories making Glocks, both under the direct control of Glock. There are now many Glock clones, but they are also being made entirely in the era of CNC manufacturing. The 1911 is an industrial product that predates numerical control manufacturing and is produced in dozens, if not hundreds, of factories around the world. It has been for over a century. Not to pick on them, but do you think the Turks (who make excellent 1911s, by the way) care whether their extractors are a drop-in-fit to an Ed Brown? Or a Springfield Armory? A Les Baer? A Wilson Combat, made under the direction of Bill Wilson, who essentially started the custom 1911 parts market? No. Another example: when the Argentines adopted the 1911, they used Colt machinery under the supervision of Colt employees. Once the Colt employees left, do you think the Argentine military cared that their production be interchangeable with Colt's? Really? As long as the Turkish (or others) extractors work in their pistols, they are happy. And the makers of extractors-as-parts know this and produce them slightly oversized, so you can fit them to any 1911 you own. (And you *will* have to fit them.)

Ditto with barrels, bushings, and a host of other parts. Grips will be as close to a standard as everyone can make them because doing so is dead simple, and there is no advantage to allowing the grip screw bushing locations to "drift" in production.

Now, take your Glock, buy a "drop-in" trigger set, and tell me you didn't have to wrestle, force, fit, or otherwise tune something to install it and make it work. Liar.

Oh, and it would be good to mention Rule One of gunsmithing, which all gunsmiths consider when facing a task: When something must be filed, modified, or altered, you work on the least expensive or most readily replaced part. An example would be a rear sight. If the new sight doesn't fit, you don't file the slide dovetail. You file the new sight. If you screw up the sight, it is as little as $40. A new slide? Or to repair the existing one? A vanilla-plain slide from Caspian starts at $260. A repair, correctly done, will run you half that.

While reading this book, you will see photographs of dozens of 1911s in process, examples of how something should and shouldn't be done. I'll use a Tisas Home Builder Kit as a base model, a box o' parts 1911 that you can purchase and assemble yourself. I'll also be using, for one detail or another, one of the 1911s I own or photos of a sample pistol or one I tested last week or two decades ago. You will not see the same pistol over and over. I have also reached out to custom 1911 'smiths for photo samples of projects or processes of my past work.

Some will complain that the 1911 doesn't have the service life of other pistols. Again, Glock. OK, what's your sample? I know personally of a bunch of people who have 1911s with 100,000+ rounds through them. (I've got a couple, myself.) Some with multiples of that. Oh yes, they had to replace minor parts. Geez, every vehicle I've ever known required oil changes, tires, and various other parts replaced, all as part of regular service. Things wear and must be replaced. Anyone who tells you, "My Glock/Sig/M&P/CZ has had 50,000 rounds through it, and I haven't even changed the recoil spring," is abusing their pistol, not using it.

One of the details you must grasp about a Browning design is that the parts and the things they do are interrelated. For example, the firing pin retaining plate does more than keep the firing pin in place. It retains and fixes the extractor in place, influences felt recoil and cyclic rate and is a consumable and easily replaceable part that takes the wear so that other more expensive parts won't. So, I'll explain what the parts are, what they do, and how they work, then how to see if they are properly installed or fitted. Finally, how to replace them if broken, lost, worn or installed improperly. Finally, for those who want it, I'll do a deep technical dive (not all subjects will call for it) and satisfy the readers who can't get enough of the techno-info.

At times, we'll veer into pistolsmithing details with a general or brief how-to, simply so you can get a sense of what is involved in a particular repair. It is all quick and easy to say (as many a gunsmith has heard), "All you've got to do is…." But often, "all" isn't easy. Or simple. Or it requires skills or practice or both.

I will also be pretty casual about referring to the book's subject. I will not type "1911" when discussing a part of this pistol. I'll refer to it as "pistol," "gun," even "blaster" because I write the way I speak, and I do not (nor does anyone I know) always refer to it as the "1911." I'll be clear when discussing some other pistol, but when it is generic or seems to be, it will always be the 1911 in this book.

***Regarding accuracy, the 1911 is the benchmark against which all other pistols are measured. This Nighthawk Firehawk sets a mighty high bar.***

Much of this info used to be common knowledge, but that time has passed. The knowledge faded, and much of it had to be relearned through testing and experimentation, historical inquiry, and even destructive testing. How common was the knowledge? During WWII, a manufacturing industry magazine published an article describing the manufacturing process of the 1911 and even listed which alloy each part was made of. Yes, they denoted the specific alloy of each part, even if they didn't do a deep dive into the heat-treatment process it underwent. Hey, it wasn't like the Germans would steal the info and start making their own.

Where relevant, I'll give you that and other info if I've uncovered it.

But, post-war (WWII), that info faded, partly because the police establishment, long enamored of revolvers, went all-in on .38 Special revolvers and because the only place 1911s got used was in Bullseye competition. But that's part of the history chapter, so without further ado, let's get to it. ●

CHAPTER

1

# A BRIEF HISTORY OF THE 1911

When the late physicist Stephen Hawking was working on his book, *A Brief History of Time*, his publisher told him that each equation he used would cut the book sales in half. He rolled the dice and risked it, including just one equation. The book was a success, and when it came time to update it to a second edition, he included a second equation. I'm no Hawking, but I will resist putting in equations unless necessary. And I'll try to be brief.

You may hear 1911 fans talk about "Saint John" or "The Mormon Genius." The period we're looking at here is the last decade of the $19^{th}$ century. Smokeless powder was still new but was around long enough that gunmakers were now comfortable with it. A self-loading pistol would be the hot new property to make some lucky somebody rich. The bolt-action rifle had been perfected (several times, in fact). While the double-action revolver was a good thing, Smith & Wesson had revealed in 1898 the frame that would become the K-Frame and the .38 Special to go with it—a self-loading pistol would be a real money-maker.

The only problem was design. And the designers of the age were stuck in the "receiver and breechblock" paradigm. The exemplar here would be the Luger, which was a receiver with a barrel screwed into it, just like rifles, and used a breechblock that cycled inside of the receiver. Another was the Mauser Broomhandle, the C96. Again, a barrel in a receiver and a cyclical breechblock. The difference is that the Luger breechblock locks itself, and the C96 locks to the lower frame.

Along came John Moses Browning. He had been designing rifles and shotguns for Winchester for fifteen years, and his latest was a self-loading shotgun. He wanted to make some real money with this one and spurned the customary process of a flat fee from Winchester for the design. He wanted royalties, a piece of the action. Winchester declined (one of the stupidest decisions ever made in the history of, well, history), so Browning headed off to Belgium, after several other problems, for a meeting with the new firm of Fabrique Nationale. Having fulfilled its Belgian Army rifle contract, FN needed new products and customers. Browning arranged for them to make his shotgun, which he would purchase for export to the U.S. and which FN could manufacture and sell in Europe.

*The FN1900 is the pistol that saved Fabrique Nationale from bankruptcy and established John Moses Browning as a pistol and rifle designer. He even developed the cartridge for it, the .32 Auto. No design aspect of this pistol made it into the 1911.*

Browning also had a self-loading pistol design, the FN1900, which FN executives fell all over themselves to acquire. Browning had been working on it for a while, and it was a transitional design—a kinda-sorta receiver-and-breech system. The barrel was screwed into the frame, but the breech looked like a slide, and it was blowback, so there was no need to lock the mechanism. It was chambered in a new cartridge, the .32 ACP, which Browning designed for the pistol. It was flat, compact, lightweight, reliable, and accurate, and, in 1900, no one sneered at the .32 as a defensive cartridge. It sold like hotcakes. FN made and sold a million of them in the next twelve years. The sales of the FN1900 slowed down mainly because Browning himself came up with better designs in short order.

But, the 1900 was already an obsolete design even before the first

one left the Liege factory. Browning was also working with Colt, for which he had designed a new approach to pistol mechanisms: the slide enclosing a barrel and the slide and barrel lock to each other, not to the frame or receiver. The Colt 1900 (yes, two Browning pistols, each called the 1900 by two different manufacturers, in different calibers. Browning was a busy and prolific designer.)

***Everyone got into the act when it came time to tool up for World War II. It was patriotic to shoulder part of the war effort, and Union Switch & Signal did a contract run of 1911A1s. They are now rarities of the first order, as Union only made 55,000.***

The Colt 1900 and its successors appear odd to us. Browning had ideas about what worked, but the end-users had their own. Things like a safety that was the rear sight and had to be pushed to permit firing didn't go over well. And that brings us to the reason for many of the details on the 1911 that we see today: the U.S. Cavalry. The Cavalry was the premier arm of land militaries in all armies of the period. They were the paratroopers, special ops, SEALs, Rangers and LRRPs of their day, all rolled into one. And they used pistols. Oh, they had rifles, but a pistol and a saber (or *sabre*) were the classic arms of a cavalryman. And while the Colt 1900 showed significant promise, there were things about it that they did not like.

First, the cartridge. In 1900, the .38 Auto was a hot number. A 130-grain bullet at 1,100 fps was plenty good enough for people, but cavalry had to stop horses. So, it had to be a .45, or they would not buy it. Second, many functions of the Colt 1900 required two-handed operation. So Browning, in the next decade, would change, alter, re-design, and ditch whatever he must to use a .45 cartridge (and stand up to hard use and long service life) and make it as much as possible a one-handed pistol. That's why all of the controls on a 1911 pistol can be managed with one hand, your firing hand. Safety on and off, magazine drop, slide release, they take one hand. To load it took two, but hey, there were limits even for Browning.

He did all this design work at a time when the average man stood five feet eight inches tall, and the word "ergonomic" hadn't been coined, yet he was a master of ergonomics. And, like the FN1900, the resulting 1911 was flat, powerful, accurate, reliable, durable, and sold like hotcakes.

Much like the original 1900, the first 1911 had some design quirks.

Bill Laughridge, owner of Cylinder & Slide, went to the trouble in the early 21st century of recreating the exact design of the first-production 1911, in the details before the various changes were made, as a centennial model. He tracked down as many un-molested original pistols as possible from the first production run and made exact replicas. These were beautiful pistols, pistols that were maddening in some regards. I tested one, and he asked me not to take the magazine catch assembly apart. "No one has ever managed to take one apart and reassemble it without scratching the finish," he said. And a beautiful, mirror-finish blue job it was, I might add, so I did not take it apart.

One aspect of Browning's design genius is that the grips aside, the 1911 is not held together by screws, pins, or other fasteners. Instead, he used interlocking assemblies, which lock each other into a mechanism and require a specific sequence to assemble or disassemble. That's part of what we'll be covering in this book.

With the manufacturing, assembly, and maintenance details taken care of, we entered World War I, and Colt made as many 1911 pistols as possible. Springfield Armory (the government arsenal, not the later company) also produced pistols. Post-war, the Army wanted changes based on feedback and use in The Great War. Those changes resulted in the 1911A1, which included larger sights (still minuscule by today's standards), a grip safety tang and hammer spur combo that didn't bite, and an arched mainspring housing.

Leading up to WWII, the government actually had some foresight and engaged the services of a few companies to let them learn how to make 1911A1s "just in case." Just in case quickly turned into "make them now, as many as you can" and they made millions.

One detail about the 1911 that might interest Glock fans is that parts interchangeability was paramount to the companies producing 1911A1s for the WWII effort. Government inspectors would look over pistols as they were being made to ensure quality. Each lot of 5,000 handguns had a certain number test-fired to more than the "magazine's worth of ammo to make sure it works" level. One in each lot was fired a whole lot more than that, and

***Even the Singer Sewing Machine Company got into the act in WWII, doing a test run of 1911A1s, all 500 of them. Finding one of these is like getting a winning lottery ticket.***

if it failed, the entire lot would be rejected, reworked, and tested again. And, at regular intervals, representatives of each company would meet and bring a box of regular production pistols with them. They would each disassemble a pistol and toss all the parts from each manufacturer's pistol into bins. Then, the handguns would be assembled by those present, who grabbed a random part from the bin until the samples were all back together again. The resulting pistols would be inspected and test-fired. If a pistol failed, an immediate analysis would determine which part was the problem, who made it, and the problem corrected.

Once the war ended, and we had more 1911A1s than we'd need for decades, all the institutional knowledge vanished. The Army immediately started looking for a replacement, which would not be concluded for over 40 years. (And this would not be the only time it would take decades to replace something. The Army is still looking for a replacement for the Browning .50 machine gun, which first saw service in 1921. My prediction is that it never will.)

During the 1950s and '60s, the only place the 1911A1 saw use (well, in the holsters of GIs and Marines, but pistols in military service are way down on the list of essential items, except to the people who are getting shot at) was in Bullseye competition. As a general rule, if a tool is used in one environment for one purpose, it will be gradually or not-so-gradually modified by the users until it is suited only to that use. A Bullseye 1911, while accurate, wasn't useful elsewhere. And with no other design driver, the choices were USGI, box-stock as it were, or a 1911/1911A1 set up for Bullseye. Then, the IPSC (International Practical Shooting Confederation) came along. The idea that a pistol, especially a 1911, could be both accurate and reliable was new to many. But it could be built that way. You might snicker, but in the early days of IPSC competition, the standard of reliability we strove for was no more than one malfunction per thousand rounds fired. Part of the learning process was the pistol, part the magazine, and part the ammunition, but we could exceed that level with work. And at that level of reliability, the 1911 delivered Bullseye-level accuracy.

A brief aside: it is now common for 1911s to be far better than that old-school "one *malf* (malfunction) in a thousand" reliability standard. These days, you might never see a 1911-induced malfunction shooting a current-production pistol. And it is typical for them to be quite accurate. Les Baer guarantees his pistols will shoot no larger than 3 inches at 50 yards, and you can pay a bit extra to get 1.5 inches at 50 yards accuracy.

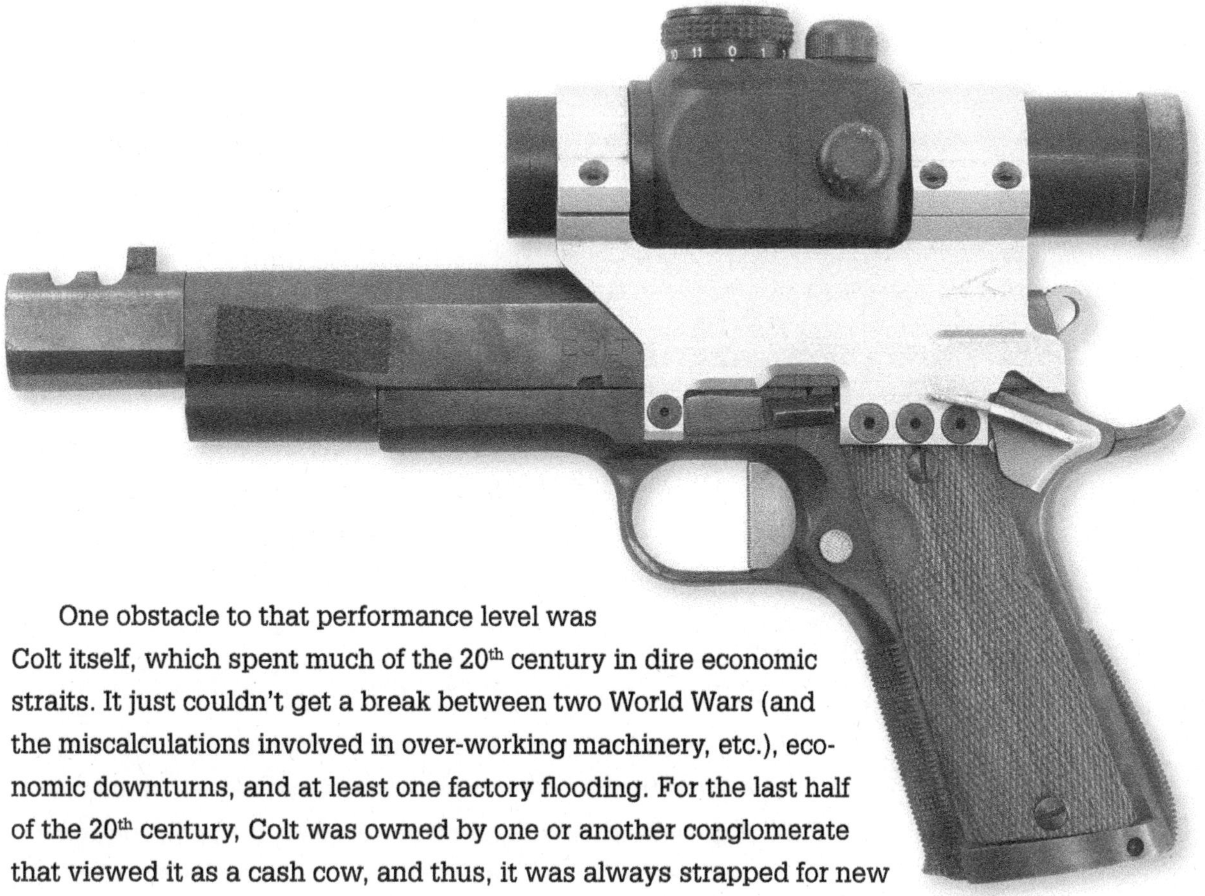

One obstacle to that performance level was Colt itself, which spent much of the 20th century in dire economic straits. It just couldn't get a break between two World Wars (and the miscalculations involved in over-working machinery, etc.), economic downturns, and at least one factory flooding. For the last half of the 20th century, Colt was owned by one or another conglomerate that viewed it as a cash cow, and thus, it was always strapped for new machines, designs, and labor. My Colt Series 70 is an example. In 1981, I attended the Targetworld National Championships. In those early years, IPSC was like drag racing, and if your match could get enough people from enough states, you'd call it a national championship. By looking over the sign-up sheet and seeing who was where (the list of top shooters was small enough that we all knew each other, not that I was a "top shooter" in 1981), I managed to place high enough as a Pro shooter to win a gun. That prize of a new-in-the-box Colt Series 70 was magnificent. And it was unreliable. One in a thousand? It wouldn't go a full magazine without a malfunction. And it wouldn't "malf" the same way twice in a row. In desperation, I learned gunsmithing to make my pistol work properly. And that was the case for all of us back then. By the early 1980s, the 1911s to build on were GI-standard surplus 1911/1911A1s or Colts. Both needed work to be competitive; they just needed different kinds of work.

*The evolution of the IPSC gun happened so fast at times that it was hard to keep up. In the fall of 1989, this was a top-end competition gun without the optics. A year later, even with the optic, it was obsolete for winning matches.*

And that is the source of the urban myths—myths now, back then, truths—about the 1911 that "It needs a gunsmith to be reliable" or "You can have reliability or accuracy, but not both." Today, no one makes an unreliable 1911 simply because they would be out of business quickly if they did.

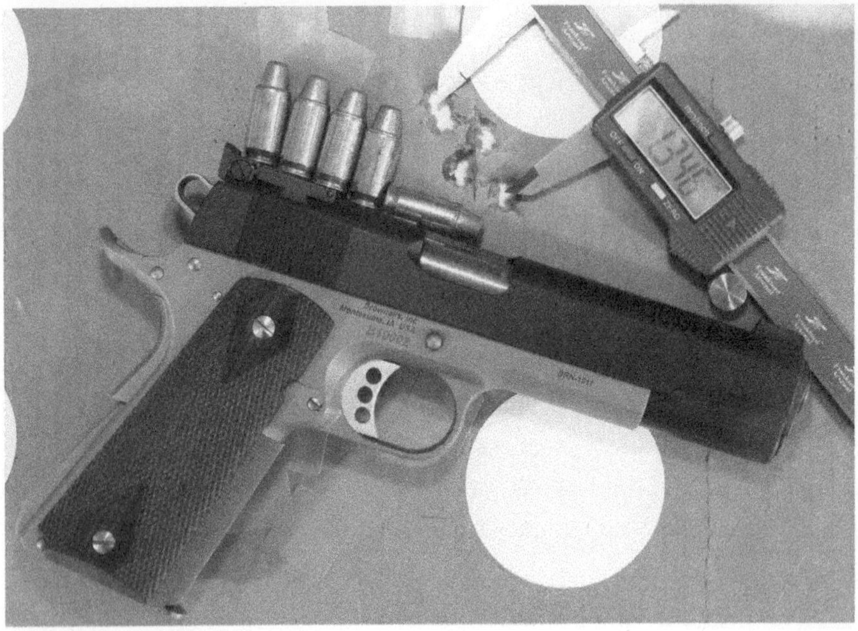

This is the kind of accuracy you could expect from an IPSC gun of the 1980s (and this is a Brownell's recreation of the same) when fed the classic IPSC load of a 200-grain L-SWC and 5.8 grains of WWS-231. This was a limited run, so don't look for it in Brownell's catalog.

Into the 1980s, the standard 1911 for IPSC was a 5-inch .45 ACP. And the Power Factor for Major was 185. (For example, a 230-grain round nose going 805 fps is now called a +P load.) But two competitors, Robbie Leatham and Brian Enos, changed that. Just as we were all learning about the advantages of a "comp," a compensator, they also switched to .38 Super. Comps work by re-directing muzzle gases. The Super runs at a higher pressure, and higher pressure gases are better than lower for comps. In short order, we had all switched over to .38 Supers; then they got red-dot optics, and then a few years later, we swapped our single-stack red-dot guns for hi-cap Supers with red-dots. By 1995, you were uncompetitive if you were not running a red-dot hi-cap Super with 28-round magazines. And the howls of "not real-world" were deafening. (I can't help but look around now at hi-cap, comped 9mm pistols for everyday carry, with slide-mounted red dots, and smile a little.)

The early 1990s saw a new 1911 design with a plastic grip and a steel rail section made by STI. Now, it is named Staccato, and there are other makers of the same approach, from overseas and here in the U.S. by Springfield Armory.

Look around you today and see how many shooters carrying a pistol for defense (and law enforcement agencies) have a red-dot optic on a 9mm holding at least 17 rounds, and with some straight from the factory compensated, and consider again the guy in your gun club who says "competition isn't real" and "IPSC will get you killed." No, competition pushes the boundaries. Determining if the changes benefit you in a defensive role is up to you.

Simultaneously, the equipment categories in IPSC (by then, the USPSA or the United States Practical Shooting Association) fragmented. The origins of "run what you brung" had proven what won, but not everyone wanted to be shooting a Super. So, competition added equipment divisions. And there, the .40 S&W proved to be—for various, arcane reasons—the alternative to the Super in some divisions. The

Production Division allowed 9mm pistols to compete and grow until IPSC/USPSA, the home of the .45 1911, had most competitors shooting a 9mm pistol that wasn't a 1911. Such is life.

In the mid-1980s, Springfield Armory saved us from Colt by offering 1911A1s. At first, they were parts kits, everything you needed to assemble a 1911A1 in the box, but no tools, assembly required, or batteries were included. I won a bunch, bought them, and built them. Springfield Armory then offered assembled pistols and sponsored competitions. Other companies entered the competition field and offered their guns, gear and equipment—so much so that you could shoot in a local club's annual championship and win a Springfield. If you practiced and were good, you could win enough loot to build a better gun, load enough ammo to get better, and then really get a leg up on the competition.

*After the 1911 and A1 were issued, they were everywhere. Here, Private Stack of 9 Commando, at Anzio, is all set with his.*

As did Colt and Smith & Wesson, Springfield sponsored a team, and smaller, specialized companies would sponsor individual shooters. The era of the professional practical shooter was born. The top shooters could travel the circuit, compete, win, get paid, and, on the side, be paid to teach other shooters. Of course, this was a gypsy life, spending most of the year on the road, and divorces and near-divorces were common.

By the mid-to-late 1980s, it looked like the days of the 1911 were over. Oh, it would still maintain a presence in Bullseye, at least as long as those using it were still competing. But the 1980s saw the rise of the "Wonder-nine" high-capacity 9mm pistols with a double-action firing mechanism and holding many rounds. A Browning Hi Power didn't much threaten a 1911 with 7+1 of .45 ACP with 13+1 rounds of 9mm. But a G17 with 17+1? An S&W M59, a Sig P226, a Beretta 92, and more to come? With the adoption of the M9 for military use and police acceptance of 9mms, ammo makers were turning to make hollowpoints that actually expanded.

The 1911's days were numbered. But they were saved by, of all people, Bill Clinton. The Assault Weapons Ban of 1994 vilified some features of the AR-15 and made magazines of over 10 rounds verboten. This did two things: First, tell Americans they can't have something and many will ask, "Where can I buy one?" By the time the ban expired 10 years later, there were markedly more AR-15 manufacturers than before.

And in the pistolverse, people rightly figured, "If I can only have

The price of USGI 1911s has gotten so high that 1911 makers are now producing GI clones. This Rock Island Armory only needs some USGI plastic grips to be a close enough copy that you'd have to look at the slide to see the difference.

10 rounds, I want 10 big ones, not smaller ones." A G17 with a 10-round magazine was just stupid. And at the height of all this, Glock 17-round magazines were offered for as high as $150 per. (No, I'm not kidding or making it up. I don't know if any sold, but that was the asking price.) The sales of 1911s jumped.

At the beginning of the 21st century, Kimber decided (after various business changes) to get into the 1911 market. But, rather than make stock guns—as Springfield had when it entered—Kimber went semi-custom. It could exploit modern manufacturing techniques and build a 1911 with mid-level custom details as a production item and sell for less than you'd pay a custom pistolsmith to upgrade your box-stock pistol. Similarly, the Dan Wesson company jumped in and offered semi-custom features on production guns. Rock Island Arsenal brought parts and pistols from the Philippines, and its catalog is full of options. The newest entrants are the Turkish makers, such as Tisas, which make custom-featured 1911s at excellent prices compared to what we paid for those as extras "back in the day."

Now, a couple of decades later, if you want a USGI-level pistol, you must hunt down that variant in a catalog of 1911s because everything else is now semi-custom or higher-featured. Of course, at the moment, the CMP (Civilian Marksmanship Program) is selling off the 1911s and 1911A1s it has, so if you get lucky and score one, you can get a real-deal GI pistol. It won't be new; it will be rebuilt, but it will also cost you less than an identical one would require in gunsmithing should you win one at an auction. Today, the details you can get out of the box on newly made pistols are often better than custom-built ones in the old days and for less cost and are ready now, not months or years after you send it to a custom pistolsmith. And yet, anything made by the hand of man is imperfect. So, your 1911 might need some work. Or you want something a bit different from what the maker offers. Or, you have worked yours hard, and it needs some TLC.

Maybe you want to know how things work, what cleaning entails, or what a given part does in the scheme of things.

That's where this book comes in.

## STUFF

You'll hear a lot of jargon and techno-babble in reading various PR handouts and advertisements, watching videos, and listening to conversations. Some may be obvious, but I suspect much is unclear, contradictory, or wrong. So, a brief background and an overview of engineering, metallurgy, and manufacturing can provide a critical perspective. Let's start with steel.

Steel is iron mixed with a certain amount of carbon. It can be "just" steel, with iron and carbon, but there isn't much of that these days simply because alloys are superior. An "alloy steel" is an iron-carbon mixture mixed with other metals and elements. These can be manganese, vanadium, chromium or sulfur; the field is so extensive you need—and those with a mechanical engineering degree get—a thorough background on alloys to keep them all straight.

Stainless steel contains higher amounts of nickel and chromium to slow down corrosion but not stop it entirely. Why not stop it completely? That leads us to the next aspect of steel: structure. Steel is a crystal. Well, it has a crystalline structure, with the metal composed of crystals of various sizes and shapes distributed through the body of the part. These crystals can also be aligned, called the "grain" of the part. If the grain is oriented correctly to the stress the part undergoes in its work, it is stronger; if not, it is weaker (another semester of instruction toward your B.S. in ME). The size and shape of the crystals also determine the alloy's hardness. Well, if you add enough nickel and chromium to the steel alloy to make it truly stainless, you cannot form crystals that produce a hard alloy.

An example is your kitchen cutlery. If you look it over, you'll

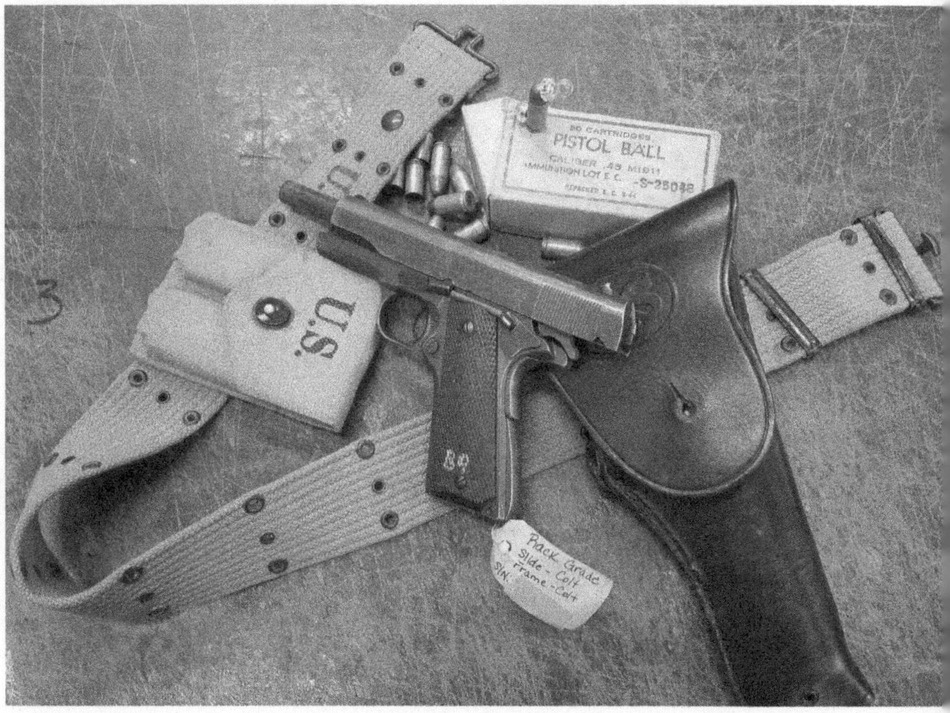


***If you get lucky and score a CMP pistol, it will be rebuilt like this Range-Grade 1911A1. The happy owner has kitted it out with the right web gear, holster, and ammo box.***

see a mark, something like "8-18" or "18-10" or such. That indicates the percentage of nickel and chromium in the alloy, which is genuinely rust-proof. But it is not hard.

*To be forged, the steel must be heated, which is done mainly by automated equipment. The job is challenging enough without working right next to the furnace.*

How do you harden steel? You heat it and then "quench" it by lowering or dropping it in oil or water or cooling it quickly. This process involves heating a specific alloy to a particular temperature and cooling it in oil, water or air at a specific rate, "freezing" the crystals in size and shape at high temperatures. "Annealing" an alloy means heating it and then cooling it slowly, which changes the crystals to a soft state.

You can create a multi-layered part by heating it to a temperature and quenching it, then reheating it and applying a different cooling rate. However, this process can be quite involved for some alloys in specific applications. Such a part could have a tough core, take high stress and flex without tiring—with the surface super-hard, so it resists wear. Doing that is expensive, however.

Certain classes of alloys have specific, useful conditions, and the class will have a generic name. A "spring steel" alloy can withstand significant flexing and stress but may not have much (relatively speaking) abrasion resistance. A "tool steel" is hard and abrasion-resistant but will not have much flex and can crack if excessively bent.

Regarding steel and steel parts manufacturing, you'll read of slides or frames that are "forged" or "billet-cut." OK, let's take a piece of steel, a rod, of a particular alloy and heat it to red-hot. (The specific color, or temperature, will depend on the alloy and the desired crystal structure.) A skilled operator then holds the part with long tongs under a forge, and a multi-ton press with a hammer die shaped like the part comes down with force. The red-hot steel is forced into the rough shape of the desired part. This is how we introduce grain into the crystalline structure of the alloy, which also makes very tough parts. The downside is that you can't forge it to the finished dimension, so carving the part out of the cooled forged blank requires machining. The machinery is expensive and requires a skilled operator to obtain good parts. Companies that have forges make the parts for companies that do not have them.

A billet is a rod or bar of steel that has been shaped to a specific contour and heat-treated to the final hardness. A slide is perfect for this, as you can get the bars very close to the final height and width, reducing machining work. The downside is that the metal is hard, so the tooling quickly wears. Why cut from billet? Forging equipment is expensive, but CNC or Computer Numerical Controlled machine tools are much less so and cleaner. For the cost of a forge, you could buy several CNC machines (which you'd need anyway, once the forged parts were cool enough to machine) and run them 24/7.

There's another method, though I don't know of any 1911 makers using it: cold extrusion. Here, the steel is forced through a set of dies that takes the original bar down in size and changes its shape to a slide cross-section. The process work hardens the steel (you need to use a specific alloy for this as not all will work), and you end up with a tough part. It isn't hard on the surface, so you must use a surface-hardening process. Let's give that hardening process a cool name; let's call it Tenifer. Yep, your Glock slide was produced like toothpaste from a tube, then machined and hardened.

Why do this? The cold extrusion process requires a significant machine investment, including forges and skilled operators. But once the truck delivers the extrusions, the machining is simple, so you can get parts in volume and not have the C-O equipment overhead and operation cost if you contract that out.

What about castings? As Ruger has demonstrated, castings can be very useful and immensely strong. But the 1911 is not entirely amenable to castings. There is no real advantage to casting slides, as many other processes readily handle the part. And the frame, due to its shape, is a nightmare to cast. As castings cool, they shift their shape. Hot metal contracts as it cools, and the 1911's thin frame walls magnify that. Trying to predict or correct for the contraction is a three-dimensional nightmare. One way to deal with it would be to cast and

***Once up to temp, the steel billets, rods, or plates are fed into the forge, where they are hit by tons and tons of force with specially shaped dies.***

Below is a cooled forged blank, and above it is the machined frame that comes from it. There are hundreds of machining steps in between, but that's all CNC now.

machine the warpage out. But that negates the advantage of casting, of not needing to machine so much. The 1911 frame is amenable to being billet-cut since you can start with flat plates almost the exact width of the finished frame.

## ALUMINUM

Aluminum is like steel; it can be alloyed, heat-treated, and made from forgings or billet. It adds surface hardness that anodizing produces and is lighter than steel. However, it is not as strong. One alloy of aluminum Smith & Wesson produces uses scandium, a rare metal that strengthens the aluminum alloy appreciably. Even so, it still isn't as strong as steel.

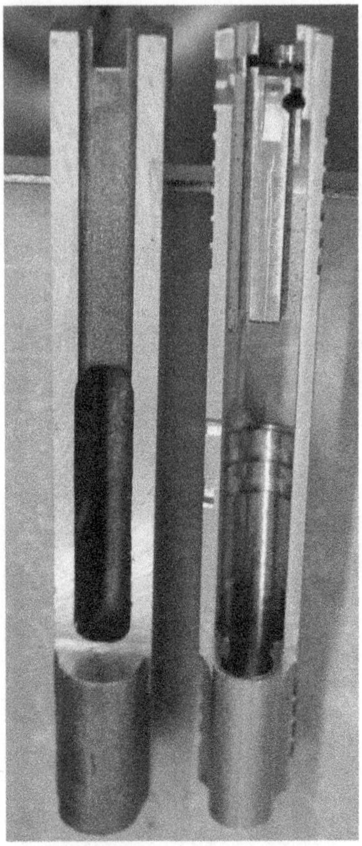

On the left is a forged slide, with the initial cut completed. On the right is a slide with all the machine cuts, but still awaiting its finishing treatments.

## THE HORROR OF MIM

MIM, or metal injection molding, is simple to describe. You take powdered metal and mix it with a polymer binder. Force the mixture into a mold to create a part. Heat the part hot enough to burn out the polymer, and the metal powder binds to itself and creates the finished part.

Advantages: you can create complex parts in volume, in whatever alloy and crystalline structure you desire (within limits, as the heat to burn out the binder can't be so high, it changes the crystals, but you have significant flexibility). For example, you can create parts that would be difficult to hold while machining. You can control the surface texture to a great extent and, as a result, have a finished product when done.

Disadvantages? There is no grain to the part. As a result, the part's strength, as initially designed, might not be there. The part may have to be subtly re-shaped to provide strength where its new crystalline structure can withstand stress. You must also be more careful in impact, shock, and abrasive resistance, as the MIM part differs from the older, forged, or billet part.

This is why the early years of MIM parts were so rocky. Not everyone producing MIM parts understood the specifics of stress and use of 1911 parts, and they broke. I am much more confident of MIM parts these days than in the beginning, and I would not shy away from a new set of parts made by MIM.

## SURFACE TREATMENTS

You can produce corrosion-resistant carbon and alloy steels by a process known as black oxide—essentially pre-rusted. USGI 1911s and 1911A1s were Parkerized—an acid-phosphate surface reaction that created a rust-resistant barrier but also porous, and by sufficiently oiling the part, you could fill the pores of the Parkerizing with oil or grease and prevent oxygen from reaching the steel's surface.

Oh, and a moment to get up on my soapbox: steel does not have pores. It is a solid made of crystals. If someone selling you lubricants tells you their product "gets into the steel's pores," they are wrong. It may be a fine product, but it doesn't work that way.

We used "industrial hard chrome," a super-hard chromium plating in the old days. Not like the decorative chrome on vehicles, this stuff was developed to plate cutting tools for the machine tool industry, and it is hard. It is also rust-resistant, and it works exceptionally well.

We now have various cyanidic processes, such as Tenifer and Melonite, that change the crystalline structure of the steel at the surface and occupy all the reaction sites of the steel. Rust forms by reacting with open sites on the alloy at the atomic level. If you have something else occupying those sites (think musical chairs, and before the music starts, all the chairs are already filled), rust can't start.

The downside to the tough surface treatments is that they are the final result. Once you have, for example, hard-chromed your frame, you can't change it. To make a change, you have to sandblast the chrome off where you want to alter something, make the change, chemically strip the rest of the chrome off, and re-plate it. That's a lot of work and cost. And I'm not sure you can do that to a Melonited part. Machining a Tenifer or Melonite part means eating up an expensive carbide cutter and chewing through the hard surface. Again, a lot of cost.

***When conditions are tough, and the enemy is near, GIs packed pistols even if the TO&E didn't call for them. That was back when we knew how to win wars, and the brass didn't care as long as our guys were safe.***

In the early IPSC years, it was typical for the inveterate experimenter or the custom pistolsmith to leave their guns unfinished. One shooter I knew invested in a bead-blasting cabinet. He was changing things on his pistols so often that he used the bead-blast cabinet to keep the rust at bay while he made changes. He shot his guns in the bare steel until satisfied, then blued them until he was certain before getting them hard-chromed.

## TALE OF THE UGLY GUN

The 1911 is the muscle car of the pistol world. It comes to us from a different era: before plastics, replaceable backstraps, and red-dot optics. It still has advanced features, like the superb trigger that striker-fired pistols are still catching up to. But like the muscle car, many people expect it to be flashy, eye-catching, distinctive in appearance, and collectible.

It was designed to be a fighting tool. And when built correctly, it delivers the goods. Let me tell you the tale of The Ugly Gun.

My gun club had hosted the State IPSC League Match, where the state-level clubs took turns hosting the match, and we'd all travel to the club holding it that month. The idea was to get to know the other shooters without attending the State or Area Championships. It also gave the people running their clubs a weekend off since the host club did all the work. I was walking the ranges after the match to ensure all the club gear was put away when I found a pistol case on one of the ranges. In it, the most unseemly 1911 you ever saw. Laying eyes on it was a wrenching experience. First off, no two parts on the exterior matched in finish. It was like the Johnny Cash Cadillac—blued, Parkerized, nickeled, chromed, painted, and rusted. The thumb safety had a piece of steel brazed onto the GI lever and shaped using a bench grinder. The grips had cracked and been glued, but the glue failed, and they were held on with a giant rubber band. The Wilson Combat plastic magazine funnel had hook tabs that were broken from use and super-glued to the bottom of the frame. Some of that glue had slopped (or been slopped) onto the grips for extra adherence.

***Built to look like a classic-era IPSC pistol, this high-end commander has a hard-chromed frame. Today's level of workmanship would have made the previous generations of 'smiths green with envy.***

The barrel was a vanilla-plain Colt, and the ejection port had been lowered using a hand-held Dremel tool and grinding wheels, with a few swipes from a file to try and knock down some of the more egregious tool marks. The sights were Bullseye Micro sights, not lowered into the slide. The rear sight had clear hammer marks where it had been forced into the rear sight dovetail. The front sight, tall as a billboard to match the rear sight installation, had been aggressively staked on. You could see the small divot on the top of the blade where the fixture had held it in place while someone had peened the tenon. It had not gone on straight, and you could see the marks from the vise jaws where the front blade had been clamped while the slide was pushed to straighten up the sight.

But the *pièce de résistance* was the magazine button. Someone had drilled the button, off-center as it happened, and then forced a flat-head sheet metal screw into it to create an over-sized mag button.

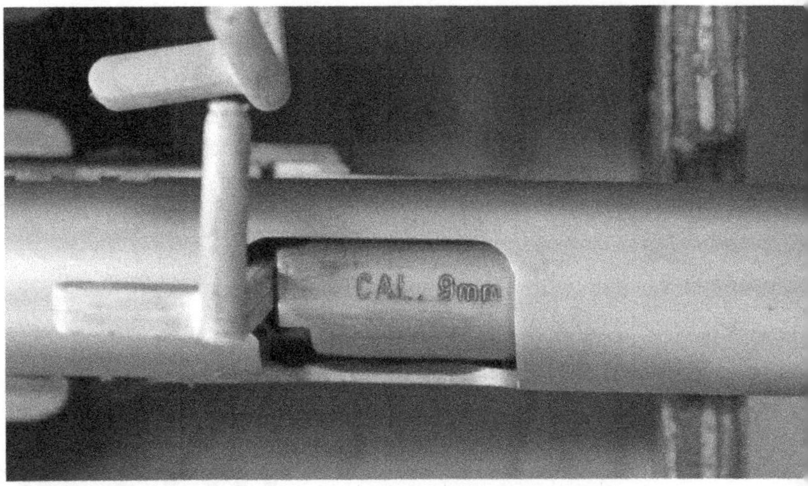


***The significant change in the last few decades is the adoption of 9mm 1911s. That would have been seen as almost heretical for the first century of its existence.***

It was ugly.

I figured whoever owned it would call me, and I'd get it back to them. After a few days, there was no phone call, so I figured it was worth some testing. I tried my match ammo in it, and it shot great. I used it to shoot odds and ends of reloading tests, loose rounds from this or that, or anything that wasn't needed in its loaded form but would be useful as empty brass. It fed everything, ejected everything, and every shot fired was in a tight enough group that every round would have stayed in the "A" zone of a USPSA target at 25 yards. It may have been ugly, but it was a star in performance.

In due time, the owner found me. "I may have left my pistol at your club."

"You might have, describe it."

"Well, it has this sheet metal screw—"

"Say no more; tell me where to ship it."

First and foremost, your pistol must perform. It can be pretty after that, but it has to perform all the expected functions of a self-loading pistol without fail and deliver groups accurately enough to solve any problem you face. Lacking any aspect of that, it doesn't matter how good it looks.

In that regard, it's like the muscle cars of the old days. There were always two groups: those whose cars ran and ran well enough to get on the street and prove it. And the cars that looked sharp but never got on the street. The latter were looking to score with the girls, so they thought they needed flash. (Curiously, the girls seemed to, often as not, end up choosing the fast cars, not the flashy ones. Hmmm, a lesson there, perhaps?)

If you want to win a match or survive a defensive encounter, you don't need flash; you need performance. This book will help you achieve it. ●

CHAPTER 2

# 1911 PROS AND CONS

I am not taking a deliberate swipe at any particular pistol when I say nothing made by man's hand is perfect, and all things have faults in design or operation. What advantages some object or process might have over others depends partly on what you expect of it—expectations defined by its inherent design faults or the environment in which it operates.

So, with that in mind, let's start by covering the pros and cons, the advantages and disadvantages, of the 1911.

## PROS

The 1911 is flat and smooth. While angular, you can round its edges, removing sharp edges that would cut your hands or grab clothing. While it is flat and was designed to contain a relatively large cartridge, the grip diameter is small enough to let even those with small hands hold, control, and effectively use the pistol. When designed, the average American man stood 5'8", and the average woman was 5'3". Despite decades of awful dietary habits, men average 5'10" and women 5'4". The 1911 is durable enough for a long service life thanks to its steel frame. Plus, you can rebuild the steel-frame version (albeit at some cost) to effectively renew its service life. I have a couple of pistols that I've put over 100,000 rounds through, and I know of others who have done more than that.

Depending on luck, use, and type of ammunition, a 1911 can have an effectively unlimited service life. Oh, barrels might (and I say *might* on all of these) have to be replaced every 50,000 rounds, slides every 100,000, and frames welded and rebuilt every 300,000 rounds, but numbers like those will cover more than a lifetime of shooting for most owners.

The grip is ergonomic and small enough to fit almost everyone. The parts needing replacement as standard service items (recoil springs, magazines springs, and magazines) are readily serviced by even the untrained-as-a-pistolsmith owner. While some tout it as fully capable of disassembly by hand, it requires only a few simple tools to take every removable part off of or out of it. Field-stripping is simple, and complete disassembly is easy enough whenever needed, so you can keep your 1911 clean and ready for use without investing an entire afternoon in service.

***The 1911 has extra parts compared to other, more modern designs, and some view that as a problem. However, those extra parts, like the bushing, can be worked on for a better fit and thus improve accuracy. So, like all designs, there are pluses and minuses.***

Magazines are quickly loaded and last a long time. They shrug off abuse and are flat, compact and easily handled. The grip safety requires no conscious effort, and the thumb safety is as ergonomic as any tool. The trigger is the apex of pistol perfection even after 120+ years. It can be clean and crisp when made and assembled correctly, affording a precise firing decision. However, it is heavy enough to require a conscious effort to fire, so the combination makes learning to shoot a much easier and more rewarding event than heavier, grittier triggers. In effect, it does not make the new shooter work to learn how to shoot a handgun.

Because the barrel comes out of the slide forward, not down and to the rear, you can take the same 1911 and install a standard barrel and one that is extended and has a comp or muzzle brake on it. You can swap them back and forth simply by doing only as much disassembly as you'd do for cleaning. That is not the case for many "modern" designs, where the barrel comes out rearward. Once you've installed a comp, you can't remove the barrel from the slide.

So, if you want a two-category pistol (say a Pin Gun and a Stock Gun for bowling pins), you can have one 1911 and two barrels. If you start with a Glock, you need two complete uppers, one stock and one with a comp.

## CONS

However, the 1911 is not all peaches and cream. The first con is capacity, or the lack thereof. A regular 1911 holds seven rounds of .45 ACP in the magazine, plus one in the chamber. You'll see that format in the specs chart, denoted as 7+1. You can get eight-round magazines (8+1) that are flush-fit and extended 10-round mags. A 1911 in .40/10mm holds eight or nine rounds. The old standard was nine rounds in 9mm and .38 Super, but they are almost all 10 these days. As far as I know, there are no 10-rounds-of-.45-length magazines to hold .40/10mm or 9/.38 Super.

There are higher-capacity 1911s, the 2011 style, or, if you come across one, the old Para Ordnance pistols. They hold more rounds but do so by giving up one of the significant advantages of the 1911, the grip size. You must make the grip larger to hold up to twice as many rounds.

The second con is weight. As an all-steel pistol, the 1911 is rather portly. You can make it lighter by changing the frame material from steel to aluminum, which saves some weight but doesn't cut as much as polymer. There was a brief excursion into titanium frames for 1911s, but the weight saved was not worth the extreme metallurgical problems it brought. The problem was that titanium would gall. Galling is when the surfaces of two metals, sliding across each other, grab and rub and tear at the surfaces of the other. My titanium-framed 1911 had shown galling just in the time it took to test-fire it for proper function, zero it, and adjust the sights. It had to be fixed, and while I found a solution, most experienced pistolsmiths had dropped Ti as a frame option due to the extra work and cost. The weight savings weren't worth the labor and materials cost. An all-steel Government Model 1911/191A1 runs in the 38-ounce range with eight or nine shots of .45 ACP. A similarly sized Glock G17, holding 18 rounds of 9mm, weighs 32 ounces.

*You can rebuild the 1911's frame because it is steel. You can also weld the rails of a "worn-out" 1911, as here, and machine it to something as good as, or better than, new.*

The third con, surprisingly, at least a con to some, is the trigger. If you're training many not-entirely-motivated people, then a clean, crisp, light trigger is a hindrance, not an asset. For people who view a pistol as just more luggage to haul and an expensive item should they lose it, as well as a dangerous instrument, a heavy trigger is a good thing: Fewer accidents by those who probably shouldn't have a firearm, anyway. (In this regard, I'm looking more at police and military than the likely readers of this book.)

This was part of the reason revolvers stayed in police use for so long. A long, heavier-than-a-1911 trigger pull kept accidental discharges off of the shift reports to a much greater degree than an equal number of 1911s would have. Not the fault of the pistol but of the training.

## COUNTERPOINT

For most shooters, a better trigger is a good thing. Weight can be handled by proper holster selection. And as far as capacity is concerned, the 1911 reloads quickly enough that another seven, eight or nine rounds will be available in short order. In most instances, the 1911 magazine's capacity was sufficient to handle whatever problem presented itself. From time to time, various gun writers have scoured the shooting incident reports to see how many incidents called for more rounds than a 1911 holds or if a reload was needed. The numbers are vanishingly small.

Of course, if we were going by statistical probability, the odds would indicate that few of us would carry handguns.

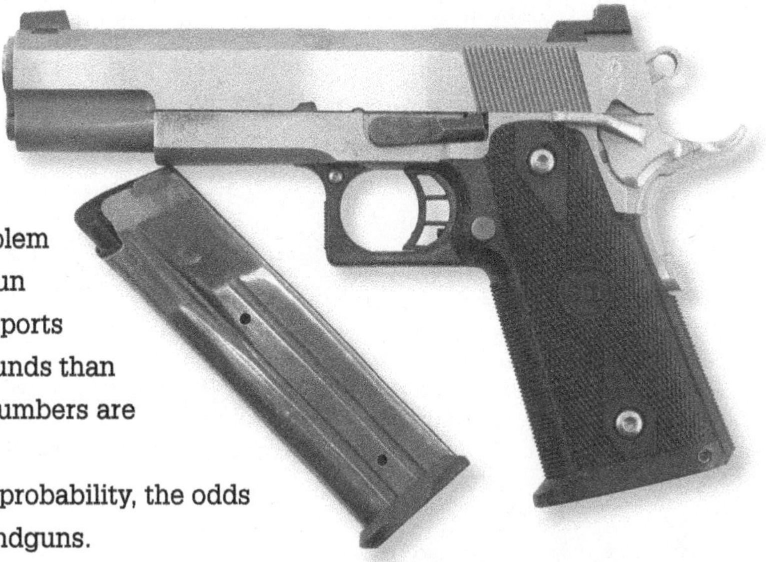

***The 1911 has another advantage that some designs don't: it can be a new caliber. This example looks like a hi-cap 9mm STI but is a .45 ACP. With the right magazine and barrel combo, it can be anything from a .22 LR to a .460 Rowland. Try that, Mr. G17.***

## COUNTER-COUNTERPOINT

And finally, when it comes to service life, all the well-built plastic-framed pistols of any design will last 50,000 rounds without a problem. If we're using that as the service life of a pistol, then there's a simple arithmetic problem: how long is 50,000 rounds? And what is the cost of 50,000 rounds?

If you shoot 1,000 rounds a year (a lot for most people), then the pistol you bought yourself as a graduation present from college is still going to be working when you collect your first Social Security check. (Assuming Social Security lasts as long as your pistol does.)

Your 1911 will cost you the same amount as your brand-new graduation present iPhone. If you're a typical user, the iPhone will be replaced next year and be obsolete in five years. The service plan will cost you $300 a year, as will 1,000 rounds of ammunition. At the end of 50 years, you will have spent $15,000 in ammunition alone (we'll ignore inflation and various ammo-buying and politically created panics that spike prices from time to time), not to mention replacement recoil springs, range fees or gun club membership, and various incidental supplies.

You will have gone through 10 iPhones and spent as much on service plans as you would have on ammunition. In the long run, it is not all that expensive. People who think shooting is expensive have not indulged in other adrenaline sports.

The cost differential of $50–$150 between this model handgun or that, this brand or that, will be inconsequential at the end of the 50,000-round/50-year run, which is my way of saying you should get what you want and not settle for something else just because "It costs a bit less." If you can afford it, always go up in quality.

*One of the advantages of an all-steel pistol is that you can weld it and re-fit it once it has become worn. Try doing that with your Glock. Photo: Ned Christiansen*

That said, pistols are like any other consumer item. You can spend as much as you want on one because someone out there will be offering it. Yes, a Glock only costs you $500-$600. But you can easily find a custom-built one that runs you $2,500. And a USGI clone, import 1911 can be had for $400. Or, if you can stand the wait, you can find custom ones that will run you $10,000.

Need I remind you? This is America. You have choices.

## SAFETY PREP AND CARRY CONDITION

You may have heard people casually talk about "Condition One" or "cocked and locked." When the time came to switch (the word "transition" has been ruined for a generation or more, so I'm not using it) from single-action revolvers to self-loading pistols, people had to work out the details of carry. Before 1911, everyone carried pistols hammer down on empty chambers. Browning changed that, intending the 1911 to be carried with a loaded magazine, a round in the chamber, the hammer cocked, and the safety on. This is Condition One. If you were to undergo the hazardous process of carefully lowering the hammer to rest against the slide (not the half-cock notch) with a round in the chamber, that is Condition Two. Hammer down, no round in the chamber, but a loaded magazine is Condition Three. And I guess you'd call no rounds Condition Four, but everyone I've ever known calls it "unloaded."

Browning designed the 1911 to be carried in Condition One. It is safe there, ready, and will not discharge until three things happen: You push the thumb safety off, depress the grip safety, and press the trigger.

Condition Two is both hazardous and awkward—hazardous in that there is no completely safe way to lower the hammer on a loaded chamber. It is awkward because there is no convenient way to thumb the hammer back while drawing.

Condition Three is the standard military carry method, at least it was previously, and on drawing, you had to retract and release the slide to chamber a round.

## WHY IS CUSTOM WORK SO EXPENSIVE?

To understand the cost of custom work, consider the example of fitting a barrel bushing. I'll go into this in more detail in the barrel chapter, but let's take an overview of fitting a new, tighter bushing to wring more accuracy out of your pistol. I'll use myself as an example of the process I'd go through in this task.

The first step is measuring the barrel diameter, the slide inner diameter, and the inner and outer diameters of the current bushing. I assume the fit is loose, or we wouldn't do this. With these specs written down, I can see if we can make a bushing fit. I need a bushing smaller inside than the barrel diameter and larger on the outside than the slide diameter. Assuming such a part exists, I order it and get it shipped. We're already into the project for half an hour of my time and the cost of the part.

Once the bushing arrives, I measure it, just to be sure. First step: Fix the slide into the lathe and polish the interior where the bushing rides, just enough to smooth out the tool marks but not enlarge it. Oh, it might "grow" a thousandth (.001 in.) or so, but that's all. Second step: lock the bushing in a bushing fixture, put it in the lathe, and turn the oversized bushing down to one-thousandth over the slide dimension. Next, measure the distance from the slide face to the front edge of the locking slot. Then, turn the bushing ledge to a thousandth over that dimension.

Next, pull the bushing out, lock the slide in the vise, and apply lapping compound to the slide interior. (Younger, cooler 'smiths, with more precise lathes, might cut both to the exact dimension, but I'm old-school and lap the last .001 in.) Lap the bushing fit, going to finer and finer grit. Once, after a thorough cleaning, the bushing can be moved with my bare fingers but not have any slop in the fit, that part is done.

Back into the lathe the bushing goes, and I turn the interior dimension (once centered) to, you guessed it, .001 over the barrel diameter. I check the fit of the barrel to the bushing and use a polishing fixture to polish them to a smooth sliding fit without any slop.

Last step: assemble the barrel and bushing into the slide and the slide on the frame. Hand-cycle it, feeling the unlocking of the barrel. If the bushing is binding (it must tip down, after all, and if the bottom rear of the bushing skirt hasn't been properly relieved, I'll have to do that now), repeat the lapping process. Once everything fits properly, strip down, clean, reassemble, and test-fire.

We're talking about at least two hours of initial measuring, machining, and hand-fitting, plus the bushing cost. And that isn't even an OCD-level bushing fit; I haven't attended to any other detail of the barrel fit, link timing, chamber size/depth/smoothness or muzzle crown. There's a reason a full-custom 1911 runs in the thousands of dollars. I can see some Glock fans in the back shaking their heads at this. Dudes, have you seen the price put on full-custom Glocks these days? You can quickly burn up a trio of Clevelands. Clevelands? Thousand-dollar bills. ●

***A custom gun is a forever or several lifetimes investment. This Yost-built 10mm will stand up to a lot of use before it needs a rebuild. By then, your heirs will be negotiating ownership. And all this time, it will be a classic.***

CHAPTER 3

# CALIBERS OF THE 1911

## .45 ACP

Delving into the numerous caliber options of the 1911 calls for a bit more history, which will help you put things into context.

In the beginning, there was the .45 ACP. As in: Automatic Colt Pistol. The U.S. Army wanted a real thumper, and they got it. The original standard was a 230-grain round-nosed, full metal jacket going 825 fps. Those who are calculating, I'll save you the trouble. That is a Power Factor of 189.7. Yowza. They were accustomed to using single-action revolvers (also Colt) in .45 Colt, with 250-grain lead bullets of a nominal 800 fps, so they were getting the same performance but in a faster-shooting package and one that conformed to the Hague Accords. (Not the Geneva Convention, as some will earnestly tell you.)

Now, the expected and the delivered were not always the same, but that's true with everything. I've chronographed military and commercial ammo in .45 ACP for nearly half a century. I've seen 230-grain JRNs from various factories or arsenals as slow as the 720s and as fast as almost 1,000 fps. It can vary from brand to brand and lot to lot, even from time of day. In all instances, the .45 ACP hurls a heavy, fat bullet at subsonic speeds. Well, most of the time. Factory ammunition goes as light as 185 grains, which can go supersonic, close in on, or creep over 1,100 fps.

In all these loads, the recoil will be noticeable. Newton's laws of physics cannot be avoided, and if you want to deliver that performance, you have to pay the freight.

The .45 bullet is .451 inch in diameter for the jacketed and .452 inch in the lead versions. The case capacity is large, but the operating pressure is low (21,000 psi for normal, 23,000 psi for +P), and the muzzle report isn't all that sharp. It's loud enough to deafen you with extended exposure, so wear hearing protection, but it isn't painful like some .38 Super or 9mm Major loads.

## .38 SUPER

The original Colt auto cartridge, the .38 Auto, predated the 9mm Parabellum and was marginally stronger than the loading with which the euro-9 came to be associated in the Luger. The .38 Auto, a 130-grain bullet at 1,100 fps, was a tad better than the Luger, which was a 124-grain bullet at 1,150 fps (more or less, it varied even more than the .45 ACP), but neither the Auto nor the Luger was ever more than a medium-bore pistol cartridge. Depending on how you measured power, they were more powerful than the .38 Special. If you used kinetic energy, the .38/9mm was more powerful. If you used momentum (which the Power Factor measures), the .38 Special occasionally topped them with a 158-grain bullet from 700 to 800 fps.

Colt wanted to leapfrog that argument, and it upped the chamber pressure of the Auto from 26,000 to 34,000 psi (this was back in the copper-crusher measurement days; now the Super is 36,500 psi by transducer) and called it the Super .38. This cartridge generated 1,300 fps with the same 130-grain FMJ. Colt changed as little as possible on the 1911, and the Super arrived in 1929. There was a new barrel, the frame had the feed ramp a bit higher, and the breechface on the slide was narrower for the smaller cartridge. The extractor and ejector were moved, so there was no interchangeability between 1911s in .45 and .38 Super. If you wanted a Super .38, you had to buy one.

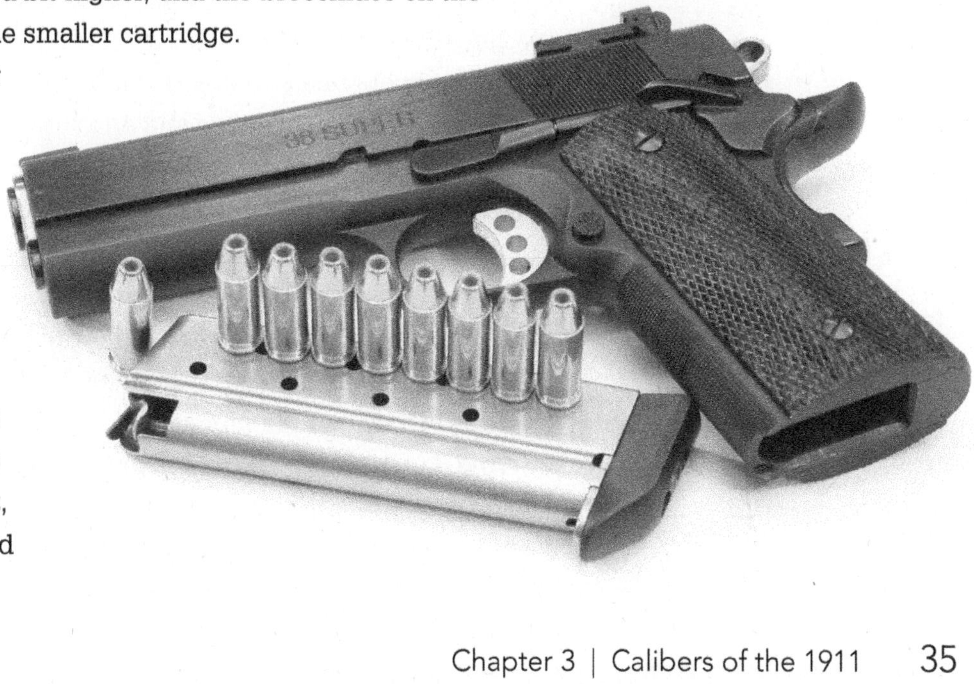

*A custom gun, like this .38 Super from Les Baer, will be a joy to shoot. Depending on the magazines used, it can hold 8+1 up to 10+1 rounds, with more on a quick reload.*

The .38 Super had its season in the sun. It was popular in the southwest, where those who traveled to Mexico or lived there could use a .38 Super (those with the pull or money to buy a permit, anyway) but not a 9mm or .45, as those were both military cartridges and not permitted. The .38 Super was also popular for those dealing with bootleggers or bank robbers, as the high-speed jacketed bullet would reach into automobiles. The Rules of Engagement were much different than today, and shooting bad guys in cars was all good as long as you got the bad guys. And before the FDIC, if the bad guys got away with your town's bank money, there was no getting it back.

The Super lost much luster when the .357 Magnum came about,

## CHAMBER PRESSURE AND AMMUNITION

A brief technical note on chamber pressure. The old method used tiny copper cylinders and vented barrels. The chamber pressure would crush the copper cylinder, and the squashed amount was measured. This method worked but had limitations. The new process uses a pressure-sensitive transducer, which measures pressure in as little time as you have the patience and computing power. Want to measure the pressure every millionth of a second? That can be done.

The copper crusher method was written as "pounds per square inch," but it was an estimate and an average of the chamber pressure over time. The transducer can measure actual psi and tell us what the curve looks like. Old cartridges will have old pressure limits in print, but the data from the copper and transducer methods do not always coincide. And some old loading data—if you're into ammunition reloading—was scary when looked at under the transducer microscope. So, old loads were dialed back or dropped. Use only the newest loading manuals to load your ammunition.

And do not believe the guy at your gun club who assures you that the ammo companies are "stealing velocity" from you and that he has safe loads that greatly exceed the performance of factory ammo. He is wrong.

and the FBI (or at least the switched-on agents) adopted it.

Smith & Wesson developed the .356 TSW in the early days of competition as a Major cartridge that was a long, high-pressure 9mm. When the USPSA changed the rules, S&W dropped its team and stopped promoting IPSC.

Up until the 1960s or so, many people felt the Super needed special-diameter bullets. If you delve into reloading articles in the black-and-white days of print magazines, you'll read of special Super bullets of .356-inch diameter, not to be confused with the .355 of the 9mm or the .357 of revolvers. Even some super-secret ones that were .3555-inch in diameter. Well, that all changed in the 1970s when barrel makers like Irv Stone of Bar-Sto just up and decided that was nonsense and settled on .355 inch for the Super, the same as the 9mm Parabellum. So, you can use any 9mm bullet in a Super.

The Super returned when IPSC/USPSA competitors adopted it in the mid-1980s. When first used, we loaded hardcast 150- to 160-grain bullets to about 1,100 fps. The early days were risky, as there weren't many powders suited to that use. And, chambers were sometimes a bit on the sloppy side (Colt, we were looking at you back then, and not with happy faces), so blown cases were not unknown. "Super Face" was coined for those who had blown a case and gotten a jet of gases and oily particles back out of the ejector slot. Then we switched to jacketed bullets and went lighter, settling on either 115- or 124/125-grain bullets. That was possible due to improved powders, tighter chambers, and more prudent loading. This required different powders to stay reasonably close to the maximum pressures (although we certainly exceeded them) and feed high-pressure gas to the comp. Then, those guns went hi-cap and soon after went to red-dot optics. When the equipment divisions were sorted out, those pistols became the Open guns and have remained the same ever since.

Open is not the hot Division it used to be, but if you were to show up with a pistol built to the best standard in 1995, you would not be significantly outclassed today. The 1995-era optic would be obsolete, but you could keep up as long as it worked and you could handle the extra weight. And you'd be using .38 Super brass, or whatever variant you used then, which is still usable today.

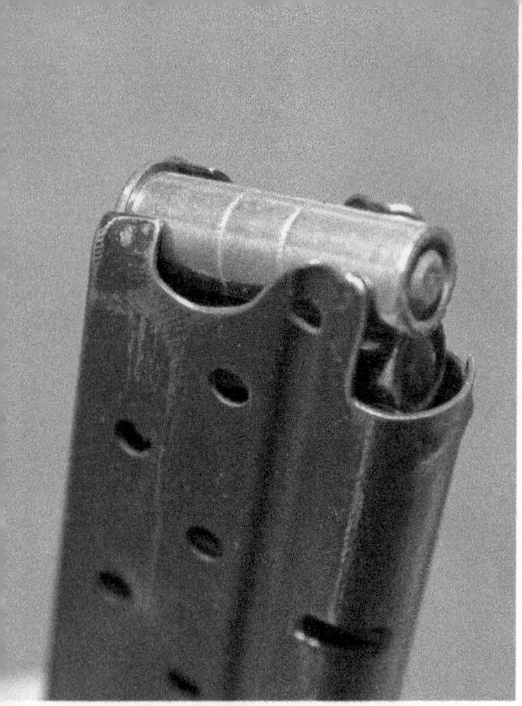

*The .38 Special required heavily modified, fragile, and hideously expensive magazines.*

## POWDERS MATTER

Even as we got new powders that worked better in the Super, we still pushed the pistols' limits. In the 1990s, it was not unusual for a serious Open competitor to have three identical guns. One would be the competition gun. The second would be the backup, and the third would be in the shop getting rebuilt. The pressures to make Major in Open were hard on the guns, peening parts and breaking things. The velocity and heat from high-volume shooting were hard on bores. A top-end competitor would easily shoot 50,000 rounds yearly in practice and match use. They might have had a two to three-year run-up of 60,000-70,000 rounds a year, getting themselves into the Grandmaster category.

Yes, that's a lot of ammo, but not the cost you'd think. I could load 9mm (not Major) ammo, with lead bullets, for something on the order of $70 per thousand. Make the bullets jacketed, and increase the powder to make Major, and maybe you'd double that, most likely not. So, let's call it $125 a thousand in 1995. Adjusted for inflation, that would be $249 per thousand today. Who among us would not risk dislocating a shoulder getting our wallet out for premium 9mm, .38 Super or .45 ACP ammo at that price today?

## 9MM

The 9mm 1911 came about because the U.S. Army was enamored of things modern. Post WWII, the Army wanted a lighter pistol that held more rounds and was safer than the 1911. Not that anyone who had been shooting Germans or Japanese had wanted any of those details on their pistols (well, more ammo, sometimes), but no one asked *them* what *they* wanted. The Army asked pistol makers, and Colt and Smith & Wesson responded. Colt even offered to rebuild every 1911 and 1911A1 in inventory and convert them to 9mm. Smith & Wesson offered its Model 39. Ultimately, the Army had other problems, like the disastrous M14 program. (The program, not the M14.) The military declined both pistols, and it wasn't until 1986 that the Army finally adopted a 9mm in the Beretta 92, a.k.a. the M9. The Colt 9mm came about in the early 1950s.

The 9mm was problematic in the 1911 because the cartridge was too short for the magazine and frame. The .38 Auto/.38 Super is essentially the same length as the .45 ACP, so no problem there. Colt solved the 9mm problem, more-or-less, by making magazines with a filler strip in the back. (Colt's magazine maker did this; Colt did not produce the mags. We'll go into this in detail in the magazine chapter.) For a long time, 1911s in 9mm were considered—and were—marginally reliable because of the geometric/feeding problem. That, and no one had asked pistolsmiths to look into that particular problem in anything like a serious way.

That did not diminish the attraction of the first Lightweight Commander 9mm 1911. Actually, at the outset, it was just the Commander because there was only one lightweight 1911, and that was the Commander. It wasn't until the advent of the steel-framed Commander in 1974 that we had to make the distinction.

Oh, and as an aside, when the Air Force (the organization first tasked with getting the military a 9mm pistol) tested the candidate 9mms side-by-side with "worn-out" 1911s in .45 ACP, it had a problem: the 1911s were more accurate. The Air Force quickly halted the testing and developed match-accurate 9mm ammo to get back to testing and "proving" the military needed 9mms pistols.

## 9X23 WINCHESTER

Think of a 9mm Luger case at the base, with the case lengthened like the .38 Super and pumped up to a potential 50,000 psi. The 9x23 Win. was another try at the .38 Major, at the same time as the .356 TSW, and it befell the same fate. Colt made 1911s in this chambering for a few years while fighting off the lawsuit by its designer, John Ricco, of CP bullets. Ricco won, but the USPSA made it all moot when it changed Major to .40 and above. Why? So people wouldn't re-chamber elderly or tired war-surplus 9mm pistols to 9x23 or .356 TSW and scatter shrapnel on the ranges.

*A Bullseye wadcutter gun with extra magazines was a significant investment when Bullseye was king; it still carries a hefty cost.*

## OTHER COMPETITION "SUPERS"

A host of 9mm-like .38 Super variants came about in the early 1990s as competitors struggled to solve the various problems of making an

Open gun reliable and lasting long enough to get a season's worth of competition out of it—and ensure the cases survived the experience, as making Major then (and to this day, in a 9mm case) requires pressures in the upper 40,000/lower 50,000 psi range. The .38 TJ, 9x21, .38 Super Comp, 9x23 Comp, and 9mm Largo had their reasons, inventors, and advocates. And if you score an Open gun at an auction or yard sale, you will want to know which chambering it is built in because the pressure needed to make a Major makes a difference.

## .38 SPECIAL

Yes, the .38 Special. This one requires a bit more backstory and explanation. Bullseye competition has three categories: .22 LR, Any Centerfire, and .45 ACP. Each is fired with a maximum potential of 900 points, and the full course is called a "2700." When Bullseye was fired mostly with revolvers, the trio would often be a .22 LR, a .32, and a .45. Some opted for the .38 Special as the middle revolver because ammunition was more readily found. Colt and S&W made models identical in handling and sized for each cartridge, so a competitor could have an identical trio. There were actually four categories, but you shot those three for the overall score and standings. Then there was the Service Pistol category, which meant the 1911—specifically, a 1911 shooting 230-grain JRN service ammo.

Shooting pistols instead of revolvers before and into the Eisenhower era was problematic because there were no accurate .32s or .38 pistols. Well, there had been some pre-war when Colt made Super Match Super .38s. But they got dropped from production for the war effort, so post-war, when Bullseye exploded as a competitive sport, those were collector's items. Colt created a 1911 built to shoot the .38 Special in its full wadcutter form. More explanation: the .38 Special had been made in a lead round-nose form from the beginning. For target shooting, ammunition companies offered a bullet with a flat face that cut a clean hole in the target paper, a wadcutter. This bullet was loaded flush to the case's mouth, both to protect the soft lead and to identify it as a target load. And it cut clean holes, making scoring easier.

As it turned out, this made it short enough to fit within the 1911 magazine tube, which the round-nosed loading could not do. The long, rimmed case wouldn't feed from regular feed lips, so those designing the new 1911 had to use special magazines to feed the pistol.

It was now possible to shoot a .22 LR pistol with a 1911-shaped grip, a .38 wadcutter 1911, and a 1911 built to be a target gun, called

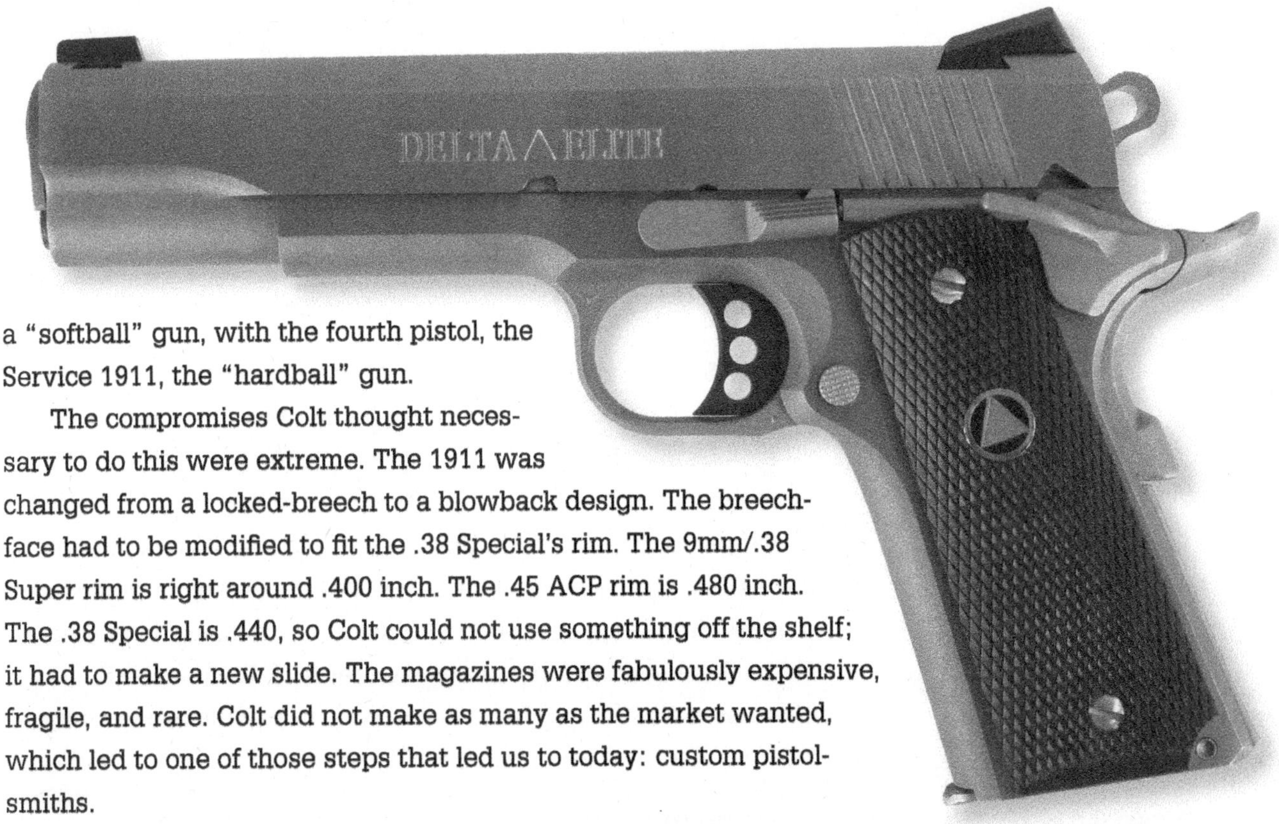


a "softball" gun, with the fourth pistol, the Service 1911, the "hardball" gun.

The compromises Colt thought necessary to do this were extreme. The 1911 was changed from a locked-breech to a blowback design. The breechface had to be modified to fit the .38 Special's rim. The 9mm/.38 Super rim is right around .400 inch. The .45 ACP rim is .480 inch. The .38 Special is .440, so Colt could not use something off the shelf; it had to make a new slide. The magazines were fabulously expensive, fragile, and rare. Colt did not make as many as the market wanted, which led to one of those steps that led us to today: custom pistolsmiths.

The late Jim Clark, Sr., a veteran of the Pacific campaign, was a successful Bullseye competitor. Really successful. And an accomplished pistolsmith. He figured out how to convert a .38 Super into a .38 Special pistol. As the story goes, he built a dozen and offered them in a small advertisement in the *American Rifleman*. They sold immediately (back then, before the Gun Control Act of 1968, you could buy and sell firearms through the mail), and he had orders to convert existing Supers, mailed to him, to .38 Special—orders that he was years catching up to. He soon made enough money doing pistolsmithing to learn to fly, buy a plane, fly to Bullseye matches, and win even more trophies. Oh, one difference: the Clark guns were still locked-breech pistols, not blowback.

*Colt rescued the 10mm from the debacle of the Bren Ten, and now the 10mm is a respected hunting cartridge. It is also a fine defensive choice as well.*

A 1911 in .38 Special of either type will be quite the rarity. You will not commonly find one lying in the display counter of your local gun shop. And if you do, it will be pricey. The magazines? How about $100 each, if you can find them, compared to .38 Supers, common as dirt by comparison, for $30? And don't drop a .38 Special magazine; it won't like it.

## A DIVERSION

I had a customer in the 1980s come to me with a project. The local ranges ran indoor leagues in the winter, and he wanted to shoot. But, the best gun he had for them was a Clark conversion in .38 Special. (I don't recall how he came to own such a rare and wondrous beast.) He had two problems, well, three. He did not have enough magazines; they were expensive and fragile, so he didn't want to drop them on the concrete floor doing reloads. They only held five rounds, while the leagues were all six-shot strings.

I thought it would be worth converting it back to .38 Super. I had a Bar-Sto .38 Super barrel on hand and was shooting a Super in the leagues, so I had magazines and ammo. Testing would not require making any irreversible changes. So, I swapped out the barrel and bushing, extractor, and ejector from .38 Special to .38 Super, loaded some test ammo in Super mags, and tried it. Dog-gone, it worked. I had already held the 1911 in high esteem, but this just put it on a higher pedestal.

So, I ordered the parts needed and made him a two-caliber league gun. He could shoot .38 Supers in the winter IPSC leagues and then rebuild/reassemble the gun for the warm-weather Bullseye leagues. No changes were permanent.

## WHY THE .38 SPECIAL?

If the .32 S&W Long offered lower recoil, why not build the 1911 in that? The problem is rim diameter. Since the magazine conversion could be done, the magazine wasn't likely the big problem, but the rims were. The .38 Super uses a case with a nominal .406-inch diameter. The 9mm uses one with a .392-inch diameter. No slide maker is so OCD as to offer separate 9mm and Super slides, so they all get a .405–.410-inch breechface.

The .38 Special rim is .440 inch, so it only takes slightly widening the breechface to accommodate the rim. (A slight widening by the terms and skills of an expert pistolsmith and machinist; for the rest of us, it's like saying, "Pilot a rocket into space.") However, the .32 S&W Long has a rim with a diameter of .375 inch. If you put that into a slide cut for a 9mm/.38 Super, the rim is slopping around with .035 inch of extra space. You *might* be able to count on the extractor reaching the rim, but I wouldn't count on it. Opening up a breechface is simpler than adding steel to make one smaller. Nope, not gonna happen.

But if someone managed it, that would be a soft-shooting pistol.

There is no need for a .38 Special 1911 anymore. You can make a superbly accurate 9mm or .38 Super and not have to go through the gyrations of building, loading, and finding magazines for a .38 Special. There's just no need. But if you find one …

## 10MM

The 10mm came about from experiments done on the Browning Hi Power in the 1970s, resulting in the creation of the .40 G&A. The experimenters could boost .400-inch-diameter bullets past 1,000 fps out of a Hi Power, and everyone was happy. The near-capacity of a hi-cap 9mm, with the near-power of a .45 ACP? That's a compromise we can all live with, right? Then Dornaus & Dixon developed the Bren Ten pistol and the 10mm cartridge to fulfill that expectation.

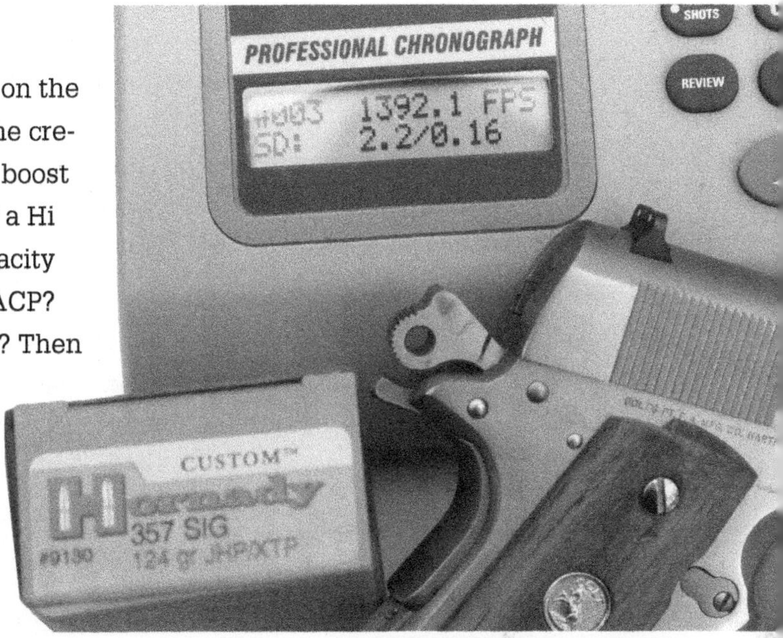


*The .357 Sig delivers. This drop-in barrel shot a 124-grain JHP to 1,392 fps. Out of an all-steel gun, it is stout but manageable. The flash from a polymer-framed 4-inch duty-sized gun is obnoxious, and the velocity drops off markedly.*

When the Bren Ten came about, D&D could not provide magazines for the pistols. (Like Colt, it did not produce magazines, and its supplier couldn't meet demand.) Worse, it was seen on the popular TV show *Miami Vice* before D&D could get production up and running at any tangible output, and suddenly, everyone had to have one. The whole episode would make for a very useful business school examination of what can go wrong when it looks like the stars are aligned for success.

In the middle of all this, the FBI experienced the Miami shootout, and there, the Bureau determined that the 9mm wasn't enough cartridge for its needs. Rather than adopt the .45 ACP, the FBI determined that the new 10mm was *the* cartridge for them. (The FBI, like many other organizations, had been wrangling over caliber selection for decades. Letting one camp or another "win" would have been too much; finding another solution would be better.) It's too bad that Norma, the ammo maker, had exceeded the expectations of the 10mm proponents. Instead of a useful 200 grains at 1,100 fps or an as-ordered 200 grain at 1,200 fps, it delivered 200-grain bullets at nearly 1,300 fps. With the Bren Ten out of the running, Smith & Wesson made all-steel 10mm pistols for the Bureau. However, S&W refused to produce an aluminum-alloy 10mm for the FBI or anyone else. The FBI designed its sear/hammer/safety variant for S&W to make and then complained that it didn't work. The result was a long-standing relationship soured and lost.

While this was going on, the FBI found another problem: recoil. It simply wasn't possible to get a workforce comprised of white-collar workers to pass a qualification course, firing what amounted to low-end .44 Magnum ammunition. Even with all-steel pistols weighing 42 ounces, recoil was stout. And packing a pistol that was almost three pounds was work. The FBI kept asking the ammunition companies for softer and softer ammunition: 180s at 1,300, 1,200, then 1,000 fps. When the FBI requested 180-grain bullets at 950 fps, the ballisticians at Winchester realized there was so much dead air space left in the big 10mm case that they could shorten the whole thing and make it fit into a 9mm-length magazine.

And the .40 S&W was born.

The 10mm? Rescued by Colt, which offered the Delta and Delta Elite in 10mm. In time, it became a hunting cartridge, and variants of the 1911, some with 6-inch barrels and slides to match, became relatively common in deer hunting and hog shooting. I scored a Colt Delta at a Second Chance pin shoot as a prize and found it fun to shoot with the FBI load. I used it as my "walking around" pistol in South Africa for the IPSC World Shoot held there in 2002.

## .40 S&W

The forty became the hottest thing since sliced bread right from its unveiling in 1990. It was the replacement for the 9mm, which had been replacing .38 revolvers in law enforcement since the mid-1980s. The promise of the .40 was 9mm capacity combined with .45 power. What it delivered was less in both categories. It did, however, take over in practical shooting competition. In the early 1990s, the USPSA added equipment divisions. One was "Limited," meaning no comps or red-dot optics. Smith & Wesson had been working on some new things, including a new cartridge, the .356 TSW, which made Major. Major is a scoring advantage, as hits off-center score more points if the load is Major instead of Minor. Built on its 59 Series pistols, the .356 TSW promised 9mm capacity with the scoring advantage of a .45. This was done by building guns that could stand up to the 50,000 psi specs of the .356 TSW. The .356 TSw was a 9x21 variant, but the 50,000 psi made all the difference. That, and having a big pistol manufacturer doing the T&E.

*The .357 Sig delivered, as these bullets, extracted from ballistic gelatin, show.*

In an episode that was quite acrimonious, the USPSA

declared that no cartridge using a bullet less than .400 inch in diameter could be scored Major. That killed all the work on various iterations of the Super, the TSW, and other cartridges in the Limited Division and caused S&W to drop sponsorship, fold the team, and walk away from the USPSA. Another relationship soured. I'm beginning to wonder if the whole 10mm/.40 episode was cursed from Day One.

It meant that the hi-cap 1911, particularly the 2011 from a new company, STI (since then, Staccato), ruled the roost. A 2011 in .40 became the default standard pistol in USPSA Limited competition in the mid-1990s and has remained so ever since. For a while, various iterations of the CZ 75 in .40 strove to push the STI off as king of the hill but never replaced it, only offering enough competition to keep the pistolsmiths working on the 2011 to keep it on top.

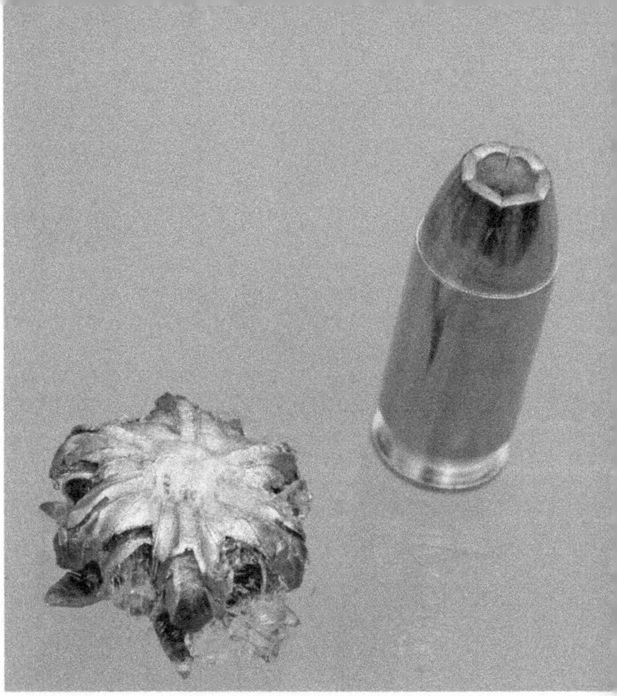

***A modern bullet design produces expanding bullets in all calibers. While a 9mm or .40 might expand to .45, a .45 will never shrink.***

The FBI would change its mind 25 years later and declare the 9mm plenty good enough. It could not see any difference in terminal performance in gelatin tests between the 9mm and the .40, and just like that, the .40 was a goner. Now, you can hardly give away a pistol in .40, and the only ones you see regularly are the legacy hi-cap .40s in USPSA Limited.

## THE FBI AND THE .40

What was the FBI's beef with the .40? I could be snarky and say that a bunch of accountants, actuaries and insurance investigators couldn't handle the recoil of a full-power .40 in a duty-sized or compact pistol. In all fairness to the FBI (and how often are you going to read my having written that?), the entire police establishment had the same problem. In a department of 1,000 officers (which is a large department, by the way, the average size is about a dozen), there will be a hundred or so who will be well below average in size. Most won't be highly motivated. Getting them all "qualified" is a major hassle of cost and time. The .40 was more difficult to get everyone qualified, and the 9mm had all the advantages: it cost less per round. It took less ammo with fewer re-quals and shorter range time. And, the same-sized pistol in 9mm held more rounds than it held .40s, so everyone was happy.

The FBI decided that having conducted ballistic gelatin tests, it could not see any difference in the wound track in the gel between 9mm and .40, and as a result, there wasn't any.

*The Guncrafter looks like another .45 1911 but is chambered in .50 GI. You can convert it to an even more durable .45, but other .45s can't be turned into .50s.*

Anyone who has had a technical education (one lacking in gender studies, DEI, or CRT courses is an excellent first approximation) could tell you it is absolute nonsense. The simple fact of rudely shoving a bullet of .400-inch diameter through gel compared to one that was .355 inch clearly shows the opposite. The other hook the FBI hung its decision on was that with modern bullet design, a 9mm expanded to the point it was equal to a .40. I vaguely recall the adage "A rising tide lifts all ships"—.40 bullets got the same R&D work for expansion as the 9mm ones did, not to forget the .45.

Oh well, it is all done now, and as a result, you will find few 1911s in .40. Most of those will be USPSA competition guns, but you might see the occasional .40 here and there. With a new barrel, it becomes a 10mm, and then life is good.

## .45 SUPER & .45 SMC

The .45 Super and the .45 SMC originated from the fertile brain of the late Dean Grennell. The idea was simple: use a case tougher than the .45 ACP and pump it up. Jumped up to the upper 20,000 psi range (I've seen numbers from 26,000 to 29,000, but I'd be leery of going past 28,000, and then only cautiously), he worked with shortened .451 Detonics cases, trimming them to .45 ACP length. He arranged for and agreed to Ace Custom 45s of Cleveland, Texas (who knew there was more than one Cleveland?) building the guns because it took more than just a drop-in barrel for the 1911 to stand up to it.

The advantage was a 1911 built to be a .45 Super that could still use .45 ACP ammunition, provided it was strong enough to run the .45 Super recoil spring. The downside was that .45 Super ammo would fit into an un-modified 1911, so you could put 28,000 psi ammo through a rattly war-surplus 1911.

The agreement between Grennell and Ace meant others had to pay royalties, so Triton Ammunition changed the name of its ammo to .45 SMC, used small rifle primers instead of large, and offered its own ammo.

Ace and Triton are now out of business, but you can still buy brass marked .45 Super from Starline and load up your own ammo if you have a gun built to the .45 Super specs.

## .460 ROWLAND

Johnny Rowland developed the .460 Rowland cartridge in collaboration with Clark Custom Guns. The process is simple in concept but had to be tricky to pull off. You take a .45 ACP case and lengthen it so it won't ever, *ever* chamber in a .45 ACP chamber. But, you keep the overall loaded length the same as .45 ACP. Then, jump the chamber pressure up to 40,000 psi, giving you low-end .44 Magnum ballistics. You can send a 230 grain up to 1,200 to 1,300 fps. A 200-grain JHP can be going over 1,400 fps, and a 185? How about 1,500 fps? Now, recoil is going to be stout. And the gun is going to be worked real hard. Part of the deal you'll have to accept with this is that you will use a 1911 whose barrel has a comp on it. The comp is needed both to keep recoil from abusing you and also to keep it from abusing your 1911.

## .50 GI

The .50 GI is the brainchild of Alex Zimmerman of Guncrafter Industries. It uses a case wide enough to hold a .500-inch bullet with a rim like a .45 ACP. The bullet weights range from 185 grains (lathe-turned copper hollowpoints) up to 300 grains. The velocities are just above the .45 ACP range, with a 185 listed at 1,200 fps (your mileage may vary; barrels differ on this and all calibers) to 700 fps for the 300-grain bullet. Pressures are what you'd expect, not going over that of the .45 ACP because the case thrust on the slide is the limiting factor. Still, a 300-grain bullet going 700 fps is enough to make Major and score highly as a bowling pin load, which is where I see it most often used.

***Left to right, 9mm Parabellum, .38 Super, .45 ACP, .50 GI.***

When knocking bowling pins off tables, momentum is a more relevant yardstick than kinetic energy. In the

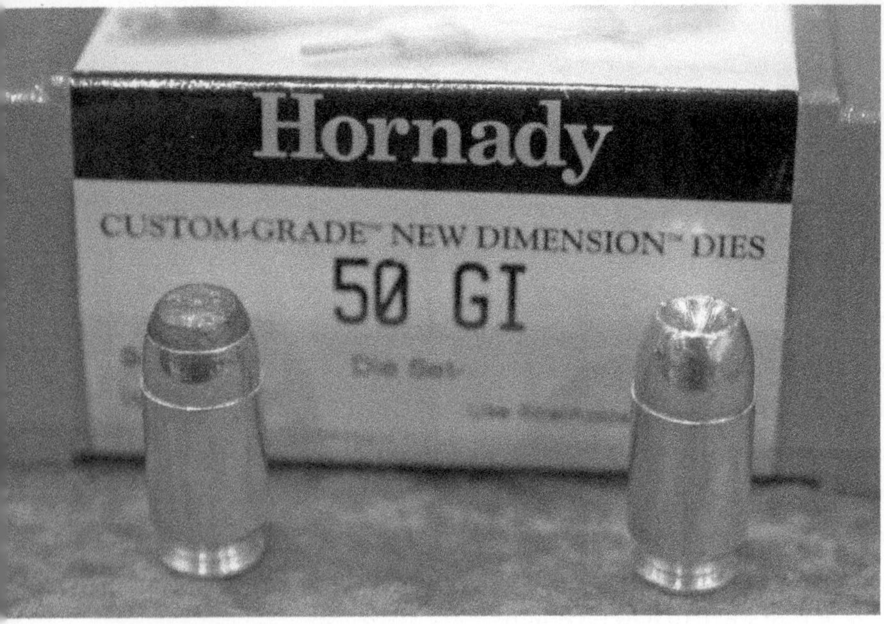


*Like pretty much every other cartridge that the 1911 has been, and can be, chambered in, the .50 is reloadable, and Hornady, among others, makes dies for it (and almost any other cartridge you can wrestle into a 1911).*

parlance, a 300 going 700 fps scores a Power Factor of 210, where 195 is considered the threshold of "good pin action."

There's good news and bad news here, however. Alex makes superb 1911s in .50 GI. They're built like bank vaults and nearly indestructible; you could spend a lifetime not wearing one out. The bad news is you can't convert a .45 ACP 1911 to .50 GI. But you can convert a .50 GI 1911 to .45 ACP, and he also does that.

Loaded ammo can be had, but only from Guncrafter; however, it's easy to reload, die makers produce reloading dies, and all you need is a .45 ACP shell holder or shell plate.

## .22 TCM: A STEP BACKWARD OR FORWARD?

The Rock Island Armory folks came up with a new one. OK, take a longer-than-normal .38 Super-like-5.56-base case, and neck it down to .22. Make the overall length just long enough to fit into a 1911 magazine, and pump the pressure up to the limits of the pistol. You've got the .22 TCM, which can deliver a 40-grain bullet at 2,000 fps. That beats the heck out of the 5.7x28 FN cartridge. The recoil is soft, but the muzzle flash is impressive, as you can imagine.

Conversion is easy: drop in a .22 TCM barrel and swap out the recoil spring, depending on your pistol. That's it.

## RIMFIRES

The .22 LR and the .22 WMR are also options in the 1911, but they both require significant deviation from the original design. Neither has enough *oomph* to run a locked-breech design, so they must be straight blowback. Colt did this pre-war with the Service Ace, a design with a lightened steel slide with a unique recoil system. Post-war, it used the Ace, which had a floating chamber, to leverage the slide (which was still lighter than a USGI 1911 slide). While it worked, the Ace's accuracy wasn't any better than plinking level, and the incredibly grubby rimfire ammo (it all is) made maintaining the floating chamber a headache. I don't know about the pre-war ones because they are all collectibles, and a Colt collector would have an attack of the vapors if you were to spend a day plinking with his pre-war rimfire.

Now, aluminum-slide rimfire conversions are common, and you can, if you're lucky, also score a Marvel Precision conversion, which can deliver Bullseye accuracy.

Rock Island Armory offers a .22 WMR version of the 1911, with a blowback upper, slide, and barrel on a 1911 frame.

## BOTTLENECKS

No, it's not a traffic jam, but a handgun cartridge that looks like a short rifle cartridge. At the end of the 19th century, velocity was king, which meant a bottlenecked pistol cartridge. That's how we got the 7.63 Mauser, the .30 Luger, and later the 7.62 Tokarev. Of those three, only the .30 Luger, a.k.a. the 7.65 Luger, can fit into a 1911, as the others are too long to fit into the magazine. But we have some that fit just fine.

The .357 Sig is one of them, and it is essentially, but not practically, a .40 S&W necked down to 9mm. Not actually, because the .357 Sig case is longer than a necked-down .40, and the neck is already short when at the correct length; make it shorter, and you'll have problems. Why do this? (A question we'll be asking repeatedly in this section.) For velocity. Specifically, to get a 125-grain JHP up to the speed of a .357 Magnum. In the 1990s, many shooters believed that that combo gave the best stopping power. Maybe yes, maybe no, but the cost was too great. The cost in 1911s was not a significant issue. An all-steel pistol can hurl a 125-grain bullet at 1,350 fps, which isn't a big deal.

*The lineup of bottlenecked high-speed demons left to right. First is the .38 Casull, then the 10mm Centaur, the .400 Cor-Bon, and finally the .40 Super.*

But, put it into a polymer pistol, and the recoil gets to be a bit much. Then—because no police officer would ever carry a pistol with a 5-inch barrel—when you put it into a handgun with a 4-inch barrel, you lose velocity and gain a bunch of muzzle flash and blast. (If you want actual speed, track down a .38 Casull. There weren't many made. It used a .45 Super case necked down to 9mm, and it got even more velocity than a .357 Sig—as in 1,600 fps with some loads. Recoil was harsh even in an all-steel 1911 and hardly worth it.)

Then there are the .40 bullets in .45 cases. The first was the 10mm Centaur from Charles Petty. That didn't get much traction, but Cor-Bon refined it and came out with the .400 Cor-Bon, which has more velocity, but the apex was the .40 Super from the now-gone Triton Cartridge Company.

These are drop-in barrels to convert a 1911 in the parent cartridge to a new one, and they are a lot of fun to experiment with. It is hard to make the case that any offers more than what regular ones do, but sometimes you have to find something new to mess around with.

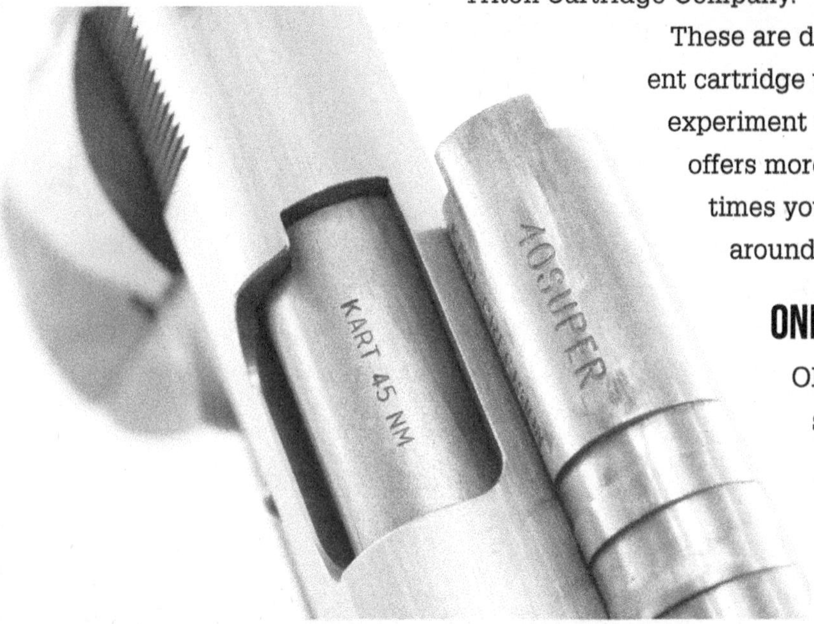


*You can convert the 1911 to another caliber with an extra barrel, so long as the breechface size for each is the same. So, the .40 Super, a necked-down .45 Super case, works in a .45 ACP-built 1911.*

## ONES YOU CAN MAKE

OK, the 1911 breechface comes in three sizes: 9mm/.38 Super, .40 and .45. (We'll leave out the .38 Special because no one I know of makes such a beast anymore.) If you can find a barrel, any cartridge that fits the 1911 magazine length and the breechface width can be made into a working pistol. I've built several .357 Sig, .400 Cor-Bon, .40 Super, .460 Rowland, and .30 Luger 1911s. If you could find a suitable barrel blank (the 8mm Nambu bore has an odd diameter of .320 in.), you could even make a 1911 in 8mm Nambu. You could build one in .380 Auto, but the hard part would be springing it lightly enough to cycle with factory loads and still have enough push to strip a round out of the magazine. The .45 GAP is a possibility, but converting a .45 ACP barrel would be work, as the GAP is shorter, and unlike revolvers, pistols are not happy with short brass in long chamber combos. The .45 Super is an overpressure .45 ACP, and the problems are more a matter of springs and barrel fit.

In the end, you will return to the same few: 9mm, .38 Super, and .45 ACP.

## EXTRA PRESSURE

What are the +P and +P+ markings you'll see on ammunition? Both the cases and the boxes will have markings that actually mean something. The standard loading of ammunition has a ceiling, a Maximum Average Pressure (a.k.a. MAP), that it is not allowed to exceed. For the 9mm, that pressure is 35,000 psi. Any given factory loading will have its tested samples average under this. And even if it averages under, a certain number or percentage cannot exceed that 35,000 psi figure. If they do, the lot is broken down and reworked.

In +P loads, the allowed pressure is raised, with the understanding that you, the shooter, are smart enough not to use it in an unsuitable firearm. For the 9mm, that MAP+P is 10 percent higher at 38,500 psi. Similarly, the .45 ACP has limits, with its standard 21,000 psi and its +P 23,000 psi.

An important detail to note: the old method of measuring pressure was not electronic. It was a tiny copper cylinder that got squished by the pressure, the "copper crusher" method. These were correctly called CUP but were colloquially called "psi."

*There is no conversion factor.* You cannot say, "A CUP of X is equal to a psi of Y," because there isn't any. So do not assume that old reloading data, using CUP, is correct, except when it is well under the pressure ceiling. Old data that runs up to the "red line" is not always safe when measured by electronics.

OK, so what is "+P+" then? There isn't a definition. It is an agreement between the ammunition makers and the big-lot buyers, usually law enforcement agencies, about what they want. Let's say a given agency wants a 9mm load where the bullet, instead of 1,150 fps for the regular load or 1,225 for the +P load, wants 1,325 fps. (These are all just for illustration purposes; do not write this down as "I can get this.") The ammo companies say, "Nope, can't do it." They haggle back and forth, and finally, the ammo company agrees to deliver 9mm ammo at 1,275 fps, which is over +P pressure, but only if the agency signs a truly ferocious contract absolving the ammo company of any problems from bad breath to hair loss, to pistols falling to pieces prematurely. What is the pressure? Only the ammo company knows for sure. But it is marked +P+ and "For Law Enforcement Only."

***Higher-pressure ammunition won't cause your 1911 heartache, but you might find the recoil a bit much. And the ammo will cost you more, as well.***

Can you buy some? Sure, this is America. Once something gets out into the market, you can buy and sell it. Will it confer any advantages? Only if the extra 25-75 fps per shot matters to you. Will it wear out your 1911? It will wear it faster, but it will take a long time. ●

CHAPTER 4

# 1911 SIZES

## GOVERNMENT MODEL

We'll start with the historic size, the original, also known as the Government, and work through them in the order of their appearance. The Government has a 5-inch barrel and slide to match, with a full-length frame and flush-fit magazines holding seven or eight rounds. This, in steel, is a big pistol and not easily carried, at least not concealed. Every USGI 1911 or 1911A1 was this size. All GI clones will be this size. It is the most reliable, durable, and easy to shoot of all sizes, and it provides as much velocity as the .45 ACP needs without going to extra pressure.

Once you get an eye for the proportions, you won't need a guide to readily see that a given 1911 pistol is a GM.

As an aside, in the engineering/pistolsmithing area, Browning designed and tested his pistol in this size, and any deviation from it required a whole lot of work and, in some instances, compromises. It is a firm opinion among makers and pistolsmiths that any size other than the Government brings the possibility of malfunctions—something the top-notch 'smith knows about, looks for, and corrects. Manufacturers have long known the changes the other sizes need to be reliable and have made them for the most part.

## COMMANDER

After the Government, first, there was the Commander with a lightweight frame. Known as the Commander then, the all-steel Combat Commander joined it in 1974, and the aluminum-framed one became the Lightweight Commander. Oh, and I should point out here that unlike the Government Model, the term "Commander" is a trademark of Colt. Only Colt can call a given 1911 a Commander, and everyone else who makes one otherwise identical to it must refer to it as "commander-sized." We all know what we're talking about, so at the gun shop, if you use the term "commander-sized" at any time other than asking to look at pistols smaller than government-sized, you might get odd looks.

*These are the basic sizes you'll run into in the 1911 universe—top, a long slide, then a Government, a Commander, and an Officer's.*

The Commander has a barrel three-quarters of an inch shorter than the Government Model's and a slide to match. However, it is not just the barrel and slide lengths that differ. The Commander's bushing, barrel, and frame were also changed from the Government to make them work properly. The Commander bushing is shorter on its skirt because of the decreased room inside the slide during cycling. The front of the barrel locking lugs, on top, have been machined back on the Commander to provide room for the shorter bushing during cycling. The slide recoil spring tunnel is shorter. The recoil spring guide rod is shorter. The barrel bottom lugs have been machined back from the front to provide more room. And finally, the slot in the frame that those lugs ride in has been pushed back in the frame.

A minor detail: the Commander frame's ejector is extended to hit the empty earlier in the slide cycle and to eject it in the shorter cycling timeframe.

In short, you cannot readily swap Government and Commander top-end parts. If you want the commander size, you have to buy a Commander (or commander-sized) pistol. We'll review the exact details in the chapters covering each. But brace yourself; these changes keep happening as the 1911 shrinks down in size.

*One of Colt's changes to create the Commander was to alter the barrel's bottom lugs. On top is a Commander, below a Government. You can't fit a Government barrel into a Commander pistol without making changes, and the lug is just one.*

## OFFICER'S MODEL

In the Officer's Model, Colt went even further. The barrel was shortened to 3½ inches, and the slide, guide rod, and bushing were shortened. Since they were making an ultra-compact pistol, Colt also shortened the frame, losing a round in capacity but making it a very compact package but one that is tough to shoot well.

## DEFENDER

For the Defender, Colt went down to a 3-inch barrel, which meant giving up the bushing altogether. The barrel is belled to match the slide interior, and the recoil system is so short it had to go to a two-spring system, one inside the other.

## KIMBER

Kimber started with Government-sized pistols, and when it came time to make something more compact, it settled on 4 inches, not 4¼. Despite losing the quarter inch, they are the same mechanically as the commander-sized pistols, and you might not even notice the length difference unless you had two side by side.

The 4-inch-even length is popular, and you can find them from Kimber, Springfield Armory, and many others.

## LONG SLIDE

In the early 1980s, there was a movement to get a long-slide IPSC pistol. This had been done before for Bullseye. Jim Clark Sr., again, was the driving force. As the story goes, he was in a government surplus store and saw a 55-gallon drum full of cut-in-half 1911 slides. (The government would rather cut and sell it as steel by weight than let us get our dirty mitts on surplus slides, then and now, the idiots.) He bought them for a song and figured out how to weld the front halves, clean up, and machine to length to existing slides, creating a 6-inch 1911. Bullseye shooters snapped them up.

***The Springfield EMP is an anomaly in the 1911 universe, as Springfield "shrunk" it in an unusual way. And it is a great little pistol, by the way.***

We thought they were just the thing for IPSC, and the impetus caught on when the movie *Thief*, starring James Caan, came out. His character carried one, and everyone had to have one. I won't go into the theoretical reasons we had to have them for IPSC and just say that we quickly found out they didn't help you shoot any faster.

You will find them on hunting 1911s, especially 10mm, where the extra inch of barrel length gets you more velocity, and the extra sight radius helps in accurate aiming. Now that red-dot optics are standard, I guess the sight radius is a non-starter, but you still get the velocity.

## SPRINGFIELD EMP

OK, what if you took a compact 1911 and, instead of making it shorter, you did something radical like take a bandsaw and slice the frame and slide into two pieces right down the center of the magazine well along the grip screw bushing. Then, shorten both halves so the remaining magazine well will hold a 9mm magazine and not a .45 mag. You end up with a 1911 with less circumference around the grip, and thus, it is better suited to shooters with small hands. This came out in 2006 and has been in production ever since in three variants.

The result is a very clever and comfortable pistol. It does, however, have several proprietary parts. The frame, magazine, slide, and firing pin are all EMP-specific. If you need a replacement for any of these, Springfield Armory is pretty much your only option, which is not a big problem, if a problem at all.

The original plan was to offer it in 9mm, .40 S&W, and .45 GAP. That didn't last long, as the .45 GAP became a Glock-only caliber, and no one else wanted to adopt it. In .40, the EMP was not fun to shoot. I tested and wrote it up when it was introduced, and at an industry event soon after, I talked to Robbie Leatham about it. I mentioned the .40 loads, and with a wince, his reaction was, "Those things hurt." When a professional shooter who grinds through 50,000-70,000 rounds a year says something is not fun to shoot, believe them.

*The slide lengths of the four sizes are the same top to bottom as before. Note that the spring tunnel on the long slide and Government are the same, and while different from those, the Commander and Officer's models are the same.*

*With the development of the hi-cap 1911 frame, the STI, USPSA/IPSC competition took a great leap forward. Suddenly, a .38 Super Open gun that held 28 rounds was a reality.*

The EMP is now a 9mm-only pistol, but Springfield Armory offers it in three variants.

## CAPACITY

Up to that point, all 1911s had been single-stack. When the Para-Ordnance frame came out in 1987, it offered higher capacity. Since we were still in the .45 era (at least, for defense, anyway), the magazines were made to hold .45 and the frames to match. When we went to .38 Supers and .40 S&W for competition, the magazine tubes got grooves stamped into them to size the interior, but the frames stayed the same. This was the only way Para Ordnance could do it, as the frames were cast. A new frame, scaled to 9mm/.38 Super or .40 would have required a new mold and magazine tubes. It was easier to crease the mag tube to adjust the volume.

The Para frames were all steel or aluminum. Chip McCormick offered us the composite frame, with a steel rail section and a polymer grip/mag holder portion, to get things going. That became the STI and then the Staccato. The Springfield Armory DS series is the latest iteration. ●

CHAPTER 5

# BUYING A 1911

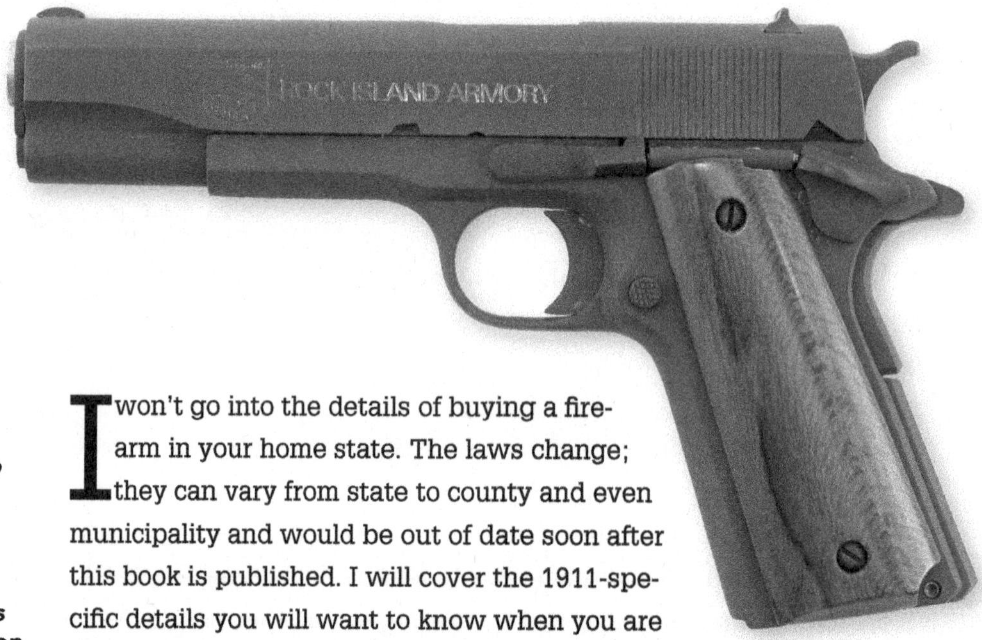


*A Rock Island GI will do if you're looking to acquire a GI or GI clone. If you want to get into competition, don't buy one like this and rebuild it for competition—get the competition model. If you want to build skills and this is a bargain at the local gun shop (LGS) counter, go for it.*

I won't go into the details of buying a firearm in your home state. The laws change; they can vary from state to county and even municipality and would be out of date soon after this book is published. I will cover the 1911-specific details you will want to know when you are standing in the gun shop or at the gun show and inspecting a pistol for possible purchase.

But first, some questions and parameters.

## WHAT ARE YOUR NEEDS?

Are you looking for something for daily carry? Competition? As a collectible? It will be a long time before a new Colt becomes collectible. A Lightweight Commander would be a great carry gun, but not so useful if you're planning on winning matches at the gun club or in your state or area.

## WHAT'S ITS CALIBER?

*Olympic Arms made 1911s in the old days. They were within spec, so if you score one at a reasonable price, you can use it to learn maintenance, rebuilding, etc.*

Caliber choice may seem obvious, but you must consider it. If you buy a .45 and have no plans on reloading ammo, you will need to buy .45 ammo, which costs more than 9mm. A 1911 in .38 Super might be a great deal, but ammo won't be as common as .45 or 9mm; it will cost more, and if there isn't any, then you're outta luck. Ditto .40 S&W. Yes, it could be a great deal, but consider ammo supply. Rare calibers might or might not become collectibles but will have more ammo supply problems.

## WHAT COMES WITH IT?

If you are buying a vanilla-plain .45, and it comes with one magazine, no problem. There is no lack of magazines; they don't cost that much, and the gun shop probably has as many as you'll need starting out. But what about that clean, low-priced STI in the corner? Or the hi-cap Para Ordnance next to it? They're both in 9mm, that's easy, right? Sure, but how many mags do they come with? One? Have you priced hi-cap mags for those lately? Old STI mags might be high-mileage and need a rebuild or tuning—when you can find them. New ones are over $100 each. Para mags are even rarer and just as pricey. Side note: since Para Ordnance went out of business (well, it was bought by Remington, which then went under), you should ensure you can get mags for a Para-framed 1911. Armscor offers hi-cap 1911s and uses magazines on the Para pattern, which is an option. But if you're going for a relatively uncommon pistol, you should ensure magazine availability as part of the transaction.

## IS THE COMPANY STILL IN BUSINESS?

The list of "used to be" companies that made 1911s isn't as extensive as those in the AR-15 market, but there are still plenty of them. And you must remember that many of them went out of business for reasons entirely under their control. A particular Colt 1911 might be rough around the edges depending on when it was made, but Colt is still in

*How many magazines does it come with, and what kind does it use? The STI mag (left) will not work in a Para Ordnance (right-hand magazine) or Para-based pistol, and vice-versa.*

business, and any pistolsmith will work on it. But show up at your local gun shop counter with a "smoking deal" Norinco 1911, and you will find as many pistolsmiths willing to work on it in, as the Lord of the Rings quote has it, "a list that grows thin." It may be within dimensional spec in every particular, but who wants to take a chance? And you have to wonder why a gun shop, knowing that, took it in on trade in the first place.

However, you might consider buying that Norinco if it is a smoking deal and if you want to learn about the 1911. If it works, you can learn your gunsmithing modification skills on it. If it doesn't, you can learn gunsmithing debugging skills.

## INSPECT IT

Depending on how much takedown the local gun shop will allow, any used pistol must be taken apart and inspected. I call it the "hammer marks and tire tracks" look. A used 1911 should show expected wear. The rails should be bright from friction, the firing pin plate should show the hammer marks, and the barrel chamber should have rubbings front-to-back where the slide has rubbed over it.

Think twice if you see hammer marks, tire tracks, or signs it has been dropped. Rust can be negotiated.

Check that the thumb and grip safeties both work properly. Look down the bore to ensure there is rifling, no rust, and no bulges in the barrel (a bulged barrel will show as a dark ring in the bore).

A grip safety that doesn't work will probably require a replacement. A malfunctioning thumb safety might be salvageable, but it, too, likely needs replacement. These are things to negotiate on a used 1911. For a brand new one, pass, as the QC from the company is lacking, and who knows what else will end up being wrong with it?

Also, if it matters to you, you'll want to know if the particular model you are considering is a "Series 70" or a "Series 80" pistol. Strictly speaking, a Colt can be either, as the company trademarked the designa-

*The Detonics pistols could be good or bad, but they are no longer made, so you are buying a pistol with no warranty other than what the gun shop provides.*

tion. But the counter clerk will know what you're asking and tell you if the model has a firing pin block.

## FIT

Prospective buyers will check the slide-to-frame fit or "wiggle." If buying a custom 1911, I'd expect little or no movement. I mean, for the price I'd pay for an Ed Brown, Les Baer, Nighthawk, or Wilson Combat, little or no play is expected. If it has come from Ned Christiansen, Stan Chen, Jason Burton, John Harrison, CT Brian, or other pistolsmiths who are at the top of their craft, and I paid for a tight fit, I expect a tight fit.

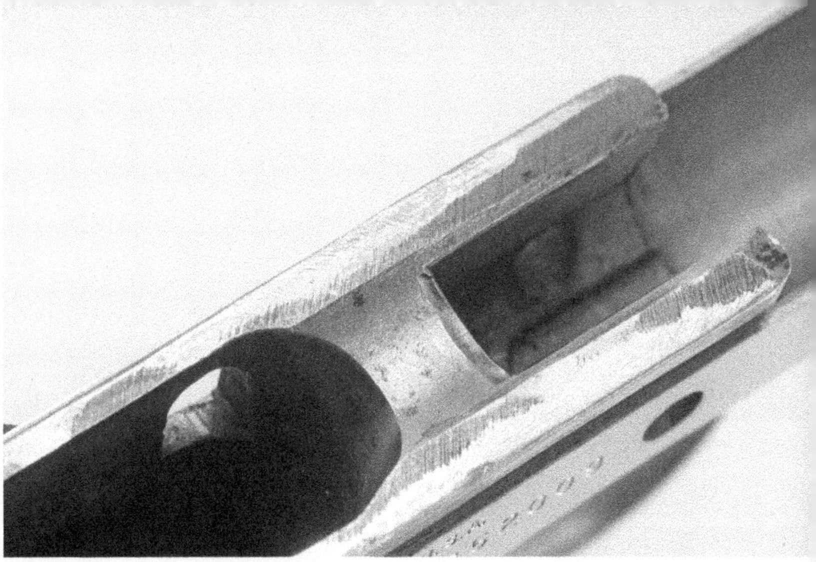

*When buying, always inspect. If you see marks like this (the literal hammer marks), you are looking at a pistol that got at least one rebuild in its career. It should be priced accordingly.*

Anything else, I don't sweat some wobble. When the pistol closes, having chambered a round, it will come together more consistently than the wobble would indicate.

The other "test" is to close the slide and press down on the barrel with a thumb. What does this check? I've been doing it for over half a century, and I'm still unclear. On a rattly old GI gun, it might indicate that the barrel wasn't resting on the slide stop pin but floating over it. Or it was being propped up by the link. But then again, not.

And most 1911s don't move when pressed that way anyway.

We all do it; we can't help it. It doesn't tell us much if anything, but it is part of the process. Consider it the 1911 equivalent of kicking the tires.

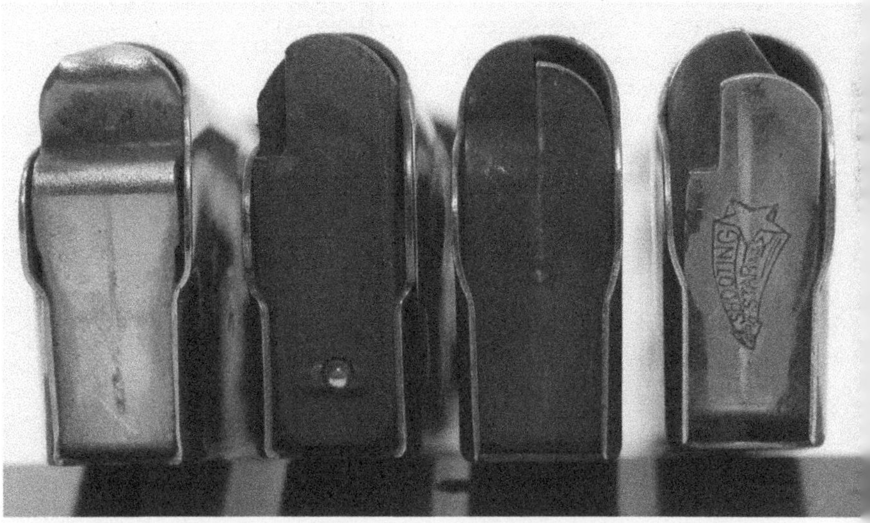

*How many magazines does your prospective new 1911 come with? Are they all the same? Don't worry about mixing brands if they haven't been abused and are of the modern feed-lip design. These are four different brands; they all work in all the 1911s they've been in.*

## TRIGGER PULL

How do you check the trigger pull? Ask the shop, counter guy or owner first, then dry-fire it. Back in the caveman days, we had all kinds of "tests" to see if a trigger job would hold, and I look back on those with a certain level of horror. What not to do?

Don't lock the slide back and trip the slide lever, letting the slide crash home with full power on an empty chamber. That's abuse, and not just of the sear/hammer engagement. That will get you branded as an idiot. ●

CHAPTER

# 6

# DISASSEMBLY FOR CLEANING

*You will see this scratch on many 1911s, where someone tried to assemble it with the recoil spring installed, forcing the slide stop into place. Geez, don't be that guy.*

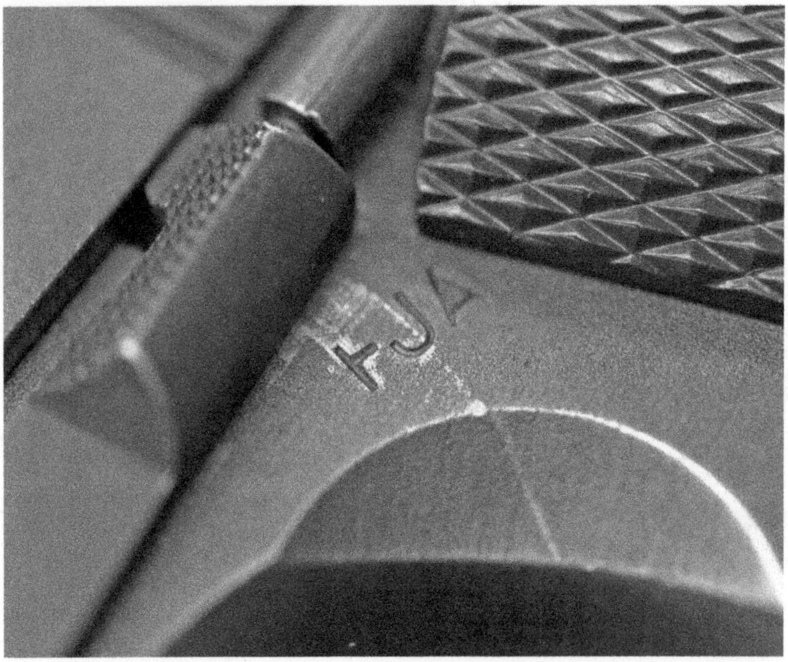

In this chapter, we'll take your 1911 apart enough to clean it. This is not a complete disassembly; that's the next chapter. Remember our discussion on the various frame sizes? Well, in the century-plus since the 1911 has been made, we've not only figured out two basic ways to disassemble it, but a couple of extra complications. You will need a few small tools and may need a bushing wrench. A brass or plastic rod smaller than the slide stop pin diameter (nominal .200 inch) and, in some instances, a bent paperclip. A small, flat-blade screwdriver can come in handy at times. As you read this, you will find almost nothing in common with how you take apart a polymer-framed striker pistol.

There are two classes of 1911, and each has variations. We'll start with a box-stock, original design like a 1911A1 USGI.

Note: We will start with an unloaded pistol in all descriptions here.

Drop the magazine and work the slide. Lock the slide back and look into the chamber. Poke a fingertip in there, to be sure. I'm not kidding. Getting it wrong can lead to a loud noise, busted furniture, a slight loss of hearing, or even valuable things being shot or bleeding. The new hole generated might be in you, so check again.

***Why take the slide apart? Because after enough shooting, your extractor, firing pin, firing pin spring, and tunnel get as gunky as this one. You've got to keep things clean. Photo: Jason Burton***

## ORIGINAL

This covers the models with no changes from the 1911. There is no full-length guide rod, but there is a bushing. Unloaded, with the magazine out? Good. Cock the hammer. Hold the pistol by the slide and frame with the muzzle vertical, braced on a benchtop. Take the bushing wrench and press it down over the bushing. The opening in the wrench will wrap around the bushing and compress the recoil spring retainer. Now, give the bushing wrench a quarter turn, or less, clockwise. The bushing flange will no longer hold the recoil spring retainer in, and it (the spring) will attempt to push the wrench aside and shoot into the ceiling. Your job is to prevent it.

Ease the retainer and spring up out of the slide until it is fully extended, and then pull the retainer and spring out of the slide. Rotate

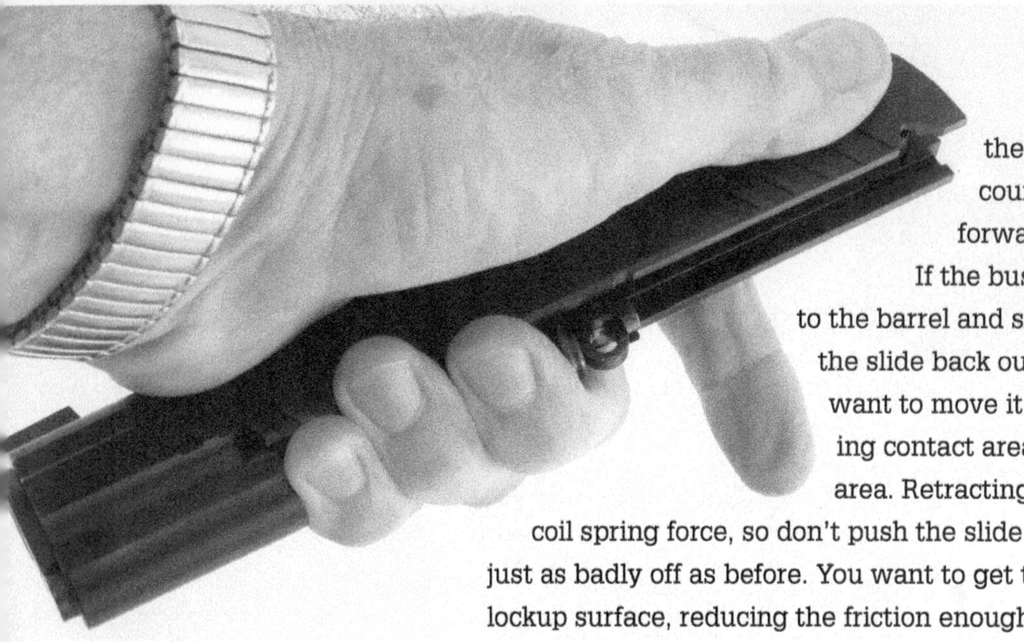

the bushing a half-turn or so counter-clockwise and pull it forward out of the slide.

If the bushing has been tightly fitted to the barrel and slide, you may have to push the slide back out of battery slightly. You want to move it enough to get the bushing contact area back of the barrel contact area. Retracting the slide increases the recoil spring force, so don't push the slide back too far, or you will be just as badly off as before. You want to get the bushing off the barrel lockup surface, reducing the friction enough to turn the bushing.

*This is how you take the slide off the frame without turning the bushing first. Keep your fingers wrapped tight, and the spring won't hurl itself across the room.*

Take a moment to look at the bushing and slide. You'll see a small lug on the side of the bushing behind its front flange. When you turn the bushing clockwise, this lug slides into a slot inside the slide, near the muzzle, and keeps the bushing in the slide. When assembled, the half-circle notch at the bottom of the bushing flange locks around the extended part of the recoil spring retainer and keeps the bushing from rotating out of the slot. That's the Browning genius at work: interlocking parts that stay assembled.

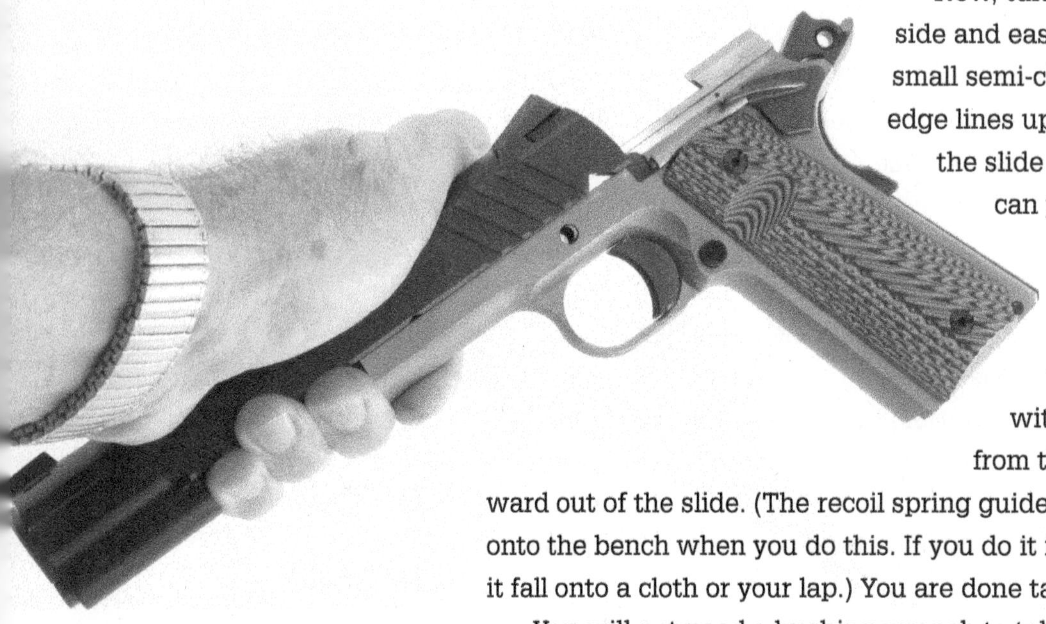

Now, turn the pistol onto its right side and ease the slide back until the small semi-circle notch on the bottom edge lines up with the retainer tip of the slide stop. Once aligned, you can push the slide stop out from the right.

With the slide stop out, run the slide forward, taking the barrel with it. Remove the barrel from the slide by pulling it forward out of the slide. (The recoil spring guide will fall out and clatter onto the bench when you do this. If you do it in the field, catch it or let it fall onto a cloth or your lap.) You are done taking it apart.

*When sliding the slide back on, keep your fingers tight and let the dust cover push them out of the way as you press the recoil spring into place.*

You will not need a bushing wrench to take apart a pistol built to GI standards or a custom gun fitted specifically to this standard. In a "finger-tight" 1911, you can (if your hand strength is up to it) press the recoil spring retainer down with a fingertip (most use their thumb tip) and rotate the bushing with your bare hands. You won't have the bushing wrench to restrain the spring from launching, but you will have your hands.

The second method makes spring retention easier and looks cool, but it comes with its own risks. Here, you hold the pistol with the muzzle pointing directly to the left. With your left hand, hook your thumb through the triggerguard, and wrap your fingers over and around the slide. By clutching it with your left hand, you can retract the slide until the disassembly notch lines up with the slide-stop retaining tip. Some people do this as a two-handed operation until the notch and tip line up and then clamp the slide in place with their left hand clutching the slide and recoil spring tunnel/dust-cover and their thumb hooked in the triggerguard.

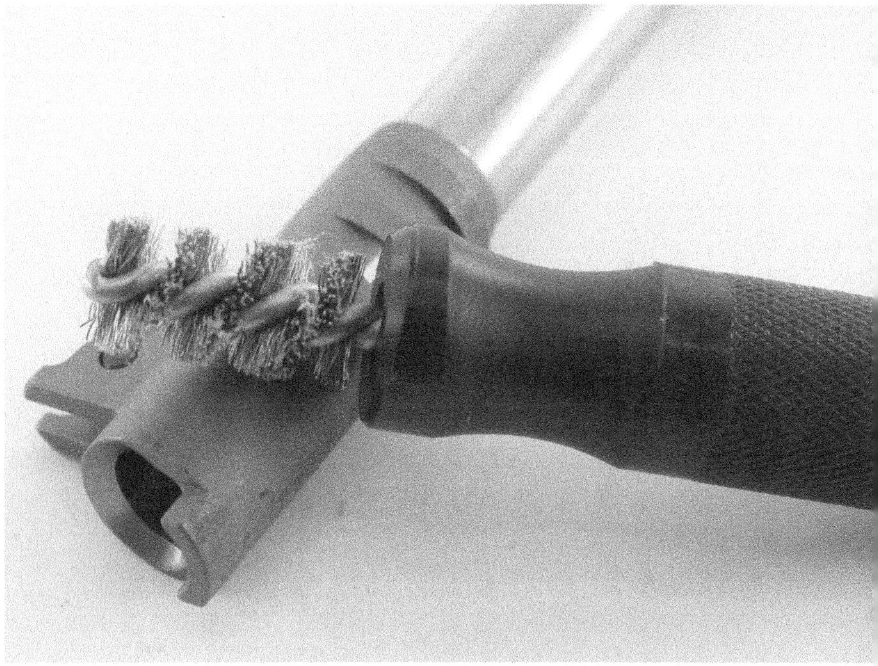

*To scrub a chamber properly, you need a chamber brush like this one from Wilson Combat. It will thoroughly scour the chamber, but do not shove it into the bore. That will ruin a brush for chamber work.*

With your right hand, reach under the pistol and push the slide stop out of the frame. It will only lift so high; reach back over and lift it out. Now, ease the slide forward, sliding your left hand with it and keeping your fingers wrapped under the slide to retain the recoil spring. Once the slide is off, you can lift your index finger enough to grab the recoil spring guide, control it, and ease the spring tension off the slide. Pull the guide and the spring out. The retainer won't fall out because on most slides (not all; it requires an extra machining step to make the slide properly), the retainer tunnel has a lip at the rear, and the retainer won't fall out the back. With the spring out, you can now turn the bushing to remove it and pull the barrel forward out of the slide. When you do so, the barrel feet will push the retainer out of the slide.

## CLEANING

Here's an overview of the routine cleaning work following field-stripping the gun. Brush the bore and use a patch to wipe out the gunk. Wipe the powder residue off the barrel, bushing, slide, and slide stop in and anywhere else it has accumulated. You can try to wipe the spring clean, but that is a Sisyphean task, best left to an ultrasonic cleaning station. Pay attention to the locking lug slots on the barrel and slide. They accumulate powder residue and petrified oil, and while they are, to a certain extent, self-cleaning, they are truly clean only with you using a small screwdriver in the slide slots to scrape the sediment out.

There is one area of cleaning that could benefit from more disassembly. If you use your brush to scrub the breechface of powder residues and notice that the extractor seems particularly gunky, press in the firing pin, drop the retaining plate, and pull the extractor out. You may be appalled at how much powder residue and stuff has accumulated in the extractor tunnel if you've gone through more than a few practice sessions. I've never seen a 1911 that failed to extract solely due to a gunk-packed extractor or tunnel, but it theoretically could happen, and I'm sure there has been at least one out there to suffer that fate.

*This is how bad some pistols can get and still work. (Well, barely, but still, in an emergency.) Not just caked on, but caked and baked on, crud. Clean yours before it gets to this point, willya? Photo: Dean Caputo by way of Ned Christiansen*

On to the frame. This will be easy. All you have to do for a routine cleaning here is use your properly fitting screwdriver (or Allen wrench or Torx bit, depending on the screws) and remove the grips. Wipe the frame clean. Wipe the feed ramp clean, and if it is particularly grubby, use a brush to scour the crud off. Here's a tip: when you scrub, don't just stick a brush in and scrub back and forth. If you do, half the time, you'll push the gunk off the ramp and back into the frame, into the area of the trigger slots. Place your brush on the ramp and then pull it up and forward. Lift, place back down and lift the ramp again. Brush the stuff out, not in.

Wipe the rail slots clean and the top deck of the frame. Interestingly (or not, depending on how engineering-focused you are), the powder residue on the top deck is somehow more compressed than the residues found in other places. Use a brush or screwdriver as a scraper to remove the tough deposits.

Unless you've been in a harsh environment (blowing sand, for example) or fallen into the water, you don't need to remove the firing system parts of the frame for a simple post-practice cleaning session; wipe off the oozing oil and powder residues, add a bit more oil, and get back to reassembly.

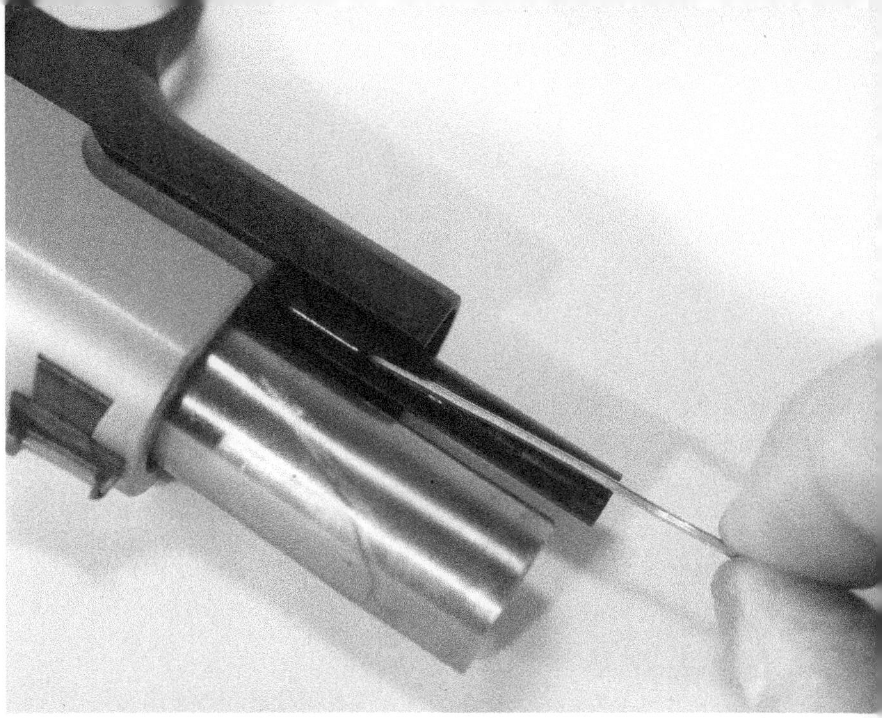

*Using a bent paperclip, lock the slide open, stick the bent tip into the lock shaft, and gently release the slide.*

## REASSEMBLY

We'll cover the reassembly of the original before we take apart the other designs. First, prep the slide by inserting the barrel back into the slide. Press the recoil spring over the guide and push the spring from the rear through its slide tunnel. Install the bushing and turn it (through the coils of the spring) until it's locked in the slide but out of line with the spring. Press the barrel back and up until it is locked in the slide. Place the spring guide against the bottom of the barrel, with the curved surface against the barrel.

Place the slide on the bench, right side down, muzzle to the left.

Now slide the frame into the slide, and let the barrel move into its frame slot. You might have to hold the muzzle and gently rotate the barrel until it aligns with the slot. You can look through the slide-stop hole in the frame and see the barrel link as it moves past the slide-stop hole. Line up the link hole and the slide stop hole, and press the slide stop shaft through. If the link fights you and refuses to align, this is where the small screwdriver comes in handy. Stick it in the slide-stop hole, hook the link, and line it up. As you press the slide back, the link will unlock it from the slide (it would not before). You can now align the slide stop clearance notch with the retaining tip.

If the slide-stop plunger also fights you, use the blade to compress it against its spring and push the slide-stop into place. Push the slide forward until it stops. Now, turn the pistol until the muzzle is pointed up.

You will be compressing the recoil spring, so do not point it at your face, nor at a lighting fixture, the cat, or anything else that might resent or be damaged by being struck by a self-hurling recoil spring and retainer. This is a two-handed operation. Hold the slide, and press the spring and retainer down into the slide. Once the retainer is fully

***The spring is contained, and you can take the pistol apart, in this instance, a Springfield Armory EMP.***

inserted into the slide, hold it in with the thumb of one hand while you turn the bushing with your other thumb. You don't have to turn it all the way at this point. The flange will hold the retainer in place if you can get it to butt up against the raised, usually knurled, nose of the retainer. Once the bushing holds the retainer, you can catch your breath and use the bushing wrench to contain and compress the retainer and finish rotating the bushing into place. ●

# GUIDE ROD COMPLICATIONS

One of the details you will hear 1911 owners argue over is the matter of recoil spring guide rods. As in full-length guide rods. Originalists argue that Browning didn't include it, so it isn't necessary. Fans want the extra weight, the "non-kinking spring," or just like the cool looks of one. I've added them to competition guns, but for a defensive gun, I'm an originalist and would not carry one with a full-length guide rod. But that's just me, and this is America.

And, since this is America, there are at least three kinds of full-length guide rods. One is the two-piece with the two halves threaded together. The others are one-piece rods. One type has a small hole (that's where the paperclip will be used; be patient), and the other does not.

*A one-piece guide rod that is deliberately short, so you can use a bushing wrench to take the 1911 apart.*

## TWO-PIECE GUIDE ROD

You'll recognize a two-piece guide rod by its end being an Allen wrench head. Use an appropriately sized Allen wrench to unlock the rod halves, unscrew and pull out the front half of the rod. After that, you are now in the same position as someone with an original design, and you can use the bushing wrench or not. Reassemble it like the original, but once together, lock the slide back, shove the front half of the guide rod into the slide, and tighten it.

## ONE-PIECE, NO HOLE GUIDE ROD

This guide rod has a peculiar design. You can't take it apart; it is one piece. You can't weasel it out of the slide if you use the original design and take the slide stop out first. So, what to do? Note that the one-piece guide rod does not sit flush with the bushing and retainer. That's your wiggle room. There's enough room to use the bushing wrench to turn the bushing, ease the retainer out, pull the spring out, and proceed as usual.

Reassembly is the same as the original bushing method.

*The Alpha Dynamics takedown tool for a one-piece guide rod. You need this, don't be cheap.*

## ONE-PIECE, SMALL HOLE GUIDE ROD

When you lock the slide back, you'll see a small hole drilled through the guide rod. Use a length of wire or a paperclip bent to a 90-degree angle and with the short end bent shorter than the diameter of the rod. This design is often used on a 1911 with a comp or one using a coned lockup and no bushing.

So, lock the slide back. Hook the short end of the paperclip into the hole in the rod. Ease the slide forward until the retainer bears on the paperclip and the recoil spring cannot push the slide. With the recoil spring captured, there is no tension on the slide; slide it back until the takedown notch aligns with the slide stop retaining tip, and push the slide stop out.

Run the slide assembly off of the frame. Pull the guide rod assembly out of the slide to the rear.

At this point, leave the recoil spring/guide rod assembly as-is until it comes time to reassemble. When disassembling, be aware that the parts are not large, the spring is strong, and you risk launching things into the ceiling.

Reassembly requires some juggling. First, insert the barrel back into the slide in the locked position. Then, insert the recoil spring assembly from the rear and place the curved section of the guide rod head up against the barrel. Make sure the link is in the proper position for assembly. Run the slide onto the frame and line up the link hole with the slide stop hole. Insert the slide stop. Until now, there has been no spring tension to work with. When you pull the slide to the rear and uncapture the retainer from the paperclip, the paperclip will fall out, and the slide will resume normal function.

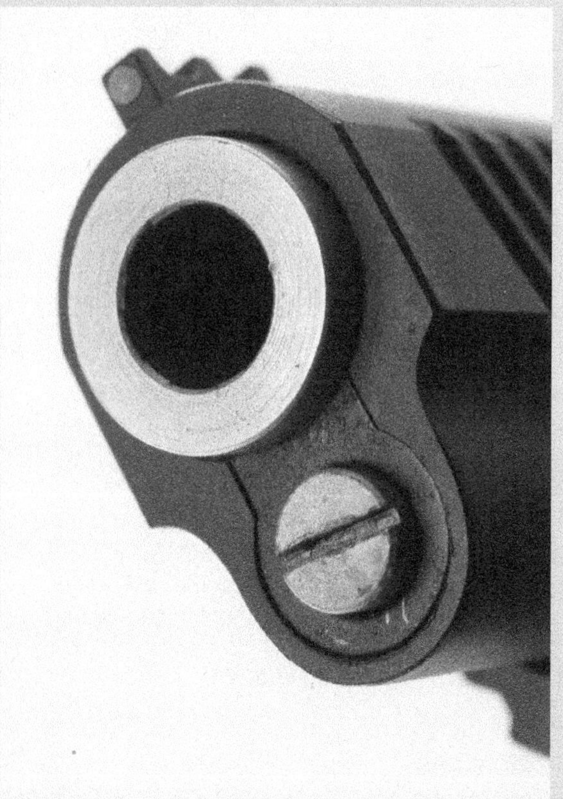

*This anomaly is one of the few two-piece guide rods the author ever saw with a screwdriver slot for unscrewing.*

In catching up on things 1911, I discovered that Alpha Dynamics makes a clever tool for this application. Think of it as Bent Paperclip 2.0. Alpha took a length of wire and bent the ends to be the catch-hook end. But, in the middle, as an offset to provide two different lengths of catch-wire, bent a loop. Clip the reverse plug retention clip (a name almost longer than the tool) onto the rod with one end in the disassembly hole. With two lengths, it works on almost any one-piece guide rod. In the current Brownell's catalog, it is $10. Yes, I know you can buy a box of paperclips for that, but this is one of those slick tools that makes life so much easier it is worth reaching into your pocket to get one, which I did.

The usual setup: a two-piece rod that requires an Allen wrench to loosen and unscrew it for takedown.

## WHY FULL-LENGTH GUIDE RODS?

The full-length guide rod became a thing back in the early days of competition. We were all running essentially identical guns, so anything, however small, that gave us an advantage was tried, assessed, adopted or rejected. The shooters who won happened to be using full-length guide rods, so it became an article of faith that you needed one. Why not have one? One-handed slide racking. If you must work the slide one-handed in an emergency or defensive situation, a full-length guide rod precludes one of the two methods. One method is to hook the rear sight on something and shove it. That's the new method. We all had "slick" rear sights in the prehistoric era and nothing to hook. So, instead, we would push the bottom face of the slide against something. A full-length guide rod prevents that.

Now, the odds of being in a defensive shooting are small. Very small. That you need to reload would be a small subset of that possibility. And needing to do it one-handed is an even smaller subset of a subset. It might happen once a decade. But the originalists hate full-length rods, and in the long run, who wants to be "that guy" who needed to do the one-handed slide rack but couldn't?

All together now: This is America, you get to choose.

CHAPTER

# 7

# COMPLETE TAKEDOWN

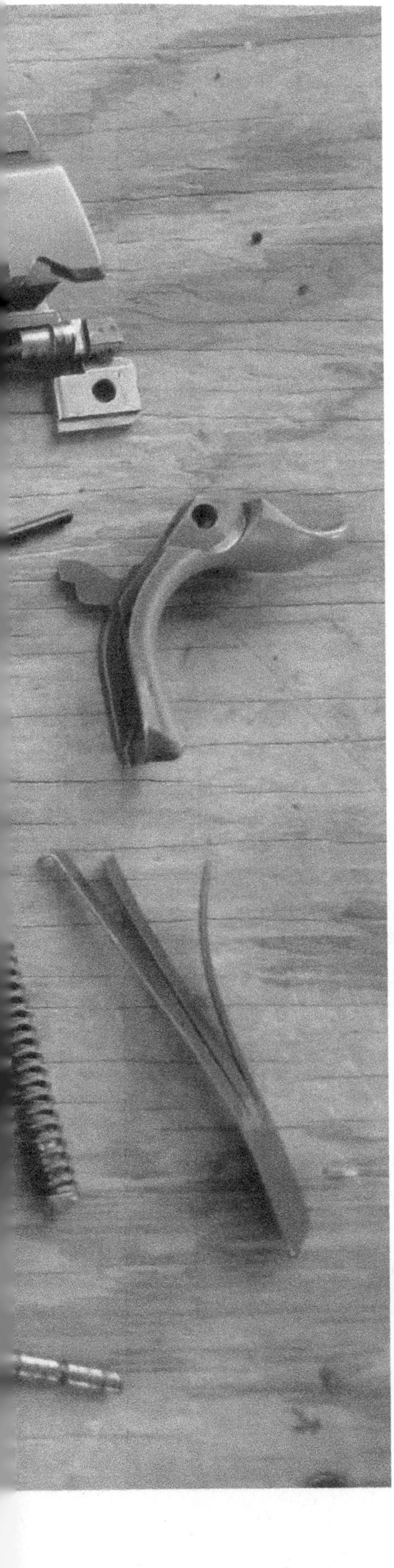

For the complete 1911 takedown, we'll continue from the field strip described in the previous chapter and remove all the removable parts, short of a replacement. Some parts don't come off without risk of damage and shouldn't be taken off short of replacement or other extreme needs. The short list would be the front sight, grip screw bushing, ejector, link and its pin.

You've got the 1911 apart for cleaning, meaning you've removed the slide assembly, barrel, and bushing. Or have you? You can leave the recoil spring on the guide unless you are replacing it.

Bushing out, barrel out, and leave the link and pin in place. Take a punch of the right size, press the firing pin into the slide, press the firing pin retaining plate down and off the slide, and ease the firing pin

***It isn't often that you'll need to take your 1911 down this far. (The left-hand grip still needs to come off.) Once a year, maybe, or if you go overboard and need to detail clean to prevent rust. And yes, this is a super-custom Ned Christiansen gun with many details attended to. Photo: Ned Christiansen***

and spring out of the slide. You can leave the firing pin spring on the firing pin again unless it's time to replace it.

That's the upper half, the easy part.

On the frame, use a screwdriver or other properly-fitting tool to unscrew the grip screws and remove the grips. This is the last of the easy stuff.

## THUMB SAFETY

Cock the hammer if it isn't already, and grab the safety with your thumb and forefinger. Wriggle it in the on-off direction while lifting it from the frame. You'll feel the orientation that lets you lift it out, but get something in the path behind the frame before you do. When you lift the safety far enough, the spring and plunger that "click" will try to shoot out. The spring and two plungers are a single unit and can't fly out if properly manufactured. But, if the rear plunger isn't attached correctly to the spring, it is free to fly, and it will. Once the spring is relaxed, lift the safety out and pull the plunger with the spring and other plunger attached out of the tube.

You might want to pull the grip safety out of the frame now. You will be foiled, as it does not clear the remaining parts unless specially modified to provide such clearance.

Place your thumb in front of the hammer, press the trigger, and ease the hammer down to rest. You do not want to dry-fire it at this time because you can damage parts.

With the hammer at rest, use a round-tipped punch in the cup side of the mainspring housing pin and punch it out. It is retained by the hammer spring into a groove turned in the mainspring pin, so it may take some tapping.

Once the mainspring housing pin is out, you can slide the mainspring housing down out of the frame. Take it easy, so the remaining parts retain their orientation. Note the three-leaf spring in the frame. It has a turned tab at the bottom that rides in a slot cut in the frame. Each of the three arms on the spring presses against a different part and performs a different function.

With the mainspring housing out, set aside the grip safety.

Look at the arrangement of the trigger, sear and disconnector. Perhaps even take a photo with your cell phone for reference. Now, press the sear pin and the hammer pin out of the frame from the right side. All that's left is the trigger and magazine catch.

Insert a correctly fitting screwdriver into the magazine catch slot on the right side of the frame. Put a small amount of counter-clockwise tension on it and depress the magazine catch in as if you were dropping the magazine. When the disassembly notch lines up with the tab on the screw-head part, rotate the screwhead tab until it stops. Then, lift the magazine catch out of the frame on the right side.

Pull the trigger straight out of the frame, and you have the frame completely apart. Oh, the ejector is still there, but unless it is broken and has to be replaced, don't take it off the frame.

## DEEP CLEANING

We'll assume that you have done, or will be soon, the light cleaning covered in the previous chapter, the field-strip cleaning. Here, we'll cover the details of all the rest, the once-a-year "man overboard" cleaning that you do because even as durable a tool as the 1911 is, it needs a complete scrubbing now and then.

I will treat my readers as adults and figure that you can do the obvious when it comes time to clean: if there is powder residue, you'll wipe or scrub it off. For this chapter, I'll go into the details of things you might not already know or the mysterious things that no one told you about because the pistol gurus at your gun club are all Glockaholics and know nothing but urban myths about the 1911.

The grubby areas on the barrel need attention, so wipe the crud off the barrel, chamber area, and barrel ramp. However, deep in the barrel, the bottom "corners" (the rim of the chamber) can collect powder and lead residue and eventually build up enough to cause problems. This is not a problem unique to 1911s, but because 1911 shooters use .45 ACP with lead bullets more than 9mm shooters, it's a lead bullet usage issue. You'll need a chamber brush, which Wilson Combat makes. If you use a bore brush the first time you run it entirely down the bore, it will be much less effective at scrubbing the chamber alone.

The locking lugs on the top of the barrel are worth a look. They won't collect stuff to the extent that the slide's locking lug slots will, but they can garner some gunk, so scrub or scrape them clear.

The slide has a pair of slots cut parallel to the firing pin tunnel on the underside to create the ejector's clearance slot and clear the magazine feed lips. These slots can collect an impressive amount of gunk, stuff, debris, whatever. (I've got to find a singular term for these residues because there are too many words to juggle.) The buildup doesn't really cause problems, but it can build up and splatter black spots on your shooting glasses, clothes and hands. The stripper rail doesn't collect any gunk, but you will notice a brass buildup on the bottom from the rail sliding across the top round in the magazine on each shot. The buildup is unsightly at worst but is not a problem otherwise.

Wipe the bushing clean, and take the opportunity to inspect it to track any wear it might be experiencing.

That's pretty much it for the barrel and slide. If you wish, you can pull the firing pin and extractor, as they can accumulate a fair amount of gunk, but the accumulation does not often hamper them. The hammer/firing pin combo has so much excess power that it will work even if it is gunked, rusty, and covered with grit. Oh, it won't be happy, but it will continue to work long after other pistols have up and quit on you.

One last thing before we move on to the frame: the brass scuffing you see behind the ejection port is not a sign of something wrong. It won't build up to become a problem, and yes, you can scrub it off with 0000 steel wool, but it will come back. Also, continued scrubbing with 0000 steel wool will wear down the finish there. Well, the blued finish, or a Cerakote finish, as stainless or hard chrome won't care. You can leave the brassing alone if you want, as it proves that you practice with your 1911.

## FRAME CLEANING

Here, we can get very involved if you want to. I wipe the oily stuff off the parts involved, look for wear, cracks, peening, or other changes, and reassemble if nothing is untoward. If I don't see any cracks or problems—and I usually don't—I oil and reassemble. But, we'll go through the various details that can come up, even if they are rare, because some will be things that won't exist on your basic polymer-framed striker pistol.

Use a brush to scrub the thumb safety lug clean, and inspect it for wear. If the lug shows signs of impressions from the sear, it is too soft (I ran into this problem once back when Reagan was president, never since, but I still check) and must be replaced.

Wipe the sear, hammer, and disconnector clean and check them for wear. A chipped sear or hammer hook requires immediate replacement (I've never seen one personally, but I have talked to 'smiths who have). Check that the hammer strut swings freely on the hammer. If not, find out why it is binding, usually due to rust. Clean the grip safety and check the front face of the tab for trigger bow impressions. There should be no impressions, but there may be rubbing through the finish of the safety, another "not a cause for concern" situation. If the trigger bounces (riding in a vehicle, the vibration can cause it to move), it will rub, but the trigger is so light it can't peen the tab.

Wipe the three-leaf spring clean, and check the slots between the three legs to ensure cracks have not formed. The slots should have been fine-blanked with the bottom ends rounded, but I've seen cheap ones with square corners, which is a stress riser, and cracks can form.

While we're working on the back end of the frame, let's look at the mainspring housing. Clamp the housing in a padded vise and use a punch to press the plunger and spring down into the body. As you ease up, it should follow your release and lift with you, not lag or slowly creep back to position. A slow response indicates petrified oil, packed gunk or grit and other residues building up. If it's slow, strip the mainspring housing, scrub things clean, lube, and reassemble.

Take the trigger, wipe it clean, and use your cleaning brush to scrub out the trigger bow slots in the frame. To check the fit once clean, turn the frame muzzle down and drop the trigger (in the proper orientation) into the slot, then hold your hand under the frame while you invert it. The trigger should fall fully forward of its own weight on insertion and fall free when inverted, again of its own weight.

Examine the grip screw bushings to make sure they are tight. No, don't grab a screwdriver and try to move them. That's a sure way to mangle the edges. Instead, if you don't have a proper bushing driver, try unscrewing them with your fingers. If they don't move, they probably won't, and you're good. If they do, unscrew them and adequately clean, degrease, install, tighten, stake, Loctite, etc., so they won't move in the future.

Look closely at the plunger tube. It must be flush with the frame along its length, top, and bottom and not move when wiggled. If it does, it must be fixed before you move on. Similarly, check the ejector for movement. It can wobble a small amount if the dimensions have not been properly held, but the design is so overkill-built that if it moves but works, it isn't a problem. If it comes out, the cross pin is missing, or the legs are broken, which might not be an easy fix.

Hold the frame up to the light and peer down the magazine well. Any debris needs to be brushed out, and if you use a cloth to do this, you will likely leave shreds hung up on the trigger bow slots. So, a plastic bristle brush is the tool if you need to scrub.

While you have the frame stripped and cleaned, give it a close inspection for cracks. You may never see one. Even those of us who have put epic amounts of ammo through our 1911s have pistols that have not cracked, so don't assume that yours will. But look anyway.

## REASSEMBLY

The order of assembly is as follows: Trigger in. Magazine release next. Place the sear onto the disconnector, lay the pair across the bow of the trigger (muzzle down), and use a small pin punch or length of wire to align the sear and disconnector holes as you insert the sear pin.

Push the hammer into the frame with the strut hinged up and out of the way. Line up the hammer hole and insert the hammer pin. Next, press the three-leaf spring into the frame and catch its folded end into the slot cut in the frame meant to receive it. Make sure the two legs connect, one to the sear (left) and the other to the disconnector (center).

Slide the assembled mainspring housing up the frame until you have trapped the bottom edge of the three-leaf spring. Swing the hammer strut down until it lines up with the mainspring housing plunger. Push the grip safety into the frame, and slide the mainspring housing up until it catches the lip of the grip safety and stops. You'll have to compress the spring in the mainspring housing with the hammer strut to line up the mainspring housing retainer pin. Oh, and the hammer has to be fully forward. If it is cocked, you won't be able to compress the spring, no matter how strong you are. Once the retaining pin is in place, you can go to the next step.

Press the safety plunger assembly into the plunger tube. Cock the hammer. Line up the grip safety hole with the thumb safety hole and press the thumb safety shaft through. You'll have to line up the thumb safety lug with the clearance lobe of the kidney-shaped hole for it. Use a small screwdriver to compress the plunger, and press the thumb safety fully into the frame.

Check the thumb safety movement by flipping it up and down. Check the grip safety movement by compressing it and releasing it. It should swing back out, propelled by the third leg of the three-leaf spring. If they do not, something is wrong, and you must check the assembly.

Last up, slap the grips on and tighten the grip screws. ●

CHAPTER

8

# NEW 1911 TUNING AND FIRST SHOTS

So, you're the proud owner of a new or a used new-to-you 1911. Now what? Well, you go to the range. If you're a member of a gun club, that's where you go. If not, then head to a rental range. A few details first.

## GUN CLUB

If you're a member, you know the club rules: Which ranges you can shoot on, how fast you can shoot, how many rounds in a magazine, that sort of thing. You might only be allowed on the 25-yard range, five rounds max in a mag, and to shoot no faster than one round per second. (Too bad, perhaps find a new club to join.) That won't be a problem initially, but it may be later if you want to expand your skill set.

*The .40 case was extracted from the .45 chamber after the wrong ammunition was used in "testing" the pistol in question.*

Will you ever be in the position to reload your ammunition? You will want to save your brass if the answer is yes or even maybe. Some clubs make this easier than others, but you'll want to know the rules before you find all your brass is gone because the range rules say you aren't allowed to pick it up.

If picking up brass is allowed, spread a tarp to your right and slightly behind, to catch spent brass.

Oh, and a quick update on .45 ACP ammunition and brass. The cartridge was traditionally manufactured with a Large Pistol primer. The Large Pistol refers to the size of the primer, not the pistol. In the last decade, some manufacturers have switched to making their .45 ACP with Small Pistol primers. While the cases and the reloading data are the same, the primer pockets are not. A Large primer won't fit into a Small pocket case and will bring your reloading efforts to an immediate halt. The Small primer won't stay put in the Large primer pocket, and the case will leak powder around the top deck of your progressive reloader.

You must either eye the primer of each .45 ACP case you salvage from the range, opting for only one or the other or sort them once you get home. Also, don't pick up steel or aluminum cases; they can't be reloaded. Well, the steel ones can, but they're a hassle and only worth reloading after the apocalypse.

These three cartridges all show off-center firing pin hits, but in the 1911, with its extra firing pin oomph, that's not a problem.

## RENTAL RANGE

Rental ranges are typically indoor facilities with strict limits on distances, rate of fire, and even what, if any, brass you may pick up. Also, indoor ranges are a lot noisier than outdoor ones. It's not unusual for regular shooters at indoor ranges to "double muff" for hearing protection, meaning earplugs inserted into the ears and big plastic muffs over them because you are essentially trapped in a phone-booth-sized firing position. Phone booths? Oh yes, in the cell phone era, they are anachronisms. A phone booth was where pay phones (phones you used by inserting coins, common currency before credit cards were standard) were kept. They were no larger than they needed to be to hold the phone and close the door. There were no roomy phone booths like no roomy indoor firing stations. What extra room is there is simply the way to get to the firing positions and to stack the empty gun cases on tables.

Most indoor ranges use powered cables to run the targets downrange.

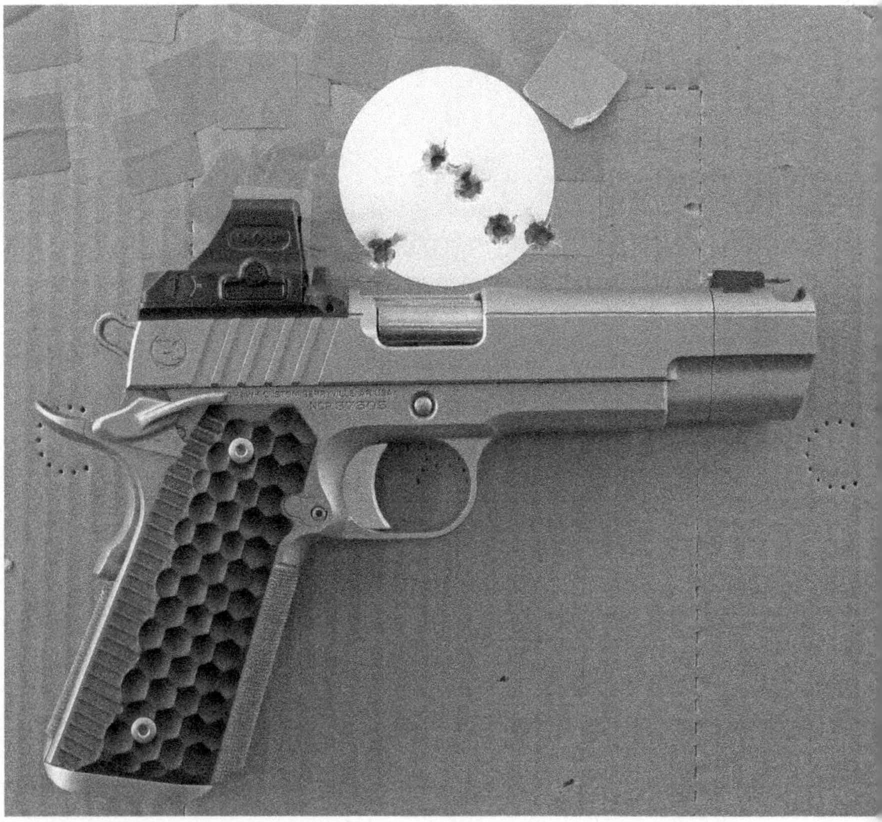

Don't quit or make adjustments on the first or second group. You are done only when you get a good group like this, and it is centered, as this one is.

## BEFORE YOU GO

Once back from the gun shop and at home, familiarize yourself with your new 1911. As at the gun shop, always ensure it is unloaded as the first step of handling it. Get a feel for the force needed to push the thumb safety up and down, how much force it takes to retract the slide, and do some dry-firing. Again, while unloaded, aim and press the trigger. In the Marine Corps, this is called "snapping in," where you learn the force needed. The ideal outcome is to press the trigger and cause the hammer to fall without the sights moving off the target's aiming point.

After working on handling, disassemble the 1911 for cleaning. It probably doesn't need it if it's new, but you should learn how to do it. It will be easier when clean and not crusted with powder residue.

Take it apart, wipe it down, make sure everything is where it should be, and what the various parts look like when clean. Run a patch down the bore, reassemble it, and pack your gear for the range.

## WHAT YOU'LL NEED

In addition to your 1911, you'll need a magazine or magazines, factory ammunition, a bag to carry stuff, and eye and ear protection; these are all obvious. Factory ammo? Yes, it is expensive, but if you're using reloads, yours or someone else's, and you have malfunctions, what is the cause? The pistol? The magazine? The ammo? You? Factory ammo (nothing fancy) removes one variable from the mix. The best choice here is standard-weight full metal jacket ammo, so in .45, that's 230 grains; in 9mm, 115 or 124/125 grains, and .38 Super 130 grains. A .40/10mm should be getting 180-grain FMJs.

Here are some illustrations of why you must be careful about ammo: I had loaded up a bucket or two of ammo for use as a bowling

*Take the screws out and the grips off, but don't remove the bushings. Make sure they are on tight. If loose, tighten and stake.*

pin load, and it worked fine in the test pistol. During the following range trip, I took along a different 1911; lo and behold, it would not chamber—the second 1911's chamber was shorter and rougher. I used that ammo for practice and adjusted the bullet seating length (and powder charge since it was now shorter overall) so the load would work in any pistol. Did I ream the chamber of the second 1911? No. As a writer, and since it was an unaltered-from-the-factory pistol, I found it more useful as a quirky test gun, so I left it alone.

The second example comes from an industry function. We were testing a new 1911, and it suddenly had the weirdest malfunction anyone had ever seen. *The fired case was backward in the chamber.* As the resident gunsmith, it fell to me to figure it out. One look and I got out the camera. Whoever had been shooting it (and it was long enough ago that I have now forgotten the miscreant's name) had mixed a .40 S&W round in with the .45 ACP ammo. The extractor held the shorter case to the breechface. The cartridge, although smaller, was large enough that the firing pin could make enough contact with the primer to set it off. But the case didn't seal the chamber, and the recoil was enough to move the slide back far enough to hit the ejector but not eject and rotate the case, which flipped end-for-end and was then re-chambered! I used a pair of needlenose pliers to grab the case and extract it from the chamber.

So, use factory ammo, use the correct ammo, and don't risk mixing ammo. Focus on the task at hand.

At the range, set up a target relatively close, say 7 yards. Yes, you are a better shooter than that, but we are not looking to train; we are testing. Insert an empty magazine into the pistol and run the slide back. It should lock open. (It has every time so far, at the gun shop and home.) Pull the magazine out, set the pistol down and insert one round in the magazine. Insert the magazine, press down on the slide stop lever, and let the slide go forward. Aim and press the trigger; the slide should lock open after it fires.

Is the hit near your point of aim? If not, don't crank the sights. You are a long way from that just yet. Now load two rounds in the magazine, and this time, to chamber a round, pull the slide back and let go. Fire those rounds, and the slide should lock back. Now that you've established that the trigger won't go "rippity-rip" (full-auto has been known to happen on brand-new pistols, not just 1911s, and it is worth easing into a new semi-auto handgun this way to avoid the embarrassment and hazard), you're ready for the rest of the testing.

If you've got the time and the area is relatively clean, see where the empties landed. If they are all in a close cluster, then life is good. If spread out, but your pistol works, that's life, and it is OK. In the old days, we'd fuss over an extractor/ejector/ejection port setup to have all the empties drop into a bucket. A high-end custom pistol might do that, but expecting it from an out-of-the-box factory gun is asking too much. And it doesn't prove anything.

OK, your new 1911 works one shot at a time, as any well-behaved pistol should. Now, it's time to lean into the details. If you have a shooting bench, use a rest (sandbags or shooting support) and shoot groups. Don't judge your new 1911 by the first group. Shoot several, and don't even think about adjusting the sights until you've gotten some small groups. And then, only if those groups agree on the direction you need to change.

How small? That depends on you and the ammo, as well as the pistol. In routinely testing handguns, I can usually shoot an accurate pistol into groups of 2 inches at 25 yards. I know people who can do better, but that's me. So, if I'm shooting 2-inch groups, and they are within an inch centered on my point of aim, I call it good, at least for the moment. For really serious work, I'll go out to 50 or even 100 yards. If the group (which, at 100 yards, will be 8 inches across or so) isn't on-center, it will show up. But remember that the sight adjustment you'd make for an error at 100 yards is one-quarter the correction you'd make for a group at 25 yards.

You've spent the day or at least a few hours at the range and fired 100 rounds or more. Pick up your brass and head home. If your new 1911 has worked flawlessly, then all you'll need to do is clean it. If there were malfunctions, then you'll have to address them. But even while cleaning, you'll want to pay attention to details.

***The bullet nose track should be centered, straight, and singular, as on this tested pistol. Custom pistolsmiths will take care of this detail. Photo: Jason Burton***

## CLEANING AND INSPECTING

Disassemble your 1911, but don't wipe anything down yet. First, you want to look at the frame feed ramp, the barrel feed ramp, the slide breechface and ejection port, and the recoil spring guide rod and barrel feet. Then there are some other details you'll want to check.

## GRIPS

Not all 1911s have had the bushing staked. Some makers seem to feel that simply torquing them down "tight" is enough. So you'll want to check to ensure the bushings are tight, and if not, stake them (I explain the staking process in detail later in Chapter XX). Take the grips off and look at the frame and bushings.

## FRAME FEED RAMP

There should be a narrow, brassy line of jacket material right up the centerline of the feed ramp. The ramp should be grubby from powder residue except for the feed track. If you see a wide path or several paths, you're probably looking at magazine changes. If you have only one mag, this is curious, but if your pistol is reliable, you are fine. If you have several different types or brands, that could be the cause, and again, if they're all reliable, you're fine.

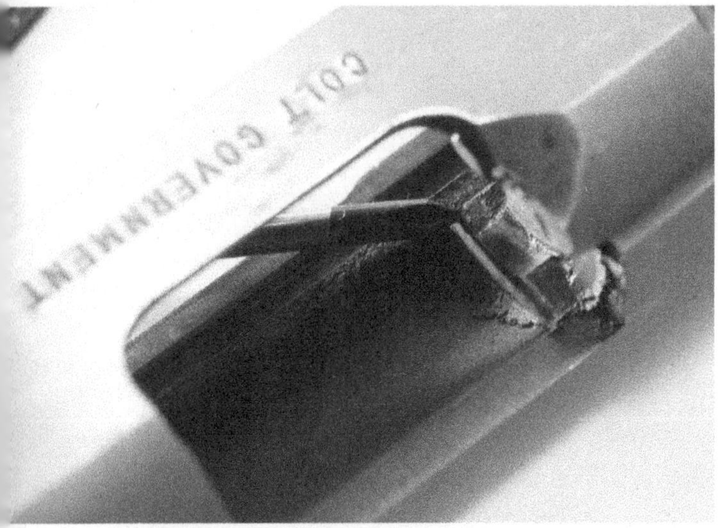


***Look at the sidewall of the breechface for brassing. Some is expected, but if there's a lot, or you have malfunctions or tool marks, it might need polishing.***

## BARREL FEED RAMP

Like the frame, there should be a single brassy track up the center of the barrel ramp, plus some brassing on the bottom edge of the chamber mouth. That will be all you'll see as by the time the cartridge gets to the chamber, everything has settled down. If it hasn't, you will probably have seen some malfunction.

## SLIDE BREECHFACE

We've got three areas to look at. Well, one area and two points. The area is the breechface itself. It should be smooth and show the sliding action of the case, plus a debris impression on the breechface from the last round fired. High-mileage pistols can show a slight depression around the firing pin hole where the primer, free to move, has slammed into the breechface tens of thousands of times at the max pressure. Unless there is a burr on the firing pin hole, or some egregious tool mark on the breechface, this will be an easy inspection.

The two points to look at are the edge of the breechface sidewall underneath the extractor and the opposite sidewall.

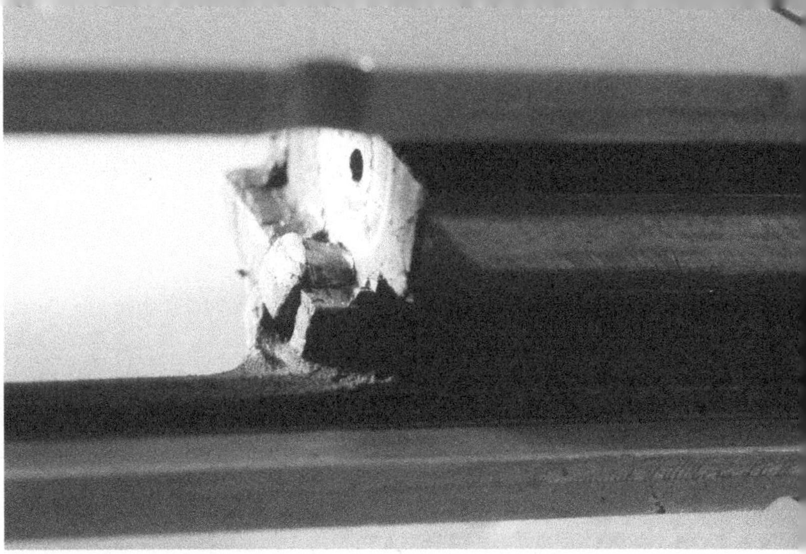

You will see some brassing here, which is unavoidable. The brass gets shoved across that relatively sharp edge at speed and under pressure, and there will be brass. But you do not want to see chunks of brass, brass shavings, or heavy rubbing. And you do not want to see an uneven surface on the far sidewall with heavy brassing—a sign of the slide working hard to shove the case forward and into the chamber. A sharp edge on these corners can dig into a case hard enough to cause a misfeed. If you're worried and want to clean things up, remember this: changing a pistol or any system working within parameters is risky business. You could make a change that alters the system's balance and causes new problems.

*The extractor should reach past the small sidewall, and that sidewall should not have heavy brassing. Don't get heavy-handed on this sidewall; it is there for a reason, and if you take too much off, you'll have problems.*

To clean up those sidewalls, use a fine stone. A fine-cut file can work, but it is too aggressive for the first-timer doing this work. A stone will be slower, preventing trouble.

To work on the extractor side, remove it first. Scrub the breechface clean and apply some Dykem (machinists' ink). Clamp the slide, muzzle up in a padded vise, and use the front edge of the stone to scrub the sidewall gently. Stone off the Dykem on the high spots of the far sidewall, stoning perpendicular to the slide rails to prevent introducing an angle to the surface. After taking down high spots, stop once 50 percent of the sidewall is clean of Dykem. That's all you'll need.

Be even more careful if working on the extractor side (which is less likely to need work). Ensure there isn't a wire edge on the extractor sidewall created when the breechface was broached. No wire edge? Then, two to three strokes of the stone and it's done.

*If a breechface looks like this, it should be a well-used pistol. If it is a brand-new 1911, there is something wrong. The erosion ring is caused by tens of thousands of rounds being fired and tiny amounts of gas leaking around the edges of the primer on each shot. A half-million rounds from Day One, and it might become a problem.*

## RECOIL SPRING GUIDE ROD

In some rare instances, the recoil rod seat is machined just a smidge rearward of where it should be. Then, when the barrel links down, the barrel feet will clank against the rear boss of the recoil spring guide rod. When this happens, you'll see a pair of nicked spots on the guide rod boss near the top. It's probably not a big deal, but it can be in certain circumstances. When the dimensional mismatch is large enough, the guide rod acts as a pre-load on the barrel, pushing it out of battery, even as it sits closed.

When I see this, I use my Brownells pillar file to angle the guide rod boss at that spot so there can be no contact. This will be a particular problem if you've installed a government-length barrel into a commander pistol because you want the barrel length or a suppressor. This was not uncommon in the old days, but there were problems. You see, the commander barrel feet have been trimmed to prevent precisely this kind of contact. In the Gov' barrel/Comm' pistol combo, the guide rod bears on the barrel feet with such force that it can throw the unlocking timing off—chipping, setting back, or busting the locking lugs. Another issue that can arise is the guide rod boss peening the barrel feet edges, hindering the link movement, which promotes early locking lug problems.

So, if you have done this kind of upgrade/barrel swap, take a look before things get any worse. Taking the edge off of the guide rod boss will do the trick for a simple mismatch in a regular build.

## SLIDE STOP LEVER

When you switch from round-nosed full metal jacket ammunition—what you should be using to do your initial testing and what it will mostly see unless you hit big on the lotto—to JHPs, you might have the occasional mysterious "early lock" problem. This is where the slide locks open before you fire the last round in the magazine.

This will happen because of one of two reasons, or maybe both. One is that your hand, your offhand thumb, hits the slide-stop lever on the recoil and bounces it up. If so, stop that. If you've installed an extended slide stop, the extra mass of the larger part can cause it to bounce even more than it usually does, and if it happens to be bouncing up just as the slide stop notch passes by, it will lock open. Remove that piece of un-

*How much is "enough" testing? With a modern 1911, if it hasn't malfunctioned in the first 200 rounds, it probably never will. After that, you are conducting a long-term endurance test, and the end happens only when you stop shooting that particular pistol.*

necessary junk, and put the original slide stop back in.

The last cause is your bullets. A large hollowpoint in a JHP bullet can cause the outside edge of the bullet nose to rub against the slide stop tab and lift it. This was first discovered in the 1980s with the then-common Speer 200-grain JHP—a bullet with an opening so wide it was referred to as "the .45 shotglass." This bullet was the standard used by bowling pin shooters, so much so that they were all very familiar with the problem. (Back then, we'd all be going through thousands of rounds of .45 ACP loaded with that bullet.)

***If your slide occasionally locks open with ammo left in the magazine, unload and take it apart. Look here on the slide stop for brassing. If there is any, the bullet, dragging on the stop, is lifting it to lock. Carefully file where the brass is, only there, and at the same angle as the existing surface. Test shoot again.***

If this is your problem, discovering it and solving it is easy. Look at the slide stop tab on the inside angled face. If you see brassing, that's the cause. Lock your slide stop in a padded vise, and, using the pillar file, file at the same angle as the brassed face, and only enough to remove the brass—no more. At the next range session, see if the problem continues. If it happens again, repeat, and again, file only where you see brassing, and only until the brassing is gone.

## TEST ENOUGH?

How much testing should you do? In the current generation of 1911s, I'd say that once you have shot 200 rounds without a malfunction, you are done "testing" it for reliability. In the old days, when every magazine was a law unto itself, we'd do much more testing than that. But today, things are better. I've conducted endurance tests, and they are not fun. The two in particular, I put (well, I had help) 15,000 rounds through a then-new Ruger SR9. One malfunction occurred because the shooter was wearing a lineman's glove because it was too hot to handle.

The other test involved 23,000 rounds through a Wayne Novak SRT Hi Power. There were two malfunctions: one was a badly loaded round, and the other was an elderly spring in a tired magazine.

On the other hand, I have two 1911s that each have over 100,000 rounds through them. However, I don't consider those endurance tests; they were all practice and competition. And that's what you'll be doing after your first 200 rounds: practice, training, competition, plinking, having fun. ●

*The 1911 can be a forgiving pistol to feed if the dimensions are correct. Even heavy bullets with wide, flat noses will feed, something other pistols sometimes won't. That can prove useful when whacking bowling pins.*

# CHAPTER 9

# FEEDING SYSTEM RUNDOWN

Let's go through the 1911's feeding cycle to understand how it works and dispel rumors. We'll start with a loaded magazine locked in place, a round in the chamber, and you about to fire.

The top round in the magazine is held down from the feed lips. The rail running down the slide's centerline or stripper rail holds the round down far enough to, oh, strip a round off the magazine.

Pressing the trigger, the hammer falls, the firing pin goes forward and collides with the primer, the primer detonates, the powder burns, and the bullet leaves. All this happens in a few thousandths of a second. At this point, Sir Isaac Newton takes over. The slide and barrel move to the rear, reacting to the bullet and the gases moving forward. Their inertial movement creates the force that drives the slide and barrel parts back.

The slide and barrel move back together until the link pulls the barrel down and out of locking engagement; at this point, the barrel bumps down to the frame, and the slide keeps moving rearward. The extractor, hooked on the case, extracts the case as the slide moves to the rear. As the stripper rail uncovers the top round, that cartridge moves up. The empty case hits the ejector, pivots, and leaves the slide, aided sometimes by the top round coming up to the magazine feed lips. The slide bottoms out, with the bottom of the slide recoil spring tunnel banging into the flange of the recoil spring guide. (Never the recoil spring itself, which must not be allowed to fully compress, a detail covered in the recoil spring section.)

Now, we're set to describe the part where the real action begins, and as we go through this, keep in mind that not only is the cartridge being acted on, but it also influences the parts it interacts with. Note that the feeding process I'll describe involves hardball ammo (round-nose bullets) and USGI-style magazines. Those are the ones with feed lips that appear to be full-length and have a taper as they extend forward. We'll cover the various other magazine feed lip styles in the magazine chapter and how they affect feeding.

## SLIDE FORWARD

At the rear of its cyclic stroke, the slide bounces off of the flange, and this bounce can be good or bad. If the slide comes back with too much velocity, it will bounce more quickly (steel-on-steel is among the fastest elastic collisions) and reach the top round too quickly. But, if it bounces off too slowly, it can hinder the timing of the rest of the process, although that is a difficult situation to arrange. However, making the slide too fast is far too easy.

Once the slide has moved back far enough to uncover the top round fully, there is a finite amount of time for the magazine spring to lift the cartridge stack and press the top round firmly against the feed lips. For all but the last round, that lifting is accomplished by the next cartridge in the stack. If the slide comes forward too soon or too quickly, and the round isn't entirely up or is tilted or cock-eyed (things can get weird in the micro-second timeframe), you will have inconsistent or unreliable feeding.

To complicate matters, the top round does not sit level in its proper feeding orientation. Due to the angle of the grip, and thus the magazine, it sits nose tilted up. So, when the stripper rail impacts the case rim, it does so at the top-center of the rim, and the round tips down at first contact.

So, the slide hits the round, the round tips down and scoots forward. Then, the nose of the cartridge hits the feed ramp and is forced up again—simultaneously sliding under the magazine's feed lips. The tip grinds on the feed ramp, the case walls drag on the feed lips, and the top rear of the rim slides up the face of the stripper rail, entering the breechface area. As if that wasn't enough, it drags along the top-center of the cartridge below it. Enough friction for you? It gets worse. As it moves forward, the cartridge nose is handed off from the frame feed ramp to the barrel feed ramp.

Now, in being pushed forward by the slide, the cartridge has also decelerated the slide. Whatever impact velocity it had when it hit the rim, it slowed once it hit. Now, as the cartridge rides up and onto the barrel feed ramp and to the tip-over line, it exerts a downward force on the barrel, keeping it from moving around in the feeding cycle.

In the next step, the case rim at the left side contacts the breechface sidewall while it slips under the extractor on the right side. We now have six contact points, adding friction to the movement.

Then, the case rim leaves the magazine's feed lips and is free to move up, but the bullet nose strikes the chamber wall at the top of the chamber. The cartridge is levered to a horizontal position by the nose impact on the chamber wall, and it must pivot and slide over the tip-over line at the bottom rear of the chamber. Only once it is completely aligned with the chamber can it be driven fully home.

Meanwhile, at the top of the breechface, that gap that is the slot for the hood clearance contacts the hood, pushing the barrel forward. The barrel feet ride up the slide stop pin (the link doesn't do anything now; it's just along for the ride) until the barrel stops against the slide stop pin.

Job done.

Things to note: The round will do its down-and-up-and-over routine every time with USGI magazines. There is no way to make the path more direct without changing magazines, and there is not much need to make it so. The extractor contacts the case rim before the case leaves the magazine (with proper magazines). The 1911 is thus a "controlled feed" in that there is no time in the feeding process where the round can do anything but go as instructed.

The process is fast. Let's do some time studies. The top shooters, the Grandmasters of IPSC/USPSA, shoot very quickly. The time between shots ("splits") for the best shooters will be something on the order of 0.12 seconds, which we would call a "twelve split." "Splits in the low teens" are very fast, and it will take a long time to get there. Most shooters consider "fast" shooting to be anything close to a quarter-second per split. Let's change splits to RPM or rounds per minute as if you were emulating a machine gun. Your fast day, quarter-second splits convert to an RPM of 240. You aren't as quick as a slow machine gun like a Vickers, running at 550 RPM. At a split of 0.15, the Grandmaster is running at 400 RPM. The best split, a 0.12, is now 500 RPM.

OK, let's go to the max and take a "runaway"—a 1911 where the hammer won't stay cocked, and it fires itself until the magazine is empty. I've had the unpleasant experience of being next to two other

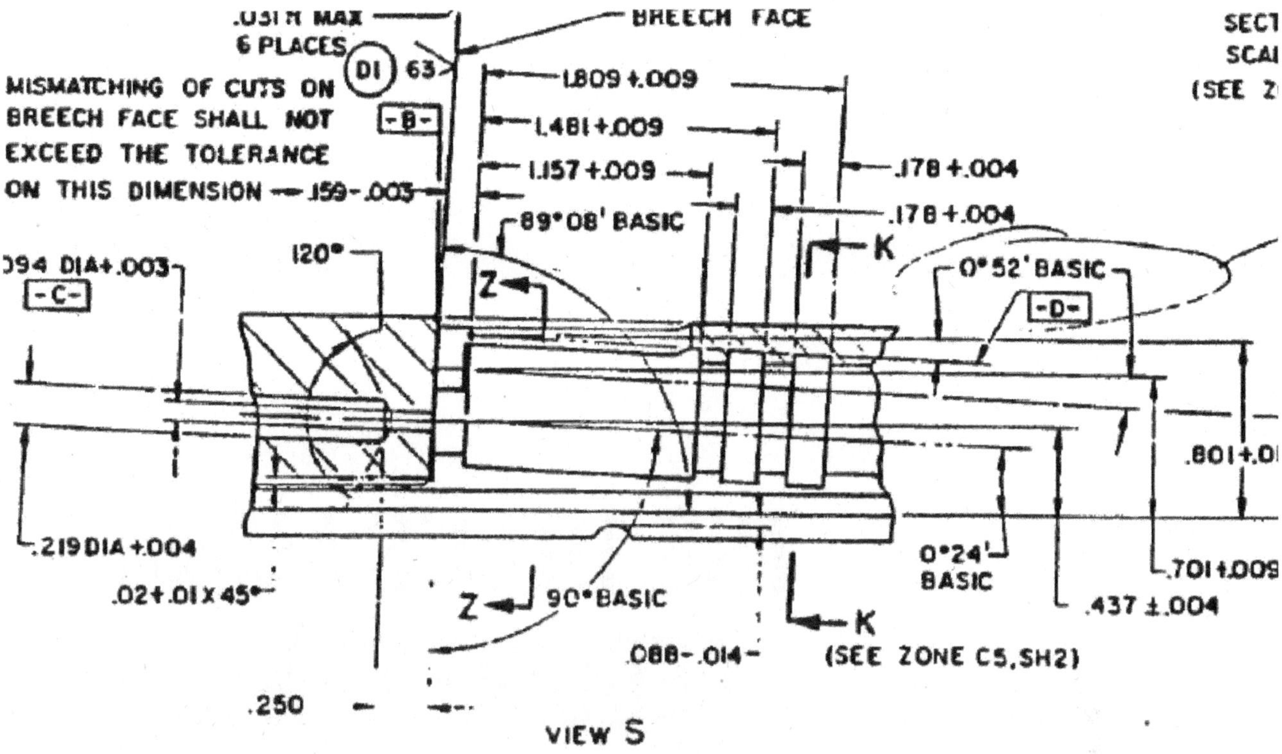


*Drill down into the details, and things about the 1911 can be surprising, including Browning's use of a very specific 89.08-degree breechface.*

shooters when that happened, and I've had it happen once to me. The cyclic rate of a runaway is on the order of 1,000 to 1,200 RPM. Yes, right up there with the legendary MG42 machine gun from WWII. That translates to a split of 0.06 seconds for 1,000 RPM and 0.05 seconds for 1,200 RPM, meaning that no one, absolutely no one, is "waiting for the pistol" when it comes to fast shooting. We discuss what is actually going on in the chapter on recoil springs and timing the 1911 for best function.

The detail of the cartridge creating a downward force to locate the barrel comes into consideration whenever we mount extra stuff on the barrel. In the old days, it was a comp, a chunk of steel meant to divert muzzle gases and dampen felt recoil. These days, it's more likely to be a suppressor, which is a lot heavier and longer than a comp. Luckily, modern 1911 makers are doing a better job than Colt did in the gory years, and the dimensions are proper, and feeding is reliable.

Oh, and speaking of dimensions, there's one you might not notice if you ever get a chance to look at the blueprints of the 1911. The breechface is not square. That is, it is not a 90-degree angle to the bore axis. Nope, it's a specific, no plus-or-minus 89.08 degrees. I'm not a trained machinist, but I spent a lot of time working on blueprints and drafting back when I thought I would be a mechanical engineer. A specification with no plus-or-minus tolerance is a huge clue. Browning knew what he was doing and made test samples that worked. If that is the angle he used, that's the angle they all should be. ●

CHAPTER 10

# THE 1911'S AMMO REQUIREMENTS

You might think that "ammo requirements" is not a big deal. You buy ammo marked the same as your pistol is chambered, right? Have you priced ammunition lately? Now, assuming you make a bunch of money and don't shoot a lot, you can buy factory ammo. Many shooters do. But, if you want to get really good or enter competition, you'll need to reload. As I've said before, and will in the future, you don't reload to save money. You reload to get more shooting for the money you would spend anyway, and in particular instances, produce ammunition better suited to your needs than any factory load.

The 1911 is very accommodating with many ammunition types. And in others, not so much. Its slide mass and spring pressure will gobble up oversized, deformed, badly loaded, and wonky ammo more than other designs. Of course, that same *oomph* means that when it wedges tight, it is tight. And you'll need more than just a hefty yank on the slide to open it. So, don't use bad ammo.

The touchy part is cartridge length. Browning designed the 1911 to be used with ball ammo loaded with jacketed round-nosed bullets and an overall length of 1.275 inches more or less, and bullets of 230 grains in weight. Not a lot more, and usually not much less in length, but we've been working on that for half a century now. Regarding bullet weight, it's slightly more accommodating and can handle projectiles from 250 down to 150 grains.

It also is not all that happy with light loads; that is, used with ammo that is too soft in power or recoil. To explore the lower ranges of recoil, ensure you have a firm grip. "Limpwristing" the 1911 is a sure way to make it choke with soft ammo.

## INTERIOR BALLISTICS

Before addressing the ammo-loading requirement, a brief explanation of how things work when a cartridge is fired is in order. Pressing the trigger, the hammer strikes the firing pin. The firing pin flies forward and strikes the primer. In the brief time before the crushed primer ignites, the entire cartridge is shoved forward a few thousandths of an inch until it reaches either the forward lip of the chamber or the case rim stops against the inside of the extractor hook. So, when the primer ignites the powder charge, the case is a few thousandths away from the breechface.

The primer detonation ignites the powder. The primer cup experiences full pressure before the powder in the case has fully burned, and, likely, the primer pops back out of the case pocket. Remember, there's a few thousandths of an inch gap there. The powder entirely burns and reaches max pressure, expanding the case, but not before the movement of the case and bullet begins. The case goes back, slamming into the breechface, and the bullet goes forward. If the primer had moved back, the case now reseats it, making it flush.

*Use tumbling media; the specific type doesn't matter.*

The barrel and slide return; the barrel tilts down, swiping the case across the breechface for a few ten-thousandths of an inch, and then, once it has cleared the barrel, the case gets hit by the ejector, pivots off the extractor, and flies away.

A lot is going on in those microseconds.

With that in mind, let's cover the details you'll want to have nailed down when you load ammo for your 1911.

## BRASS CLEANING

Your brass must be clean to commence reloading. Using dirty, gritty, or otherwise unclean brass is a sure way to accelerate wear on your dies, decrease accuracy and reliability, and make shooting not fun. Whatever process you choose, be sure to use it.

*It takes time to clean brass, but it's worth it, so do it.*

## RESIZING

Resize the brass. As in full-length. There is no "neck sizing" or other rifle-reloading tricks of the trade that make your handgun ammunition more accurate. (Not that anyone neck sizes anymore, even for hunting rifles; that went out of style when Nixon resigned.) Resize the brass down as far as the sizing die can reach. Even if you only use your own brass (not stuff picked up from the gun club), you still need to full-length resize. Unless your chamber is hopelessly oversized or your sizing die is criminally undersized, sizing should not work harden or shorten the useful life of your brass.

I have a bin full of .38 Super brass from shooting in the USPSA Open Division. While the extractors chewed up the rims, and some of the headstamps are hard to read because they have hit the ejector so many times, and the nickel is worn off, I did not have to reject them in any quantity for being overworked.

What are the signs of overworked brass? Simple: cracks running along the length of the case. Cracks at the mouth are from a different cause.

*Remove the brass from the media once clean. This tumbler from Berry's does a first-rate job of getting the kernels out and not spewing them all over the floor.*

## BELLING

You'll need to bell the case mouth to keep it from catching on or shaving bullets being seated. If you don't sufficiently bell your cases, you'll encounter one of two problems: Jacketed bullets can catch on the case mouth and crush the case. You can salvage the bullet, sometimes the powder, but you've lost the case and primer. Lead bullets present other issues. The case can cut into the lead bullet and shave off a thin lead wire or ring. Here, you've lost the bullet but can salvage the case and primer (sometimes).

If you see these problems, adjust your belling die an eighth of a turn deeper to bell a bit more. Can you bell too much? Yes. If you bell too much, it can overwork the case mouth, creating mouth cracks after a few loadings. If you go extreme, the case might not enter the crimp die. Since cases vary in length, this will be a "try it and see" setting you'll have to learn over a few reloading sessions. Once you find the "Goldilocks" setting, you'll never have to change it, at least on that die, for that caliber.

## CRIMP

An important detail: Seat the bullet in one step and crimp in the next. A die that does both at once does neither well. With the seating/crimping die, those last few thousandths of the bullet travel into the case occur as it is seated, which is also when it is being crimped if you do both at once. That is a recipe for unhappiness.

In the case of the 1911, belling is not difficult. The trick is to use a taper crimp—not a roll crimp, as some revolver loads require. The taper crimp is expressed in the finished diameter. For the .45 ACP, that is .468 inch. The 10mm and .40 should be .416 inch and the 9mm and .38 Super, .372 inch. Measure this with a set of dial or digital calipers across the case mouth of the finished cartridge at the very top of the case mouth.

The load data for the .45 Auto is well-established, and deviating from it will lead to ammo that isn't as accurate or reliable as you'd like. The 10mm and .40 are almost as forgiving, but the 9mm and Super are a law unto themselves (bullet type in particular). Experiment with your 9mm or .38 Super pistol and your loading setup, starting at .372 inch, and see how things work out. The 9mm and .38 Super are especially touchy about crimp for plated or coated bullets. Too little results in poor feeding or bullet setback. Too much, and accuracy declines from cutting too deeply or through the plating or coating. This is not the 1911's fault. These problems occur with any other pistol, or PCC chambered in 9mm or Super, but since we're talking 1911s here, understand some research and testing may be needed.

Oh, and while many pistol bullets are not equipped with a cannelure, it is there for a reason. If, for example, a bullet maker offers a bullet specifically for the .45 ACP, and it has a cannelure, that groove is where to crimp the case mouth—it is more than a hint that loaded to that length, it will be the correct length for proper feeding. If it does not have a cannelure, load it to the same length as a cannelured bullet with the same profile.

## READING PRIMERS

Let's get one thing out of the way right now: Anyone who tells you they "Read primers for pressure signs" is someone whose reloading advice you can ignore, at least as far as handguns are concerned. (I'd skip their advice altogether, but that's just me.)

Why? Simple: pressure, as in pistols don't have much. As in primers don't show signs of pressure problems until they are well past the safe line for pistols. The top-rated ammo for pressure is the 9mm+P. That loading runs at a maximum average pressure of 38,500 psi, compared to the standard of 35,000 psi for regular 9mm. The .38 Super is 36,000, and the .45 ACP? Regular ammunition is 21,000 and +P 23,000 psi. If we go up to the big bores and higher pressures, the .460 Rowland, .40 Super, and others are in the upper 20s—26,000 to 28,000 psi.

Rifles run from the low 40s (the .30-30, the .35 Remington, or other oldies) up to 50,000 to 55,000 psi, such as the .308 or .223. Some new rifle magnums run into the 60,000 range, and a few handgun cartridges are also at 60,000. So here's the skinny: none of those cartridges show "pressure signs" when properly loaded and fired in firearms made for them. So, we can say that it is unlikely to see "pressure signs" under 60,000 psi.

And you expect your primers to tell you when your pistol cartridge load has wandered from 35,000 to 40,000? Oh, you optimist.

But your primers can tell you other things, such as off-center firing pin hits, rings around the firing pin hit, a pierced primer, or a flattened primer. They don't necessarily tell you pressure, but they can offer other valuable tidbits of information.

## OFF-CENTER PRIMER HIT

This means that your chamber's center isn't aligned with the firing pin. This condition does not necessarily mean that something is wrong with your 1911. You are good to go as long as the barrel and slide lugs have sufficient overlap and the lockup is tight. It probably means that your barrel/slide/frame lockup is on the "tall" side, and the barrel is high to ensure lockup, putting it a few thousandths over the firing pin center. But you're all set as long as no other dimensions conflict with the frame, slide, or barrel, and you get 100 percent ignition. The off-center primer hit is commonly seen on the models with barrels shorter than the Commander.

## PRIMER STRIKE RINGS

"And one ring to rule them all." OK, I couldn't resist. A ring around your firing pin strike is not a reason to suspect excess pressure. It most likely means that your firing pin hole is too large or your firing pin is too small.

In rifles, it can (but not always) indicate excess pressure, but there's far more likely a dimensional problem in a pistol. However, as long as it works, it works. Now, if you were to be using a 9mm-dimensioned firing pin in a .45 slide with a .45-dimension firing pin hole, then you really ought not to be doing that. It will lead to problems. Is there a solution to a mismatch? Not an easy one. A ring can also mean your hammer fall is too light. How so? If you've installed a weaker hammer spring for a lighter trigger pull (this will also increase felt recoil), the firing pin might not have enough inertia to keep the primer from flowing back into the clearance hole.

*On the left is a belled case. On the right, a crimped round. Bell the case to avoid crushing it or shaving bullets. Taper crimp to lock the bullet in and to reduce feeding drag.*

If your hammer spring is standard, and you have a gap creating a ring, then the question is this: Is it a problem? If it is, then you need to fix it. If not, then you don't. The fix can be expensive. One way is to find an oversized firing pin. I don't know of any, but they must exist. However, that oversized firing pin in another 1911 could wedge forward and create a malfunctioning pistol. Or, a pistolsmith can install a new bushing in the slide. That is not a do-it-yourself project. It involves drilling/milling the firing pin tunnel from the rear, fitting a new bushing, and soldering it. Next, the breechface gets dressed down until flush. You're right to think the cost of all that approaches a replacement slide.

So you live with it.

## PIERCED PRIMERS

A pierced primer occurs at the impact dent, blown through. This is not a "blown primer," which is when the primer is blown out of the case and is usually caused by an oversized primer pocket (itself caused by excessive pressure on a previous firing).

This problem is usually caused by the firing pin not retracting promptly. So, you've got a firing pin tunnel packed with gunk, and the pin is sluggish in retracting. Or the spring is tired or broken and can't get the firing pin back in time. How does that happen? Remember the primer skooching out of the primer pocket for a few thousandths? The firing pin is also retracting, and the two move back together. If the firing pin binds, is sluggish, or is not spring-powered, it can linger long enough to pierce the primer. Basically, the primer impales itself on the sluggish firing pin.

It can also signify excessive pressure or the wrong powder, but it is usually mechanical.

## FLATTENED PRIMER

At firing, a flattened primer backs out of the primer pocket with the case slammed back over it. It indicates one of two or three things (sometimes more than one). One, your chamber is too deep, and the case can go farther forward than it should, so the primer pops back out too far, pressing it against the breechface. Or, the extractor hook is too open, allowing the round to be driven forward too much—a situation aggravated by an excessively deep chamber, as a regular-length one will stop the case before the extractor.

As a brief aside, if the chamber is too deep and the extractor stops forward movement, it's likely to add stress to the extractor and shorten its service life.

The third cause is excessive pressure. The primer moves back, but the pressure is so great that it slams the primer hard on reseating it, expanding the cup and flattening it.

Solutions? You can't shorten a deep chamber. You can properly fit an extractor. And you can give up the hot loads and stop abusing your 1911.

## CLEAN BRASS

If you reload, you need a proper manual on the subject. Gun Digest Media offers the regularly updated *Handloaders Digest, 19th Edition* by Phil Massaro and my contribution on the subject, *Reloading for Handgunners, 2nd Edition* (available from GunDigestStore.com). One detail about which you must be near OCD is cleanliness—both the loading area (messiness leads to mistakes, accidents, and other unfortunate things) and the brass. Do not load brass without cleaning it. Clean brass means a long life for your loading tools. Also, clean brass is free of objects in the case, such as mud, dirt, pebbles, or other debris that reduces capacity. (For example, dumping that same amount of powder into a half-filled case with dirt can easily double the pressure on that round. So, your safe, easy, 17,000-psi .45 ACP load is suddenly 34,000 psi. How so? The dirt, pebbles, or whatever cuts the combustion chamber volume in half. The Ideal Gas Law states that decreasing volume increases pressure.)

That combination will likely blow the case, trash the magazine, split the grips, and cause you to have learned a flinch. It could take a long time to get over the flinch, and you'll have to buy a new magazine and grips.

## DON'T BE CHEAP

Brass for reloading is easy to come by. My home gun club has the ranges carpeted in brass (mostly 9mm, I'll admit, but there are enough others there to keep you going), and found brass, sorted by caliber and properly cleaned, is functional brass. However, any brass case with a cracked mouth, body, or primer pocket that won't hold primers must be ditched. It doesn't matter if it's yours or found at the range, pitch it. A cracked mouth will work OK, but it won't be as accurate. However, if the crack extends far enough down to decrease neck tension on the bullet, the bullet can set back into the case on feeding. A smaller combustion chamber, with the same powder charge, again means a higher chamber pressure. That's the same as mud/dirt/debris in the case, and another magazine trashed.

***The primer ignites the powder, but the chamber pressure also pushes the primer. So, when the round goes off, it slams back against the breechface and shows the evidence of that work.***

## THINGS TO NOT WORRY ABOUT

Your brass will get mangled with use. I have brass that has been fired so many times the nickel is worn off, you can't read the headstamp from the ejector dings, and the extractor has nipped the extractor groove so many times you'd think it was a cannelure, not an extractor groove. I use it as long as it isn't cracked and holds a primer.

How about mixing headstamps? Don't worry about it as long as they are of the same caliber. Rifle reloaders worry for two reasons: accuracy and pressure. Different brands of the same caliber, mixed, can have slightly differing neck tensions, which can affect accuracy. They, however, are working toward groups less than one inch at 100 yards. Mixed-headstamp .45 brass, instead of all the same brand and lot, for example, might open your Les Baer 1911 groups from 2.5 to 3 inches at 50 yards. Can you see that? Can you shoot well enough to notice that? Then don't worry about it.

As far as pressure, again, the rifle shooters are working in the 50,000+ psi region. Let's say they get a single case in the mix with a slightly smaller interior volume, increasing the pressure from 50,000 to 55,000 psi. Still, no big deal. (As long as they aren't running their loads to the redline. Then an extra 5,000 psi might be a deal, big or small.) The problem isn't pressure but velocity. The 55,000-psi round

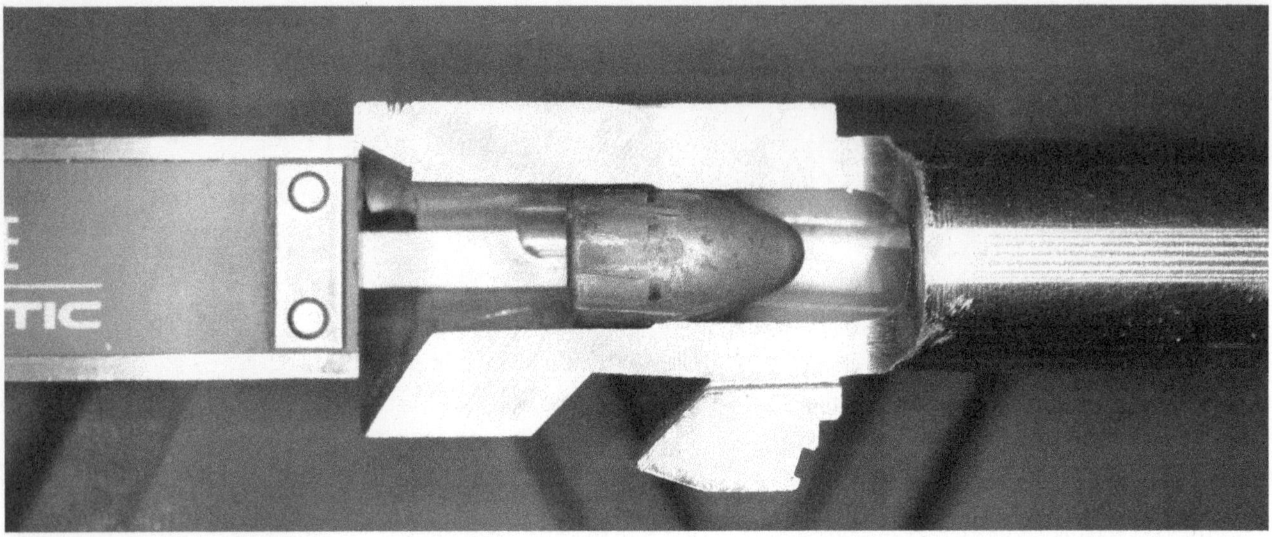

*While the magazine interior limits how long a loaded cartridge can be, it might still be too long for the chamber in your pistol. Drop the bullet you are using (just a bullet) into the chamber and let it stop on the rifling. Then, measure to the base of the bullet, like this. That measurement, plus the length of the bullet, is your maximum overall length to touch the rifling. Load your cartridges shorter than that. The 1911 is not alone in this, it is a good idea to make this measurement for all pistols you will be loading for.*

will have a higher velocity. This means less drop at a distance and on a target range, a mysterious "high nine" instead of the ten-ring hit they expected.

Even at 100 yards, the velocity change that mixed brass can create in a pistol round would be immeasurable as a change in the point of impact of the various bullets.

## BULLET SHAPE

The original cartridges, the .45 ACP and the .38 Auto/Super were designed around jacketed round-nose bullets. And the bullets were not hemispherical. They were more pointed than the half-sphere of something like the old .455 Webley Auto. When we shifted to JHPs for defense, the ammunition manufacturers and the 1911 makers adjusted. Initially, the 1911's feed ramps were narrow and not particularly polished. For FMJ ammo, that was not a problem. Through WWII, the feed ramps were narrow, but the commercial guns had a better polish than the GI guns. But, after that, Colt and the later makers widened and polished the feed ramps, and you will likely not have a problem with any of them today. And if you do have a feeding problem, it is more likely the magazine. Or, if using reloads, the reloaded ammo.

Do not worry about bullet shape if the ammunition is .45 ACP factory or the maker lists the bullet as suitable for the .45 ACP. In the 9mm and .38 Super, about the only thing you must avoid is a full-wadcutter bullet, typically used for .38 Special ammo. However, you won't load those bullets for target competition since the .38 Special bullet is longer than the 9mm or Super case.

In researching the 1911, I've encountered half a dozen "correct" sets of blueprints. Most of them agree on the essential details, which no doubt lack the particularities of production, things the machinist running this or that machine knew but didn't annotate on the blueprints. However, one from the Rock Island Arsenal, dated 1965, has some interesting details. It specifies the bullet length and shape. The 230-grain JRN bullet is listed as a maximum length of 1.275 inches, but curiously, there is no plus-or-minus specification or tolerance. I can't believe that the need for length was so precise as not to allow for variance in length. So, to load your ammo, we will take that as the maximum allowed. Any longer, and it might not fit into the magazine, where an excessively long cartridge will drag on the interior and not lift in time.

The wadcutter bullet listed is a wide-nosed style, longer than the typical factory wadcutter, which I find curious. The bullet, weighing an unknown weight (another curiosity), is listed with a cartridge overall length (COAL) of 1.255 inches long; again, there is no plus or minus. The match chamber on the drawing shows the wadcutter round (the ball cartridge has its own chamber dimensions) and differs from the GHI chamber only in the throat angle. There, the rifling start is steeper than on the ball cartridge. These drawings were signed off and approved by the chairman in March (ball) and August (wadcutter) of 1965. I figure that, by then, the various arsenals and teams knew what they were doing, at least regarding Bullseye competition.

Still, interesting data points.

## RELOADING DATA

The loading data for the cartridges you'll use in a 1911 are well-known and easy to find. Load data for the .45 Auto has been around since the beginning; the original .45 ball ammo packaging even listed the charge and weight, typically 5.0 grains of Bullseye powder and 815 fps. The .38 Super languished until the 1980s, but since then, every reloading manual includes current data, even if it doesn't list loads that make Major. As for the 9mm, it, too, languished for a long time but, in the last two or three decades, has come on strong, and if a powder maker offers a powder even remotely useful in the 9mm, they will list it, since so many people now shoot the 9mm even in the 1911. ●

CHAPTER 11

# SLIDES

*The induction-hardened front end of a slide. This one got polished sometime in the past when clean GI guns were relatively cheap. If you do this to a CMP 1911A1, collectors will hate you.*

The 1911 slide is the second most complex part of the pistol after the barrel. It feeds the rounds, locks and unlocks the barrel, holds the extractor and firing pin, and times the trigger disconnector so your 1911 is a semi-auto pistol, not a runaway machine gun. We will discuss the bushing and barrel in the barrel chapter, so let's work on the slide, firing pin system, and disconnector groove first because they are simple.

## SLIDE MANUFACTURE

In one example, the 1942 production list indicates that the slide was made out of SAE 1050 steel and came in unannealed square bars. SAE 1050 is a carbon steel, but unlike the frame, it contains more carbon. Its components are .6 to .9 percent Manganese and of low sulfur and phosphorus (less than .05 percent S and less than .04 percent P) content, but the carbon content is between .47 and .55 percent. This permits a much greater degree of hardening than the frame can take, which the slide needs, with the high-stress locking lug design. However, we have some disagreements here. I have a copy of the 1928 blueprints, when the 1911 was upgraded to the 1911A1, and the slide is more exotic. It's made of 4140 steel, and the locking lug and bushing areas were hardened to between 40 and 46 Rockwell C.

So, what changed? Most likely, production rates. The GI slide in WWII had to be produced at a much higher production rate than prewar, so the alloy selected was changed to be easier to machine and

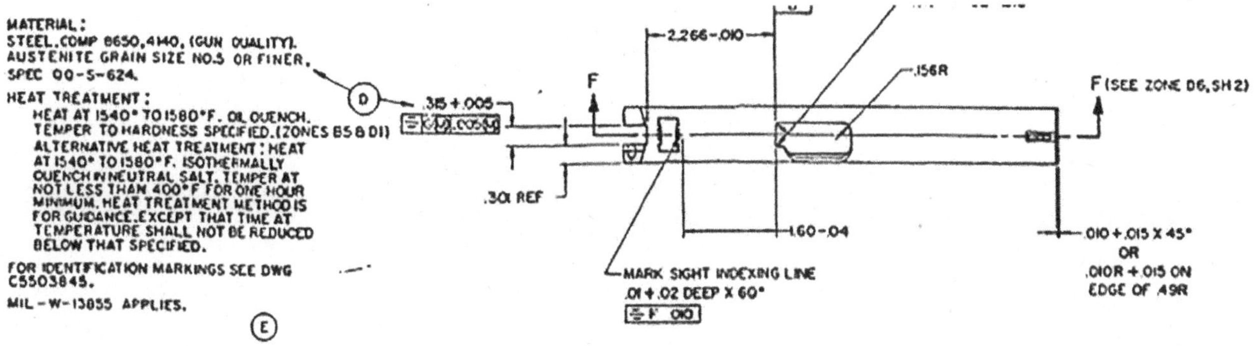


spot-hardened to strengthen the lugs and bushing area.

Today, we have a vast array of alloys suitable for use as a slide in the 1911. Like the 1898 Mauser, the 1911 is strong because of its design, not its alloy.

***When the 1911A1 was updated, the slide was to be made out of 4140 steel. Along comes a world war, and suddenly, it gets made out of 1050 and is spot-hardened. When you need millions of them, those things happen.***

## SLIDE SHAPE

The original was a flat bar with a radiused top. Well, what with the ease of change using CNC operations, you can have a slide of pretty much any shape or contour you wish. Flat-topped used to be a rarity; now, it is expected. Tri-top, side sculpting (started in production guns by Sig to echo the shape of its P226 slide), holes in the slide, and extra cocking serrations are all cosmetic. The slide will cycle like any other if it is close to the original weight. If anyone tells you they must have a lightened slide for the pistol to keep up with their incredible trigger finger, they are blowing smoke. The difference is minuscule, and the gun is much faster than any shooter.

Other than length, any change from the original is simply cosmetic. If you like it, knock yourself out. If not, move on to the next one, as there is no point or reason to argue over this or that shape, at least not as a mechanical issue.

## A COSMETIC ISSUE

OK, let's talk ball-end cuts. The front of the slide is machined with two swooping cuts. This is to adjust its mass and balance and to make it easier to holster. The original cut was a more-or-less ball-end cut. During the increased production rate for The Great War, Colt changed the two-passes-with-a-ball-end cutter to one pass with a single, two-flanged cutter. That shape stayed after the war and continues to this day.

Now, some factory guns come with the ball-end cut. Many pistolsmiths have worked out the details of machining the slide to have

The holes, sculpting, lines and cosmetics are just that: cosmetics. They may look cool, but they do not change the function of the 1911 in any way.

ball-end cuts. This is not a home gunsmithing job; it requires a large, powerful milling machine and the skill to use it properly. The ball-end cuts make no difference in function, but I find I like their appearance, and if at all possible, I get them on a pistol if I can.

## LENGTH

The commander-sized pistols have a shorter slide, but they also have a shorter recoil spring tunnel, which provides enough slide travel to let the slide uncover the top round in the magazine, get behind it, and give the magazine enough dwell time to lift the cartridge. You can't swap uppers on frames between Government Models and Commanders.

## FIRING PIN

First up, the firing pin. The 1911 firing pin uses an inertial system. That is, the firing pin, when pressed back by the firing pin spring, is not long enough to reach the primer. Even when the hammer rests on it, it still doesn't reach the primer. This design is in contrast to the Colt SAA, where lowering the hammer presses the nose of the firing pin against the primer. That's why you must carry a traditional Single Action Army or SAA revolver with the hammer down on an empty chamber. More modern designs, or those with an adaptation such as a transfer bar, are safe with a round under the hammer, but the originals are not.

The 1911, meant as a replacement for the SAA in the first decade of the 20th century, did away with that constraint.

The front of this slide has ball-end cuts. The tighter radius and alignment with the dust cover are the clues.

The firing pin spring is a return spring. At rest, the firing pin protrudes from the back of the slide through the firing pin plate. When the hammer strikes it, it is driven forward until it is either stopped by the fully compressed spring (when dry-fired) or striking the primer. During the time the firing pin moves forward, the firing pin plate stays where it is, pinned in place by the hammer resting on it and by the friction of its fit in the slide. By the time the slide starts moving, the firing pin is likely back into the plate, and even if it isn't, the initial movement of the slide puts the hammer underneath the firing pin plate, keeping it from moving down and out of the slide. Mostly. We'll see when it doesn't in a bit.

OK, here's some trivia on the timing: Igniting a primer generates a certain amount of "chamber" pressure. That is, the ignition pressure pushes back against the indentation of the primer cup. That's also part of the firing pin return. Bouncing off the primer cup, the firing pin has retracted from protruding past the breechface before the barrel and slide have moved from rest and can begin unlocking. If, in your fired brass, you see that the primer indentation is circular, things are fine. If, on the other hand, the firing pin indentation is tear-drop shaped, you have one of two minor problems. The teardrop indicates that your firing pin is protruding when the barrel begins to unlock.

One probable cause is that your firing pin tunnel is packed with gunk, or your firing pin spring is weak from use, age, or some combination. It's unlikely that your firing pin is too long, as getting the firing pin length correct is such an easy dimension to track. So, the first check and fix is to strip the firing pin and spring out, scrub the tunnel spring and pin, replace the spring, and check on the next range trip. If that solves the problem, good. If not, look at your recoil spring. How old is it—how many rounds does it have through it? For a complete rundown, go to the recoil spring section of this book, Chapter 16, where there are charts, suggestions, equations, and observations.

The real cause may be your loading. If you're shooting some of the real stout loads, a .460 Rowland, a .45 or .40 Super or the 9x23, you may not be able to go with a heavy enough recoil spring to eliminate the teardrop. Going too heavy there causes other problems in feeding and reliability, and you may have to live with the teardrop impressions.

## FIRING PIN REMOVAL

You may ask yourself, "Wait, how do I remove the firing pin?" That's a relatively easy task.

You can do it with the slide on the frame, but most people remove the slide and work on the firing pin as part of a disassembly and cleaning process. At the rear of the slide, press the firing pin tip down into the slide through the firing pin plate with a small screwdriver or pin punch. Now slide the firing pin plate down and away from the rear

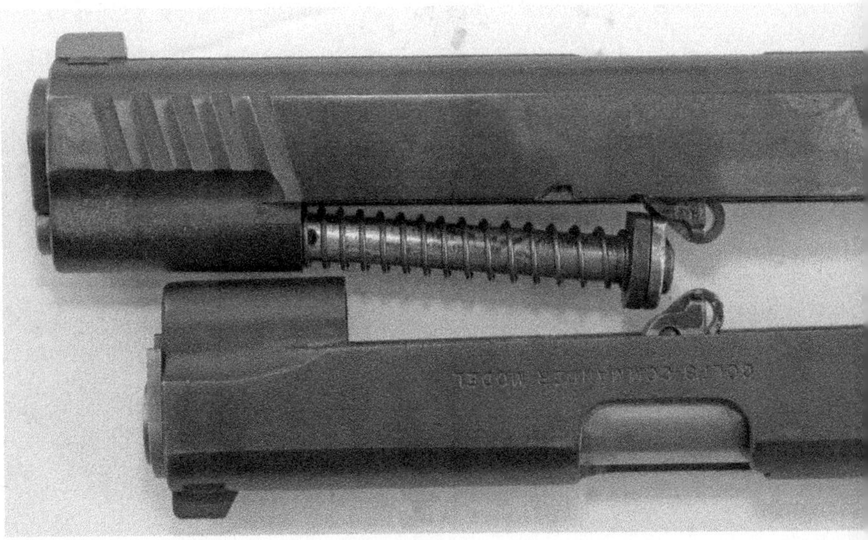

***On top is a government-length slide, and below is a Commander. Not only are the slides different in overall length, but the recoil spring tunnels differ.***

***A government-length 1911 slide is in front, with a long slide in the rear (both 10mm). The extra inch of the barrel gains useful velocity for a hunting gun. The extra inch of sight radius is even more advantageous if using iron sights.***

sight, and off the slide. The firing pin, driven by its spring, will attempt to hurl itself to freedom, so don't let it. To scrub the tunnel, use a cotton swab on a stick of a particular brand name, and try not to be surprised at how much gunk comes out. For a relatively sealed location, the tunnel seems to be a gunk-magnet. The firing pin spring has one end crimped smaller than the other. The smaller end is meant to be a press-fit over the firing pin, so you must weasel the spring off the pin on a well-made 1911. If it slips off, either the spring wasn't crimped or it was assembled at the wrong end on the pin.

Wipe the pin and spring as clean as possible (you can't get it completely clean short of an ultrasonic bath), and add a drop of oil. Set them aside, as we will look at the firing pin plate and extractor afterward.

## FIRING PIN SIZES AND TYPES

While firing pin length is standard, diameters are not. When Colt added the .38 Super to the lineup in 1929, it had to make another change: the firing pin. The .38 Super, like the .38 Auto before it, uses a small pistol primer, not a large one like the .45 ACP. It also was running at more than half-again the chamber pressure. The firing pin Browning designed for the .45 wasn't going to work. First, the big, round nose would not have adequately struck the small pistol primer. Underneath the primer cup is a three-legged anvil. In between the anvil and cup is the priming compound. The impact of compression is what sets off the priming compound.

The blunt nose of the .45 pin would likely not properly compress the priming compound, leading to ignition problems. I haven't tried it, but it doesn't look right doing a mental 3D simulation.

The big problem is primer flow. When the primer goes off, it has its own "chamber" pressure. That, and the higher 9mm/.38 Super pressure (maxing out at 36,000 psi), can cause primer flow. With the larger firing pin clearance hole in the breech, I suspect that the Colt testers back in the mid-1920s found primer flow a problem. So they made the firing pin tip and the hole it passes through smaller.

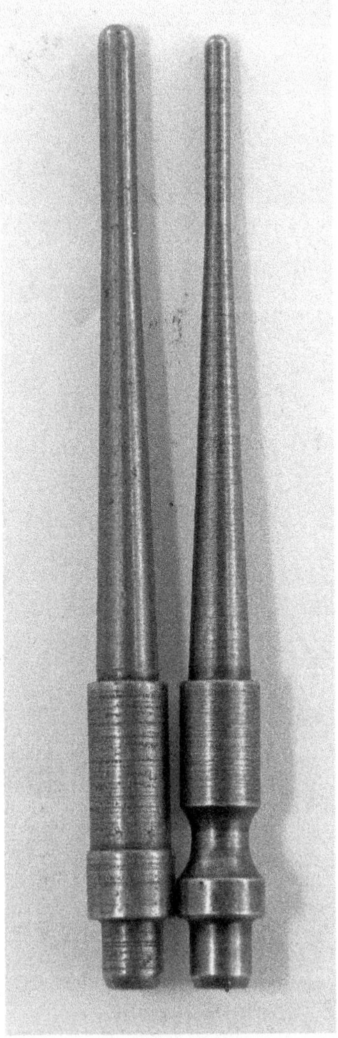

*The 1911 has three diameters of firing pins, but all models and sizes use pins of the same length. Here is a standard .45 on left, with a Series 80 9mm right. If you will stock a spare, measure yours to be sure of what you have.*

A .45 firing pin will not work in a 9mm/.38 slide. Some 10mm/.40 slides, depending on when and by whom they were made, might. A 9mm/.38 firing pin will work in a .45 slide, but it will be an unhappy mix. You will definitely have primer flow, and it may even be bad enough to tie up your gun.

There is one mix, however, that does work: a slide with a .45-dimensioned breechface and a 9mm/.38-sized firing pin hole. It's a combination some makers have gone to, as it simplifies manufacturing (all slides get the same-sized firing pin setup) and does not cause problems in a .45. If you have one and only one 1911, you'll have to measure the firing pin hole. Or, pull the firing pin out. The 9mm/.38 will have a step in its forward third, which the .45 does not. If you are ordering spares, you'll want to know which you have so you have the correct one on hand when needed.

There are three sizes of firing pins, and you can see slides with all the combos. The smallest-diameter firing pin—at the tip, they are all the same on the back end—is the Colt .38 Super pin, with a tip diameter of a nominal .068 inch. This pin also fits Caspian slides for 9mm, .38 Super, and .40. The original ones are .093 inch in diameter and work in 1911s and 1911A1s from Day One, and clones and copies, except for newer-production Springfield Armory .45 ACP pistols. The middle one has a tip diameter of .075 inch, and those go into Springfield Armory 9mm, .38 Super, 10mm and the newer-production .45 ACPs. Yes, Springfield found a Momma Bear middle-size that works in all of its pistols and started using them.

So, the quick advice here is: if you stock a spare or replace an exist-

*On the left is a standard or 70-Series firing pin. On the right is the Series 80 style. Note the groove turned into the Series-80 pin, which is the clearance for the safety plunger.*

ing one, get out the digital calipers and measure before you order.

You'll also want to ensure you have the correct series firing pin. In its Series 80 pistols, Colt added a firing pin safety activated by the movement of the trigger. The Series 80 firing pin has a groove machined around the rear boss for the trigger-activated plunger to clear. A non-80 firing pin, an original, will not clear the plunger. You can't assemble a non-80 firing pin into an S80 slide and still fit the safety parts.

On the other hand, you can install an S80 firing pin into a slide lacking the Series 80 parts, and it will work just fine. It won't provide the firing pin safety feature, but it will work. If you have multiple 1911s, and some are S80, you won't need both; get the S80 firing pin and use it in your non-80 pistols if needed. Stainless versus blued? No big deal; use whatever you want to.

## TITANIUM

You'll see titanium firing pins in gunsmithing catalogs. Titanium is a lighter metal than steel but stronger than aluminum. For a short time, replacing aluminum frames on lightweight pistols would be the big new thing. However, it didn't take long to find the shortcomings of titanium in that role, primarily its refusal to work in any function involving sliding friction. It galled, badly and quickly, so quickly that using it in frames ended up being a big "Nope, not gonna happen" event. (I know of one custom pistolsmith who had begun taking orders for Ti-framed pistols. He had started his first when he had five such in the queue, and as soon as he realized the magnitude of the galling problem, he stopped taking orders and let the other four know what the deal was in case they wanted to change their order.)

A lightweight titanium firing pin lessens inertia, reducing or eliminating the dropped-pistol problem. We'll cover this in detail at the end of the chapter, but by using a lighter pin and a heavier spring, the chances of a dropped 1911 going off are essentially eliminated.

## SERIES 70, 80, WHATEVER?

I've already touched on the Series 80 pistols. You'll also read of Series 70 vs. Series 80 1911s, which has to do with a firing pin blocking safety. Colt developed this feature (other makers used it later) to deal with the dropped gun "problem." I discuss the testing elsewhere, but we're concerned with the parts here. The Series 80 (the one with the firing pin safety) uses a spring-loaded plunger in the slide that rides across the firing pin tunnel. The firing pin has a notch turned into it, and the plunger rides in this notch.

When the plunger is at rest, it blocks the firing pin movement. When you pull the trigger, its movement cams a lever that lifts and presses the plunger out of the way, and the firing pin can move when struck by the hammer.

The Series-80 design adds parts, friction and trigger pull weight to the system. At first, everyone hated it, but pistolsmiths learned to manage the system, and you can get a decent trigger pull out of an 80-Series pistol. It is not without problems, however. If the trigger movement isn't long enough, it won't lift the lever far enough, and the plunger barely clears the pin or doesn't clear it. But the hammer force is significant enough to drive the pin past the plunger—the cause you might see in some Series 80 pistols where the firing pin has seriously gouged the edges of the plunger.

In the course of this book, I discovered an interesting fact: I do not own a Series 80 pistol. None of the loaners I have on hand are Series 80. So, I don't have photos of the parts. Hmm, that should be, as they say in law enforcement, a clue.

By removing the plunger and spring, you can make an 80 into a 70 (the model without the parts). You have to leave the lever in place, as it rides beside the sear and disconnector, and if you remove the lever, it can slop around and cause problems. You can buy filler plates to fill that gap after removing the Series 80 parts.

The firing pin can stay as it is; there's no problem with a Series 80 pin in a Series 70 pistol.

## FIRING PIN RETAINING PLATE

The firing pin retaining plate slides up into the slide recess, and it is meant to be a snug but not binding fit. Notice that the firing pin plate also retains the extractor in the slide. Removing the extractor properly requires both hands. Use a small screwdriver to pry the extractor from its tunnel. However, remember that a hook on the other end will catch on the breechface when you pry. Use a fingertip or thumb to press the extractor hook away from the firing pin hole as you pry to prevent damage. Once the extractor is out, you can scrub its tunnel (more gunk) and wipe the extractor clean.

## REPLACEMENTS AND TUNING

A firing pin or firing pin spring replacement is easy: plug in the new parts. Neither needs tuning or adjustment in any way. The rest? They will all need, or likely need, tuning in one way or another. Let's start with the firing pin plate.

Why would you replace the plate? Three reasons. One, it is broken. Two, it supports and locates the extractor. Three, recoil. The plate takes the full impact of the hammer every single time the hammer falls. The plate has a notch in it, clearance for the ejector, and it is not uncommon for the plate to be cracked from the corner of that notch to the firing pin hole. I've seen plates with a chip knocked out from the initial crack and later breakage. A cracked plate may not stay entirely in place during cycling, and when it drops down, it causes a bad malfunction. It may even fall out. So, cracked or chipped plates need to be replaced.

Secondly, the plate holds the extractor. If the plate is too narrow or the slot in the extractor is too deep, the extractor can rotate slightly in its tunnel, which can change (usually for the worse) how much it grips the rim on extraction. A rigidly held extractor is more consistent in function and has a longer service life than one that moves. This is a detail that a custom pistolsmith will fuss over for what might seem to be an excessive amount of time. And if you have a top-end custom gun built, the 'smith might even fit two extractors to your 1911, a spare in case the first one breaks, because your fit is so custom that a drop-in won't drop in.

Third, recoil. When the slide begins to move back, one of the first functions it performs is to begin cocking the hammer. Since the point of contact of the slide on the hammer is above the axis, the hammer pin, you have a lever at work. As with all levers, the longer the lever arm, the easier the work. If you look at the bottom of the firing pin plate, you'll see it is machined to a curve. The larger the radius of the curve, the longer the lever arm. That is, a "swoopier" curve is easier to cock. If the radius is smaller, the curve is sharper, and the effort needed to cock is greater.

Why is it curved? People who use 1911s like to have an easy time racking the slide. But the longer lever means the slide uses less energy to cock the hammer, so there is more left to cycle the slide, bottom out, and feel sharper in recoil. If you replace the original with a sharper-radius firing pin plate, the lever arm is shorter, and the slide uses more energy to cock the hammer. That means less leftover to bottom out the slide and less felt recoil.

Recoil can also be managed with a heavier recoil spring and hammer spring. But those both come with other costs. So, what is the cost of the short-radius plate? For one, racking the slide will be a bit more difficult. The initial effort will be greater, and some shooters don't like it. The other is that, in extreme situations, it can cause malfunctions. If you're building a competition 9mm to be used with light loads and you do not have a "crush" grip, adding a short-radius plate could cause a malfunction in some situations. This is something you may have to test for yourself.

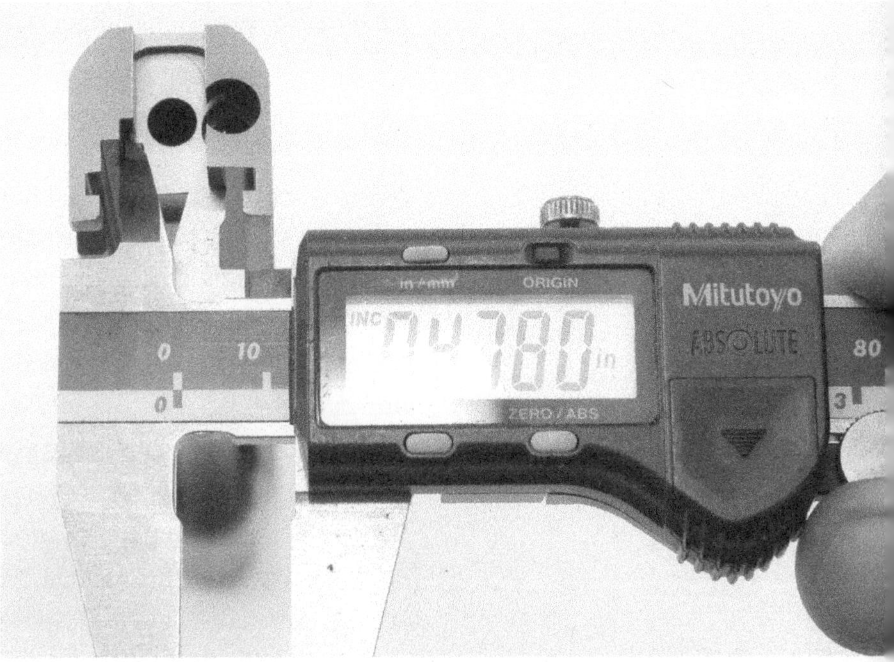


To fit a new firing pin plate, measure. If the plate slides in, you're good; if not, measure before filing.

What is a "crush" grip? A vise-like hold, hands *and* arms. I have an example from experience. In the 1980s, I shot in a PPC league at the local sheriff's department range. Even with the lightest .45 loads I could get to function, I used a pistol much more robust than the .38 Special wadcutter ammo the others were using. (I was not a member of that department, but I was shooting there because that league was 10 minutes from home, and the league of my department was over an hour away, one-way.) So I built a 1911 in .38 Super and tuned it to run with loads as light or lighter than their wadcutter ammo. My load was a 125-grain lead round-nose, and I was pushing it maybe 900 fps. I'd have to dive back 40+ years in chronograph loads to find out.

A course of fire was 60 rounds. I'd commonly shoot three courses, the best one of them being my league score. (Those were the league rules.) I could shoot 180 rounds of super-light, really grubby ammo, and the gun would run just fine. None of the deputies could shoot a single magazine without a malfunction because they did not have a vise-grip. They didn't need one for their duty .38s or the PPC .38s they used. If you don't have a vise grip, your light-load 9mm, especially if you have built a Government Model, can malfunction. You'll have to test to be sure.

When would you install one, then? If you will be shooting a lot of .45+P ammo or one of the hot numbers I've been mentioning. It will make the felt recoil less sharp and also tame the vibration and slide-bounce of bottoming out at high speed.

## FITTING

Fit the firing pin plate first. If the replacement is a drop-in, there's no fitting. You'll have to take potluck on how it gets along with the extractor, but unless your extractor worked marginally to begin with, you'll likely be fine.

You will have to do some measuring if your plate is oversized. EGW makes a gauge to measure this, but if you're doing a one-and-only plate fit, investing in a gauge might be a bit much. A good set of digital calipers will suffice. Measure the width of the slot in the slide and the width of the new plate. How much over the plate width to slide slot width tells you how much filing to do. You also have the question of the plate thickness—the slide slot and the plate flanges. If the plate is under, life's good; there's only one dimension to file. If both are under, you must relieve the flange thickness first, or you'll never correctly fit the side-to-side dimension. It also requires a bit of practice, as the flange thickness can be a smidge under the slide and still work, but the width being under brings you back to a drop-in fit.

You know how much you need to reduce the plate, so clamp it in the vise and file it straight (another learning skill you'll be getting on the way) until you are just under halfway. Do the side away from the extractor first. Measure the plate width top and bottom. File a few passes, then measure again. If they are not evenly reduced, you are not filing straight. Adjust your technique and continue. If you mess up a firing pin plate, it is relatively inexpensive practice; grab another (you did order two, didn't you?) and start over. Wait, don't. Flip the scrapped one over and file the other edge, getting in more practice before you go to your second one. Don't practice on the original; you may need it for testing later.

Then flip it over. File the extractor side until it exceeds the final measured slide width dimension. Check it for fit. At this point, you are in "file and check" mode. A few strokes, check in the slide—a few more and check. You'll get to the point where it starts to fit; break the edges of the plate. Filing creates a sharp burr on the plate. With a single stroke on each edge, break that burr and check again.

Oh, one last detail: if you have a Bomar sight installed on your slide, the top of the firing pin plate must be filed down to clear the sight. The old plate will show you where and how much, but you must do it. The new one won't fit otherwise.

You want a plate that presses up into the slot with finger pressure, won't drop out of its own weight, and won't wiggle when it is in place. Job done so far.

## EXTRACTORS

OK, you've now fitted a firing pin plate to the extractor. Wait, why would you? If your extractor is working just fine, why fit a replacement? Well, things break. If you have an already-fitted extractor in your gear bag, and your 1911 decides this particular match is the place to break, you're out of luck. You can maybe borrow another firearm to finish the match with (been there, done that, it sucks, but our team still won Gold despite the broken gun), but chances are the loaner will be someone else's backup gun, and it may not be much like yours.

If you have a spare extractor, you only zero one stage, not it and all the rest in the match.

Unless you're operating in a military environment and can back out of the fight long enough, I can't see swapping out a busted extractor in a fight and getting back into things. No, in a defensive situation, you'd better have a backup, as in, another working firearm.

*A set of Weigand extractor tension gauges. Use these by inserting the appropriate caliber gauge into the breechface and letting the extractor get a hold. Then, use a trigger pull gauge to see how much force it takes to pull the gauge out. Competition shooters use them, some often. Most of us use the "drooping round" test.*

And, one extra, more minor reason for another extractor. This one from your custom pistolsmith. He probably has serrated the back of the slide (because it was included in the package or you requested it). A new replacement extractor won't be serrated to match and will be flat steel. He will fit a spare and serrate it to match, so it matches when you need a spare. (These things matter on a custom 1911 costing $5,000 or more.) Once you've swapped in the spare, you'll have to schedule sending your 1911 back for the new spare to be fitted because each one is hand-fitted.

Before we can fit and test a new extractor, we need to know how to test them, period, to see if your current one is up to snuff.

With the bare slide off the frame but with the extractor, firing pin, and retaining plate installed, pick a loaded round. Yes, yes, you should not have loaded ammo on hand when you are cleaning a firearm. So walk into the next room, get one round, and bring it back. Slip the round up and underneath the extractor hook, simulating its path when fed from a magazine. Let go. The round should stay in place, held in the breechface by the extractor's tension. There should be a bit of "droop." The round should not be held fast and tight to the breechface. Lift the nose of the cartridge, and if the tension is correct, it should drop back down when you take your finger away.

There are tension measuring gauges. The EGW ones use a brass plate of the correct rim diameter that you slip under the extractor. Then, use a trigger pull gauge to pull the EGW gauge out from under the extractor and record the force needed. I used to obsess over tension, as we all did. When I wrote my first 1911 book, I had a couple of dozen factory-built pistols and the gauge on hand. So I measured them all. The measured tension ranged from 0 to about 4 pounds, and all the guns worked flawlessly during testing. After that, I gave up being picky. The "droop" test is good enough, along with test-firing (the only real test of extractor function, when you think about it) and haven't measured any since then, around the year 2000.

## WHAT MATTERS

OK, what do I obsess over, then? Fit. Let's take the contact points of the extractor from back to front. First, it is held in by the retaining plate. I want that to fit tight so the extractor can't "clock" or rotate inside the tunnel. Next, I want enough bend in the extractor, so it has to be pried out of the tunnel on disassembly. It can't just be allowed to fall out; that's not the way it was designed to work. That bend is also one of the two things determining extractor tension. Next, I want the bearing pad, right behind the hook, to be the same radius as the tunnel so it bears evenly. If it is smaller in radius, it contacts one point; if it is larger, it hits two. Both let the extractor do squirrely things.

*When a pistolsmith serrates the rear of your slide (or you do), it is crucial to get them started square. And to have the extractor already fitted since it will also get serrated.*

The hook pad, the interior surface that contacts the case rim, needs to be slightly under the rim diameter as it rests in the slide: the distance from the far wall (opposite the ejection port) to the pad must be a couple of thousandths under the rim diameter, a nominal .480 inch for a .45 ACP. This dimension ensures it controls feeding and keeps the other edge of the rim tight to the breechface wall/shoulder.

In many instances, the hook needs to be trimmed so it doesn't dig into the extractor groove. If you look at much-fired brass, you'll see a series of nicks, or dings, in the groove ahead of the rim. This is where the extractor hook has dug into the case and keeps the extractor hook from bottoming out, as above, and while it's not always a bad thing, it's not ever a good thing. I've seen 1911s that ran for tens of thousands of rounds, where the hook dug into cases and never failed. But it is wrong and asking for trouble. It can be fixed, so I make sure it is.

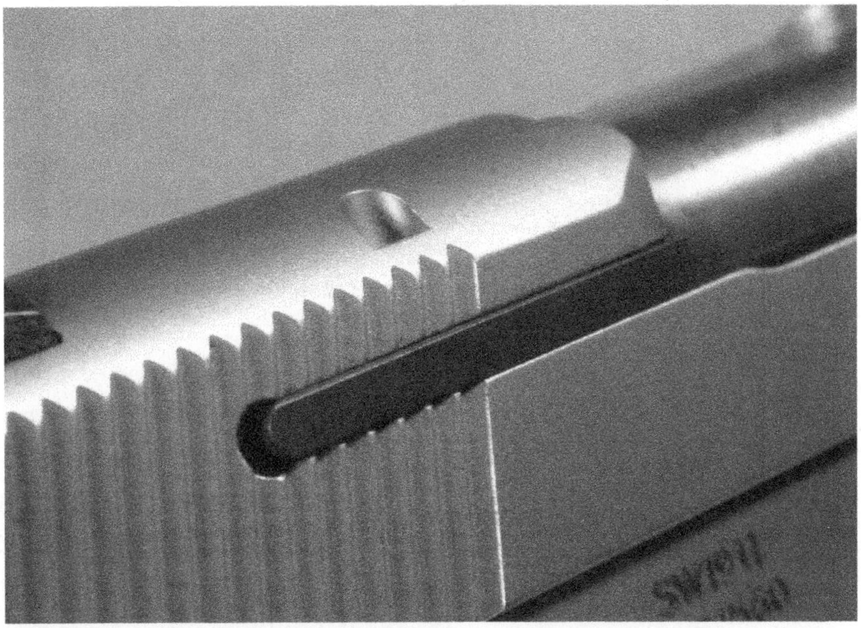

*The external extractor, found on some models of 1911, like the S&W series and Sig. Is it better? Maybe. Is it what they know how to build? You bet. Does it work just fine? Certainly.*

Last, the extractor tip cannot touch the barrel. Unlike the hook nicking the case, this is bad, and if the extractor hits the barrel too hard, it will break in short order. Remember, the slide slams shut with the full force of the recoil spring every single time. If the extractor touches the barrel, then it takes that hit.

## EXTRACTOR FITTING

OK, the first thing I do, even before I pick up a file, is to stuff the new extractor into the clean slide and conduct the droop test. Someone may have put the extractor into the wrong package. It might have been incorrectly machined or otherwise damaged between when it was made and when it arrived in my mailbox. Secondly, I heave a sigh of relief because the modern extractor, coming from those who know their stuff, has many of the small details we used to fuss over already done.

I don't know if the old ones were unfinished because they were expected to be fitted and fine-tuned, and armorers of the time were expected to know that. Or, more likely, modern manufacturing practices permit the makers to put in those details and produce a final product that is less likely to be screwed up (or need fitting) by the end user. I am reminded of a long time ago reading a lament by an experienced samurai of the late Edo period, who complained bitterly that modern samurai didn't know how to properly sharpen their swords and had to have a specialist do it for them. Well, the top competition shooter at your gun club, who may be nationally ranked, probably doesn't know how to fine-tune an extractor. But he knows it matters, and he knows when it hasn't been done right.

Your extractor likely comes with the retaining plate slot already milled. You can order one without the slot, and custom pistolsmiths do when they need to fit an extractor to a slide that isn't within specification. You'll likely get a spare or two back with your gun when they have to do that because a drop-in won't do. You do not need one unless you have a milling machine or a burning desire to learn the intricacies of filing a square, axially aligned, precisely located slot by hand, an onerous task.

Install the extractor in the tunnel. Install the firing pin and spring and the retaining plate. Do the droop test. Most of the time, you are now done. Oh, you might want to add a little more tension to the extractor fit, but there won't be any metal removal required.

Examine the radius of the extractor pad in the tunnel at the breechface. It should be the same as the tunnel, and knowing that makes it easier to adjust extractor "reach" if need be.

Tensioning? There are two ways: the simple and the exacting. The simple way is to remove the retaining plate and firing pin and pull the extractor halfway out of the tunnel. Rotate it 180 degrees, and put your thumb against the plate end. Press the extractor out, bending it, using the tunnel as your lever. Simple, yes, but how much should you bend it? The short answer is "Just enough." It can take some time, a bunch of pistols, and a fistful of extractors to learn how much is just enough.

Next, hand-assemble the barrel into the slide and check the extractor length to ensure it doesn't touch the barrel. If it does, a few file strokes on the end to shorten it does the trick.

Barrel out, clamp the slide in a padded vise, muzzle up, and use an empty case for "reach" and contact inspection. In this context, "reach" is the distance the lip of the extractor hook extends toward the firing pin hole. It is the grip of the extractor on the rim. The extractor hook should reach as deeply into the groove as possible for complete rim contact, but the hook should not gouge the groove taper. Nicking the taper of the extractor groove is not good, and it also indicates an extractor hook that doesn't have the proper front face angle. You can't change the angle without risking weakening the extractor, so decrease the "reach" while maintaining as much rim contact as possible. Make sure the hook groove also contacts the rim. The hook should catch the rim on its front side (toward the muzzle), and the extractor hook groove should contact the rim on its external radius.

Last is the take-up angle. This is the hook's bottom corner and the contact groove's bottom lip. Both need a slight bevel to prevent a sharp edge from biting into the brass of the rim and slowing feeding (not much, as removing metal means decreasing contact or grip).

*With much use, the breechface of a 1911 (or any pistol, for that matter) will show the wear. In this case, the erosion of the firing pin bushing edge may become a problem in another half-million rounds. Photo: Ned Christiansen*

## BREECHFACE WORK

While we're fussing over extractors, attention to the rest of the breechface is in order. If you have bought/inherited/won a high-mileage 1911 at auction, the firing pin hole might have a peened lip around it. A minute's worth of stoning or using an abrasive cloth with a hard backer will even it and smooth it out. Just smooth it; there's no need to make it a mirror, and in trying, you could alter the breechface detrimentally. Other than that, the breechface probably doesn't need your attention, but the sidewall does. The sidewall is the face opposite the extractor that locates the far edge of the case rim. That surface is difficult for the manufacturer to machine, and there was a time (probably several times) when Colt pistols came with that surface rough.

There are two parts of it to inspect. One is the bottom edge. The other is the contact face on which the rim rides. The bottom edge is where the case rim rides up into the breechface, and it cannot have a sharp lip and certainly no machining "wires" or tool marks. A pass or two with a fine-cut safe-edge file will remove such problems. The sidewall might need some stoning to smooth out machining marks or a rough surface. You do not want to remove any more metal than you need to make it reasonably smooth. A mirror surface isn't needed here.

If your 1911 has been recalcitrant in feeding, a look here will tell you volumes. If you see heavy brassing or, worse, bits of brass here, then the sidewall and its bottom edge are a big part of your problems. Knocking off the sharp edge on the bottom and smoothing the sidewall will make your 1911 run 100 percent.

## DISCONNECTOR

OK, as your slide moves, it must disconnect the firing parts from each other so the sear and hammer can reset. It does this using the disconnector, the strangely shaped part that rides in the middle of the sear. The center leaf of the three-leaf spring under the grip safety pushes on the disconnector. The stripper rail keeps it pressed down and engaged with the trigger and sear. When the slide cycles, the small dished section in the stripper rail allows the disconnector to ride up into the groove—delinking it from the sear/trigger engagement and allowing the free movement of the sear to intercept the hammer as the slide closes.

*Check the sidewall of the breechface for tool marks and brassing if you have problems feeding. There can be significant brassing here requiring judicious polishing.*

What can you do here? Not much. Usually, nothing at all. It does what it does; it is where it needs to be, and as long as it works, life is good. I know some pistolsmiths who are the exemplars of OCD who will polish the stripper rail for smoother feeding and also polish the disconnector dish as part of a primo trigger job. Does it make a difference? Not that I can tell, but when someone is paying $5,000-$7,000 for a fully custom 1911, no surface is left un-inspected. They also polish the stripper rail and the slots on either side because that is a typical place to mark a slide. They might do a serial number match, or a date of build and their initials, that sort of thing. Having stamped the numerals and letters into the rail, they will polish the rail to remove the "halos" the stamping produced.

## DROPPED GUNS

All modern striker-fired pistols are made with a "drop safety" to ensure they cannot fire when dropped. This feature is required in a striker-fired pistol because at ready-to-fire, the striker (at least on some models) is held partway or entirely to the rear. If the striker's tail slips off the sear tab, the striker should hit the primer. So, there's a drop safety of some kind (or two) in the slide to prevent that. The 1911 was deemed safe enough with the inertial firing pin design, but there have been instances when it seemed to go off when dropped. I don't want to sound too critical, but many "dropped gun" discharges are probably something else. When a firearm goes off at the wrong moment, and there's damage or injury, the typical reaction is, "The gun just went off." (Alec Baldwin comes readily to mind, but it happens a hundred times a year in one police department precinct house or another.) So Browning built an extra safety into the setup besides the inertial firing pin.

The hammer has the full-cock notch, the one that the sear contacts for firing. Below that is a "half-cock" notch, a safety notch. If the hammer at full-cock gets jarred enough to slip off of the sear, the hammer will rotate, but the sear is designed to intercept the hammer at the half-cock notch. That's the intent. Suppose you were to compare a classic 1911 to a current production one. You'd see minor differences in the parts, as the desire over time was to protect an expensive trigger job from damage, and manufacturers and 'smiths made minor changes.

If, when dropped, the sear was jarred out of contact with the hammer notch, then the half-notch safety shelf should catch the hammer on the sear. The supposition of "dropped gun discharges" goes that it is the firing pin flying forward (Newton's Laws are unavoidable regardless of how good your lawyer might be) that hits the primer with sufficient force to discharge the pistol, even if the hammer stays cocked, or falls to the half-cock notch.

***The shelf under the extractor may need attention, a detail that most manufacturers have sorted out long ago. Still, check for brassing.***

This theory has been tested many times over the previous century-plus, and I'm not sure anyone has come to a conclusive opinion. (Or if they have, they've kept it to themselves. I suspect there are reports of each decade of such tests somewhere in the depths of Colt's filing cabinets, but then I just might be a bit overly suspicious.)

I've tested the theory myself a few times and have not been able to create a discharge, but the best test is one I'll recount. The sample pistol was an all-steel Para Ordnance hi-cap factory gun. So, the heaviest a 1911 pistol could be. It was an evidence gun and was slated for the smelter since the court proceedings were all over, so we could

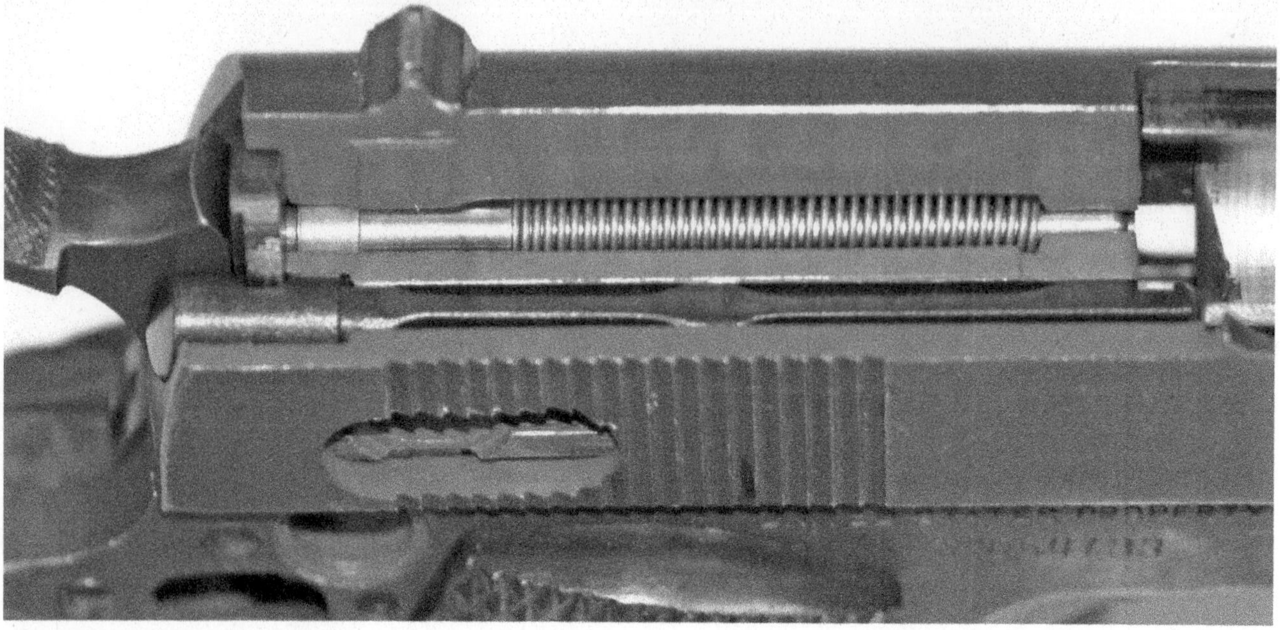

***Note how the firing pin spring pushes the firing pin back away from the breechface, and how the impact of the hammer drives it forward enough to set off the primer. Even when the hammer is at rest, it doesn't push the firing pin far enough to reach the primer.***

heinously abuse it, and as long as the serial number was legible when it came time for destruction, no one would care. Well, we cared; it was an excellent pistol or had been at one time.

My friend Ned threaded the barrel interior and fabricated a muzzle weight we could screw into the barrel. The steel weight, screwed into the barrel, brought the pistol up to the total weight of a fully loaded magazine and ensured it would fall with the muzzle straight down. We inserted a primed, empty case in the chamber, cocked the hammer, left the safety off, and proceeded to drop it onto the concrete floor of the indoor police range. The ceiling height limited us; we could only drop it 8 1/2 feet, but we could never get the primed case to go bang. Max weight, a hard surface, safety off, no discharge.

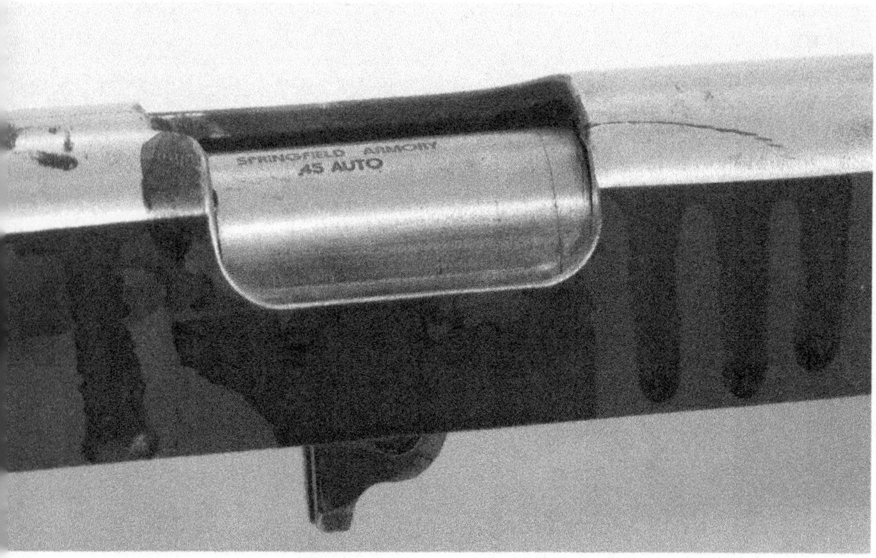


***This was common back when a USGI pistol was standard and not expensive. The ejection port here has been milled lower. Today, doing that to a clean USGI slide would be blasphemy, removing one more historical item from its original status.***

I, for one, am not worried about a dropped 1911 going off. However, if I were worried, replacing the firing pin with a titanium one or using an extra-strength firing pin return spring would put my mind at ease.

## EJECTION PORT SIZE

The original ejection port has a "high wall" on the slide flat. That is, the port is as it was initially made. During the heyday of Bullseye competition, then later IPSC, the ejection port grew in size. The Bullseye shooters did it first—only on the "softball" guns—because the lighter loads they were shooting did not offer the *oomph* of ejection that hardball did, and while they could get a re-shoot if they had a malfunction, it was better not to have a malfunction in the first place.

***Shooters used to lower the ejection ports on early commercial and GI slides. Now, unless it is a full-house custom, doing that reduces the value of any collectible 1911. Photo: Jason Burton***

IPSC shooters, not shooting soft loads, wanted reliable function and used an extended ejector. The ejector, a rib riding in a slot in the slide, was a fixed post that the case rim hit. The originals were angled to toss empties up and out of the smaller, original ejection port. But by making that face vertical instead of angled back, IPSC shooters caused the case to intercept the ejector sooner at a higher velocity, and eject it more vigorously. Making it vertical also changed the ejection angle to the side, which required lowering the ejection port. Extending the ejector blade forward made the case hit earlier, adding energy to the ejection, but still required lowering the sidewall.

***A pair of Nighthawk T4s, a build that does not use a bushing. The barrel diameter is increased to match the slide interior, and the recoil spring retainer is captured from behind.***

It used to be expected that, to lower the sidewall, a milling machine was required (doing it by hand was possible but onerous). However, that is uncommon these days. First, because all modern-production 1911s will have a low sidewall. Since it is already lowered, there's no reason to lower it more. Second, the only reason to lower a sidewall is because you have a mil-spec slide. Well, if you have an unaltered USGI 1911 or 1911A1, it is more valuable than anything you could make it into. You can sell a non-rare 1911A1 USGI pistol for $2,000 (2023 dollars) and buy a fully featured brand-new Tisas 1911 for $1,200 or less—$800 buys you a lot of practice ammo and magazines and saves you from the enmity of collectors for having butchered an increasingly rare pistol. ●

CHAPTER 12

# SAFETIES

The 1911 has two safety mechanisms: thumb and grip safety—the thumb safety blocks the movement of the sear. Theoretically, the 1911 could still fire inadvertently if the sear were to break catastrophically and the parts failed to block the falling hammer. Yeah, no. Not gonna happen. The grip safety works by blocking the movement of the trigger. So, if the grip safety isn't working, and the thumb safety is in the off position, a sufficient force could jar the sear out of the hammer notch (actually a shelf, not a notch, but we call it a notch, so get used to it) and fire the pistol. Again, it's not likely, as the half-cock notch will catch the hammer.

While the 1911 is well-equipped with safety parts, many shooters fuss over their fit and function, and if you aren't careful, you can fuss them into not working. So let's go over how they work, how to check their function, and how to adjust if need be or replace them because you want to. We'll start with the grip safety because it's the easiest to work with and more likely to need adjustment, at least for some shooters.

## GRIP SAFETY

The moving lever behind and below the hammer, the grip safety must be depressed for the 1911 to fire. This was not a problem when Browning designed it, nor for a long time afterward. In the beginning, handguns were fired one-handed. Shooters did not work as hard (nor did they see the need) to get their hands as high up on the pistol as we later developed for IPSC competitions. In the old style, one-handed, thumb middle or low, the grip safety worked just fine. However, when we learned to position our hands as high as possible, shifting the point of contact on the frame upward and reducing the leverage on the grip safety. For many shooters, that meant the grip safety wasn't being depressed far enough, and the pistol would not fire.

Before we move on, it's time for a mechanical discussion and illustration of how the grip safety works. If you have yours disassembled (and you should at this point, or be looking at a drawing, diagram or photo), you'll see that the grip safety rotates around the thumb safety shaft. Projecting forward from it is a thin tab that comes to a blunt point. If you slide the grip safety over a pin punch, you can rotate it or move it through a short arc. You'll see that the point of the tab lifts or lowers. When the actuation spring arm of the three-leaf spring pushes the safety out, away from the frame, the point of the tab rotates down to behind the rear of the trigger.

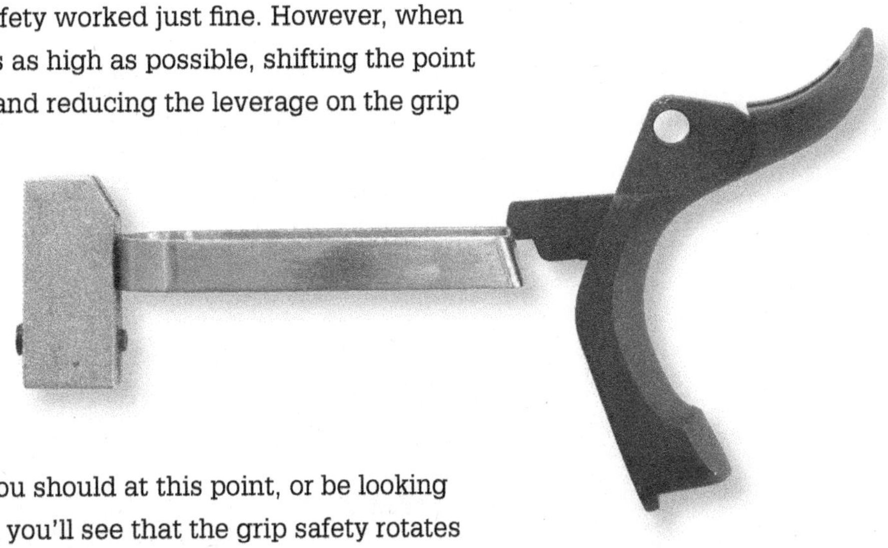

***When the grip safety is at rest, it hinges down, and the tab on the front of the safety blocks the back of the trigger.***

OK, it's time for some 3D mental modeling. Imagine the safety with the point behind the trigger. The point keeps the trigger from moving. Yes, there's some gap, some slack, but as long as it isn't enough to let the trigger push on or move the sear, the grip safety is working. Now press the grip safety in and note how the tab rotates, lifting the point from the trigger. The trigger can now slide under the tab in the clearance space.

The tab is important. First, its length determines where it stops the trigger from moving. That is its *security.* How far down it rotates determines how far you must depress the grip safety to fire. That is its *sensitivity.* Once the shooter depresses the safety, the smoothness of the bottom edge, or clearance of the tab, rotating it out of the way, determines trigger pull *cleanliness* (or at least one aspect of it).

Lastly, the strength of the three-leaf spring determines how quickly the grip safety returns to the safe position. It doesn't matter for your grip; you will have pounds and pounds of grip pressing it down, where it has ounces of pressure up. So the "obvious" solution to grip safety problems, decreasing three-leaf spring tension, gains you nothing.

You can see all this if you detail strip your frame, grips included.

Install the trigger and magazine catch. Place the grip safety into the frame and press the thumb safety shaft through the frame and grip safety, but leave the thumb safety body hanging out in space, not inserted into the frame. Lay the frame down on the right side, mag opening towards you. You can now look through the grip space into the trigger slot and see the grip safety at work. Move the grip safety and see how it engages the trigger. Push it in, move the trigger, and watch the clearance under the tab.

***When pressed, the grip safety lifts the tab, giving the trigger bar clearance to move.***

For more grip safety engagement, counterintuitively go to its opposite end. Two tabs at the bottom of the grip safety engage the top lip of the mainspring housing. Carefully file off the grip safety and mainspring housing engagement surfaces to give the grip safety more pivot. Carefully, because you don't need much to make a big difference, and there isn't a lot of metal on those tabs, you want to leave enough metal so it's strong enough to do the job. This is a rarely-needed adjustment—I think I did it twice as a gunsmith—but if you need it, this is the place.

More often, you'll need to increase the sensitivity. If, now and then, your grip doesn't depress the grip safety enough to fire, you have to make it more sensitive. The sensitivity test requires a fully assembled but unloaded pistol. Hold the pistol without depressing the grip safety, cock the hammer, and gently press the trigger until it stops, bearing on the grip safety. Watch the frame edge where the grip safety enters, and, while still pressing the trigger, gently and slowly press the grip safety into the frame. Notice the moment the hammer falls, and note where the grip safety is in that movement.

Let's consider the grip safety movement distance by percentages. If you have to have the grip safety depressed 90 percent of the way before the hammer falls, you have a very safe pistol, but perhaps a not-so-useful one. Any slight difference in your grip means the pistol won't fire. On the other hand, if the grip safety only needs a 10 percent movement for the hammer to fall, it really isn't much of a safety. Anything that bumps it provides clearance for the trigger.

Discussions over where the grip safety should trip and the percentage for best function are like debating how many angels can dance on the head of a pin. Me? I'm happy if the grip safety releases just shy of 50 percent, which works well for me, given my high grip on the frame.

So, how do we increase sensitivity? That is, decrease the percentage of depression for actuation. The bottom surface of the tab is your area of focus. Take the grip safety out of the frame, turn it upside down, and use a clean, fine-cut file. Take a couple of passes on the bottom of the tab, clean the edges, and re-do the test. This is a sneak-up-on-it, file-and-test process because it doesn't take much, and you can't put metal back.

## SPEED PEDALS

One extra detail that has been built into grip safeties since the old days is what I call the "speed pedal." This is the raised tab, or the raised rib on the grip safety, that gives your hand additional leverage and ensures it gets fully depressed when you grasp it. Unless you are buying a specifically GI-type 1911, it is pretty much a standard item now to have the pad or rib on the beavertail grip safety. It works and is expected and customary.

## HISTORICAL

In the early days, when we were gripping the pistols higher and higher, those with inconsistent grip safety clearance had few options. One was to pin the safety. Today, this is not just discouraged but prohibited in some competitions. If you encounter a 1911 with the grip safety blocked or pinned, it is a historical curiosity. And all the usual methods are easily reversible, so don't sweat it. But if you inherit an IPSC pistol built in the 1960s-'80s, it could have a pinned safety. Check before you go to the range. How to check? The easy one is that the grip safety doesn't move; it is locked in the depressed position. The other check is to see if you can dry-fire the pistol without pressing the grip safety. That's the more difficult one to update, as the tab has been shortened or removed. In that instance, let's now see about installing a new grip safety.

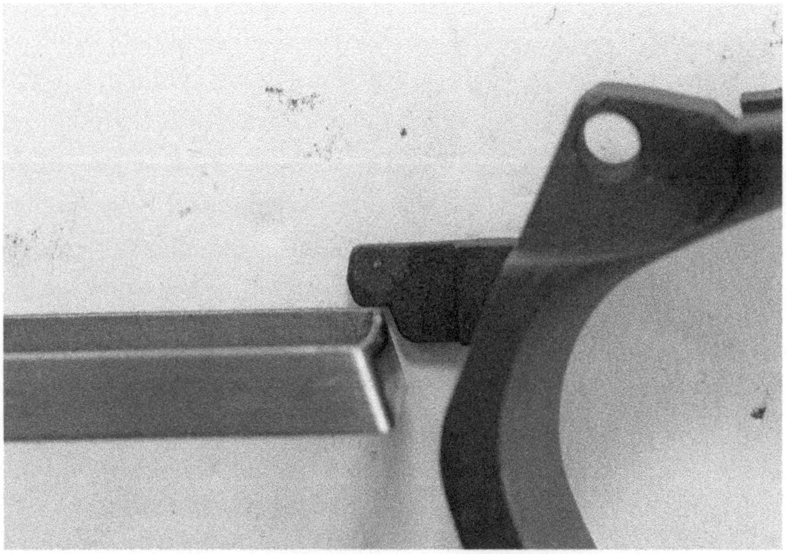

*When you fire, the trigger bar travels under the grip safety tab. This is the surface to relieve if you want to sensitize your grip safety. It must also be smooth so the trigger bar won't clatter if it rubs the grip safety.*

## GRIP SAFETIES AND INSTALLATION

There are three kinds of grip safeties based on the frame. The original is the extended tang with the standard grip safety sticking out behind. We would occasionally install a Commander or Rowel hammer into a full-sized 1911. The Commander pistol used a shorter grip safety to accommodate the Commander hammer. Compact, but not always comfortable. The Government Model's longer grip safety tang was more comfortable but did not have clearance for the Commander hammer. So, as part of building a competition gun circa 1982, we'd install a Commander hammer for looks (you've gotta look stylish, always) and machine the grip safety to create clearance for the hammer. This also included smoothing sharp edges and corners; the result was pretty good-looking.

The other two styles of grip safety are the Wilson and the Ed Brown—a.k .a. the "beavertail" safety. They are wider and higher than the original and let you get your hand higher while spreading the impact of recoil over a larger area. However, to do that requires frame modifications.

The Wilson is easy. Bill Wilson carved the rear tabs of the frame tang off at a .250-inch radius from the thumb safety shaft hole. This mod is simple if you have a milling machine and a fixture. The fixture is a block with a post the diameter of the thumb safety post. I'll describe the process so you will understand what your pistolsmith is doing when he installs it, and you'll be in on the secret.

First, clamp the fixture in the milling machine, post vertical. Move the milling machine bed until the cutting tool, a simple endmill, is .260 inches from the center of the post in the fixture. Turn on the machine (at the appropriate RPM and cutting speed), slip the frame over the post through the safety hole, and then hand-pivot the frame against the cutting tool, machining the tang to a .260-inch radius. Pull the frame off, turn off the machine, knock off the chips, and deburr the edges.

Check the fit. Of course, the grip safety won't fit. Move the bed .005-inch closer, and repeat. Adjust in small increments until you can just force the thumb safety shaft through the frame and grip safety. The machine work is done. Apply Dykem to the newly machined surface, force the thumb safety shaft through the holes (your custom pistolsmith will have a drone safety for this task or a special pin with a head), and then pivot the safety up and down. Take it apart and see where the Dykem has been rubbed off. Those are the high spots.

Ideally, you would remove the friction by knocking down the high spots on the safety. But the area is in a tight curve and not easy to reach. So carefully file the high spots on the frame until the grip safety moves smoothly but not so much that it wobbles on the shaft.

You are now ready to fit the tab.

The beauty of the Wilson grip safety is that you are done fitting it and only have to adjust the tab. You don't even have to refinish the frame. If you are careful, the bare steel is covered by the grip safety and won't be seen. But, it gives you that by not providing the highest possible grip on the frame. To do that, you need the Ed Brown treatment.

***To check a grip safety's sensitivity, unload and check. Then check again. Cock the hammer, press the trigger hard enough to fire it, and then gradually press the grip safety in. When the hammer falls, you can see how much the grip safety had to be depressed to clear.***

The Ed Brown starts similarly, cutting a radius and fitting the pivot. But, the grip safety is sculpted to ride much higher into the frame, requiring steel removal under the tang. When first radiused, the Ed Brown leaves pyramidal steel blocks on either side of its lever. Once you have cut the radius and fit the pivot, lock the grip safety in its depressed position (masking tape or rubber bands do this well) and get out the power tools. I even used a bench grinder and a light touch to grind the pyramids down most of the way before finishing it with the Dremel tool and the grinding wheels. Once I had them mostly flush, it was time to break out the strips of sandpaper and crocus cloth and finish the blending and polishing in a shoeshine process.

After all this, your frame will need to be refinished. And all of this is theoretical. Well, mostly. If you have (and I've written this more than once in this book) a USGI 1911 or 1911A1, and it is in unmolested condition, it is not a candidate for custom work. It is worth more as a collectible, and you can get many of these features on a new 1911 out of the box. Once you learn what each type of grip safety looks like, you can opt for a regular-, Wilson-, or Ed Brown-pattern safety on a regular production gun that is better featured than a custom gun. And cheaper, too. Having a custom pistolsmith install a Wilson grip safety on a frame that does not already have it will cost you a couple of hundred dollars. An Ed Brown? A hundred or two more than that. So, it is just not economically prudent to change a USGI pistol. Now, if you have an older Colt, Springfield, or some other vanilla-plain pistol and want to do this work yourself, go for it. But do not labor under the illusion that you're saving money.

## TUNING THE NEW GRIP SAFETY

You have somehow come across a bargain of a 1911, but the grip safety has been knarfed. (Technical term: Knarf, to butcher, chop, alter, or otherwise make ugly or less-than-useful.) You know the pattern: you buy a new one from Brownells and want to install it. Lucky you, it drops right in and doesn't need fitting to allow it to pivot smoothly. Now to time and sensitize it.

Again, detail strip the frame, including the grips, and lay it on its right side. With the trigger installed, press the safety into the frame with the tab up as high as it goes and see if there is room to fit it. You will likely find that you can't quite fit the grip safety in, clear the back of the trigger, and still press the thumb safety shaft through. Pull the grip safety out and look at the nose of the tab. Clamp the grip safety in a padded vise and take one pass on each side of the angled nose with your file. Then, check the fit. Repeat this, maintaining the original shape of the nose while gradually shortening it until you can force the grip safety into the trigger and shove the thumb safety shaft through the frame and grip safety holes. Almost there, you are. One more top-and-bottom pass, then reassemble the frame without the grips. Check the spring-powered movement of the grip safety. It probably hangs up a bit now and then or maybe doesn't entirely engage. Take it apart and file another single pass.

This process is essential to get right, and there is no clock on you. It is not a timed event. Do it slowly until you get it right. The correct adjustment is for the grip safety to pivot smoothly by spring pressure into engagement and disengage smoothly when you press a fingertip. At this time, your press with a fingertip will be fully in the frame. Do not sensitize the grip safety until it properly works with near-90-percent depression, or whatever the max is with this particular safety in your frame.

Once that is set, then sensitize it. Again, use single passes of the file along the bottom of the tab until it clears the rear of the trigger when depressed halfway.

## THUMB SAFETY

Unlike the grip safety, which will not need replacement unless it is damaged, mucked with, or has gone out of tune, the thumb safety could legitimately need a change. One would be to install a larger thumb safety for competition, providing an advantage. Or install an ambidextrous one for lefties, or if you want one "just in case," you need to shoot left-handed.

Unlike the grip safety, the thumb safety has a slew of things that must be fitted to function correctly. Let's look at the safety parts before we begin fitting it.

The safety is a plate with a shaft, a lever pad, and a lug to engage the sear. It slides into the frame through the kidney-shaped clearance hole machined into the left side of the frame. The plunger clicks it up and down into place, sticking out of the plunger tube on the left side of the frame. Let's go through this step by step.

*The stainless safety on the left has the shaft broken off. This happens occasionally. To address it, install and fit a new safety.*

First, detail strip the frame, removing the plungers and springs from the plunger tube. Now, check-fit the thumb safety into the frame with just the grip safety in place. The thumb safety should be completely flush with the frame and rotate smoothly, with its clearance slot in the lug passing under the frame wall without binding. If it won't, that is cause for some careful inspection. Is the plate flush? If not, a tool mark or casting bump could keep it from flush, and you'll have to find that and smooth it out. Is the clearance slot on the lug the problem? Here, a machining chip could be binding, and you'll have to use your diamond needle file to remove it without altering the lug.

The thumb safety and grip safety should rotate smoothly at this point. What might keep them from doing so? The thumb safety shaft could be rough. Or have machine marks or—horrors, it's a MIM part—a mold line. If so, a fine-grit polishing cloth, wielded like a shoeshine cloth, will smoothen it. Don't be heavy-handed; use a fine or very fine grit. You want smooth movement with no wobble. Does the extended or oversized safety pass cleanly over the plunger tube? You'd be surprised that some don't, but I've seen it.

With the safety smoothly fitting into the frame, reassemble the frame, but leave the grip safety off and the plungers and spring out.

Coat the safety lug in Dykem, and once dry, attempt to press it into the frame. It should insert but not rotate to the safe position. Try this with moderate force a couple of times and pull it out. Note where the Dykem has been rubbed off from the lug—this is where the lug is binding on the sear foot. Now, compare the shape of the new safety lug to the one that came with the pistol. Note where and at what angle the new lug should be filed for fit and function. Take a few passes with a file, recoat with Dykem, and try the fit again. If you thought the grip safety file-and-fit process was delicate and took a while, then the thumb safety will set a new standard (because you want it to fit smoother and tighter than the grip safety).

When fitted, the thumb safety must fully engage the sear foot with no slop. It has to release smoothly when pressed to the Fire position. It has to slide back into Safe when pressed and not bump on the sear foot, bind, or fail to engage. There is no "close enough" here. Keep at it until you get it right and see in the Dykem that the lug is rubbing on the sear foot on most of its surface, not just on one high point.

## THE CLINK TEST

Once you have it fitted (and as a check for other 1911s to see if their thumb safety is fitted correctly), do the "clink" test. You'll need a quiet environment, so turn off the radio, TV or whatever is on speaker. First—and we're not done fitting all the details of the thumb safety yet, so don't think you're done here—cock the hammer. Press the thumb safety to the Safe position. Press the trigger (not hard, but a pound or two firmer than the trigger pull weight. If yours is a 4-pound trigger, put 6 pounds on it). Now let go. Next, lift the pistol to your ear, muzzle up. Press the safety to the Fire position and slowly thumb the hammer back. If there is no noise, you've done it properly. If you hear a tiny "clink" as you ease the hammer back, you've overdone it. The clink indicates that the lug-to-sear foot engagement has a thousandth or two of an inch slop. When you press the trigger, the sear moves. The sear, pressed on by the hammer, stays slightly out of contact on the shelf (the shelf will have .018 to .020 inch of engagement) until you ease the hammer back. Once the pressure eases enough, the sear, pressed by the three-leaf spring, snaps back to full engage-

*The thumb safety lug comes up behind the sear foot and blocks its travel. If the lug has play, peen it to fill the gap.*

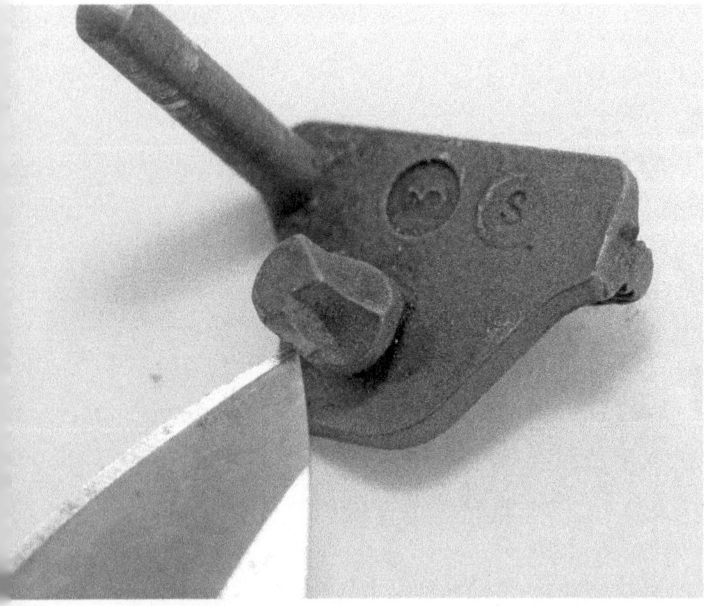

ment. That's the "clink" you heard.

"Oh no," you're thinking, "I have to buy a new safety." No, not just yet. You can salvage things if your overage is just a thousandth or so. Take the safety out and place it lug up on a padded vise. Keep the flat plate of the safety riding across the tops of the vise's jaws, with the lever in between the faces of the jaw. The shaft the safety rotates on should be pointed straight up. Close the vise jaws just enough to hold the safety firmly. Hold it in with one hand, and take a ball peen hammer and whack the lug at the engagement face to bend down one edge or corner of the lug. You get one chance at fixing this, but you can take multiple hits with the hammer if the first one isn't firm enough. Peen the edge and check the fit. If the lug doesn't fit, you have enough metal to file or stone again. Go easier this time, and fit it properly.

*A custom 1911 with a well-fitted safety. It clicks up and down correctly, and its curve matches the frame at the grip safety.*

You may think, "Waitaminute, the lug depends on the peened edge to hold the sear." Nope. The lug holds the sear (in this example) for .017 of the .018 thousandths of engagement on the hammer notch. The peened portion takes up the last thousandth. And, if you were to press the trigger as hard as possible, you could not generate enough pressure to shove that steel back out of the way, using the trigger as your leverage.

While working on many 1911s, I saw quite a few that had been fine-tuned this way before they arrived at my shop. And they all worked just fine.

## PLUNGER FITTING

OK, the time has come to fit the plunger. Look at the front corner of the safety plate. Notice how the plunger rides over that corner to lock the safety up or down. Swap out your new safety and watch the original one as it clicks up and down. Most people prefer the safety plate briskly but evenly clicking up and down. I'm different. Now, you don't want to reduce the force needed to click it either way because you need a certain amount to keep it under control. Too easy off, and you will find your 1911 in your holster is safety-off, not comforting. And too easy up, and you might find it has bounced up in recoil and now won't fire.

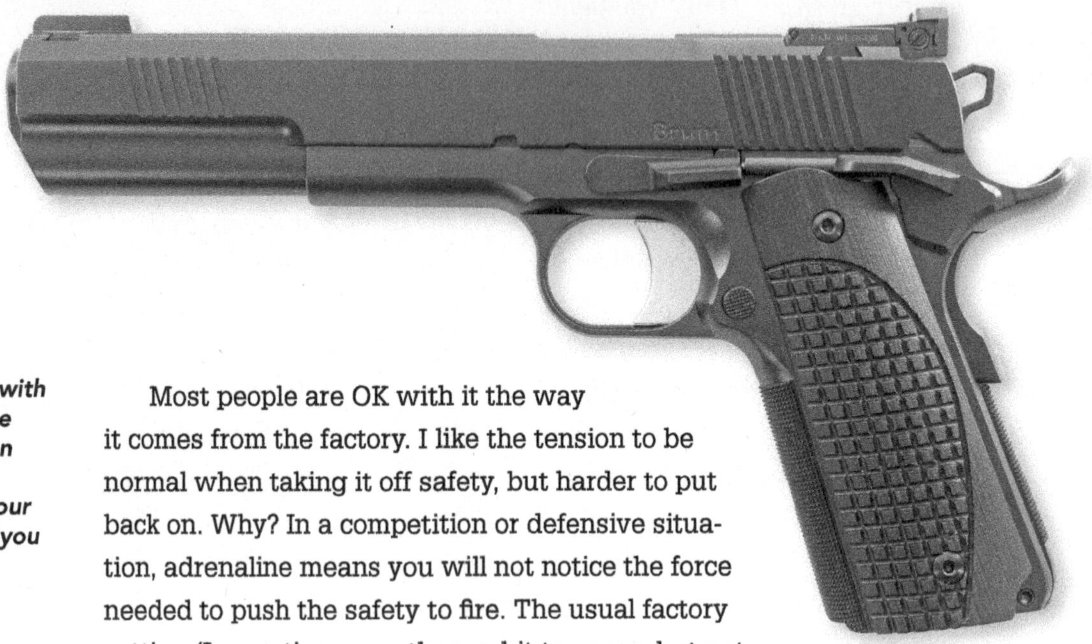

*A long-slide Dan Wesson with the thumb safety and slide correctly fitted and a clean line along the top of the left-hand grip. If you fit your replacement, this is what you are looking for.*

Most people are OK with it the way it comes from the factory. I like the tension to be normal when taking it off safety, but harder to put back on. Why? In a competition or defensive situation, adrenaline means you will not notice the force needed to push the safety to fire. The usual factory setting (I sometimes see them a bit too easy, but not often) is good for this.

However, once it is off, I want it to stay off. Recoil, bouncing or jumping, wrestling for the gun, I want it to stay off so it's ready to shoot when needed. If I have to switch to left-handed-only shooting, the safety is unlikely to get jostled up to the safe position if it has been set to require more force, and if I'm truly shooting left-handed-only, a safety that is on is a real problem to get to the fire position. Once I am done, there will be plenty of time to push it to safe. I can even use both thumbs to do so if need be. So, I set up a carry or competition gun's thumb safety to go on hard and come off easy.

Adjusting the click setting is easy enough. Shape the leading edges of the safety plate nose to make it more or less difficult to cam over the plunger. Take it easy as you can't readily put metal back, and too much back-and-forth filing can remove the plate nose, and now you're into the cost of a new safety. Round and half-round diamond needle files are what you'll need here.

## LAST CHECK

After you've done all this, there is one more potential adjustment. If you have a frame with an Ed Brown grip safety, when the thumb safety is pressed to the fire position, the safety plate's bottom edge might overhang the frame's edge where it has been sculpted for the grip safety. This was more of a problem in the past, but now that the Ed Brown is so common, thumb safeties come with the bottom edge adjusted, so it's not a problem. But if it is, you'll need to fire up the Dremel tool. With the safety hanging over the edge, use a sharp scribe to mark the edge of the frame on the back of the safety plate. Take the safety out, and follow the line with a grinding tool until flush with the frame when fitted. Then, it is simply a cosmetic task to blend the curves of the safety and polish the newly cut surfaces so they match the rest.

If a pistolsmith had installed the Ed Brown grip safety on your frame, he would have fitted the thumb safety and blended the safety to the frame before even considering refinishing the frame and other work. If yours is a finished frame or pistol (blued, plated, coated, whatever) with the Ed Brown already on it, be more careful in blending the new safety into the existing curves.

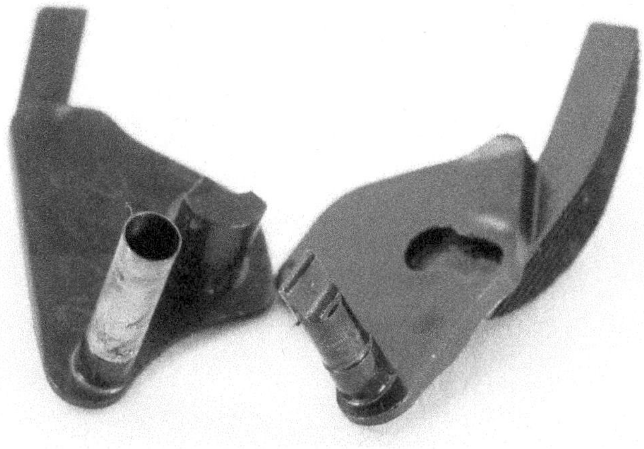

***A neat trick on the ambi safety fitting problem. Instead of a tab and slot, this one has the shaft relieved to accept a sleeve that rides over the tab and slot interface to add rigidity.***

## AMBIDEXTROUS

By ambidextrous or ambi, we really mean bilaterally symmetric, identical on both sides. But everyone calls safeties and other controls on both sides of a handgun "ambidextrous," so that's what we'll do. The ambi thumb safety has a lever on both sides, which isn't easy to do if you think about it. Most of the ambi safeties have a half-shaft for each paddle or shelf, and the two shafts join in a tongue-and-groove or tenon system. Fitting the ambi set is the same as the single side in that you must fit the left side as if it were the only one. Then, fit the right side to the frame, flush to the sidewall, and under whatever keeps it in place.

The "keeping" part is the fussy part. The right-hand lever does not have the internal lug to interact with the sear, so there is nothing to keep it from falling out except the friction of the tenon unless some other restraint is built in. There are a few methods. One is to use an extended sear pin, where the extension protrudes out of the right side of the frame with a slot cut into the end. A front-edge shelf or tab on the right-hand safety rides in the slot in the pin, keeping the safety

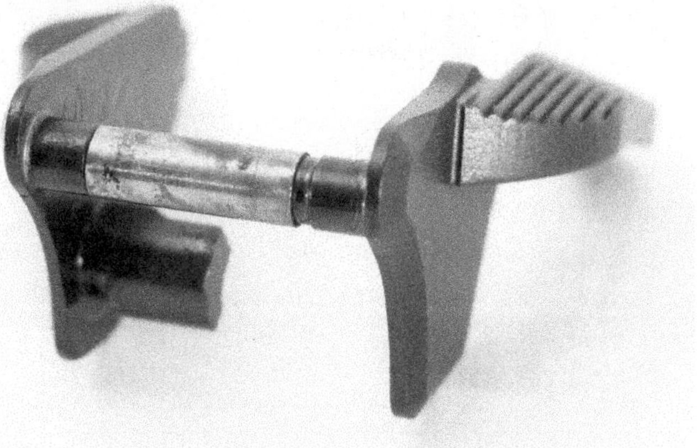

***Once assembled, the sleeve is the same exterior diameter as the shaft would have been, and it all rides in the frame as expected.***

from falling out.

Another more elegant method is to use a thinner extension of the right-hand plate that extends under the right-hand grip. The back of that grip is relieved to provide room for the extension. If you buy aftermarket grips, you probably will find that they have been made with the relief cut on the back edge of the right-side grip, just in case you want to install an ambi safety.

In the early days of aftermarket accessories, I saw a few other approaches, some resoundingly ugly. One was a screw threaded into the main safety shaft, holding the right-hand plate on. The problem was that it wasn't very strong. Another was a clear and wild modification. Someone had taken a regular safety, machined off the lug, welded a new thumb lever onto it, reversed it to fit on the right, shortened both shafts to accommodate the pair, and then—this was the ugly part—drilled and tapped the frame side to use a small cap screw to hold the right-hand lever on, pre-dating the extended sear pin approach. It was a Herculean effort to make an ambi safety setup, and it was ugly.

*A low-rider safety the author built for his brother. It involved milling the shelf off, silver-soldering on a new block, and shaping it before nickeling the part. Now you can buy one ready to go.*

## SAFETY SIZE CONSIDERATIONS

How big a lever is the right size? Well, that depends. It depends on your hand size, your intent, the penalty for failing to press it to fire when needed, and the penalty for having it inadvertently wiped off when not desired. There are three situations, and the existing sizes of safeties will cover them all. One is non-action competition, like Bullseye (even PPC, as the time frames are so generous they might as well not exist). Here, the old GI thumb safety is plenty big enough.

Action competition calls for as big a safety as it takes to consistently get the safety to fire on the draw or off the table. For most shooters and needs, the largest of the "combat" safeties will be plenty. I have an excessively large safety on one 1911, my bowling pin gun, because it's also useful as a recoil lever. It might be too big if I were using it for Single Stack competition in USPSA (then again, it might not be). It would probably not pass muster in an IDPA match, being an obvious competition part.

For daily carry, you want something large enough to be reliable but not so big it binds in a holster, gets rubbed to the fire position by movement, or catches on clothing. There is no "perfect size" for this; you must choose for yourself. Luckily, the 1911 makers have some experience with this and get user feedback, so you will likely find the size is just fine.

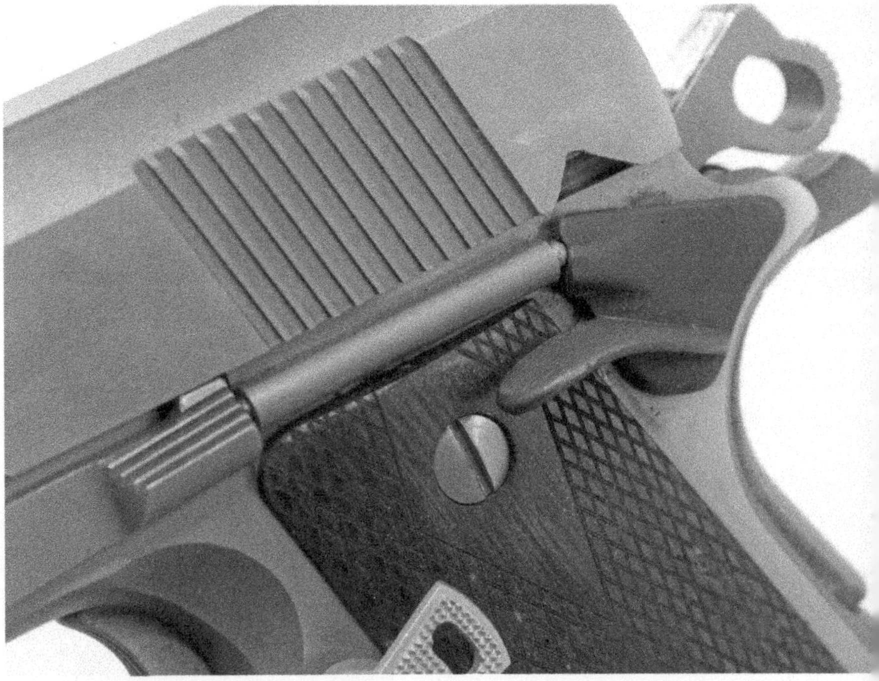

*You don't have to make a new low-rider safety. You can get them right out of the catalog now.*

Fit and angle can matter. I find that some shapes and sizes (the Ed Brown in particular) are very comfortable and fit my hand nicely. I also have a problem with some ambi safeties. My grip is a bit odd. I learned how to shoot the 1911 before Ronald Reagan was elected president, and my grip is very high on the gun—so high that my trigger finger does not come around to the trigger; it comes *down* to the trigger. My shooting hand's first knuckle is high, and an overly large ambi paddle will bind on or be stopped by my knuckle. For me, an ideal ambi safety is one that barely exists.

## LOW-RIDERS

There is one other safety that some shooters may consider: the low safety. Instead of a paddle at the top edge of the safety plate, the low safety attaches halfway down or lower on the plate. This design is useful for shooters with small hands who can't get their shooting hand high enough to use a regular safety and still reach the trigger. Everything about it is the same as a regular trigger, except for the location of the shelf. ●

CHAPTER

# 13

# BARRELS

First, let's review barrel basics and the types you'll encounter. Note that this will be an extensive chapter because the barrel is the heart of any pistol, and in the 1911, it interacts with just about every other part of the handgun. Or at least influences their function. So hang on, there's a lot here.

An article on 1911A1 manufacture, published in 1942, provides us with a pretty interesting data point: the 1911A1's barrel was to be made out of SAE 4150 steel. That's right: the USGI barrel in that surplus pistol is made out of the same alloy as your mil-spec AR-15 barrel, with a tensile strength of 106,000 psi—the drawing for the pistol barrel even details the heat-treatment process. The desired result was a Rockwell (I don't see a scale, but the numbers and use strongly suggest the "C" scale) of no less than 53 and no greater than 56.5. So, if anyone tells you that GI barrels are "soft," they are not entirely up to speed. Sure, early barrels may have been softer than modern, top-quality ones, but they were hard for the time. And hard enough to stand up to extended use.

*USGI barrels, in addition to being made out of 4150 steel, were proofed and marked as having passed. These are good barrels, even if they are not "match" quality.*

To give you the full import, barrels were proof-tested, magnetic particle-inspected, and marked as tested. They were not making "disposable" barrels to be used for a short while, tossed, and replaced. Pistols may not have been the primary weapon, but they wouldn't be shortchanged in production.

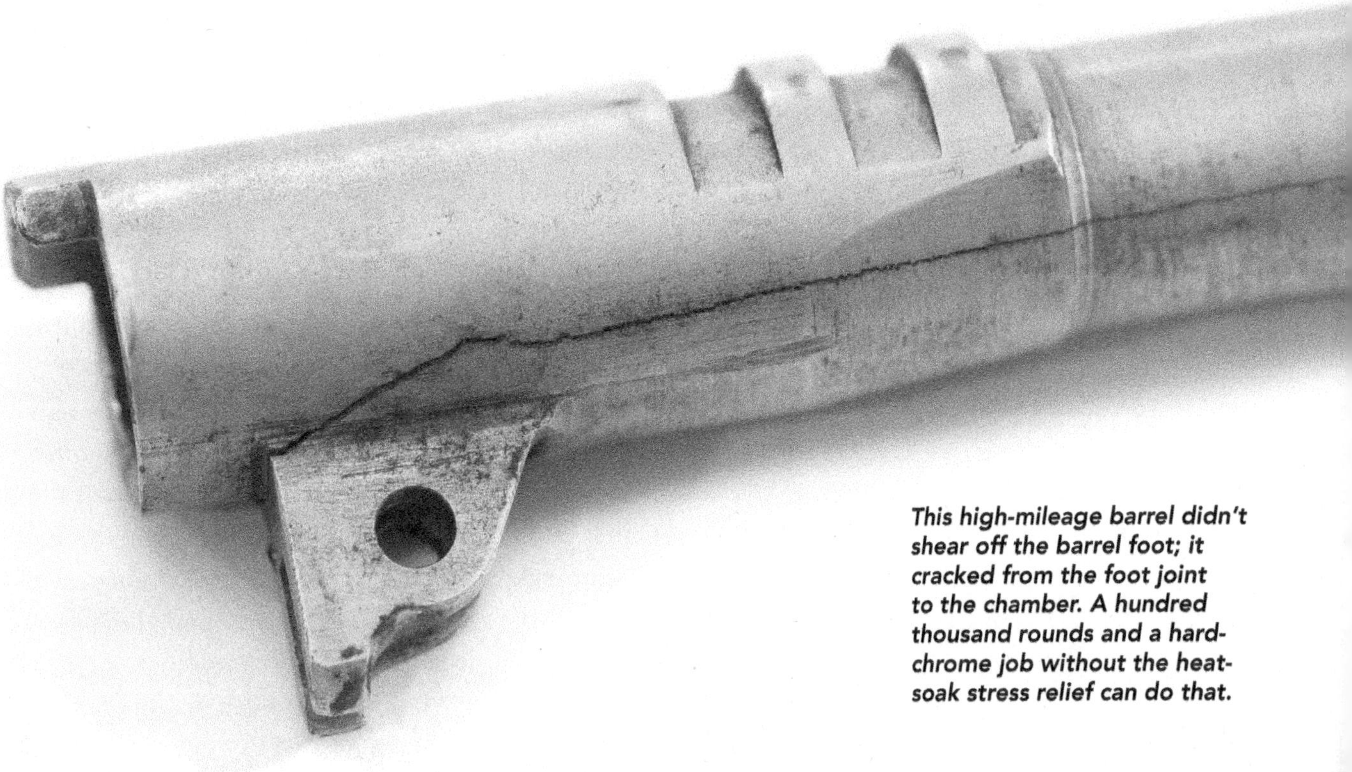

*This high-mileage barrel didn't shear off the barrel foot; it cracked from the foot joint to the chamber. A hundred thousand rounds and a hard-chrome job without the heat-soak stress relief can do that.*

## JUST SITTING THERE

At rest and closed, the barrel contacts the other cycling parts this way: At the front, the barrel rides in the bushing, which is not, as you might think at first glance, a simple cylindrical holding part. The bushing has many subtle details that we'll cover. At the opposite end, the barrel hood rides between the breechface shoulders, with its rear against the top end of the breechface. Well, held in a tightly fitted pistol, in most instances, it has a few thousandths of an inch gap there, which is of no consequence as far as accuracy is concerned but very consequential for reliability.

In between, the barrel bears against one or more of the locking slots on the top and rides on top of the slide stop pin on the bottom. The link doesn't support the barrel in its locked and rested position in a properly fitted barrel.

Let's examine the details of the interior first.

## CHAMBER

The chamber is a cylindrical resting place for the cartridge. The chamber depth is greater than the length of the longest case, so every round made will fit any chamber ever made. The maximum case length is supposed to be .898 inch. I was curious about that at one time, so I started measuring the lengths of fired cases (they get a bit shorter once fired), and the longest one I encountered was .890 inch long. I then measured the chamber depths of the .45s I had at the time and found the shortest one was .905-inch deep. So, right there, I had a minimum "headspace" gap of .015, where the maximum allowed for rifles is .006 inch.

So why does this work? How does it work? Simple: The .45 ACP's operating pressure is low enough that case stretching, like in rifles, doesn't occur. Too, the firing pin has enough reach to contact the primer even if the case is at the maximum forward position the extractor allows. Yes, the extractor is the limiting factor in the round going too deeply into the chamber. And the .015 inch of "slop"? The firing pin has enough travel in it that it could reach multiples of that allowance. All of that is to say that we've been using the 1911 for over a century (well, not any one of us, but as a group) and in that time, there has not been a problem with firing pins reaching primers or excessively long chambers, at least not as reamed by barrel makers.

*Note how the barrel's locking lugs and slide lock together in this cutaway.*

In the .38 Super, there was a problem for a few decades. The initial Supers were quite accurate, and there were even fabulous collector's pieces and match pistols built by Colt before WWII. If the status of reloading had been as great pre-war as it became post-war, those might well have become the defacto Any Centerfire pistols in Bullseye competition. But something happened at Colt post-war, and the later Supers were not nearly as accurate. The chambers apparently were not reamed with a definite stop-shoulder at the front but some sort of cone.

Irv Stone of Bar-Sto Barrels solved that problem by making barrels with proper chambers, and everyone since then has followed his lead. As a result, you can have a very accurate .38 Super pistol. You need to go to the 9mm for the absolute accuracy max. Yes, a 9mm. When building a 1911 for long-range shooting for an article—I would shoot to at least 300 yards, more if I could manage it—I asked Stone which would be more accurate, a 9mm or a Super. The 9mm, hands down, was his reply. So I built it, and it was and is truly accurate.

For much of my gunsmithing career, I was faced with sub-par barrels. The factories' chamber reamers were routinely being used past the point where they should have been replaced or sharpened. I got into the habit of using a standard chambering reamer (one I kept sharp and used for nothing else) to check each chamber. It was appalling how many were short, rough, or both. It was also gratifying how accurate and reliable they became with that simple step. Today, I'd probably not need to do that as much. As with so many other details, barrel makers have learned what matters, what works, and what customers demand. But, if you want to invest in a chambering reamer, you'll need a Finish reamer from Brownells that will run you $75 or so. However, be sure you need it first before you invest.

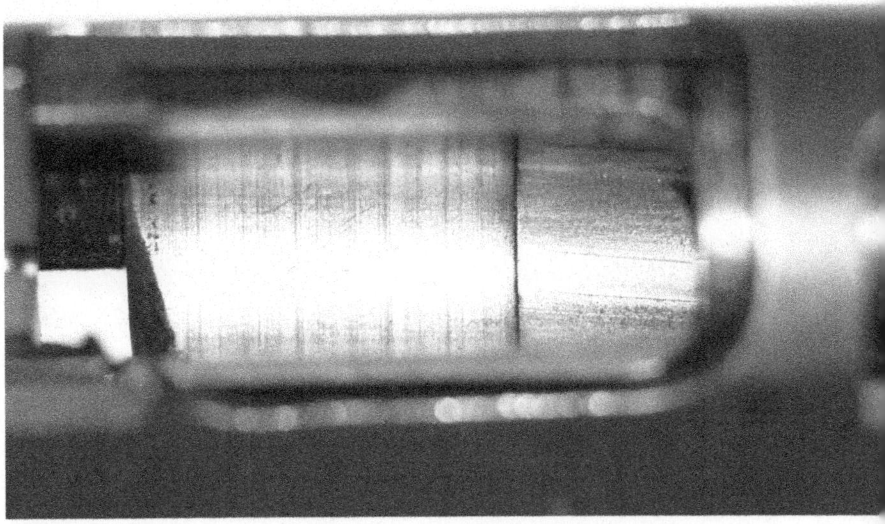

*The chamber of your barrel is a simple cylindrical resting place for the cartridge. The front edge determines headspace, a detail that is usually not a problem in the 1911, except for the historical problem of the .38 Super, which is now long-solved.*

The groove diameter of your .45 (the others will have different specs) will be made to .450 +.002 inch, so up to .452, which is the diameter of the lead bullets you'd be using if you loaded your own ammo. The tops of the lands will be .442 +.002 inch with six evenly spaced grooves and a twist of 1:16 inches or 16 inches for one full rotation. The twist rate can significantly affect accuracy in rifles as bullet weights vary. Still, in the .45 (and the other 1911 calibers), the difference in bullet length between the lightest and heaviest is not enough for twist rate considerations.

The total length of the bore plus chamber is 5 inches on a government-sized pistol. On the commander-sized, 4-1/4 inches. Other models are even shorter, but in the .45, at least barrel length is not a big deal for velocity. The .45 works using diameter and mass and doesn't need mega-velocity.

The 10mm/.40 barrel has a groove diameter of a nominal .400 +.002 inch, and the 9mm and .38 Super (the Super now uses 9mm specs) of .355 +.002 inch.

*A comp or muzzle brake jets gas out the top to reduce muzzle rise and felt recoil. In this instance, it is also a way to mount the front sight farther forward for a longer sight radius.*

## RAMPS

The original barrel has a frame ramp and a barrel ramp. The cartridge jumps up from the frame to the barrel and, when properly fitted, feeds with 100 percent reliability. However, IPSC shooters developed and adopted the ramped barrel or integrally-ramped barrel. Here, the frame ramp area is machined away, and a new barrel with an integral ramp is installed.

This design is not new. The original Browning/Colt M1900 pistol

used it. That early model also had two links, one at the front and one at the rear. As an interesting historical detail, the M1900's barrel ramp had a groove machined, which was part of the cartridge headspacing. The .38 Auto's rim (a "semi-rimmed" design) contacted a groove in the hood and the groove in the ramp and was held in these two places for firing. Since the only bullet being used was a jacketed round nose, the bullet never noticed the ramp groove and just slid right over it.

***The muzzle of this .45, shooting hot bowling pin loads, stays down thanks to the comp. It's excellent for competition, but too long for daily carry.***

The problem with the M1900 was two-fold: it wasn't a .45. So Browning changed it and made the M1905 in a .45. Then the second problem arose, which had been noticeable before: the front link meant the slide had to be open. There was no other way to make it. The recoil spring was held in, and the slide held onto the frame by a cross-wedge at the front of the slide, which broke often enough that Colt replaced slides right up to and even after it stopped making the 1900 line of pistols—at least until the supply of extra slides ran out, sometime in the 1920s. Browning was almost injured when a slide broke during the early-production test firing, and he quickly abandoned the design.

Somehow, in the change from the Model 1905 to the 1910 and then 1911, while the front wedge disappeared, so did the ramped barrel. Too bad.

***The two ramped barrel designs now standard in the 1911 are the Para (blue) and the Wilson (stainless). They are not interchangeable, so if you have a ramped barrel and want to replace or upgrade it or add a new one, you*** must ***know which one you have.***

Why did IPSC resurrect the ramped barrel? Case support. The barrel ramp takes steel from the chamber, and the cartridge case is unsupported. In the .45, this was not a problem. The ramp wasn't big, the case was tough, and the pressures were low. However, we had to greatly increase the chamber pressure to make Major with the .38 Super. Instead of the typical pressure ceiling of 36,000 psi, we had to run into the mid to upper 40s. I have pressure-tested 9mm Major—even worse than Super for pressure; the 9mm is a smaller case—where the *lowest* average chamber pressure of the three standard loads tested was 42,000 psi. That is close to the Proof Load pressure for the 9mm or .38 Super. The highest was in the mid-50s, which is well over Proof Load. No, I will not provide the loading data.

Without full case support, the thinnest portion of the case can't regularly withstand the pressure, and it blows out. This typically meant a trashed magazine, cracked grips, and a high-pressure jet of oil and gases squirting out of the ejector slot, leading to "Super face." Using an integral ramp allows the barrel maker, in essence, to push the ramp back slightly, putting steel under that thin portion of the case and supporting it against the increased pressure. The thicker portion of the case can then withstand the pressures.

The trick is designing and producing a ramped barrel with the link and bottom lugs. The real trick is in machining the frame to accept it. Depending on the machine tools available and the fixture you've made (in the early years, each pistolsmith had to make his own fixture, or holding jig, to machine frames), there are two ways to do this. The barrel makers settled on two patterns, the Wilson/Nowlin and the Para Ordnance/Clark. If your 1911 has a ramped barrel, it has one of these, and you cannot make it work with the other. And, you cannot use a traditional, non-ramped barrel short of fitting in a spacer to fill the gap the ramp otherwise occupied.

Is there an advantage to one or the other design? Not to you. It is only a detail that matters to the frame or barrel maker.

## BULL BARRELS

Two barrel features qualify it as a "bull" barrel, but you'll only find one in a commercial gun. Initially, it meant a barrel with thicker walls that needed a special bushing, and this extra weight meant the barrel was stiffer and had more weight in the initial cyclic movement.

Nowadays, it means a barrel that does not have a bushing. (Back in the old days, we called that a "coned" barrel because, to get it, you had to thread the barrel outside, thread a cylinder inside to screw onto it, then lathe-turn the cylinder/sleeve to a cone shape to fill the slide and provide a lockup. Now barrels come that way, no sleeving or threading.) The pistolsmith who taught me the trade, Dan McDonald, didn't do it as a separate sleeve. He fitted a steel cylinder to the barrel, cut

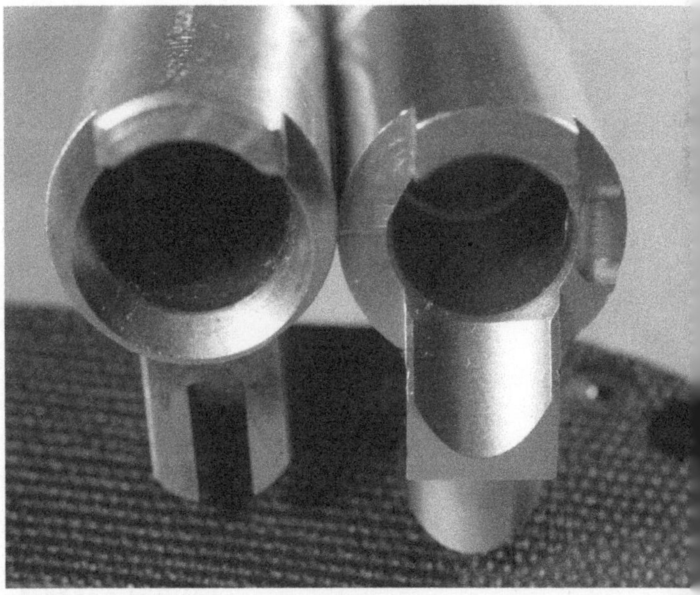

*The barrel on the left is a typical frame-ramp barrel. On the right is one with an integral feed ramp. Neither works on a frame made for the other, so pay attention to which one your 1911 has.*

the cone to fit, slabbed the cylinder forward of the cone, and finally filed it to match the slide contours—a cone integral to the comp. That's a lot of work. It didn't take long for commercial parts makers to provide kits. You'd get an oversized cone or comp and thread a barrel to accept the cone, fit and time it all, and not have to start with a 2-inch diameter steel cylinder.

Today's bull barrels fill the slide at the muzzle and do not have a bushing. Why do this? Several reasons. It has the potential to be more accurate. Half a dozen dimensions on a bushing must be precisely fitted for best accuracy. A bull barrel merely (as if anything accurate is "merely") fills the slide without any movement up front. Another is that it puts more mass into the initial movement of the cycling parts, slowing unlocking while maintaining slide velocity. It also makes short-slide 1911s more reliable, as the builder doesn't have to account for the room needed for the bushing on the interior spaces.

*Note the difference between the two ramped barrel designs in the bottom lug contours.*

Now, all is not sweetness and light. Since there's no bushing, there's nothing to keep the recoil spring assembly in place. As a result, a bull barrel also requires the use of a "reverse retainer." This part is a recoil spring retainer not installed from the front, as in the traditional method. Instead, the retainer goes into the slide from the rear and is held in place by the rear flange of the recoil spring hood or loop. Ideally, the retainer has a half-loop on it, and the slide loop has been relieved by the thickness of this lip, so the hood's overall length is unchanged. Moreover, it's a half-loop, so there's clearance for the recoil spring and a guide rod. All this can complicate disassembly and reassembly. And that is covered elsewhere.

## WHICH STEEL?

Many barrels are now offered as stainless steel simply because "stainless is better." Well, maybe, sometimes. When stainless was new, there was still some—though not much—corrosive surplus. All the USGI ammo loaded since the mid-1950s was loaded with non-corrosive primers, so the chance you will encounter corrosively primed ammo today is slim. I have a box of early GI ammo dated 1917 and 1918 that I've been testing, which is corrosive. It has all gone bang, all of it. Anything loaded in WWII is corrosive. But ammo from that era is approaching collectible status, not to be shot. There was a brief time when a supply of French surplus ammo came in green pasteboard boxes of 25 rounds each. Now *that* stuff was corrosive. It was so bad I swear it would rust the bore of the guy next to you on the firing line. But it was probably all shot up decades ago, as it came into the country in the 1980s.

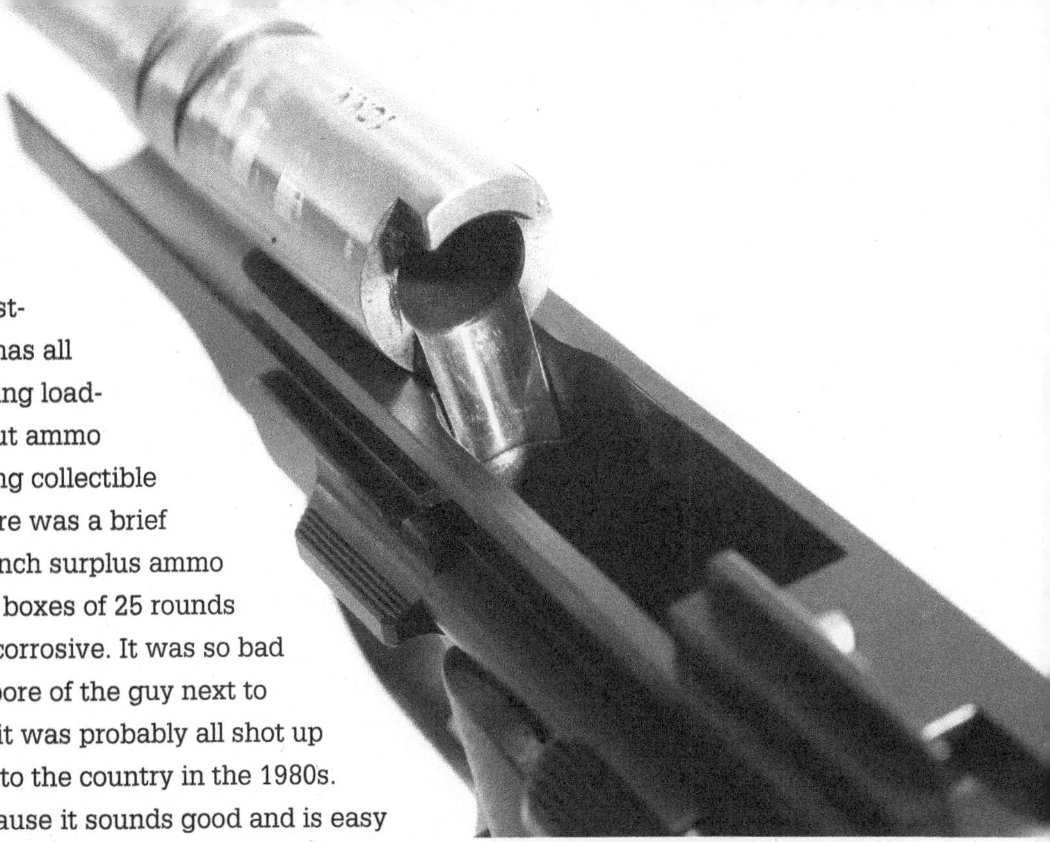

*The integrally ramped barrel has no gap between the frame and barrel that the bullet must jump over.*

So why stainless? Because it sounds good and is easy to machine. And it works. I quickly checked at Brownells for 1911 barrels; of the 25 barrels you can choose from, two were *not* stainless. The stainless ones were either 416 or 17-4, but the carbon steel barrels were 4150, the original GI, pre-WWII spec, and the same as your AR-15 barrel.

Stainless works.

## BARREL CYCLE

OK, you have just dropped the hammer (literally) and fired your 1911. Let's dive into the microsecond realm and follow things step by step. The powder burns, creating pressure, and the bullet begins to move. In the .45 ACP, the bullet is heavy enough, and the powder charge is so tiny that the powder has likely all been consumed before the bullet leaves the case. But, the moment the bullet moves, recoil begins to work.

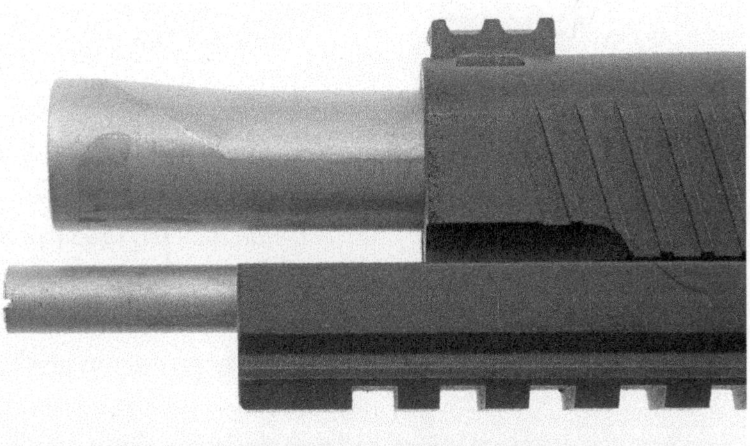

*The bull barrel does not require a bushing, but it must be elaborately machined to fit the slide and unlock when fired.*

The barrel and slide are locked together, but the slide is not locked to the frame. So once the inertia of the slide/barrel mass has been overcome, they begin to move. The bullet has probably not left the muzzle yet. The feet of the barrel, where they bear on the slide stop pin, are machined with a short, flat section. The barrel and slide move as one for a few hundredths of an inch, a critical distance. But once the barrel's movement has taken all of the slack out of the link fit, the link (pointed back toward the rear of the assembly by this time, where before it had been vertical or very slightly pointed toward the muzzle) begins to lever the slide down and out of the locked position. Once unlocked from the barrel, the slide continues to the rear, decelerated by the recoil spring, only coming to rest when it impacts the rear face of the recoil spring retaining hoop and the front face of the recoil spring guide.

That is why and where you install a shok-buff. We'll debate the pros and cons of that in the recoil spring section.

The barrel, released from the slide, has its own tasks. Having linked downward, it must come to rest. The impact (everything in a firearm bangs into something else; that's how it works and why the metal must be heat-treated to withstand the punishment) is essential. Vital, even.

*As long as it fits properly, don't be concerned about tool marks and such on the bushing. The one on the right looks like it was brazed to enlarge it, then turned or filed to fit, so the brazing filled the gaps and made it snug. Modern bushings don't need that much work, but back in the "good ol' days," sometimes that was needed.*

Look at the back face of the barrel feet. Notice that it is a flat surface. Also, note that where the feet and chamber meet is a generous radius. (It better have if you expect it to last more than a few magazines.) Now, look at the frame behind the guide rod seat. If the frame and barrel feet have been appropriately machined, the barrel will hit the vertical surface of the frame behind the guide rod seat on the upper half of the barrel feet. Many frames will have the guide rod seat machined (with a boring bar or an endmill in a CNC machine) with the bore slightly deeper than the vertical face. This leaves behind a shoulder called the "bowtie," the surface the barrel impacts. If the frame face isn't recessed, it still works, as long as the barrel feet impact *at the top half.*

If the frame is not recessed and the barrel feet hit at the bottom, this improper fit will not last long. Oh, it may last many years of plinking, but it will not last forever. Eventually, the leverage of the impact striking the bottom ends of the barrel feet will shear the feet off of the chamber. The recess creating the bowtie prevents that even if the barrel feet would have otherwise been the first impact.

The problem is the backs of the barrel feet or the heels, if you will, are hitting. The solution is simple: carefully file the heels (you don't have to take much off) so the impact is now in the upper half. Where does this problem come from? It could be the barrel or frame maker got the angle off a degree or two. Since you can't bore the recess, file the heels.

Do you know what else breaks barrel feet? A short link. If the link is too short, the barrel can't go to the rear far enough to impact the frame on the bowtie and slams down in the frame saddle, swinging by the link. The saddle is the curved recess you see in the top deck of the frame ahead of the feed ramp. A short link is not common, as links are used (correctly) only to link down the barrel, and it is easy to keep them within spec. It's more likely to have a link that is too long, which is noticeable when you try to assemble the pistol and can't close the slide. Or, having closed it, it binds on the unlocking cycle. Why would someone use a longer link? As a makeshift way of improving accuracy by forcing the barrel up and into the locking lugs. However, the problem with this approach is that the link now takes all the force of locking, and it isn't big enough to do that.

***A close look shows where this .38 Super barrel's feet were relieved so it would unlock, bounce off of the bowtie, and not hit the bottom of the feet.***

Once linked down and released from the slide, the barrel rests in the frame saddle and, positioned by the top curve of the guide rod and the bushing, stays put until the slide collects it again.

The round being fed gets shoved up the feed ramp and into the chamber. The barrel remains where it is until the slide contacts the hood, and then the slide pushes the barrel forward. You might think the link pivots it up, but it shouldn't. The barrel should cam up the feet, propelled by the slide, and lock into place. The locking lugs slide up into position, and the barrel feet move forward until the stop pads at the rear of the feet bring it to a halt.

The barrel should slide/cam up the slide stop pin in government-sized pistols, even without a link. However, the commander-sized 1911's barrel feet are much more vertical in the front to accommodate the shorter slide and make the pistol cycle properly. So, if you're amusing yourself by closing the slide/barrel/frame assembly without a link, you can't do the same with a Commander. However, don't worry; the link will take over.

## OTHER ACCURACY IMPROVEMENTS

The bushing does a lot for accuracy. If your bushing is loose, or the barrel is loose in the bushing, you can gain accuracy by fitting a new bushing. But first, inspect and measure. Strip the slide and scrub it

*An example of a cleanly installed bushing and a properly crowned barrel.*

clean. Look closely at the bushing lug. Is it peened and out of shape? If so, the problem wasn't a worn bore but a gradually (or not so gradually) peened and loosened bushing. A replacement bushing will help, probably a lot. Look closely at the slot in the slide where the bushing lug rides. Is it OK? If it's peened, then you are in a bad spot. You'll either have to replace the slide, as the peening slot can't be fixed, can't be made harder, and won't stop peening even with a new bushing, or you can fit a new, coned barrel to the slide. That is more difficult than a traditional barrel replacement and also involves a new recoil spring retaining system since there won't be a bushing to hold those parts in. Either way, it is a bunch of money.

Let's assume you only need a new bushing. Get out your Brownells catalog and your dial or digital calipers. Measure and record the diameter of your barrel at the muzzle. Then, measure and record the diameter of the slide on the inside, where the bushing fits. No, don't bother measuring the old bushing. It was a sloppy fit, anyway.

You need a replacement bushing as close to an exact fit on the barrel and inside the slide as possible. You will not have an infinite choice of combos, so come close. Do not think, "Oh, I'll get a bushing that is way under the barrel size and way over slide size and fit them together." Not unless you have a lathe and know how to do it, you won't. A thousandth or so is all you need, want or will manage. You will also need the Brownells file I refer to as "the perfect file" and some fine lapping compound, as well as a bushing wrench or two. (If you get the plastic wrench, count on breaking at least one in your lifetime, so get two.)

*The bottom lugs of a Government Model (left) and a Commander (right), which you cannot swap. They match the frame made for each model.*

A quick aside. Some bushings are made for a specific purpose, and that purpose has the name Para Ordnance. For reasons known to no one, the interior of the Para slides was bored to a larger diameter than any size bushing before. To fit a new bushing to your Para slide (and that will be a real legacy operation, as Para was bought by Remington, which went out of business), you'll need a Para-sized bushing. The last Remington-made Para-branded pistols might have dimensions in the normal range, but the thing is, you don't know what size you'll need until you measure your slide.

Some replacement barrels come with a fitted bushing, saving you that inside fitting. In many instances, the drop-in barrel will come with a bushing that is also a drop-in fit, and installing a new barrel is simply a reassembly job, not a pistolsmithing task.

A snug fit is perfect. If it won't fit at all, the proper way to make it fit is with a fixture and on a lathe. Sure, you could try to polish it down with crocus cloth or careful filing, but you'll probably end up with a lot of practice and need another new bushing.

Bushings can be had in a wide array of sizes, so careful measuring and ordering will see you to good results. In the days before aftermarket parts, we'd solve such problems in various ways. One was to use a special "bushing expander" fixture. This was a cone-like wedge that flared the rear of the bushing skirt. It created a tight fit, but it quickly wore since the edge of the rear skirt bore on the slide. As that wore, the old, loose fit returned. Another was to hard-chrome the bushing, which could only add a few thousandths before it became too expensive. A hard-chrome shop can plate up to .040 inch but that costs a lot. Putting 40 thou' onto a crankshaft so you can re-grind it back to spec is one thing, but doing it to a 1911 bushing borders on the absurd.

And the interior? I've seen bushings worked on by the old-timers, who bored them out, silver-soldered new interiors, and lathe-cut them to spec to match the barrels. It's amazing what you can do when there are no other parts, and you are skilled, clever, and obstinate.

So, buy your bushing from Brownells.

You'll sometimes find that, while it is a snug fit into the slide, you can't turn the bushing to lock it into place. You'll have to do some more measuring now. Find the distance from the slide's front face to the slide slot's front edge of the bushing. Compare this dimension to the gap between the bushing flange on the front and the front edge of the bushing lug. You'll need to file the lug back .001 inch or so it takes to

***One more detail between Government and Commander barrels: The Commander's shoulder forward of the front locking lug is turned a smidge farther back for bushing clearance.***

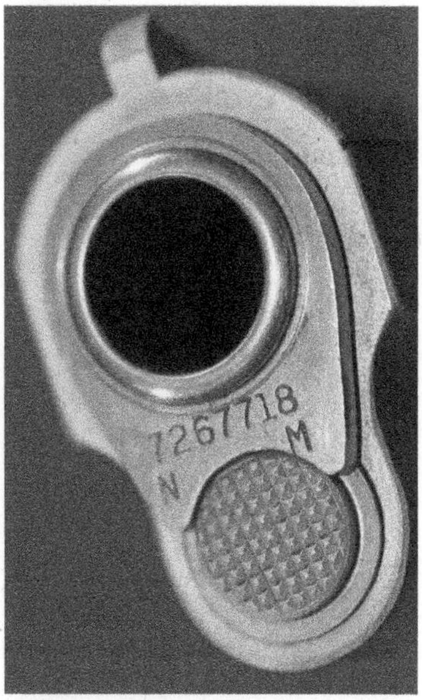


***This bushing started as a national match part, but that wasn't good enough for the 'smith who built this gun in the 1960s. He bored it out and silver-soldered in a sleeve to refit it to the barrel. That's a lot of work and not needed today.***

make them fit. Resist the temptation to file the leading edge of the lug at an angle to get it to slide in more easily. That will leave you with less than the full lug to act as a bearing surface.

Carefully file the front edge of the lug—keep it square to the bore, so its full face absorbs the stress—then fit it for assembly. Some custom 1911 'smiths provide a bushing fit so tightly that you need a wrench to rotate it. You can't do it with your fingers. Others pride themselves on precisely fitting a bushing so there's no movement, but you can disassemble it with your fingers. If tight and can't move is OK with you, and that's the fit you have, you're done. If you want to disassemble it without a wrench, you need some lapping compound from Brownells. Those in a hurry will use varying grades, starting coarser for a quick "cut" and then the final lapping with finer grits. Since you're not on the clock, start with what you'll finish with and get the fine or ultra-fine. Take your 600-grit lapping compound and apply some to the exterior of the bushing. You don't need much; don't goop it on.

Press the bushing down into the slide, and take a moment to be not-messy. Use a cotton swab to wipe the excess off of the slide. When you rotate the bushing, the excess will grind the finish off the slide's front face if you don't. There will be some finish wear, but you can minimize it by being neat. Use your bushing wrench to rotate the bushing once to the past-locked position and wipe the excess off again. Use the bushing wrench to turn the busing back and forth a few times. Pull the bushing out, scrub the lapping compound off the bushing and barrel, and check the fit. Repeat until it moves with finger pressure, but no more.

***Left to right, a standard bushing, a bushing for a Commander, and one of the collet bushings Colt tried and dropped decades ago.***

## COLLET BUSHING

Colt had a great idea in the 1970s: the collet bushing. Collets are not new; they are used to hold machine tools in milling machines and other devices. Colt put "fingers" in the bushing and mated it to a barrel with slight swelling at the muzzle. As the slide closed, the collet fingers flexed, holding the barrel firmly, which would improve accuracy. Great idea. It, however, had problems. Occasionally, a collet finger would break off on some guns, which would tie it up. It usually required a pistolsmith and a new bushing to get it apart, assuming nothing else got damaged.

I'm not sure anyone ever got to the bottom of why, but the problem of "tolerance stack" is the most likely culprit. If the dimensions are a bit off but within tolerances, and they all stack one way, one collet finger could get flexed more than the others, more than it can take.

*Barrels break for many reasons. The 1911 is not immune, nor more prone than others. When it happens, replace the barrel and possibly the bushing. Now that you have to fit one, you might as well step up to a better barrel.*

If you buy a 1911 (Colt would be the only one unless someone installed it in another brand) and intend to do some shooting, be aware the collet could break on you at some unspecified time. If it is a collectible, leave it alone. If not, swap out the collet for a regular bushing, as described elsewhere.

## BARRELS

What if you want or need a new barrel? Want is up to you, but what about need? People talk about "worn-out" 1911 barrels, but that is hard to do. Well, hard to do in .45. When we were learning about the .38 Super in IPSC, we discovered it was an entirely different animal than the .45, even more so than the 9mm. Again, in .45, we'd been shooting lead 200-grain bullets at just over 900 fps, and barrels lasted a long time, if not forever. We loaded 160-grain lead bullets in the first Supers at 1,150 fps, and the barrels lasted. (I'm not sure anyone stuck with the 160s long enough to find out how long barrels lasted; things changed so quickly.) But, to get more muzzle blast gas to the comp, we moved down in bullet weight and had to go to jacketed bullets. The extreme was when we got down to 115-grain JHPs and ran them at 1,525 fps! (Thankfully, the Power Factor had been lowered from 185 to 175; otherwise, we'd have had to drive those bullets to 1,610 fps. Ouch.)

The worst example of that I ever encountered was a local shooter who had built a matched pair of Supers for himself and his wife. He had scored a batch of harder-than-linotype lead and cast his bullets. They were running 108-grain bullets. To make Major and have a "reasonable" cushion when it came time to be tested on the chronograph, he was pushing them close to 1,650 fps. The load was so obnoxious that everyone left the range when we were shooting indoors in the winter. Only the Range Officer was with them; no one wanted that job.

Super at Major with jacketed bullets—many of us went to 125-grain bullets at 1,400 fps to save on barrel wear—toasted barrels quickly. Unlike the .45, where a barrel bore lasted a long time, and the pistol needed a tightening every couple of years, we shot out barrels in Super. Between the friction, the abrasive gases, and the heat, they just died unless you were careful.

Today, that's not going to be a problem. If you are shooting USPSA and running a Super or Super-like cartridge in Open Division, you know about this. Everyone else shooting a .45, 9mm, or 10mm will not be toasting bores.

But, perhaps the barrel that came in your 1911 just isn't as good as it could be. A quality replacement barrel will run you $150 to $300. There's no point in replacing it with anything but a good barrel, even if you can find cheap ones these days. However, be sure the barrel is the problem before you spend money, time, and effort. You might find that the new match barrel you installed doesn't shoot any better than the old one. That could be because of the barrel, the barrel fit, the ammo, or the shooter.

However, sometimes a new barrel is needed. I have one where I was doing abusive tests and shooting 1911s underwater. (Do not do this. No, I'm not kidding, *don't do it.* It is hazardous and abusive, and I've proven the point: they work, but sometimes they break.) I bulged the barrel, which trashed the bushing but didn't harm the slide, so it got a new barrel.

*The bushing's interior can be turned on a lathe to make the dimensions work out, or you can lathe-turn the barrel's exterior—a pistolsmith's choice. Or do both. Photo: Jason Burton*

So, let's consider the levels of barrel swap available.

## USGI

USGI barrels used to be a thing. Back when Reagan was president, you could still find new-in-the-wrapper USGI 1911 .45 ACP barrels for not a lot of money. When a new Bar-Sto would run you $100, you could find a USGI barrel for $20 to $30. And it would probably drop right in. Now, a new-in-the-wrapper barrel like that would be pricey, and collectors would hate you for using it in a USGI gun.

What did we do then? We'd weld or silver-solder the hood and the barrel feet ends and cut them to fit a slide/frame. Then, put it into the slide in a match bushing for improved accuracy. The extra work we put

When it comes to getting things precise, being able to measure before, during, and after the cut is essential. Photo: Jason Burton

into such barrels more than offset the price break from a drop-in match barrel from Bar-Sto, but we all had to learn, and that's how we did it.

By 1990, Bar-Sto had a half-dozen competitors making match barrels, and they were all good.

## DROP-IN BARRELS

The drop-in type is a unique barrel in that the dimensions of the fitting areas are larger than for a fully parts-interchangeable barrel but not so large that you will have to fit it. At least, that's the plan. If you took 100 1911s at random, made over the last 20 to 40 years, I'm sure you'd find at least one, maybe more, where the barrel wouldn't fit. The more off the beaten path the maker of that 1911 is, the more likely the "drop-in" won't ... drop in. However, using a name barrel and a current-production name 1911, the fit will be excellent and probably more accurate than the existing barrel. The current 1911 makers know 1911s have a reputation for accuracy (just as they have a reputation for good triggers), so they will spend the extra $10 for a better-grade barrel. That is if they don't make it themselves.

Some 1911 makers produce their barrels, and that's a good thing. On the other hand, installing a new barrel before the 50,000- or

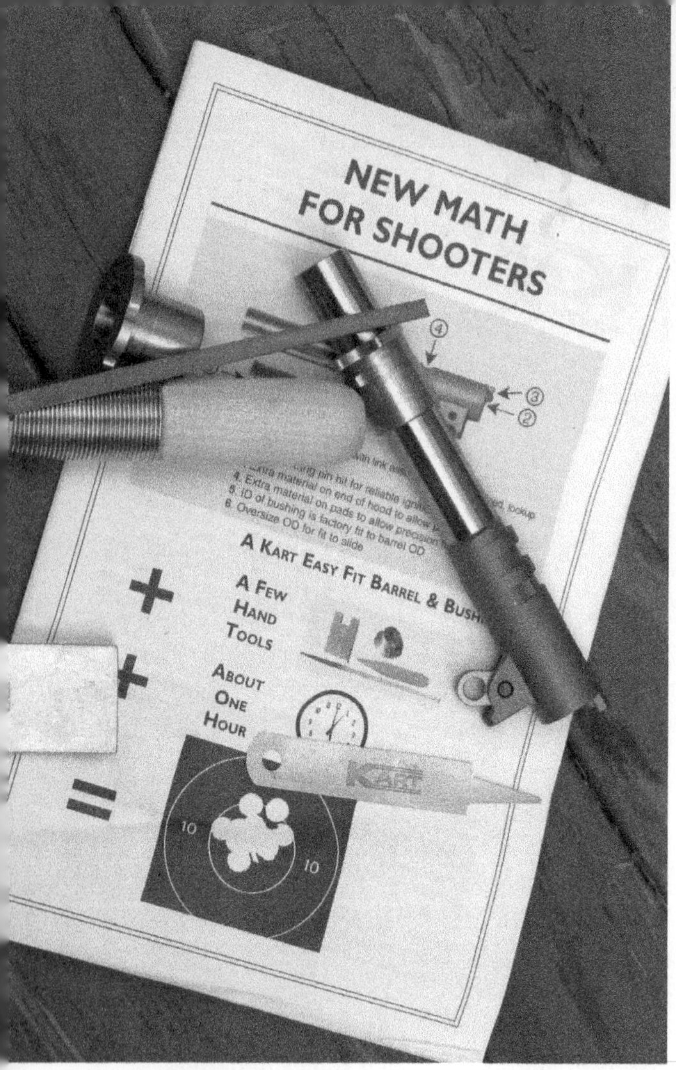


The Kart XACT Fit barrel kit (formerly the EZ-FIT Kit) is a complete barrel, bushing, link, and the tools to fit it.

100,000-round level is pointless if you have a pistol from one of them. If you're building your own, say from a Caspian Arms slide and frame you've ordered, you're not likely to find a drop-in barrel to drop in. It may, but it isn't Caspian's fault if it doesn't.

A drop-in barrel will come with a link, link pin, and bushing (in most cases, anyway), and you fit it the way you would any other barrel. First, check to ensure the bushing fits your slide. If it doesn't, check the fit of the new barrel in the existing slide. Once you have a working bushing, assemble the barrel, slide, and frame, and check the function manually. Once it passes that test, plan a range trip.

## EASY-FIT BARRELS

OK, here we have the in-between barrel. It is small or close enough dimensionally almost to fit in, but it has special prep, so it will be easy to fit. The exemplar is the Kart XACT Fit (formerly EZ-Fit) barrel kit. It comes with a barrel and the tools you will need. The process is easy and fully described in the booklet that comes with it, so I'll give you the highlights.

The kit comes with a fitting bushing, which is not meant to be the one you shoot with but the one with which you fit the barrel. Slide the barrel into your slide, install the bushing, and check the hood fit. It should drop in. If it doesn't, measure the distance from the breechface to the first locking lug so you can carefully file the hood to length. A lathe is much better, as you can "nip" a few thousandths off the hood and keep it square to the bore axis.

The Kart XACT Fit barrel has two raised pads to control the barrel's lift into the slide.

You must file clearance if the barrel hood is too broad or your hood clearance is insufficient. No, you do not want your hood touching on the sides. It has to have some clearance. The Kart kit has a feeler gauge for this; use it. There is also an alignment block that keeps the barrel centered while you inspect and decide which side, if any, to file.

Once the hood fits, adjust the "lift," which you do with the slide off the frame. Lift is the upward vertical distance the barrel travels into lockup. A match barrel will have some means of controlling this, so the barrel comes to a hard stop, not just floats on top of the slide stop pin, kept under control by the link.

On the Kart barrel, this is done with the two pads you see in the slot created when the locking lugs were machined. To fit this correctly, you'll need a sized and deprimed case of the proper caliber (a clean one would be nice), and you'll need to remove the firing pin plate, firing pin, and extractor from the slide.

Slide the barrel open enough to stuff the empty case into the chamber. Close the barrel and push it up and into the locking lugs. Now, turn the slide around and peer down the firing pin bore. You will most likely see the top edge of the primer hole but not all of it. This means your barrel is too low for a centered firing pin strike. You will also be able to see the locking lug engagement since the fitting pads are below the surface of the locking lug edges.

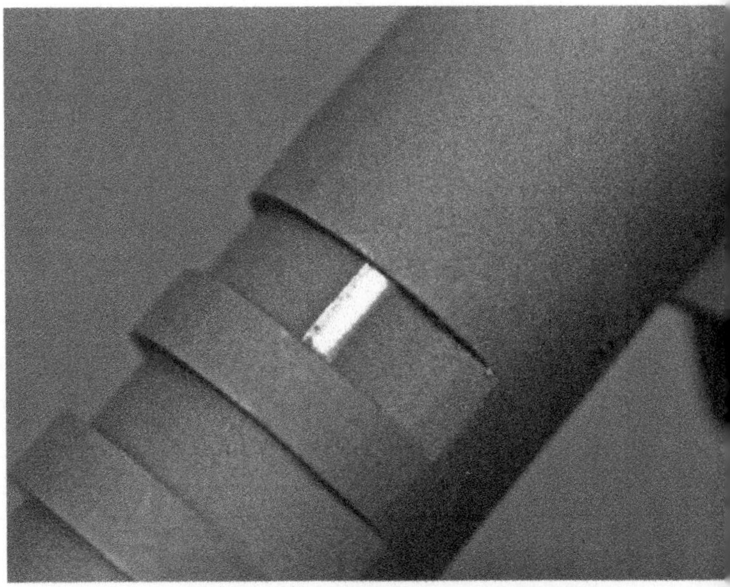

*A stop pad on the Kart barrel was filed before checking the fit.*

With the Kart-supplied file, remove a small, equal amount from each pad and recheck alignment. This is a slow, gradual process; there is no way to determine what filing you need to do, and you only get to do it once. Once centered, you are done.

Next is the barrel feet. This will probably be a no-problem detail, as the barrel feet will, once the barrel lift has been properly done, slide right over the slide stop pin, and you are finished.

If not, you have two choices: Lift the barrel more if there's clearance to be had. A slightly off-center firing pin hit isn't a crime. The 1911 will still work. But you might run out of lift to file into the fit. Or cut the barrel feet, but that requires an additional tool, a lug-fitting kit.

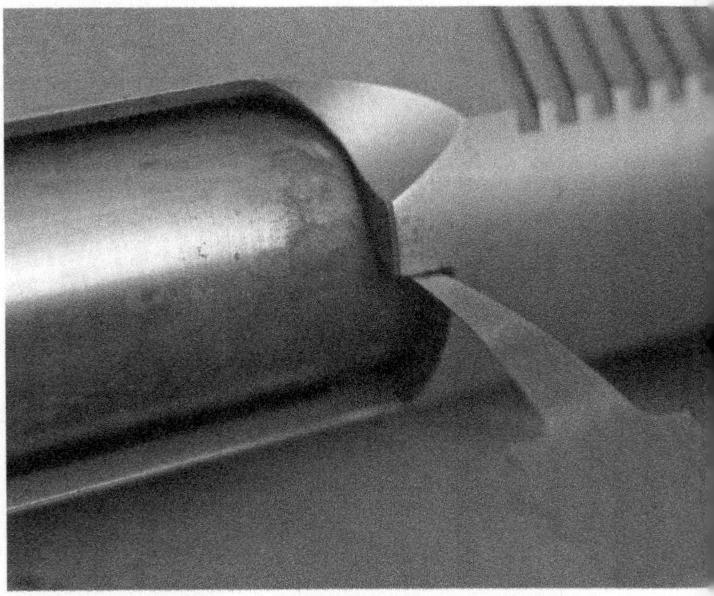

*The Kart kit also has a feeler gauge to check the needed gap on the sides of the barrel hood.*

## GOLD CUP

I would be remiss if I didn't mention another hood detail: the Gold Cup. When Colt made its top-end Bullseye pistol, it added a rib on the top of the slide. Well, to make the rib continuous, the hood could not have the same width. So, the Gold Cup has a narrower off-center hood. You can cut a regular barrel to fit a Gold Cup slide, but a Gold Cup barrel won't work in a regular slide. If you have a Gold Cup or a Gold Cup slide on your parts gun, keep that in mind if or when you decide to replace the barrel.

## FITTING THE LUGS

The bottom of the 1911 barrel, the feet, are also called lugs. You need the lug-fitting kit, a cutting tool that replaces the slide stop pin to fit them. Fitting the lugs is the last thing to do. Everything else must be correct for this to work.

The process is simple: with the link and pin out of the barrel and the pistol assembled with the slide, barrel, and frame (bushing, too), hold the action open and insert the lug-cutting tool. Push the slide forward (there's a lever for this) as if it were chambering a round, and rotate the cutter to cut the lugs to the exact dimension you need.

The rest is clean up.

*Some barrels are made with the rear slot for the locking lugs machined at a different radius, and the ends of the slot are made as the lift stops for that barrel. It requires a bit more finesse to fit, but it works fine.*

## PISTOLSMITH BARRELS

Pistolsmith barrels are oversized in the hood and barrel feet but are the correct dimensions at the muzzle. That way, there's no extra work involved in fitting it to a bushing. However, a detail-oriented custom pistolsmith will probably use a bushing that requires complete fitting: fit in slide, fit in slide lock slot, and fit to the barrel diameter. That's why it takes a couple of years to get such work done because all the people ahead of you get the same work done at the master level.

You may think, "Oh, cool, that will deliver all the accuracy my pistol can get; I want that." It probably will when properly fitted to your pistol. But, to fit it, you'll need many tools and skills, which may take you from two to 10 barrels worth of practice. I recall that there was a master pistolsmith who was giving 1911 building lessons. He could distill the work to a couple of days and have people who arrived with a box of parts leave with a working 1911 and know how it all worked. But the barrel fitting? That was an extra day that came after the other work and knowledge.

There is at least one more barrel grade, which Bar-Sto produced back when the Marine Corps still ran its fleet of 1911s for Recon and others. They were special runs of a handful of barrels where every dimension was grossly over-spec. The Marine builders would call on these few barrels when they had used up all the in-spec frames and slides and were left with the ones that were so worn, abused, and off-dimension that the barrel had to be epic in its dimensions to be made to fit. All this to get one more working 1911, of which the USMC never had enough. You do not need such a barrel, and the USMC doesn't either, so I suspect when the last of those goes (or went) into a 1911, that was that. So, how does one fit a barrel?

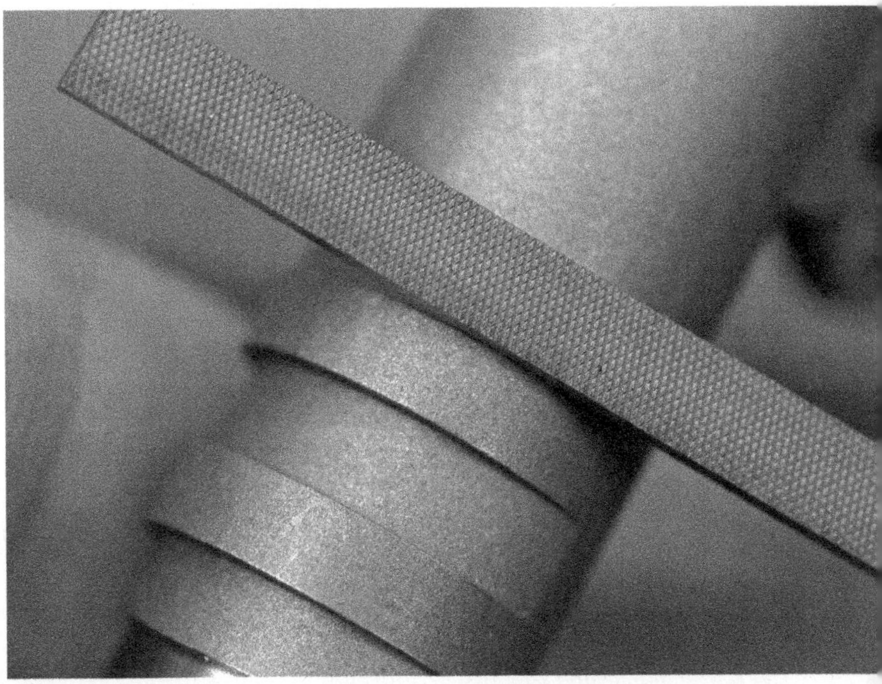

*Once you've determined that your Kart barrel needs more lift, carefully file (evenly on each side) the stop pads to lift it.*

## BARREL FITTING

I won't describe barrel fitting as a blow-by-blow, step-by-step process, so you can do it. A raft of books is already devoted to that, and they spend dozens of pages laying it all out. I'm simply going to give you the overview so you will know why the person you are paying to do this charges so much—or to provide you with the foundation to explore more detailed gunsmithing manuals on the topic.

Barrel fitting includes bushing fitting, which we've described before and must be done first. The barrel fitting is the last thing done after the slide-to-frame fit has been addressed, welded, fitted, etc. Then, the bushing, breechface, and bowtie are completed before barrel fitting, except perhaps the cosmetics, because how the barrel fits may create a slide-to-frame lineup mismatch at the rear when closed.

*The Kart kit has a barrel alignment gauge to keep the barrel centered while you check the fit and hood gap. Use it and keep it for the next barrel fitting job.*

Your custom pistolsmith will cut the barrel hood using a lathe and delicate measuring equipment. But before doing that, he will first work on the breechface and ensure it is square and perpendicular to the bore. If that means he has to dress the breechface back a thousandth or two on one side to make it square to the bore, so be it. Then, he'll use the lathe to trim the hood back to length, and then it's off to the mill.

He'll use the milling machine to dress the sides of the hood and make them the correct stand-off distance from the hood clearance. There are several ways to measure and do this, some proprietary. In the past, we'd use an alignment gauge, pretty much like that of the Kart kit, and file the sides for clearance.

The hard stop for lift adjustment on high-end barrels (actually,

Kart is high-end, but we're past the EZ-Fit/XACT Fit ones now) is more subtle. It took me a barrel-fitting lesson to notice, but it was a Bar-Sto with the features. Yours may have it or not. Look at the locking lugs of the barrel. Two slots are machined in the barrel's body, forming the locking lugs. Notice how one of the slots has its endpoints on each side, ending higher on the barrel body? Those are the stop points. The slot is machined to create the stop points on the outside ends of the slot. When fitting the barrel, the custom pistolsmith will use these points as his hard stop points on the lift.

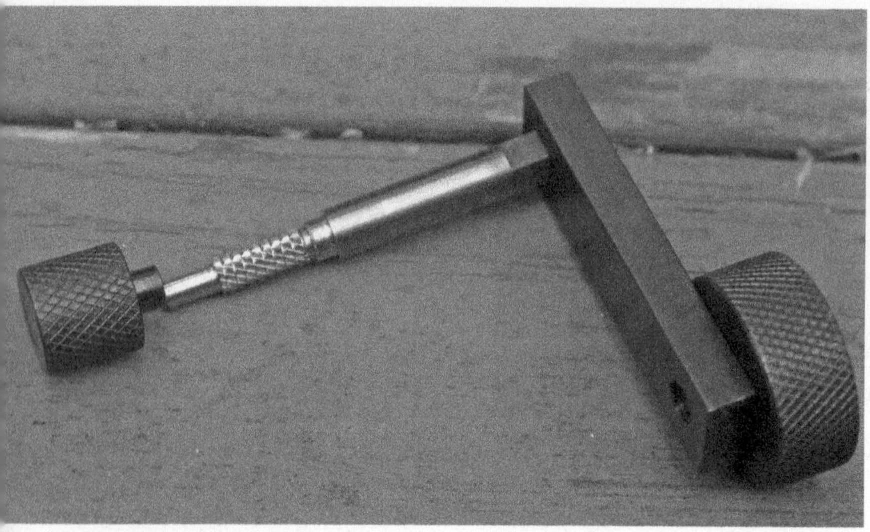

***The barrel lug-cutting tool fits into the frame through the slide stop shaft to cut the barrel feet for the correct fit.***

Now it's time for the barrel feet, the lugs.

This step requires a milling machine and a fixture. The fixture holds the barrel on its side, and it locates the barrel in the fixture within .001 inch. The pistolsmith will assemble the slide, frame, and barrel and attempt to close it. It won't close. But how close it comes to closing will tell him the task ahead. The barrel will get clamped into the fixture, and he'll use a cutter that is the diameter of the slide-stop pin to machine the barrel feet where they ride on the slide-stop pin. He'll take less than the indicated amount and test-fit again. This might require a few passes or be happy-happy-joy-joy on the first one.

***The lug cutter in the frame without a barrel shows the cutting teeth.***

Important detail: He will not machine the barrel feet that last thousandth so he can polish them to remove tool marks. And, he will not machine the feet to the point that the slide closes flush to the frame at the rear.

Instead, he will machine the feet (he is not just machining it to let the feet rest on the pin, but how far forward it travels to come to a stop) to the point that the barrel is just past dead center on the pin. The short—very short, the ideal number is .030 inch—flat that over-center creates allows the slide to move back about .100 inch with the barrel still locked to it, which gives the timing needed to let the bullet leave the muzzle and to soak up the recoil before the barrel slams down and the recoil spring has to do all the work.

What if the back of the slide and the frame don't match? Then, he will hand-file the surface to a proper fit and either polish, serrate, or checker, as your build order requires.

A barrel with the bottom lugs shorn off due to hitting the bottom of the lug feet, not the bowtie, as it should.

Again, if you're spending thousands of dollars on a custom 1911, this is the attention to detail you expect. And the proper fit of the barrel means the built-in accuracy will last much longer.

So, to get the absolute maximum out of your expensive barrel takes more than just some hand tools. It can all be done with hand tools because it was for many years, decades even. But the modern method is machine tools.

## COMPS AND BRAKES

How do muzzle comps and brakes work, and why and when should you have them? First, nomenclature: when we started using pistols with extra "stuff" on them, they were called compensators or "comps." The same thing on a rifle was called a muzzle brake. They work the same way, and I use the terms interchangeably, except in historical references. (An IPSC pistol in the mid-1980s would have a comp on it; now it is whatever the manufacturer calls it.)

How tough is the 1911? This barrel cracked, but aside from the occasional malfunction, it still worked fine for its owner until he took it apart for cleaning. Photo: Ned Christiansen

When you fire a round, the expanding gases push the bullet out of the barrel. The exiting gases create the muzzle blast and noise. A suppressor slows and cools those gases, decreasing noise. A comp is an expansion chamber in front of the muzzle, with an open port or ports on the top. It works by having the gases hit the sidewalls of the expansion chamber and pushing on them. Yes, you can think of it as jetting gases out the top, and they do, but that's only part of what it does.

The more gas you push, the better the comp works. The higher the pressure of those gases, the more it works. So, when the .38 Super came along, it was the obvious choice over the .45 due to gas pressure. As handloaders, competition shooters could select powders that produced more muzzle blast than others, increasing the comp's effectiveness.

Design matters. The more wall area the gases have to push on, the greater the effect. The differences are minor, so you can have

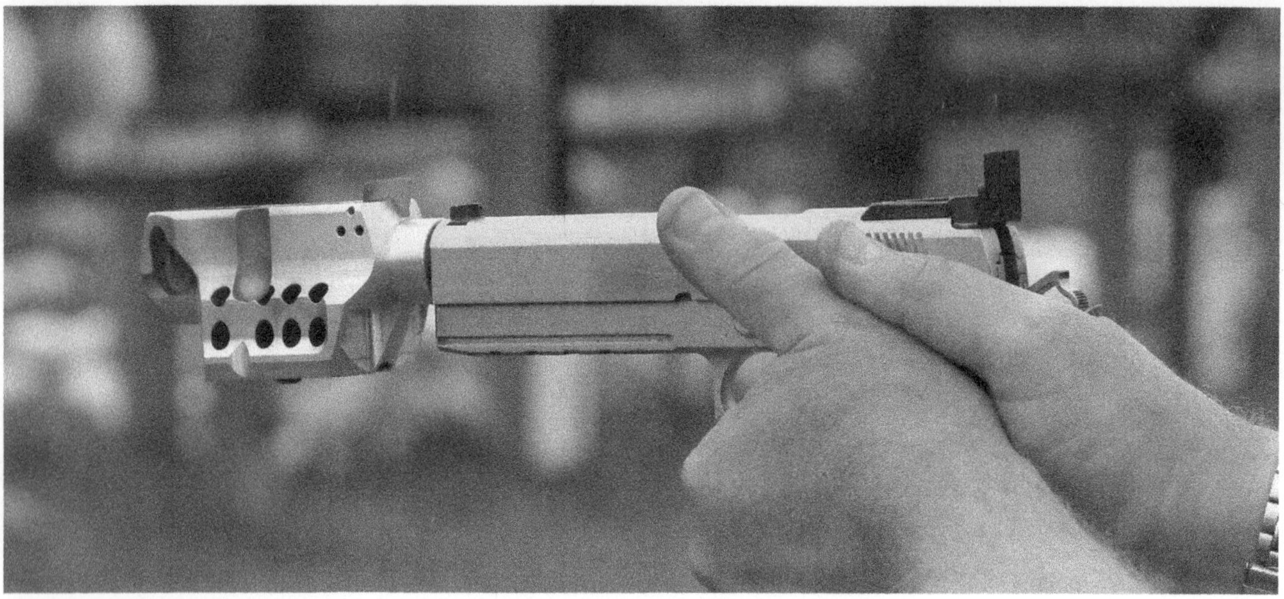

*Regarding muzzle brake size and intricacy, some is good, more is better, but can you have too much? Not yet, but this is getting close.*

many designs that all feel similar. One aspect is not the same: a comp that makes the gun "shoot flat" or another that makes the gun "shoot soft." You can't have both; there isn't enough gas. The flat-shooting one puts more into the downward push, lessening the muzzle flip. The soft-shooting one puts more work forward, decreasing the recoil jolt in your hand.

You benefit from recoil reduction not by making it go away but by handing it off to the shooter next to you. The more effective your comp/load combo, the more the shooter next to you suffers. Can you have it both ways? Well, you can, but you won't like it. For a brief period in USPSA/IPSC competition, some competitors tried to have it all. The 9x25 Dillon was a 10mm case necked down to 9mm. It was possible to pile enough slow-burning powder into the case to make Major and get both soft and flat. But the cost? Oh, the cost. The comp's bark was so bad that no one wanted to be the timer or Range Officer for a shooter with a 9x25. And barrels didn't last an entire season of competition and practice. You had to give up magazine capacity due to the larger case. Those who tried it almost all built one gun, tested and used it, and gave up on the idea.

*A comp or muzzle brake on a pistol was a competition thing. Now, it's typical on carry guns.*

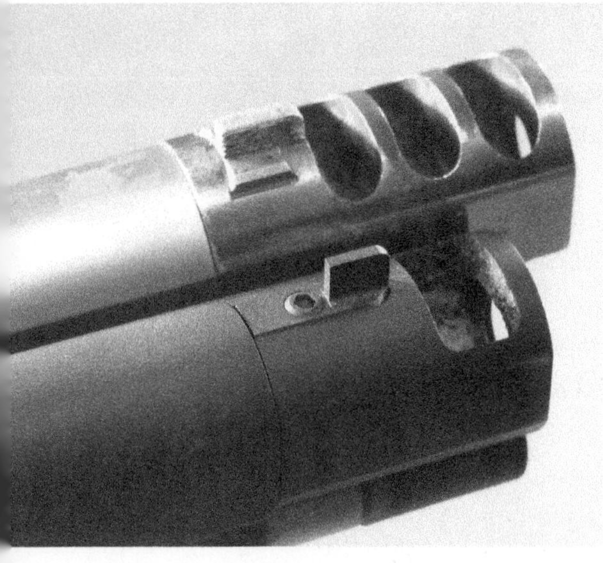

## SUMMARY

What are the odds, the chances, the likelihood, that you will need a new barrel in your 1911? How long does it take to wear one out, and how bad does a barrel have to be before you consider replacing it? When I started gunsmithing and IPSC competition, I would have said "pretty high." And for a few years, new makers entered the field and tried to get a piece of the pie. But by the early 1990s, barrels were improved. Pistol makers realized that shooters demanded more. The aftermarket barrel makers became so numerous and worked at such a high level that the firearms makers had even more pressure put on them.

Today, it's typical for an out-of-the-box 1911 (or many other pistols, for that matter) to outshoot their new owners. You will likely find that you will have to practice a lot and spend money on premium ammo or load your own to find the limits of the pistol. I test guns for a living; many easily shoot under 3 inches at 25 yards. The better-than-average ones in build and cost will often shoot down to 2 inches. Now, I'm not obsessing over groups. I do not spend all day shooting groups to wring out all the accuracy of a given pistol. I'm just giving it a reasonable, full-faith effort and calling it as it happens, and I can't remember the last time I tested something that was, "OK, this has to go back; it is so bad."

Some will think that gun writers get special, custom-built, hand-tuned, and tested samples to write up. As if. Any gun writer you mention that to will likely laugh out loud, if not snort in derision.

I don't use a machine rest because it takes too much time, and the results are not as predictive as you'd imagine, which leads me to the last part of this chapter: the machine rest.

The name you will know is the Ransom Rest. The Ransom Rest is a

***With jetting gases from a comp, you get jetting smoke.***

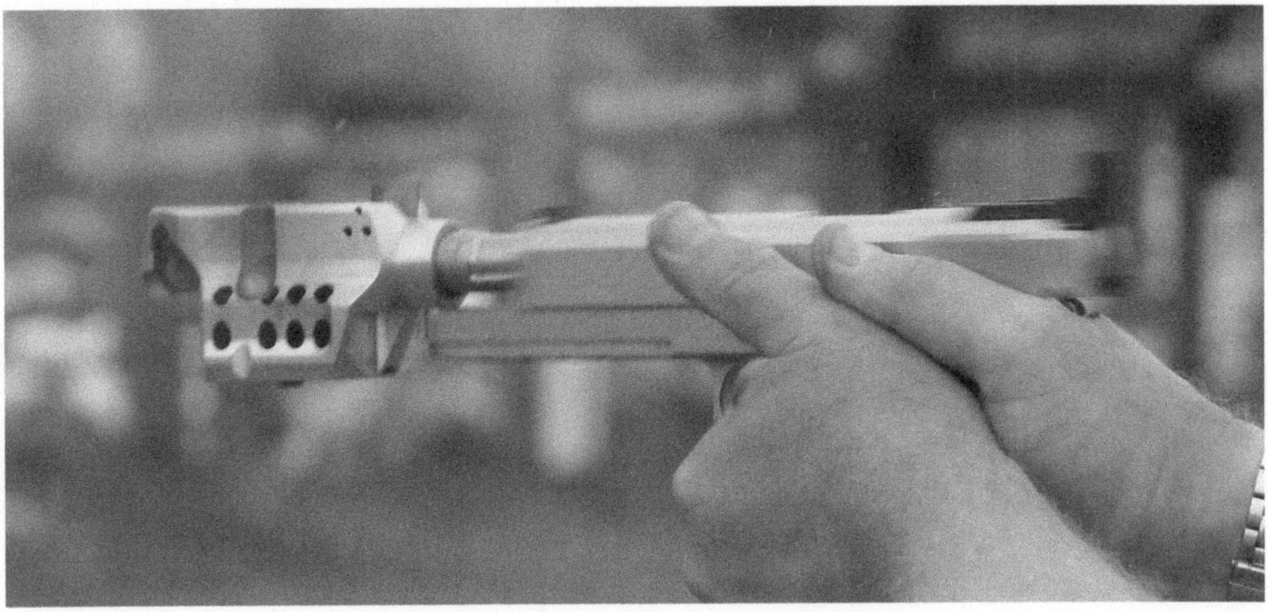

***The bushing must be snug but movable inside the slide, which can mean polishing or turning on the lathe to remove more than a smidgen of steel. Photo: Jason Burton***

friction-dampened, spring-loaded holder for testing handgun accuracy. However, when it comes to pistols, it is a slightly problematic tool because it "aims" the frame, not the sights. Let's take our accurate rack-grade 1911A1 from the armory. All the moving parts slam up and close the same way, so it is accurate because you are aiming with the sights, which are always in the same place relative to the other parts.

Clamp it in the Ransom, and you might see accuracy drop off. Why? Because the frame is being returned to the same place after each shot, the slide and barrel, despite locking up the same to each other each time, can "float" on the frame and point to a slightly different point on the target. A revolver in a Ransom Rest is an absolute measure of accuracy, as the frame and sights are attached. But in a semi-auto pistol, it's not always definitive. And it takes excessive time to get set up, settled in, and test anything. So, I rarely use it.

I did use it testing a Les Baer pistol, my Heavyweight Monolith.

The frame has the entire width and size in the dust cover to the muzzle, and the slide is made without the front scallops. The slide/frame fit in the front looks like a steel 2x4.

The test was to see what it did out of the Ransom, compared to what I could do over sandbags and offhand. I tested it with a 200-grain lead semi-wadcutter bullet. Earlier in my shooting career, I put between 3 and 4 tons of lead into backstops across the country, shooting in competition and practicing for the same. Back then, it was loaded with 5.8 grains of WW-231. The new load (well, new as of the 21st century) is 4.5 grains of Vihtavouri 310. At 50 yards, the Heavyweight Monolith delivered 3-inch groups from the Ransom Rest. That is center-to-center. The Monolith can deliver every shot into the 10-ring on a Bullseye target, with half of those touching the X-ring. If I were willing to change my "random brass" to a single source and one the Monolith liked, I could shave those groups down. And if I were really OCD, I'd weigh the bullets, not use those markedly off the average weight, and probably get a 2-inch center-to-center group regularly.

What about shooting off the bench without the Ransom Rest? Once settled into an assemblage of sandbags, I could produce groups between 4 and 5 inches at 50 yards. Before you go and "dis" that, let's quickly check reality: Fifty yards. You are going to find a judge quite leery of your need to have shot someone at that distance. So tactically, it's a mostly unrealistic distance for testing. Then, sight width. The front sight is typically .125 inch wide. What it looks like on a 50-yard target, how much apparent width it subtends, is 6 ½ inches. I was shooting groups smaller than the width of the front sight.

Offhand, Bullseye style? Do I really have to say? Sigh. I shot *1-foot* groups at 50 yards, one-handed. No serious Bullseye shooter will brag about that, but keeping four of the five shots in a group inside the A zone of a USPSA target is pretty darned good for me.

The lesson here is scaled back to 25 yards, the Monolith could do a group of 1.5 inches. On the other hand, I could shoot a 2.25-inch group over sandbags, which is right there at the limit of my skills when testing pistols. Testing over sandbags, I can expect to get a realistic measurement of what a pistol can do. So that's how I do it. ●

CHAPTER

14

# GRIPS AND FRAMES

This will be a long chapter because a lot is going on with the 1911's grip and frame. We'll begin with the grips only because they are the easy part to start on in the frame and also because they are the most customizable part. There seems to be no end to grip makers' offerings, and since this is America, where we have choices, then choice abounds. However, we'll go way beyond grips and into other areas of the frame. We'll examine everything below the frame rails that isn't safety-related or fire control work.

***Government and Commander frame screws are a nominal 3 inches apart.***

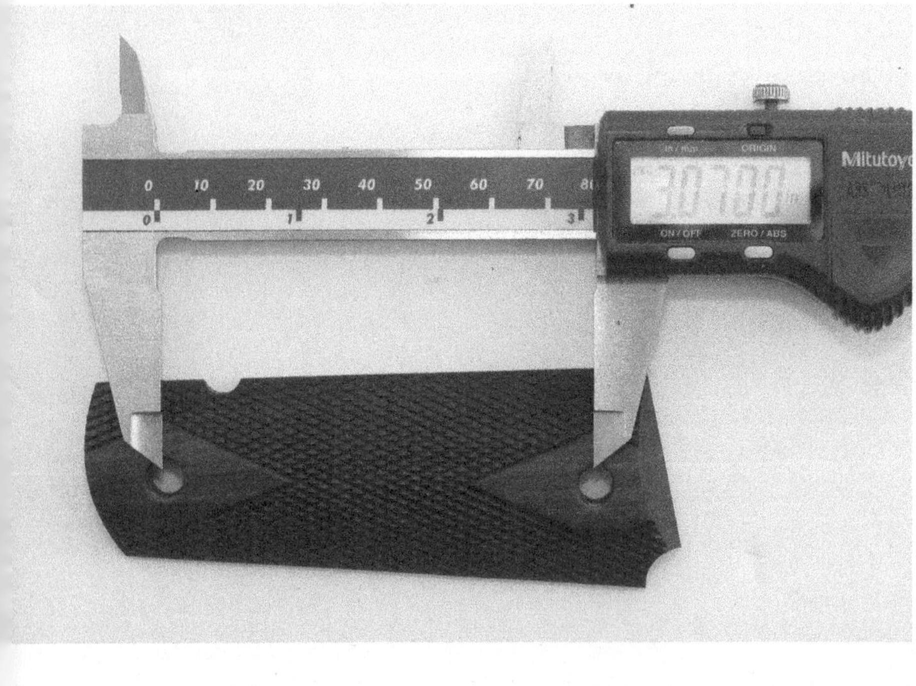

## GRIP SHAPE AND FUNCTION

The grip panels are mirror images, more or less. They sit on the sides of the frame, and the bottom edge has a circular cut for clearance of the mainspring housing pin. The left grip rides a bit higher to come over the safety/slide-stop plunger tube in a vain attempt to keep it in place should it come loose. (It tries but fails if the plunger wishes to cause problems.) The top edge is curved, and the panels are not rectangles or rhombuses—they're kinda-sorta rhomboids, narrower at the top than the bottom, and the top and bottom edges are not parallel. A drawing of the grip panels has all kinds of extra measurements and dimensions than you'd think something so simple as a grip would need.

There's a small scallop to provide clearance for the magazine catch and two holes for the grip screws. The grips provide a non-slip surface and shape the frame for the human hand without adding weight. Yes, the whole thing could be steel, but back when we were trying to add weight with steel grips, we found that it could be too much of a good thing. So, wood it was in the beginning.

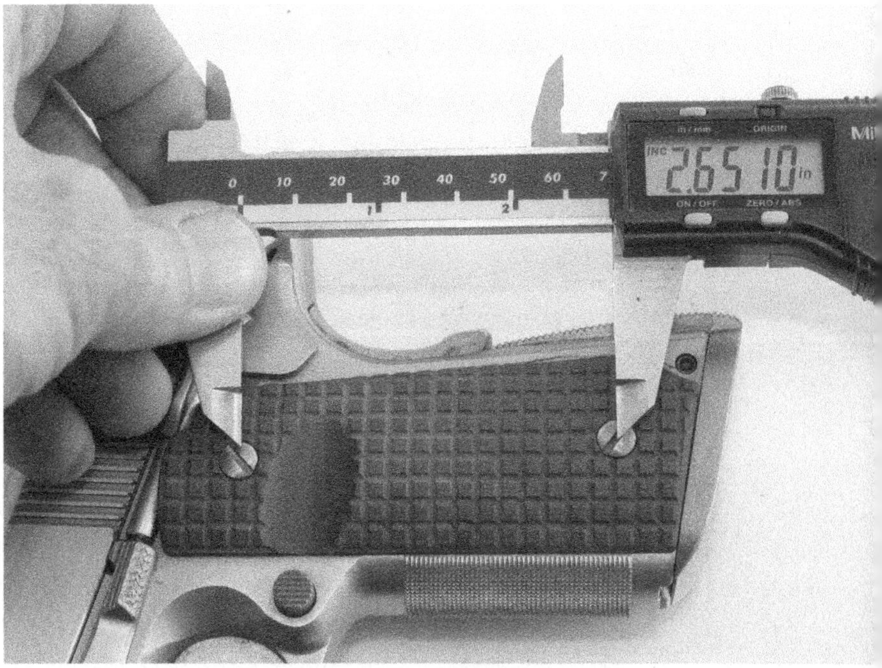

***Officers model frames are shorter, and the grip screws are 2.7 inches apart.***

## GRIP SIZE AND EXTERIOR

Which grips do you need? There are two primary sizes and a dizzying array of contours, colors, materials, and shapes. The Government Model one is easy. The distance between the grip screw centers is more or less 3 inches. The blueprints show the distance as something different, but they don't measure it center-to-center but at an angle. Go figure. The commander-sized frames are the same. The Officers frame has the screws about 2.7 inches apart. That's it. If you want replacement grips, use a ruler and see which you need if it isn't apparent.

Grip screws hold the grips on. But, once you take them off, you see that the grip screws thread into bushings attached to the frame. Wait, what? Why not just thread the frame? Simple: Browning was a frontier gunsmith and designer. He started designing firearms when the American frontier was still open (it wasn't declared closed until 1898), and those in the West expected durability. If it wasn't, they were not too keen on it, regardless of any advantage it might confer on the owner.

If the screw loosened or fell off, it meant lost grips. With the bushings, the grips held position if a screw fell out. If both were lost, a length of twine could keep the grips on until new screws could be bought. Also, the bushing provided more threads for the screws to thread into, making it more secure. Without bushings, if a screw loosens a couple of turns, it will fall out. With bushings, it takes four or five complete rotations for a screw to fall out. And if it moves enough almost to fall out, you'll feel it when you grip the frame. So, the grip screws are threaded into the bushings, and the bushings are threaded into the frame and staked from the inside to make them a permanent (or at least semi-permanent) part of the frame.

Now, the great thing about the 1911 is that the grip screw threads, spacing, and sizes have not changed one bit in 112 years. The bushings are still 3.074 inches center to center (on a properly made 1911), and the bushings are the same.

A brief history lesson. In the 19th century, the U.S. was the machine tool industry and manufacturing leader. Making parts to a standard size and thread pitch, with plus-and-minus tolerances (designated +/-), inspection gauges, and industry boards to determine standards, was referred to as The American Method. That's how you can go to your local hardware store and buy 8-32 screws and nuts to match, regardless of where in the country you live; they will fit.

Ouch. This frame has been hammered, filed, abused, and "fitted" to the slide: ugly work, but work done by a "name" pistolsmith back in the 1980s. Things were different back then.

Firearms? Well, in some regards. Unfortunately, the thread pitches that will work for industry are too coarse for firearms. As a result, the thread pitch of the bushing into the 1911 frame is .236-60, and the screw threads in the bushing are .150-50. You will search in vain for any hardware store to stock anything in those pitches. The big industrial supplier, McMaster-Carr? Nope, not a chance. You will have to go to a firearms-specific supplier; Brownells, Midway USA, and others have what you need.

Grip screws are slotted, Allen socket or Torx. The type of grip screw head doesn't matter, except that you'll need a matching tool for that type of head. You also don't need to torque the screws; they will stay in place for the most part. We'll review the exceptions when we get to grips.

## GRIPS ON, GRIPS OFF

Use your tool (screwdriver, Allen wrench, Torx tip) to unscrew the grip screws. Set them aside. Lift the grips off. If they are tight on the bushings, stick a finger into the magazine well and press the grip through the frame opening. Scrub the frame and grips, then press the grips back onto the frame, index the screws, and tighten them.

***The 1911 frame uses bushings and screws to hold on the grips. Here is a frame, bushing, and screw with the bushing driver you can get. (It saves knarfing the bushing.)***

## GRIP MATERIALS AND CHECKERING

In the beginning, grips were wood. They were checkered for a non-slip surface, and the originals were known as a "double diamond" pattern. There, the checkering rows were skipped around the grip screws, so there would not be little pyramids of wood next to the fasteners and exposed to damage. In WWII, the grips were changed to plastic, deemed superior and impervious. Alas, not so much. The plastics formula had a miniscule shrinkage rate, and after 80+ years, some of the grips have shrunk enough to be problematic. Thus, 1911 collectors are loathe to remove the grips, which can be damaged by cracking or snapping down to the shrunk size and not fitting back onto the frame.

Modern materials don't have that problem, but they can pose another. Aluminum grips are susceptible to loose grip screws. Wood, being compressible, acts as a sort of crush washer to grip the screws. The compressed wood resists screw rotation. Aluminum doesn't compress, and screws sometimes won't stay tight. Other uncompressible materials can have the same problem.

A popular grip material is G10. This is the name given to a specific epoxy and layered material sandwiched in very thin layers, like plywood, of very durable materials—requiring power machinery to shape and checker. By alternating colors, we get interesting, even gaudy combinations when carved to the contour of grips.

Any wood, plastic, rubber, metal, combinations, and laminates can work as grips, and since they are easy to swap, all kinds of shapes have been conjured in the previous century of use.

## GRIP SHAPES

The nominal thickness of grip slabs is .240 to .250 inch—the thickness of

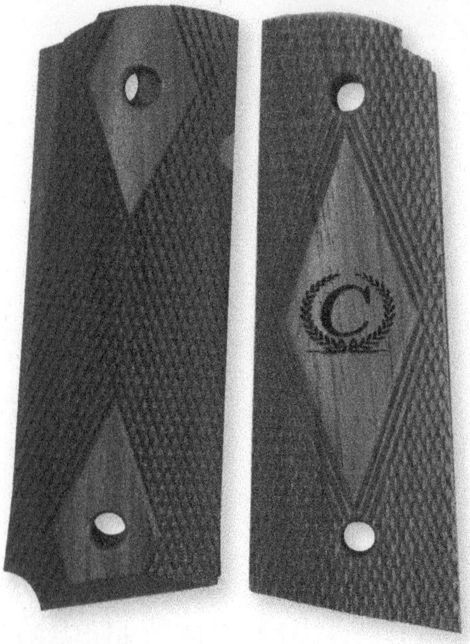

On the left are Spegel double diamond grips, which you'd use if you were restoring a 1911 or looking for the pre-WWII GI look. On the right are Caspian grips, which fit an S&A mag well funnel.

USGI wood or plastic grips. However, the thickness and shape are up to the end user. When Bullseye was popular, it wasn't uncommon to see "orthopedic" grips contoured to the shooter's hand with a big thumb shelf on the left side, providing as much contact as possible with the pistol. These required a light grip to make the hold consistent. They're not of much use on an everyday carry gun; they're more of a historical curiosity. But you may still see such grips if your gun club holds Bullseye matches.

The big difference now is grip thickness. When shooters were learning IPSC, many came to it from PPC, initially a revolver-only competition. Revolver shooters preferred rounder grips, a shape more like the revolver. New shooters stayed with the USGI shape. I and many others preferred thinner grips than USGI but not shorter front-to-back, which allowed us to "index" the pistol faster and more consistently. Indexing is not point-shooting, but rather, by having the frame feel more like it had flat sides, we could get the muzzle on center and the sights aligned faster, with the flats to guide us by feel. With the stronger G10, it's possible to make flat-sided grips. If you have experience with other pistols, this might initially feel odd. Then, you either learn and don't notice or love it. Some hate it, and since grips are easy to change, swap them for what feels right.

There are also "slimline" grips. These are thinner but not flatter and often require shorter bushings. The idea is to make the 1911 frame slightly smaller in circumference so those with smaller hands can more easily use it. I find this interesting, and also it is a personal thing. I know of IPSC competitors who stand all of 5 feet tall and do not need them and taller shooters who prefer them. Like clothing, if it fits, it's better; when it comes to shooting, fit does matter.

Techwell makes a set of aluminum grips with a mag funnel as part of the ensemble. The grips clamp the mag funnel in place, and so as long as your grip screws stay tight, your funnel remains in place.

## BOTTOM END

You'd think something as innocuous as the bottom of the grips would be a no-brainer. However, the originals had a small bevel cut, probably to keep them from abrading the flap of leather holsters. But, if you put a mag funnel on your 1911, the bevel now looks odd. So, some grips are made without the bevel, so they blend into the mag funnel. It's just one more detail to know when ordering your new grips.

## CHECKERING PATTERN

In the past, this would have been a treatise on how to checker grips. Not anymore. Grips come in such a bewildering array of checkering and other non-skid patterns that no one checkers their grips anymore, not unless they plan on starting a grip company. And, many of the patterns are identical to the non-slip ones machined or filed into the frame itself, so we'll cover those there and leave the idea of checkering patterns as whatever you think feels good, looks good, and doesn't chew your clothing to pieces.

*The idea of "orthopedic" grips is that they snug onto your hand, and you don't have to be as conscious of holding consistently. This, of course, is not a good choice for everyday carry.*

## REPAIRS

Let's assume you need to repair the bushing or tighten the grip or grip screws. If you're going to do any grip screw or bushing work, take the slide assembly off of the frame. (I assume you have already taken to heart unloading before doing any maintenance, cleaning or mods to your 1911. If you haven't, don't blame me for the unpleasant results of not following basic safety guidelines.) Simply tighten any loose grip screw. If the screws won't stay tight, order a set of "O" rings from Brownells that are specifically sized to fit under the screws and keep them tight.

What if the bushing is loose? Well, if the screw is out, but the bushing is loose, tighten it. Brownells carries a special "bushing driver," a hollow tube with a screwdriver blade. The tube keeps the blade from slipping out of the bushing slot, which mars it. However, you can get by with a regular, properly fitting screwdriver if careful. Or, you can modify your screwdriver on a bench grinder and file to make a center stub that fits into the bushing and keeps the blade from slipping out of the slot. It won't be good for anything else, but for the cost of a regular screwdriver, you'll have a specialized tool that will serve you for years.

The more likely prospect is that you unscrew the grip screw and find that the bushing came loose and it is still on the screw with the

grip stuck in between. There are two ways to solve this problem.

First, carefully degrease the frame hole for the bushing and the bushing threads. Then apply a drop of Loctite to the bushing threads and screw it back in. Let the Loctite set, and then unscrew the grip screw. This does not always work, as the bushing and frame may have collected enough gunk and corrosion that the Loctite can't hold enough to stand up to the torque needed to unscrew the frozen grip screw.

The second method is to use a pair of bull-nose pliers and tightly grip the bushing at the threads. Unscrew the grip screw, which usually comes free with a snap. It was likely stuck in place by dirt, grit, petrified oil, and rust. You now have a marred grip screw bushing, which needs to be replaced.

*The grip on the right side is notched for clearance for the tab of an ambi safety.*

As an aside, I managed to salvage grip screw bushings as, back then, they weren't all that common, and a 1911 owner often wanted it fixed, not repaired with a mismatched replacement part. I would use my all-purpose fine-cut file to file the marred threads flat. I'd then go to the next steps in bushing replacement. I did this when it was a USGI pistol, and the owner didn't want a blued bushing or a stainless gun and, again, did not want blued parts.

Before installing the bushing, we need to discuss screwdrivers. As in, using a screwdriver is a good way to mangle a bushing. Yes, there is a slot, and a screwdriver fits it, but you will knarf the bushing if it slips. Brownells makes a bushing driver that is essentially a screwdriver inside of a tube, and the tube keeps you from slipping in the bushing slot. If you are only ever going to install/replace one bushing, you can risk it. But if you do more than that, it is worth investing in the right tool. Heck, it is always worth investing in the right tool.

Whether replacing or salvaging the bushing, the next steps are as follows:

Use a tap for the bushing threads to clean out the threads in the frame. Check the new bushing for fit if you're replacing it or the old one, just to be sure. Unscrew, degrease, apply Loctite—blue is OK, red is better—and screw the bushing into place. Stake the bushing. Staking? Oh, yes. This is a pointed, star-shaped tool you insert from the top or bottom of the magazine well, index on the bushing, and stake it in place so it can't rotate. How to do this? Simple: There is an inset cup on the back of the staking tool. Insert a steel punch of the correct size through the bushing on the far side, set it in the cup, place the staker on the bushing, and give it a whack.

Let the Loctite set, but we aren't done yet. If one grip screw is frozen, the others are close to it. So use a grip screw thread tap, and clean the threads of each of the bushings, including the one you just installed. This tap cleans the threads *inside* the grip bushing, not the frame threads. You will be surprised, and perhaps even a bit alarmed, by how much gunk you extract from each bushing, gunk that could seize the grip screw in place sometime in the future.

Nope, not done yet. Pull a shop cloth through the magazine well and hold the frame up to the light, looking through the well with the light glancing along the sides. If the new bushing protrudes into the well, insert and drop an empty magazine to see if it drops free. If you feel any slight dragging on the bushing, file down the bushing. This next step might involve some cosmetic altering of your pistol, so if you'd rather live with the drag than the cosmetics, that's OK.

Use a wider file than the bushing but narrow enough to fit flat into the magazine well sidewall. Hold the file flat against the inside of the magazine well on the bushing side and push it back and forth, filing down the bushing until flush. It's difficult to do this without the file contacting the mag well at the opening edge, which will remove the finish.

Of course, doing hundreds of magazine insertions when loading or practicing reloading will do the same, so most people don't care or notice the file marks. I'm just giving you a heads-up.

And, since you're replacing or reinstalling the bushing, you might as well do all the others. Hey, since this work creates filings, and they will gum things up, now's the time to do a detailed strip of your frame, file all the bushings, scrub, wipe clean and reassemble.

Do you need to file down the grip screw bushings? No, not unless they create drag on your mags. However, being careful, you can't create problems doing this.

***You can see the difference here. It matters when you are trying to make your 1911 style harmonious.***

## NEXT-LEVEL PROBLEM

What if the bushing is loose because of stripped frame threads? (You might get lucky with only a stripped bushing, but it is usually both. Such is life.) This happens for several reasons, including ham-handed installation, which cross-threaded the bushing. The frame threads might survive, but probably not. Another cause: Over-enthusiastic bushing tightening. That's your fault. Over-enthusiastic grip screw tightening? That's doubly your fault. Being just a smidge too enthusiastic, and having a 1911 with an aluminum frame. That's not always your fault, but the problem is still the same. Where the original bushing threads were .236 inch, the new tap cuts threads of .255 inch.

The process uses an oversized tap held perpendicular to the frame surface to cut new threads in the frame. Once you have the threads cut, use a fine-cut file to knock off the wire edge on the inside of the magazine well (the burr) where the tap cut through. Then, install the new bushing the same way you'd have replaced one that loosened or a new one on a new frame in a build project.

If your frame is stainless steel or nickel, you have no choice: you will use the blued bushing that Brownells provides as the oversized bushing.

## BIG TROUBLE

What if the stripped bushing you must replace is already oversized? Alas, Brownells does not make a 2X oversized tap and bushing set. You're in deep water. I can see a few solutions to this problem (which only happens once or twice in America each year as a SWAG). You will need the services of a professional pistolsmith familiar with the problem. They may use a low-temperature silver solder to hold the old bushing in place. The exacting ones will high-temp solder it in place, then machine or file it flush, drill and re-tap the tube to the original thread pattern, and install a fresh, correct-sized bushing.

I must warn you that anyone skilled enough to accomplish this—you don't want the unskilled "learning" on such a project—will charge you as nearly as much as a vanilla-plain new frame would cost. So why do it? Well, if the original frame represents a considerable investment in custom work already—checkering, mag funnel work, fitting the frame and slide to a perfect fit—then re-doing all that work on a new frame would be cost-prohibitive. And, in some jurisdictions (California-stan, we're looking at you), replacing a frame may not be easy, advisable, or even possible.

Brace yourself! Finding someone up to the task won't be easy. They will be backlogged to forever. They will charge exorbitantly. It will be worth it.

## MAGAZINE CATCH

There's not much to be done with the magazine catch or crucial details to know. You can swap it out for a taller one or a larger bolt-on head. We used to make extended magazine catches the hard way: We'd take the catch out of the frame, remove the spring and retainer by rotating the retainer and relaxing the spring, lock the mag catch in the lathe (obviously, professional pistolsmiths or advanced hobbyists only), and dress the grooved surface of the button down until smooth. We'd remove it from the lathe and put a piece of rod steel in the lathe, cut off a section of rod larger in diameter than the mag button and a bit longer than we wanted the finished product.

*The plunger tube usually has two holes for stacking studs. Caspian has milled a slot, so it has a bit more support. M-Guns has a better idea.*

The following steps: Degrease the parts and apply flux to the bonded surfaces. Heat up and silver-solder the extension onto the magazine button. Once cool, clean off the scale and lock it in the lathe again. Dress to the proper mag button diameter, and trim smooth for length. Reassemble and install in the frame, and lay the pistol down on the left side for a quick test. If the mag button touches the tabletop, remove and shorten it in the lathe until it has clearance. Why? Because in a match with a "table start" (where your pistol, loaded or not, rests on a table at the beginning of a stage, not in your holster), if the button touched the tabletop when you grabbed it, you risked depressing the button enough to release the magazine, which resulted in an embarrassing malfunction right from the beginning of the stage.

That's a lot of work, but that's what we did then.

Today, you can buy them oversized, even with a wider head bolted on after installation. If you do that, use a drop of blue Loctite. If you use something stronger than blue Loctite, you'll have to remove the mag catch sooner or later, and the task will be difficult. If you don't use Loctite, it will loosen and drop off with use.

## MAGAZINE CATCH EXCESSES

In rare instances, you may notice that magazines don't fall free when you press the magazine button. There is one of two causes, with different solutions. (Do this test with the slide removed and the magazine empty.) Lock a mag in place. Press the button and hold it down. Does the magazine fall free of its own weight? If so, your job is done. If the magazine falls a short distance, stops, and falls again when you release the button, you have an overtravel problem. Solve it by carefully polishing the left-side curve of the magazine button where it presses on the magazine tube. What's happening is the button travels too far when you push it, trapping it in place by pressing the button against it on the left side. Polishing can solve that, but there's a better way.

The inner diameter of the mag catch spring should not be any larger than .091 inch. From McMaster-Carr, order a packet of hard wear-resistant 52100 alloy steel balls, catalog number 9528K52, a package of 100 steel spheres of .083-inch diameter (with shipping, $10 or so). I wish you could order fewer, but that's the smallest amount I've found.

Reassemble your mag catch by inserting the spring, then drop one of the steel balls down the interior of the spring. Now press the retaining rod in and rotate it into the locking slot. You may ask, "What if I've gone too far, and the one I've used is too big? I'll never get it out of the frame, right?" Nope. If the one you've used is too big, you won't be able to get the retaining rod in and rotate it into the slot. The ball reduces the distance the mag button can be pushed into the frame and will probably solve your problem. Even if it doesn't solve it entirely, it should reduce the binding so any drag on the mag is unnoticeable.

The second problem is a bit more involved. Here, the flat face of the magazine button, the part inside the magazine well, is rubbing on the front face of the magazine tube. The solution is to remove the mag button, clamp it in your vise with padding so you don't mar it, and remove a slight amount of steel. All you want to do is polish the flat of the magazine button (and you'll probably only have to do this to the very center of the flat, where the radius of the mag tube bears on it) to allow mags to fall. You could find that the surface of the mag button, where the mag tubes bear, has been rubbed enough to remove blueing or scrub the stainless, so you'll know exactly where to do this.

Use a fine-cut file, crocus cloth, a hard backer, or even a careful application with a Dremel tool and a polishing bob. This is also a "hit and fit" process. If your mag button binds on magazines, test all of them and use the one that does it the worst as your test case. Take the button out of the frame, do some polishing, put it back, and test the worst binding mag sample. Once the worst mag falls free, the rest will as well. Job done.

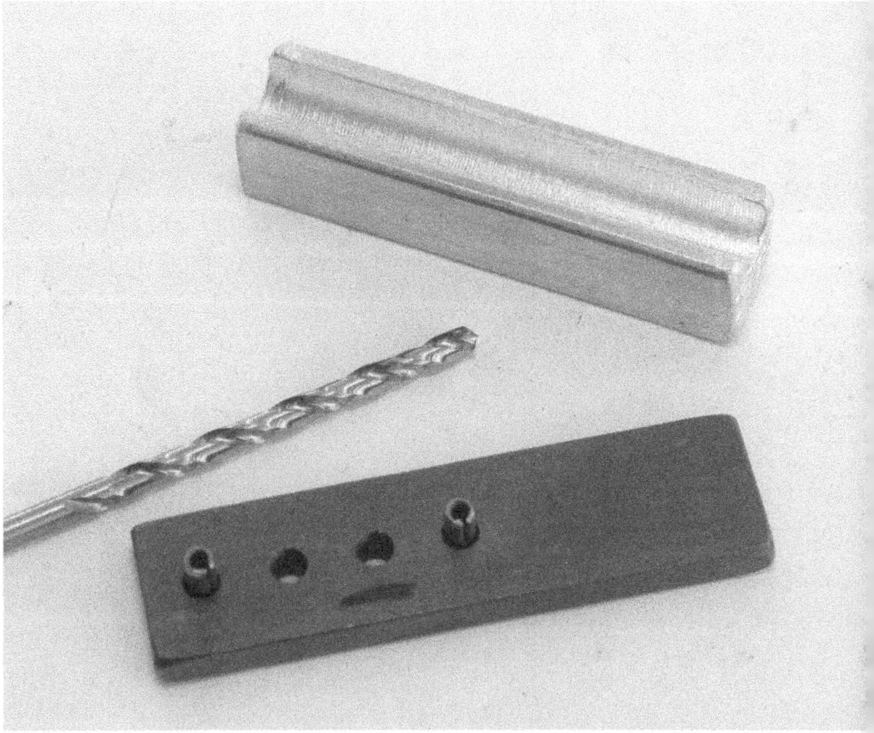

*The M-Guns locating fixture and drill. Clamp the fixture in place (the existing holes locate it), then drill the extra holes. The curved block on top is the outside support when staking the studs.*

## PLUNGER TUBE

We could call it by a more specific name, but since it is the only plunger tube in the 1911, more verbiage is unnecessary. So, plunger tube it is. It's the tube on the left side holding the two plungers and spring. These plungers bear on the slide stop lever and the thumb safety. We'll cover each function in the safety- and barrel-fitting sections, but for now, we're concerned solely with the tube itself.

It is a steel tube of intricate manufacture secured to the frame using brute force. The tube has a curved exterior with a flat face against the frame. On its obverse are two hollow studs. To secure it to the frame, the manufacturer drills a pair of holes through the frame, presses the tube onto the frame with the studs entering the frame holes, and stakes the studs from the inside. This simple process seems to have been too intricate for some manufacturers at times. There were periods of Colt manufacture when they would routinely come loose.

I solved the problem one way; my friend Ned Christiansen solved it another way.

My solution was to use a ball-end carbide cutter in a Dremel tool. I would reach down into the magazine well with the cutter and cut a relief funnel into the holes in the frame at the edge of the magazine well wall. The relief angle would allow the open end of the plunger tube studs to expand to a broader flare and lock them into place more securely. This, combined with thorough degreasing and application of the strongest Loctite made—the dark green 680 Shaft and Bearing locker—meant they never came loose. Of course, it also meant that if the plunger got damaged in the future, the only way to remove it was to cut it off with a milling machine or surface grinder and punch out

*If using the Nedster four-stud plunger, drill two more holes using the provided guide plate. Photo: Ned Christiansen*

the stubs of the locking studs.

Ned's solution was two-fold. One, he makes a tougher plunger tube. It is made with a thicker wall and out of more robust steel, and I'm not sure you can damage it short of using a ball-peen hammer. And he makes it with four studs, not two. Two are the original holes, with two more evenly spaced. This design requires a fixture to drill the two extra holes and is a pistolsmith-level upgrade, but if I were building a fighting pistol with no detail left untouched, it would have a Nedster plunger tube on it. Of course, if you have one on your 1911, and something goes horribly wrong and has to come off, you can still install a standard two-plunger.

What happens when the plunger tube comes loose? And why doesn't the grip keep it from coming loose? The last part first: the grip simply doesn't have the mechanical strength or leverage to keep that from happening. You'd have to make the grips out of aluminum or steel and fit them so they bear hard on the plunger tube. That would put more stress on the top grip screw, which was not designed for the task. No, it isn't the solution.

When the plunger tube comes loose, it lets the rear plunger ride up over the thumb safety plate, binds the safety and keeps it from working. If the plunger loosens when the safety is on, you won't be able to get it off. If it comes loose when the safety is off, you won't be able to get it back on.

How likely is this to happen? Not very. When I was gunsmithing, I encountered it maybe half a dozen times in 20 years, in working on the carry guns of customers in and around Detroit and on competition guns of high-volume shooters. It isn't common, but it is a hassle when it happens and will require some work and special tools to fix. As a data point, I found that the pliers tool to swage the plunger tube stud wasn't up to the task. Instead, I cut the recess, Loctited the parts, and used a bar-with-a-pointed-stud tool and a good-sized ball-peen hammer to keep them on forever.

Even so, let's solve this once-in-a-lifetime problem. First, disassembly. With the pistol unloaded (which might be difficult if the plunger tube came loose when the pistol was loaded and the safety on), use a small screwdriver to press the plunger back into the tube enough to clear the safety. Move the safety to the center position and lift it out of the frame. This is enough of a hassle that you might need three hands. One approach I have taken when I didn't have an assistant is to lay the 1911 down on its right side and use a sandbag or a bag of lead shot as a clamp. I put the weight on the slide forward of the trigger area and could compress the plunger with one hand and remove the safety with another. You could do the same by clamping it in a padded vise, but getting an angle of approach for your hands and seeing things wasn't as easy for me as having it flat on the bench.

Detail strip the frame. Clamp the frame in a padded vise just below the top grip screw bushing. To avoid squishing the frame, you don't need or want much force. With a large pair of bull-nose pliers, grab the plunger tube and wrestle it off the frame. No, you're not going to salvage it. I've tried that, and the repaired plunger tube didn't last. Plus, I've talked to other pistolsmiths with the same experience. Once the locking stud (either of the two) weakens and loosens, you can't re-stake it.

Now, use your Dremel with a ball-end cutter or small-diameter grinding ball to relieve the edge of the stud hole on the inside of the frame. Check the fit of your new plunger tube, make it fit flush, apply Loctite, and stake it. As mentioned, I found the pliers not up to the task and used the staking bar, but not according to the instructions. Instead, lay the frame on its side with the plunger tube below in its holding form. Stick the staking bar the length of the magazine well and hold the bottom end of the bar up against the upper edge of the frame. The bar staking cone now rests in the stud opening so you can strike the end of the bar down toward the benchtop briskly—maximum staking force. None ever failed once installed that way.

*The four-stud plunger tube, with the holes drilled, is ready to be staked in place. Photo: Ned Christiansen*

## EJECTORS

We're now up to the top deck of the frame and the ejector. This is as

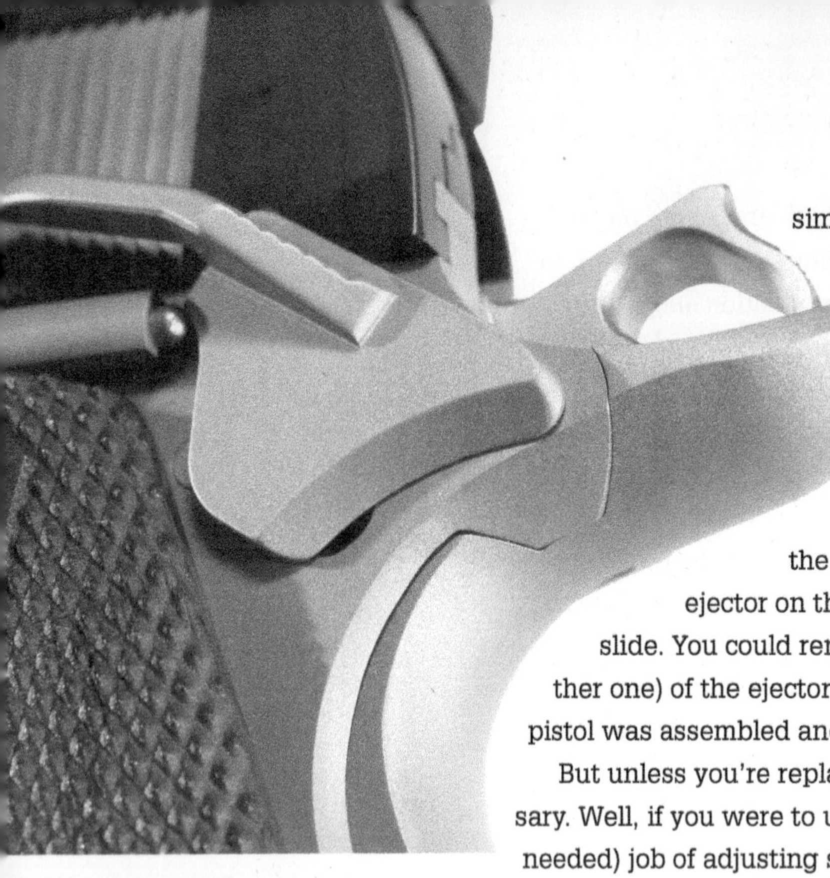

*The fit of this grip safety to the frame, along with everything else, is superb.*

simple a part as you'll ever find on a Browning design, and even at that, it has "belt-and-suspenders" smarts. The ejector has two legs inserted into holes drilled down on the frame's top deck. One of those legs has a notch, and a cross pin holds the ejector in place. When on the frame, the slide keeps the cross pin in place and the ejector on the frame—the ejector rides in a slot in the slide. You could remove the cross pin and break off one (either one) of the ejector legs, and it would stay in place when the pistol was assembled and still do its job.

But unless you're replacing it, removing the ejector is unnecessary. Well, if you were to undertake the onerous (and these days not needed) job of adjusting slide-to-frame fit, you'd have to remove the ejector. But that's another chapter and a task of more than a small chunk of time and effort.

To replace, use a drift punch less than the pin spec of .063 inch to drift the locking pin out. It should not be under much, if any, tension, so you might even be able to push the pin out without tapping the punch with a hammer. This is a small-diameter punch, so be gentle, or you'll bend or break it. Once the lock pin is removed, lift the ejector out of the frame. After years or decades of shooting, carbon, petrified oil, lint, dust, dirt, grit and even some rust might make it challenging to lift out. The easy way is to clamp the frame muzzle-end up in your vise *on the ejector*. Then, tap the frame with a rawhide mallet or plastic-faced hammer to free it.

*The grip safety keeps the trigger from bouncing and tripping the sear so it won't discharge when dropped. This is how you test it: with an unloaded 1911.*

Check the new ejector for fit. It should just slip down into the frame holes. If not, the best approach is penetrating oil and compressed air. The oil loosens the gunk, and the air jets it out. (Make sure it isn't pointed toward you as the gunk comes out with vigor.) Or, force it in, tapping it into place with your plastic-faced hammer. Do this only if it starts and is snug on sliding the rest of the way in.

If it doesn't go flush, you have another step: use a drill bit larger than the hole and rotate it clockwise by hand to bevel the ejector pin hole on the top deck. You can always remove the new one as you removed the old one. More likely, it will be slightly loose. Not a problem. It'll still work loose, and the locking pin will remove some slop. If being loose bothers you, carefully bend the longer leg, providing some friction in the fit. Do this carefully. It's absurdly easy to bend it too much. You'll have to bend it back, and if you overdo that, you weaken the leg, which will break and have to be replaced.

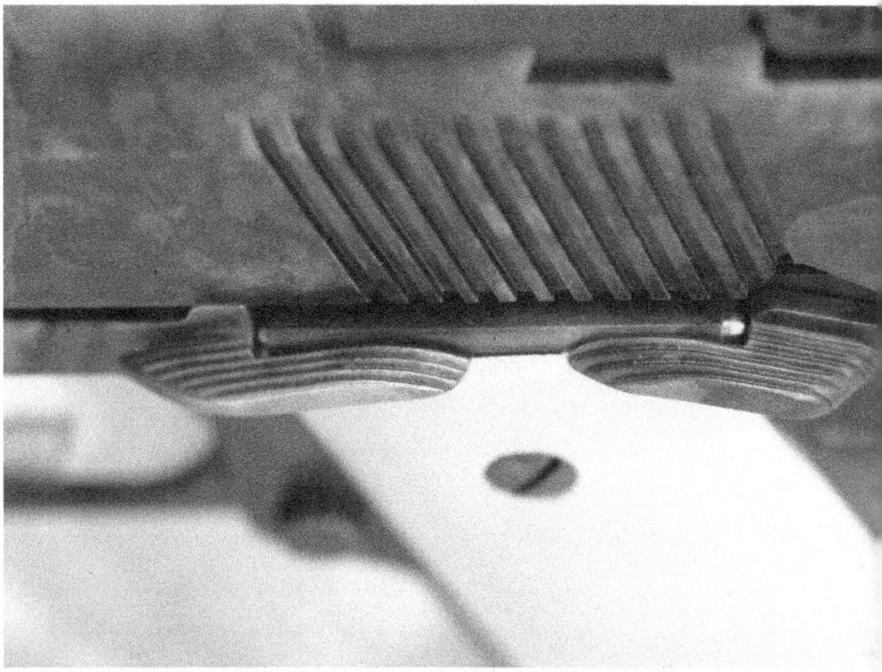

*Avoid an extended slide stop lever. It'll hook on your clothes, add mass that creates problems, and be ugly. Oh, they were a fad in the 1980s, but so were shoulder pads, big hair, and two-day stubble.*

If the new ejector's leg is too large to fit the frame hole, clamp it in your vise (padded or some other protection) and use an abrasive cloth to polish it with a shoeshine motion. This is yet another "cut and try" process, although it is polish and try here. Polish, check the fit, and keep at it. Turn the ejector over each time and check that you're polishing it evenly, not just on one side.

## EJECTOR HORROR STORY

A customer tried to install an extended ejector. It wouldn't fit, so he thought he'd drill the hole in the frame to match. He did everything right except for the idea of actually doing it: he measured the ejector leg, found the right-sized drill, and even used a drill press. It was all hopeless, though, because the drill grabbed the sides of the existing hole, seized and snapped off. My first thought was to have my welding guy weld onto the protruding drill stub so I could back it out. "Nope, not gonna weld on that," was his reply.

Sigh. I told the customer he was in for a hefty charge because this would involve open heart surgery. The frame was, of course, a fully-customized one (ca. 1988, if you're curious) and a replacement was out of the question.

I took it in several steps: First, I used a carbide endmill to mill right at the side of the ejector (with not much room, so a small, delicate cutter) until I could free the stub. Since the disconnector hole was right next to it, I had to come in from the magazine well side. Once free, I could make a new slot, fit a piece of steel to fill the gap, and low-temperature silver solder it.

What remained was the work of filing the filler flush with the top deck and with the magazine well opening. Then, I had to drill a new hole at the correct diameter (the blueprints call for it to be .1245 to .1270 inch, which is a 1/8-inch drill bit) and polish the leg of the new ejector to fit.

Don't be that guy.

OK, fitting the locking pin. Use your dial calipers and measure the distance down from the top deck of the frame to the ejector pin hole at its center. Now, measure the distance below the bottom edge of the ejector. Use your round diamond file to file a groove in the leg at that point. Use the old ejector as a guide. File lightly, press the ejector into the frame, and attempt to push the locking pin across. If it won't go (try it from the left side, so you have enough pin to hold on to as you try), pull out the locking pin, remove the ejector and file the leg a bit more.

Once it fits, push the locking pin in flush on both sides, and the job is done.

If you are considering using a drill, re-read the horror story above.

## GOVERNMENT AND COMMANDER MODELS

*The Commander ejector rides closer to the centerline than the Government ones.*

One more detail: while ejectors can be had in various lengths, from the angled GI to extended for ferocious ejection, they also differ between commander- and government-sized and smaller calibers. The Commander and smaller ones have the ejector built to ride more toward the centerline than the .45 ones. I assume this was an outgrowth of the .38 Super back in 1929. The smaller-diameter .38 Super would be right on the margin of ejecting were it built with a .45 ejector. So, Colt put it closer to the centerline. As far as the Commanders go, I figure that came about because Colt was trying to entice the Army into 9mm 1911s as replacements after WWII.

Your ejector configuration has to match your slide slot geometry, or it won't work. So, if you plan on having a switch-top 1911 with a .45 and a .38 Super upper (possible with an integrally ramped barrel), you'll also have to swap ejectors each time.

## FRAMES

An article in *Machinery* magazine, December 1942, lists the receiver

of the 1911A1 as being made out of SAE 1035 steel. Those familiar with steel alloys will read that and react, "What? Really?" because 1035 is an alloy of steel that was then, and is now, about as common as dirt. It is carbon steel and contains .6 to .9 percent Manganese, less than .05 percent Sulphur, and less than .045 percent Phosphorus. Its carbon content is between .31 and .38 percent, with a tensile strength of 84,000 psi. It can be formed cold-drawn or hot-rolled with no extra corrosion resistance or alloying additions for improved machining. It can be hardened up to about Rockwell B of 89, which means in a thin-wall segment, you can practically bend it with your bare hands.

*The newest thing on 1911 frames (not really the newest, but a must-have in a makers' lineup) is the accessory rail—a place to put a light or laser.*

If it is such a plain steel, why make 1911s out of it? Because it forges well, machines relatively easily, has decent abrasion resistance and stands up to impact stress. And, in 1910, when Browning was finalizing the pistol, 1035 was a damn fine steel. It isn't his fault that the automotive industry went crazy in improving steel today, so we are accustomed to everything being high-alloy this-or-that. The standards have shifted so much that 1035 isn't alloyed enough to be considered a low-alloy steel. Attempting to heat-treat a frame of 1035 would be a waste of time, as the gains would not be worth the effort, assuming there *were* any gains.

Today, a manufacturer would use something more alloyed than 1035, if only because alloy steels have alloying constituents in their content, making it faster and smoother to CNC machine and thus less expensive on the tooling. A small thing, but a profitable operation is made up of a large number of small things, and the more you can bend to your benefit, the better. So, if you're machining forgings, you'd go with what the forge company recommends. If cutting from billet, use a pre-hardened plate that cuts to a smooth finish, and if casting—some frames were cast, even into the 2010s, like the Remington R1—then use whatever alloy cast to the smoothest finish desired on the unmachined final surfaces.

For making frames today, it is more a matter of the engineers and machinists' art than "Which alloy works best?"

It's all the same for us, as you will be using your home milling machine (If you have one) or files, Dremel and crocus cloth, and the differences between alloys won't matter. And you'll probably have it hard-chrome plated or DLC-treated once done.

## MORE ON FRAME SIZES AND TYPES

As a review and expansion of the frame size discussion from Chapter 4, the original is the Government Model, the 5-inch barrel, and the one against which all others are compared. The frame is a flat plate; the rails are the same width as the frame body—not smaller or larger. The blueprints show it to be .751 -.003 inch wide, but that varies. I've seen them as wide as .755 and as small as 747 inch. I suspect some makers (mainly in the past) simply used whichever plate steel they could source, and the steel supplier's tolerances determined the dimension to which they machined their slide rail slots. The rails and frame width are the same for all models and caliber of the single stack, with one exception: railed receivers.

Let's get one bit of 1911 lingo out of the way: the 1911 frame has rails. But a "railed receiver" has an accessory rail on the dust cover. So, before we delve into the various frames, let's get the accessory rail out of the way.

## RAILED RECEIVERS

If you want to put a light or laser on your pistol, the modern way is to slip it onto the rail built into the receiver. The 1911 wasn't made originally with rails. When lights became the new thing, various 'smiths worked on attachment methods. One, Dave Dawson, developed a small rail bolted to the bottom of the dust cover to attach a light. The problem was that it had to be attached, and it was proprietary. Dawson Precision made it, and if you wanted one, you had to have Dawson make and install it. Or, your gunsmith could acquire a rail from Dawson or make one.

The next step was to knock off the "Picatinny" rail (so named because Picatinny Arsenal adopted it, not because it designed it) and bolt an adapter to the dust cover. The Rail Wars heated up so quickly that it seemed like overnight every pistol had a "Pic" rail, and 1911s had to keep up. The problem was that it required significant changes. If you were building your 1911s from forgings, you had to have a die sinker

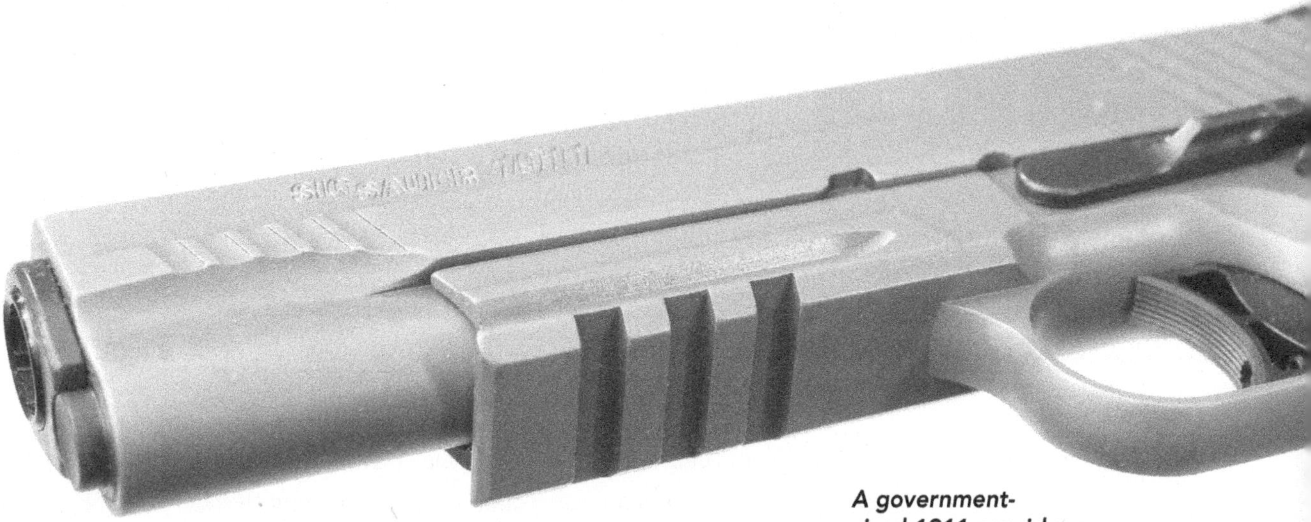

A government-sized 1911 provides a lot of rail for your accessories. So you can fit pretty much any one of them you wish.

update an old (or new) forge die set to include enough metal for a rail. If working from plate/billet, you had to order new stock thick enough to handle the extra width of the Pic rail. Casters had the same sort of problem as forgers. Then, you had to update your cutter paths on the CNC machining stations to carve the rail out of the forging or billet.

Today, it's just another option on a model array or a box to tick on a custom order/build.

While we're at it, let's also look at the heavy dust cover timeline. The original dust cover was machined as a shroud to keep the recoil spring from escaping and gunk from entering the system. If you change the cutter paths and don't carve as much steel away, you have a heavier dust cover, adding weight forward of your hands and below the bore. This was something done in two areas: competition and custom guns. USPSA shooters building Limited division guns on 2011 frames often opted for the full-width, full-size, and full-length dust cover. More weight was more better. In the custom arena, Les Baer made his Heavyweight. At the max, it was the Heavyweight Monolith, with the frame full width, length, and width, and the slide not cut for front flutes.

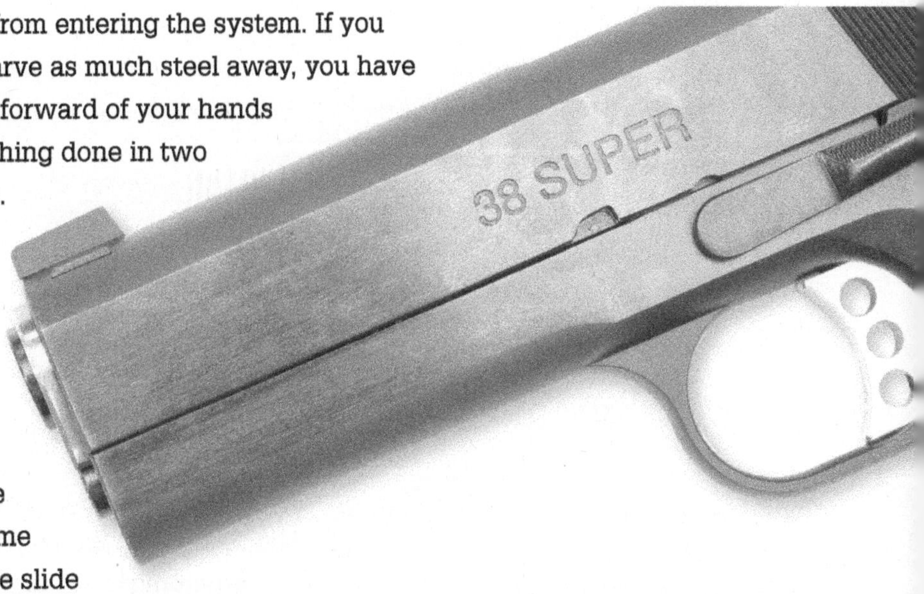


The full-length dust cover, the Monolith, from Les Baer.

Competition and custom are now a box to tick on an order or build. That's how progress works; in America, you can get what you want.

## BACK TO FRAMES

When it came time for Colt to make the Commander, it wanted a shorter barrel. But that required some changes, some of which we cover in the barrel and slide chapters. In the frame, Colt drilled the recoil spring tunnel deeper to give the slide enough travel and shorten the recoil spring hoop. The frame part, the recoil system abutment, was machined .100 inch farther to the rear than the Government Model. Colt also shortened the dust cover, so the slide/barrel assembly on a Government Model and a Commander are not interchangeable. You can cause some real operational and service life problems by mixing components, and this was a situation custom pistolsmiths had to deal with when building compensated pistols. It was not uncommon in the early days for someone to want a commander-length slide on their "compgun" because they wanted it to be faster, have less recoil, or handle and balance better.

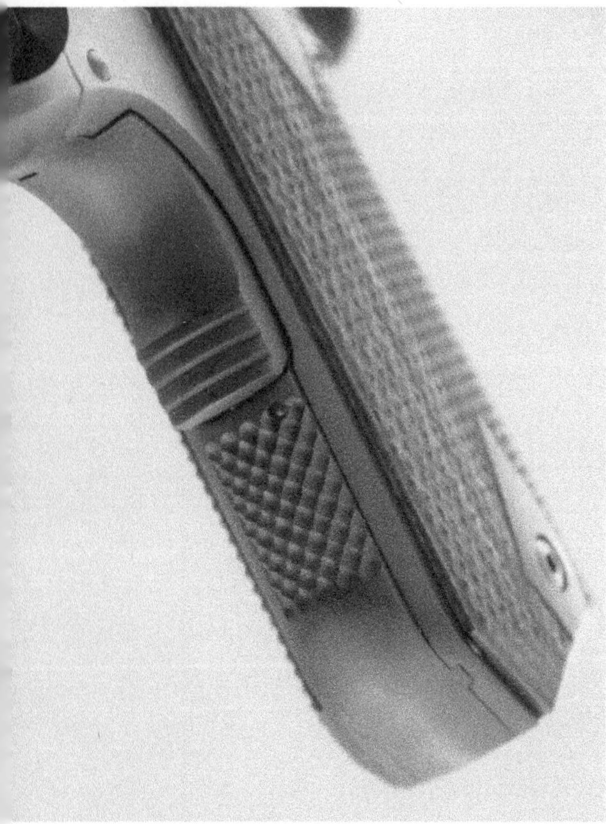

The 1911 "bobtail" rounded frame makes it more concealable.

Fitting a government-length barrel into a commander-length slide meant some changes, almost as many as chopping a Government slide to commander-length. Either way, the recoil spring and guide rod system must be rebuilt to match. The differences also carried over to the bushing, which is shorter in its skirt so it won't bind on the barrel, and the front of the barrel chamber reinforcement is also shorter.

So, in summary, you can't mix and match Government and Commander slides, frames, barrels, and bushings.

## BOBTAIL

In 1911, when it was going to be a Cavalry sidearm and an Army backup, that didn't matter. Men's clothing was much heavier than it is today. You could get away with packing a Government Model without people noticing. The exemplar is the movie "The Maltese Falcon," where people are packing all sorts of ordnance, and no one notices until they produce the same. Now, not so much. One way around that is the bobtail, where the frame is rounded.

Rounding the frame also required the mainspring housing to be changed, the retention pin moved, and the interior altered since there was less room. But it does make for a more concealable pistol. However, some shooters find it changes the frame enough to affect their grip, so you should test-fire one with a bobtail frame before you invest in one. You might not like it, and it would be an economic hit to find out *after* buying it.

## FRAME FRONTSTRAPS

With your 1911 in hand, look at the line of the frame from the dust cover down along the triggerguard and the frontstrap. In the original, and all Colts, those three lengths (dust cover, triggerguard, frontstrap) were machined to three different radii. That is, the curve of the cupped cutter differed for each one.

Once the frame comes out of the forge or the casting annex, the CNC (back in previous days, a fixture in a manual mill) had a single radius of cutter pulled along the entire length. This left the frontstrap and dust cover with an exterior radius that did not match the interior; the larger external radius left the frontstrap bulkier. We called those the "fat frame" guns, and the early Springfield Armory series were the primary ones. Well, *primary* in that the sheer volume of Springfield guns, compared to others, meant you'd see more of them.

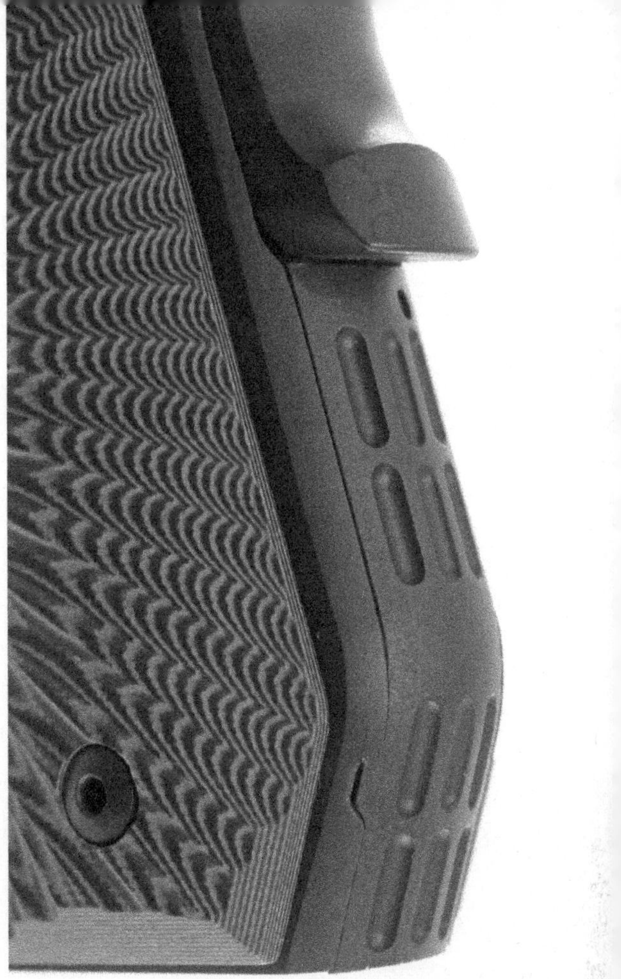

***The bobtail, a rounded-end 1911 frame, makes it easier to conceal. The round surface is less likely to catch on clothing, and it prevents drape. The traction grooves on this Tisas 1911 also prevent a shirt or coat from draping.***

If you have a fat-frame 1911, an old Springfield or something newer, it will slightly complicate your home gunsmithing. A pro will chalk it up to an extra hour of work, which we'll get into in a bit.

One of the details that wasn't a big deal years ago, but is for many now, is the radius of the curve blending the frontstrap to the triggerguard. When shooters fired one-handed and only one-handed, it was fine. When shooting speed became a measure, getting your hand higher on the frame became more critical. That larger radius pushed your hand down. So, it became customary for custom pistolsmiths to "lift" the frontstrap or "undercut" the triggerguard.

## LIFT THAT CURVE

Early on, pistolsmiths had individual ideas of how to do it and what looked good. (Oh, you'd better believe that for what we were charging back then, customers cared a lot about what looked good.) Much of that went away when Colt started offering undercut triggerguards, which it did using the most straightforward method (the ugliest, to many eyes), but it became the default standard.

If you have a milling machine, the process is simple: use a fixture or do a lot of indicting with levels and dial indicators, and lay the frame on its side on the mill table, flat and level. Indicate the frontstrap to be straight in line with the table travel. Lock a ¾-inch endmill in the chuck. Fire it up to the appropriate rpm, and index the cutter to the face of the frontstrap. Move the cutter toward the rails, milling a dished section of the frame radius. How much? Enough to matter, but not so much to weaken the frame. This is a matter of taste and wall thickness, and unless you're doing it as a production operation on 50 frames per hour, there is no "cut X hundredths of an inch" measurement.

Colt cut, used whatever tumbling machine it used to clean the sharp edges off the machined frames, and called it done. What some pistolsmiths did, to Colts and others, was to get out the Dremel or big files and put a secondary radius on the cut, smoothing out the corner edges of the machined dish. Those lacking a milling machine did the whole thing with a Dremel and files, working until it looked and felt right.

Today, so many come with a lifted frontstrap in various styles that it's just another feature. If you want to try it, do not use a USGI gun. But there is a bunch of steel, relatively speaking, in there, so you can have at it and not worry too much about weakening the frame.

*Checkering has come a long way. This was high-end checkering when it was done in the late 1980s. Today, it shows a lot of work left undone and details that need to be cleaned up.*

## CHECKERING

Pour more of whatever you're drinking and settle into your chair because this will get long and involved. The original 1911 was smooth. No checkering, no grooves, no nothing on the frame, just checkered grips. In adopting the 1911A1, the mainspring housing not only got arched but also grooved. Bullseye shooters did some non-slip grip work on some of their pistols, but they could not on the Service Pistol because the issue guns didn't have it, so such external changes were disqualifying. However, the Any Centerfire and .45 softball gun sometimes received it. The customary one was called "tiger's tooth" or other names.

The pistolsmith used a sharp center punch and hammer. He'd slide a mandrel into the magazine well to support the steel and whack the punch into the frontstrap to create a burr, which kicked up a curl of steel. Since there was no such thing as "on the draw" in Bullseye, it didn't take many of these burrs to create

a non-slip surface for one-handed shooting. For IPSC, this didn't do enough. The constant draws rubbed the curls off. The few and far-between (relatively speaking) burrs didn't provide enough grip, so the frontstraps were checkered.

*A frame being checkered, where the center lines have been established. Note the flat plate on the side as a guide for the file, which keeps it straight as the first cuts are made. Photos: Jason Burton*

Checkering is simple: file rows of V-shaped grooves with other grooves at a right angle, creating rows of pyramids. These are denoted by how many rows per inch have been filed. So, 20-lpi checkering is 20 lines per inch, which, if correctly done, is incredibly aggressive. Made with even and sharp points, 20 lpi will almost draw blood.

*All vertical lines have been established; now it's time to do the horizontal ones.*

The customary method is a checkering file made to the desired lpi pitch out of file-hard steel. We'll learn how to do that shortly, but first, we need more background.

The traditional file pitches are 30 and 40 lpi. The 30 lpi pitch was done on the frontstraps of 1911s to show off one's skill as a pistolsmith, as making the rows and crosses that fine was much more difficult than 20 lpi. And it provided a less aggressive but still plenty of non-slip surface. Also, 30 lpi was the standard for the Browning Hi Power, as there wasn't enough wall thickness on its frame to withstand 20 lpi; 40 lpi was reserved for the back of the slide, creating a non-glare matte surface for improved aiming.

## HOW TO CHECKER

OK, are you sure you want to do this? Really? A hot tip: if you start and it doesn't go well, this will get ugly. While learning to checker, I bought used shotgun barrels and practiced on them. So, if you want to do it or know how it is done, here we go:

You'll need a checkering file, a following file, a frame mandrel, and a checkering guide. A file card or needle pointer and filing chalk will prove useful. Before we begin, you will have to make some cosmetic decisions. You will checker the frontstrap fully side-to-side. However, you'll need to decide what to do at the top and bottom. If you checker all the way down and "out" of the frame, it will be easier, but it might not appear professional. If you will stop, you'll have to indicate your stop point so you don't file down past that point, similarly, at the top. You must have a stop point so your checkering ends evenly and cleanly.

*If you're going to have a checkered frontstrap, you need a checkered magazine button.*

Use your dial or digital calipers to measure the width of your frame. Divide that in half, and scribe your index line down the center of the frontstrap. Put the frame on the mandrel and clamp the mandrel in your vise so you can comfortably work on the frontstrap. Clamp the file guide on the frame and adjust it until one row of the file (I used the outmost row, not any inside the cutting face of the file) bears directly on the index line. Carefully push the file forward, cutting a single groove on the index line. You will have filed a groove deep enough to be self-guiding in a short time (which will seem like forever as you're learning).

Remove the guide, and using the index groove, tip the file slightly and begin cutting the next groove. Once that groove is deep enough, tip to the next groove and repeat the process until it feels like your fingers will fall off and your hands cramp up. I'm not kidding. This process is hard work, requiring a strong grip, a careful eye and patience. Do not try to bring each groove to a sharp point.

Once you have a complete set of grooves vertically across the face of the frontstrap, install the guide again. Start at the bottom or the top, at your stop point. Follow the same process, establishing a self-indexing groove and work your way up.

You will reach the point where you have a complete set of grooves in both directions, but not sharp, ending in various-sized flat-topped pyramids. Now, the really fussy work begins. Use your following file to deepen the grooves until they are sharp points on the tips, with evenly crossed grooves on the bottom. Making a non-slip pattern isn't enough: you will be judged—and you *will* be judged—on the grooves' evenness and the points' regularity and sharpness. As the rows come around toward the sides close to the grips, you cannot make them disappear under the grips. The curve of the frontstrap will end at the flat of the frame, where your checkering ends. The location of this line is beyond your control. Depending on how well the manufacturer made the frame, you might have a clean line, a half-set of pyramids, or a line of checkering that tapers off, top or bottom, of the frame.

Checkering used to take a lot of work; it meant many hours of fussing over points and grooves, and we charged a lot of money to do it. As I recall, my last price list had a 20-lpi checkering job charged at $250 in 1993; 30 lpi was $325.

All that is history due to CNC machining. The CNC process doesn't use a checkering file but a cutting wheel with a 60-degree groove as the cutting tip. OK, a bit of machine tool lingo and info here. The cutter you think of as a milling machine cutter, which looks like a fat drill, is called an endmill or endmill cutter. Like a drill, you can cut straight down with it, but it's designed to cut to the side. One with a round end is called a ball-end cutter and can be a hemisphere or have a flat end and rounded corners—the desired cut dictates the shape. On the frontstrap and the "fat frame" ones we described earlier, imagine an endmill that is fatter to make it stronger, with a dished face that looks hourglass-shaped.

The "Woodruff" cutter is another type. Think of a shaft with a wheel on the end. The Woodruff cutter is used to mill a groove instead of using an endmill tip to cut. Why do it this way? The tool lasts longer between resharpening or replacement since there are more cutting edges on a Woodruff cutter. For checkering, take the Woodruff cutter, and instead of the edge shaped to cut a round-bottom or flat-bottom groove, angle it so it cuts a V-shaped groove. Voilà! You have a checkering tool.

The machine cuts a groove, lifts, moves over 1/20th of an inch, comes down, cuts another groove, and so on. The big hassle is fixturing and making the frontstrap a consistent surface. Also, because it is computerized, you can have any spacing you want. The compromise is 25 lpi: 20 lpi is too aggressive, and 30 lpi requires follow-up by hand, even with CNC. But 25 is machine-only, not overly aggressive, and looks good.

Computer Numerically Controlled machining also opened up other approaches. Since it is simply a matter of what kind of cutter you are using and what kind of spacing you use, you can cut pretty much any pattern you want, and as long as it provides a non-slip surface, you're good to go. And the patterns are many.

One of the earliest approaches to a CNC-cut non-slip pattern was made by Colt, which machined vertical grooves down the centerline of the frontstrap. It worked, and for the time, it was a good approach for a factory-done method. But pistolsmiths hated it because making hand-checkering fit into and onto the Colt grooves was always a hassle. They weren't always centered on the frontstrap—that mattered when you got over to the edges of the frame side flats—and not quite 20 lpi.

Now, you can get many checkering options on factory-built guns. Oh, and if you want hand-cut checkering, Les Baer still offers it. He has an employee who loves doing it, and as long as that (or another) employee is up for the work, Les will offer it.

## CHECKERED MAINSPRING HOUSINGS

Checkering the mainspring housing is so easy that new 'smiths learned by checkering it first. The vertical grooves are already done for you. Today, if you want a checkered M-S, you can easily select from dozens of them, in blue or stainless, in the checkering pattern you prefer. You can even buy an inexpensive one with cast-in checkering and learn to chase the grooves with a finishing file to sharpen them. For the practice value, you might even want to get the least-expensive, roughest-appearing M-S available and get a feel for filing by cleaning it up and fitting it to your 1911.

The checkering part is easy. The only tricky thing is getting the horizontal grooves you'll be filing (on a standard M-S) precisely square to the existing grooves. Here's how. Start your index groove, tip to the second, and work down to the bottom. Follow up with the finishing file and clean up all the grooves.

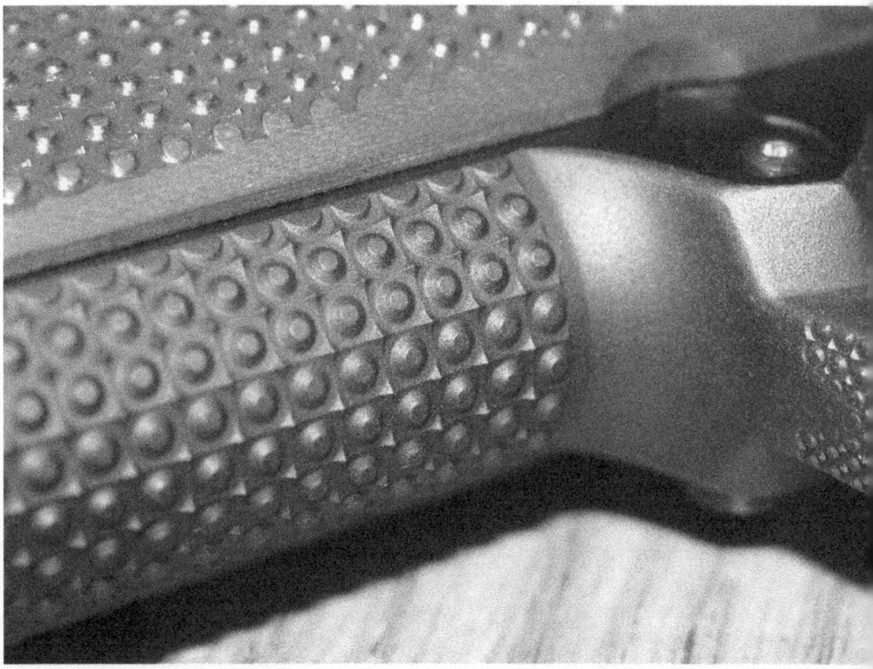

*One of the cleverest and neatest non-slip treatments is Conamyds by Ned Christiansen.*

If you look at a checkered mainspring housing and notice that the outermost pyramids are rectangles, you are looking at a grooved M-S that got checkered. If the outermost pyramids are pyramids, that M-S either was an original grooved one that the person who checkered made pyramids, or it was a made-from-billet M-S (Wilson, Ed Brown, etc.) machine checkered.

## CHECKERING FAT FRAMES

If your 1911 is a fat frame, your checkering won't curve around and almost disappear under the grips. It will end at the corner of the frontstrap, "high" up from the grips. Can you reduce a fat frame? Yes, but unless you have a milling machine and have built a fixture to hold the frame, you won't get it done in less than several weekends of nothing but filing. Custom pistolsmiths look forward to a fat frame because, with machine tools and fixtures, they can lock it in and make the frontstrap straight, square, and even. This means their checkering is perfect, with no tapering-off lines or partial rows of pyramids.

If you think you can scribe a line on the flat and file the frontstrap even, I have to give you a heads up: this will be hours and hours of filing, and the last parts will require extreme care.

What makes checkering and other treatments work?

People will discuss the "grippiness" of this or that pattern and whether it works with soft office workers' hands or hard-callused farmers' hands, but the details are the same. A pattern increases in non-slip as the sharpness of its edges increases. So, a 20-lpi checkering job, with flat-topped pyramids and uneven edges, won't be as grippy (that's the term I'm going to use from this point forward) as a 30-lpi checkering job with razor-sharp edges.

The second detail is the depth. How far can your hand press into the pattern, creating what amounts to tread on a tire? Depth is the key to how dull 20-lpi checkering works so well, as the depth lets your hand sink in and resist slipping.

Last is the spacing. This attribute aids depth, and if unsharp or shallow grooves are spaced correctly, the effect increases grippiness.

## ED BROWN CHAIN LINK

Chain Link and many, if not all, of the custom patterns on the frontstrap, are now done via CNC patterns and individual cutters. The Woodruff cutter used here is our wheel, but the outside edge doesn't cut a flat-bottomed groove. Instead, it has a slight radius and cuts a round-bottom groove. Then, instead of pulling the cutting tool the entire length of the frontstrap, the guys at Ed Brown dip it, lift, move, dip it, move in an interrupted line. The following line is offset in the sequence of dips, so you have a regular pattern that creates a non-slip surface.

*An example of the Ned Christiansen Frag pattern. It provides a superb, non-slip surface. How does he do it? Exactingly. Photo: Ned Christiansen*

The Ed Brown pattern is proprietary, and you could (were you doing this cutting as a production process) adjust the side-to-side spacing of the cuts, the depth of the cuts, etc., to create this or any variant of the pattern.

That's precisely what several manufacturers have done, as the pattern is good-looking, easy on the hands, simple to cut, and doesn't take much time to produce, unlike machine-cut checkering.

## M-GUNS, CONAMYDS AND FRAG

Ned Christiansen has crafted some spectacularly exotic patterns, and they are all very good at being non-slip. The original exotic is what he termed "Conamyds." OK, the original, classic checkering is rows of pyramids, like the pyramids of Egypt, but row after row of them. Ned machined rows of cones, with the cutting head not cleaning the bases of the other cones that the machine cut entirely off. This created a pattern of cones with small conelets/pyramids in between them, the pattern of which will lock into your hand like you wouldn't believe. Unlike checkering, where you can lower the cutting head and run it along the surface, the cutting tool here is more like a chain link: it goes down to the surface, cuts one cone, lifts, steps over to the next location, lowers, cuts, lifts, and so on. Yowza, but what a pattern.

The next was easier to craft, looks notable, and locks on tight. Called Frag, it looks just like the surface of a WWII fragmentation grenade or "pineapple" grenade. Christiansen worked out the spacing, height, angle, and edge details. Unlike Conamyds, which are much more difficult to make, Frag was popular enough to be copied by several pistolsmiths and manufacturers.

Then, he developed Barb Wire. This pattern looks like short sections of, you guessed it, barbed wire, laid side by side, and again provides a non-slip surface. While it works as a non-slip pattern, it is undoubtedly distinctive, so it isn't for everyone. And, once it has been done, you can't cut some pattern over it and change it to a less cosmetic pattern. If this is what you want, remember this: like a tattoo, it is likely permanent.

## GOLF BALL

Let's take another tack. Remember that ball-end cutter I described? OK, take one that is smallish in diameter (¼ inch works well) and drop it onto the frontstrap in rows, overlapping each other, to produce a surface that looks like, you guessed it, the surface of a golf ball. Out of Rogers Precision (another pistolsmith who is booked apparently to the end of his working career), it's about as grippy as you can get, marrying the aggressiveness of 20-lpi checkering with the depth of Frag.

***The Golf Ball pattern is produced with a ball-end cutter touched down repeatedly until the pattern is complete.***

## SCALES

Ed Brown calls it Kobra, others snakeskin, or dragonskin; the appearance is just like scales. The process is to take the indexed and level frontstrap and tilt either the milling machine head or the table. Then, the endmill is brought to the surface, "kissed" into the frontstrap, lifted, moved, dropped to kiss again, and repeated. This is the kind of thing that CNC excels at. Could you do this by hand on a milling machine? Yes. Should you? Nope. Misread the measurements on one cut, and you have an oops that will be obvious.

## STAN CHEN

Stan Chen, to no great surprise, does things a bit differently. His ProTrac, or Progressive Traction Checkering, is not like others. First, his machined grooves are at a 60-degree angle, not square to the frontstrap. The pattern is centered on the frontstrap, creating the "X" pattern. He also uses the pattern on the mainspring housing, and if the pistol has a magazine funnel, the pattern goes right down onto the funnel extension. When you first handle a pistol with ProTrac, it might not seem all that grippy. But the depth of the cuts and the spacing lock it onto your hand. For those who do not have callused hands from working with tools, this is a way to get grippiness without the risk of bleeding.

*A frontstrap with the scale pattern Ed Brown calls Kobra; others describe it as dragonskin. Hundreds of individual plunge cuts by an endmill produce it; if you mess up on one, it will show. So this is done CNC.*

## STIPPLING

One of the old standards, stippling, is sometimes now seen done on the tops of slides to knock down glare. It is also the customary treatment of Browning Hi Powers, as their thin wall thickness makes deep checkering impossible. Stippling is easy, but it requires a learned hand. The best way to learn how to stipple is to buy a steel rod of ¾-inch diameter. You can also buy a used and abused shotgun barrel, and this will do as well.

The process requires a sharp, pointed punch and a way to re-sharpen it once it dulls, plus a ball-peen hammer, safety glasses, and a willingness to build hand strength through lots of hard work.

Clamp the part to be stippled in a padded vise (I used a shop cloth as padding). Brace your hand, holding the punch half an inch from the surface you wish to stipple. Put a bit of away-from-the-work tension in your hand. You do not want the point resting on the metal. Strike the punch with the hammer hard enough to drive it to the work and make a mark, but when the hammer bounces off, the punch comes away from the metal. In essence, that's it. All you have to do now is learn the details: how hard you strike determines the size and depth of the punch mark. Moving your hand distributes the punches across the surface. Not doing them in exact lines, so you have a random pattern, is another trick. Stopping and resting your hand so the punch doesn't slip and making a gouge instead of a strike is another thing you must learn by feel.

Practice on the bar or barrel, then once you have a feel for it, go to work on your frontstrap. One good thing about stippling that isn't possible with checkering is that you can re-do it. By the time you are halfway done with your frontstrap, you will likely have a good feel for the process and like the looks of your work. The scrap part you've already done at the beginning? It might look a bit ugly or amateurish. So go back and re-stipple it.

*The crack in the frame has been welded and dressed down. The unavoidable change in the crystalline structure of the steel shows the repair.*

## COSMETICS

What looks good? Well, in one way or another, it all looks good. However, some combinations are considered better than others. The lines, the finish, the checkering: some combinations are "just right," and some aren't. To take a page from automobiles, curb feelers are appropriate on a 1950s family car but not on a gull-wing Mercedes. That spoiler wing that fits onto a Plymouth or Ford muscle car from the late 1960s? Don't even think about putting it on a 1950s street rod.

A classic polished and blued Government Model cries out for 30-lpi checkering, not scales or golf balls. But a matte-Parkerized 1911 with an accessory rail will look odd with checkering and needs golf balls.

Each custom pistolsmith has his own "look and feel" (in the trademark and patent lingo), and once you learn who is who, you can glance at a pistol and be pretty sure about who made it.

## FRAME FAILURES

What breaks on a frame? Well, with enough shooting and abuse, pretty much everything. But then, that describes every other pistol out there, as well. There are a couple of known and relatively common use-related ones.

## DUST COVER CRACKS

Inside the recoil spring tunnel, the thicker portion of the frame blends into the thin tube we call the dust cover. It is not uncommon for high-

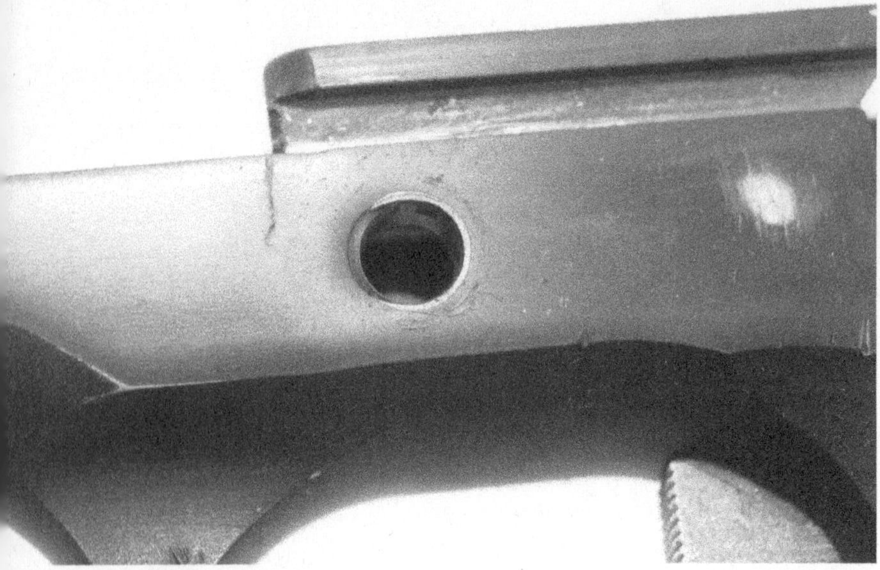

Sweeney's Lightweight Commander with a cracked frame. It's an aluminum frame, so there's no welding it. Not a problem; it was this cracked when he got it, and tens of thousands of rounds later, it hasn't cracked more.

mileage 1911s to show a crack there. How does this happen? Everyone has a pet theory, but it comes down to several potential causes. One is the blend has not been machined with a large enough radius, so the joint is a sharper corner than it should be. Sharp edges are stress-risers, which can lead to cracks with enough use. The other is dust cover flex. When the slide bottoms out, the frame is jolted to the rear, and the dust cover flexes down and up. (Down? Yes, when the slide hits, it jolts the frame back and pivots in your hand. This leaves the dust cover to catch up, flexing it down.)

Some people think the crack happens due to the dust cover not having enough vertical clearance, slapping it against the slide. Hmm. Others say it has too much clearance and can move up too much, magnifying the downward movement and making it a dual flex.

In any case, some dust covers will crack, and some won't. And some will crack quickly, while others take forever and forever. Question: is it a problem? Answer: only if you want it to be. The crack usually only goes so far and then stops. It happens more often on aluminum frames than steel and more often with .45 than 9mm.

Solutions?

Not many. One approach is to weld the crack. This means delicate TIG or laser welding, dressing the weld bead to flush, and refinishing the frame. The other is to stop-drill the crack. This fix requires a drill press or milling machine—you can't do it with a hand drill, no matter how steady your hand is. Using a 1/16-inch bit, drill the end of the crack. Cracks propagate by extension of the fissure. By drilling it, you present the stressed surface with a no-stressor obstacle (there are no stress risers in a circular hole), and the crack usually stops. I say "usu-

The STI pistols were all the rage and about the only thing for competition in the mid-1990s. Well, if you wanted to win competitions, anyway.

ally" because I'd bet there's one out there that got drilled and still cracked more.

The belt-and-suspenders approach is to stop-drill and weld.

I've got a bunch of 1911s with 50,000+ rounds each through them and a couple past 100,000. I have a Lightweight Commander, round count unknown, that is cracked. It was cracked when it came to me, and it has been to Gunsite four times and a daily carry gun for a decade-plus, and the crack has not enlarged. I didn't stop-drill it because I wanted to see what would happen, and as for welding, well, welding aluminum is a lot dicier than welding steel, and the person who handled my welding then wanted nothing to do with it. "I don't know the alloy," he said. I couldn't blame him.

*The STI frame is a steel rail and hammer/sear/safety section with a bolted polymer magazine holder. It is a clever design and a way to get hi-cap magazines into a frame without excess bulk.*

*A beveled magazine well can be as simple and straightforward as using a file to put an angle on the opening.*

That said, I have a friend who has even more ammo through his gun (He's worn out half a dozen extractors, several barrels, and two slides that I know of) who had his frame crack many years ago. It has been stop-drilled, welded, and welded again. He breaks things, and as I've never had to swap out an extractor, and the only slide/barrel changes I've had to make involved a USGI slide that was too soft, I shake my head. When it cracks there again, he just keeps on shooting.

## RAIL CRACK

Examine where the slide stop tab goes through the frame on the left side. The section of rail

Note how the Techwell tabs on the funnel engage the slot in the grip. When screwed down, the grip holds the funnel on.

that extends across it can crack. People get all fluttery when they see it, but it is no big deal. Anyone with enough rounds through their 1911 in a .45 or 10mm will have that crack. It happened so often and quickly with the Colt 10mm pistols that Colt just machined the rail. I suspect the company got so many phone calls and warranty requests that it decided "what the heck" and took it off. That part of the rail doesn't do much, and it isn't a problem if it is cracked, so don't sweat it. Can it be repaired? I suppose so, with a deft enough welder, but it will crack again, so why bother?

Why does it crack? Firing up the mental 3D CAD/CAM software, we can see that the barrel, slamming into the slide stop pin, tries to drive the pin forward. The inertia drives the frame down, in effect pushing the pin upward. That's a lot of slamming around, and the shock waves propagate throughout the frame. Because the closest part is weak, the rail vibrates on each shot.

Ignore it and move on to cleaning your pistol.

The rail section above the slide stop lever opening is prone to cracking. Cracked, it is no big deal, and no one bothers about it. This one isn't, but who cares if it cracks?

## MISCELLANEOUS CRACKS

The frame can crack at the bottom of the magazine well, but this only happens when it is dropped on a hard surface. Typically, the result is that something gets bent, and the magazine becomes difficult or impossible to insert or remove. Bent is tough, as straightening it can be a real hassle. Cracked is easy, as long as your welder knows how to deal with thin-wall parts and doesn't pump so much heat into the weld that he warps the frame, which is the same as it is bent—a hassle.

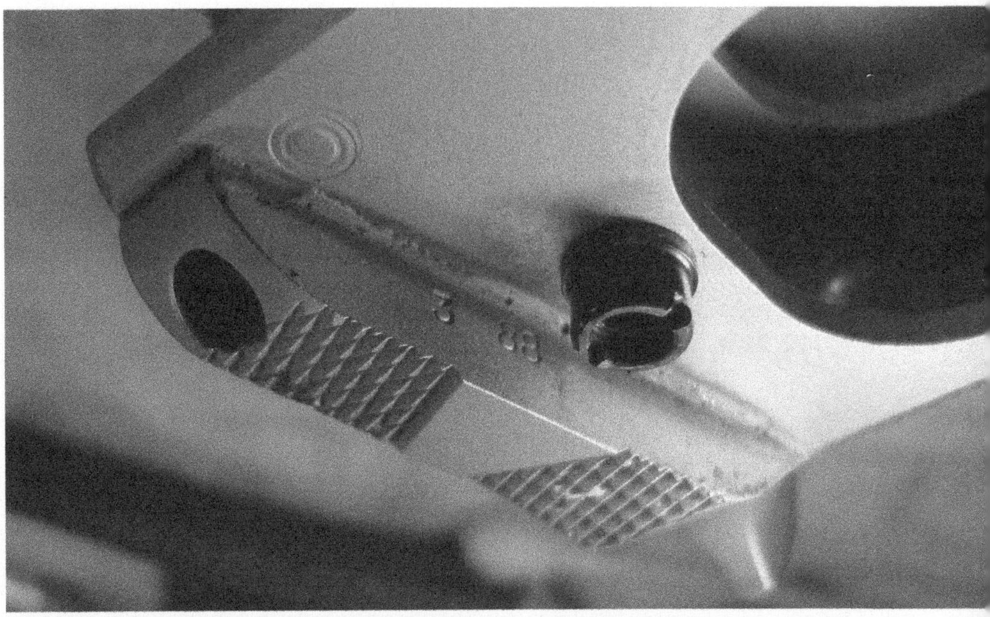

*An old-school mag funnel with welded-on side plates, filed and machined to fit the contour of the grips. Yes, the build date is stamped into it: March of 1988. A well-built 1911 is a lifetime pistol. Photo: Ned Christiansen*

## MAG FUNNELS

To make reloads faster, we all had mag funnels, and they were considered "competition" things, nothing a serious pistolero would hang on his gun. Now? They are common because they are useful. The old-school method was to weld or silver-solder steel to the bottom sides of the frame and then machine, grind, file, and polish it until it was a funnel. Today, many pistols come that way. There are even grips that are extended and shaped to be used as funnels.

Techwell offers an aluminum set of grips with an aluminum mag well funnel. The grips have a recess for tabs on the funnel to lock into. When you install your grips, hold the funnel against the bottom of the frame and press one grip in place. Use the screws to hold it on. Flip the pistol over and install the other grip, ensuring the grip slot engages the funnel tabs. You now have a one-piece grip and funnel setup. It adds some weight (not always a bad thing), so you might find it too much or a good addition. ●

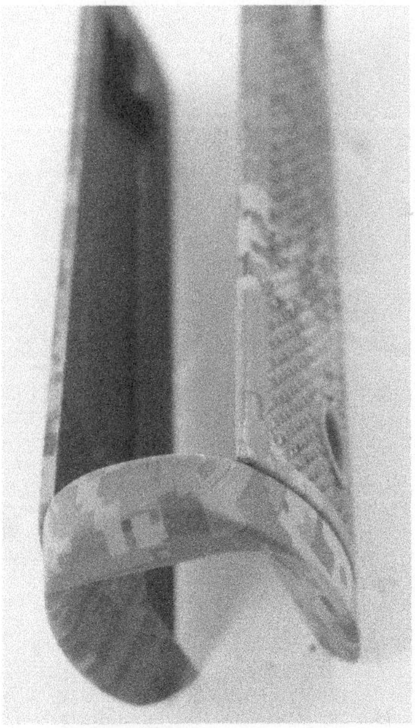

*If a frame existed between the grips, you'd have a mag funnel on your frame. This shows how the whole assembly fits together on the frame.*

# USES OF THE 1911

The 1911 is a classic carry gun and has been since the first one left the Colt factory in late 1911 or early 1912. However, carrying a full-sized, all-steel 1911 is not easy. You really have to want to be packing a classic, in a big bore, to do it. Most people who carry it opt for either an aluminum-framed, compact, or both. The Lightweight Commander, or an Officer's model, steel or aluminum frame, is much easier to pack. They are not, however, easy to shoot in .45 ACP. So, many 1911-carrying shooters have switched to the 9mm, which was not a reliable combo in the past. Today, it is.

If you want more capacity, then a partly polymer frame, like the STI/Stacatto or others, will give you lots of capacity and can be had in a compact size.

*Shooters like Robbie Leatham have spent a lifetime running 1911s, and even he would have to work to wear one out.*

## COMPETITION USES

Much the same thing has happened in Bullseye circles, as in everyday carry. Oh, not the compact or aluminum-framed pistols, but the switch from .45 to 9mm. Since the Beretta was and the Sig P320 (M17) now is the Service Pistol, that's the choice, not a 1911. But for those who

have them, like them, or shoot them well, the 1911 is still on the line at Bullseye matches.

At The Pin Shoot, you can quickly burn through gallons of ammo. A 1911 will shrug that kind of shooting off.

You won't see a 1911 at a Glock match, but the name of the competition should give you a clue as to why.

In USPSA competition, the 1911 or its derivatives, are well-represented. The Divisions where 1911s are allowed under the equipment rules are Open, Limited, Limited 10, and Single Stack. The Open guns will be .38 Super or 9mm Major with extended magazines, comps, and red-dots. The Limited, Limited Ten and Single Stack pistols used to be .40s, but now many are 9mm for lower recoil and ammo costs and more capacity. Limited Ten is a pistol restricted to 10-round magazines for use in those states that are not free. Limited means no comp or dot, and shorter, extended magazines. So, an Open pistol might have a magazine with 29 to 31 rounds. The Single Stack gun (just what the name says) is a .45 in 8+1 or a 9mm in 10+1 capacity. The .40 offers no advantage over the .45, but you can load it to Major, unlike the 9mm in other than Open.

The big one is Limited. These are double-stack magazine uncomped and no-dot pistols. In .45, such a beast has a capacity of 13+1. I built one because I had all the spare parts, but there's no point in it for competition. As a carry gun, were I to pack a full-sized pistol, it would rock.

In practical shooting and competition, capacity matters. So you'll see magazines like these. On the left is an STI with a magazine extension. On the right, a vanilla-plain Para.

A full-house Open gun can run well over $6,000; shooters have spent $10,000 getting what they wanted.

The same-sized pistol in .40 holds 17 rounds in a mag, and we've fussed, rebuilt, and crossed our fingers to get 18+1, and some even managed 19+1. Change it to 9mm, and you're talking a 27–28 round magazine, which in a big-round-count stage can mean no reload or one to the other guy's two. That matters.

An Open gun has been extensively overhauled and shoots like a laser. This is full recoil in an Open gun.

In IDPA, there are several divisions in which a 1911 is entirely suitable and allowed by the rules (after all, the competition was originated by none other than Bill Wilson).

As a handgun in the various 2-Gun, 3-Gun, Multi-gun, and "Outlaw" matches, the 1911 can serve you well, but be advised. Well, be advised here and in all other forms of competition that the rules matter. And if you show up with something that doesn't fit the rules, you might not be allowed to compete. Or if you are, it will be for "no score," meaning that even if you best everyone, the prize and the glory go to the guy behind you, the one with equipment that fits the rules.

The last competition that I'll mention is the bowling pin shoot. The format is simple: The competitor starts at the shooting line, gun touching the rail. The table is full of pins, in whichever layout the event calls for, 25 feet away. On the buzzer, lift and shoot the pins off the table faster than anyone else. The fastest shooter gets to walk up to the prize table first at the end of the match.

There are single-stack, double-stack, .45, 10mm, and 9mm events. Oh, and there's also the Power Factor (PF), which the pins determine. Basically, in the Major events, you need to generate a PF of 195 to do well. That means a 200-grain bullet at 975 fps or a 230-grain at 850 out of a .45 or 10mm. The .40 can't generate enough oomph to get the job done. In the 9mm-specific events, the jury is still out, but I suspect that a 140 PF will be needed, so you'd best have your 147-grain bullets up to 950 fps, or suffer the indignity of "deadwood," that is, pins left on the table. For the 9mm events, a downloaded .40 would be just the ticket if you have a suitable pistol and a few gallons of empty brass.

***An Open gun is not built for daily carry; there's no way to comfortably hide and wear something like this daily.***

***Competition accounts for equipment differences, so a shooter using a Limited gun like this is not scored against an Open shooter.***

*This Nighthawk went to The Pin Shoot, where it acquitted itself well. If you compete with what you carry, you will be well-served by the experience.*

## TRAINING

The classic locale to train in pistol use is Gunsite. I've been there four times in classes (three "E" tickets, one M1, and a banged-up knee) and more times for industry functions. The classes seem expensive at first glance, but if you want expensive, try skydiving or anything with an internal combustion engine. (Price a rebuild job on a blown dirt bike engine sometime and get back to me on how "expensive" shooting is.)

*The first optics-equipped pistol to win an IPSC World Shoot. This is Doug Koenig's pistol; alas, it isn't a 1911.*

The task of Gunsite is not to prepare you for competition. This statement requires some explanation. A class devoted to competition will push your skills to the limit (the instructor will be better or worse at it, and you will be more or less capable of it). You win by being that last percentage point of performance better than the other shooter.

Gunsite looks to make your performance not the apex of competition but stress-resistant. For example, the classic El Presidente drill is three targets at 10 yards. Start with your back to the targets. On the buzzer, turn and draw, place two hits on each target, reload, and place two hits on each again. If you want to win at your average club, you'd better be able to do it in

8 seconds with all "A" hits. A club of competitors, 7 seconds. A USPSA Area championship, 6 seconds. The USPSA Nationals? Under 5 and close to 4, unless you are in Open Division, where it had better be under 4 seconds.

The Par Time is 10 seconds at Gunsite, with all "A" hits. A par Gunsite run is a skill level better than most SWAT teams, 99.9% of the bad guys out there, and after a week at Gunsite, you can do it in the rain, cold, dark, just having been awakened, etc.

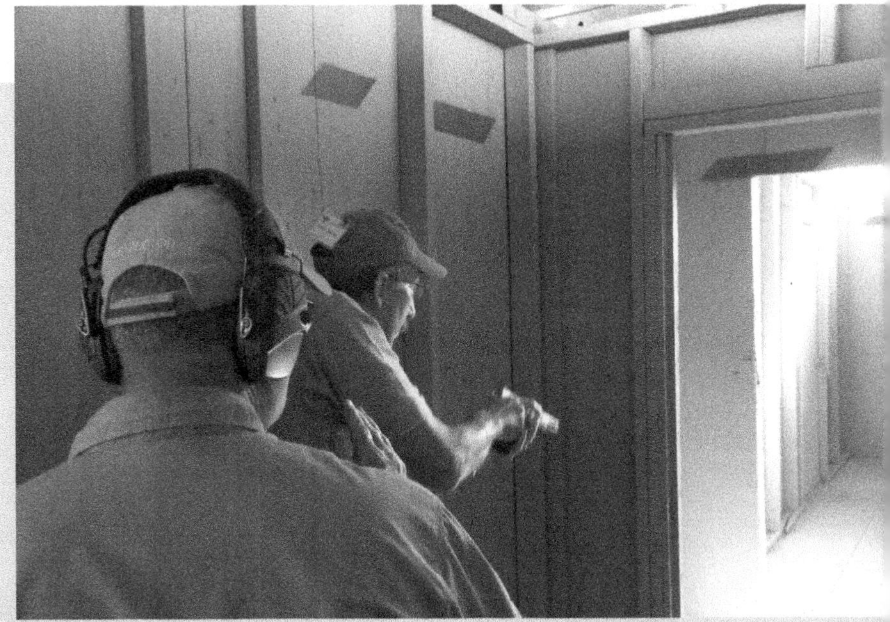

*Your author, going through a shoot house at Gunsite, learning about corners and the evil cleverness of instructors.*

They want your skills to be solid and stress-proof.

But whatever training you get, between training and practice, you'll go through a lot of ammo, and the 1911 will be up to it.

In summary, there are a lot of 1911s out there. Many 1911 shooters want to compete. So, 1911s in competitions aren't going anywhere. And there will always be training.

*Training means shooting, and 1911s shrug off volume shooting. The first M9s died under the kind of volume to which American shooters subjected them.*

CHAPTER

# 15

# MAINSPRING HOUSING

The mainspring housing is the part on the bottom rear of the frame, and it does several things: It works as a filler for the frame at the rear. It holds the hammer spring and the plunger, which combo drives the hammer by means of the hammer strut. And the spring and plunger are held in by a tiny pin that retains the spring and plunger combo. The shape of the mainspring housing also influences the pointability of the 1911, at least for some shooters. The M-S also traps the three-leaf spring in place, which works the grip safety, sear, and disconnector. In typical Browning fashion, it does multiple tasks while being nearly indestructible. Some parts on the 1911 wear and need to be replaced, and others that wear need a rebuild. The mainspring housing is one of three or four lifetime parts. In fact, if you were to take a mainspring housing off of a Great War gun that had been used heavily during the century-plus since, unless it had been hacked on by an incompetent, you could plug it into any existing 1911 and be good to go.

## MAINSPRING HOUSING DISASSEMBLY

Since we've just done a detailed strip of the frame, we might as well look at the mainspring housing. Again, it's the part at the bottom below the grip safety. Ease the hammer forward (we did this in the complete takedown chapter) and punch out the retaining pin. Slide the mainspring housing down and off of the frame. You'll see a small pin head on the inside face—its base is on the exterior face. *I have to*

*point out that the mainspring, or hammer spring, is strong.* If you slip, things will fly, so you must, and I mean *must,* wear safety glasses at this point.

***The mainspring housing funnel was a competition-only part and is now a common daily carry feature.***

Most shooters, most of the time (as in, most of their lives), will never have to take this apart. I'm giving you this info so if you want to fine-tune a trigger job, you'll know how to get to the relevant parts. Clamp the mainspring housing, open end vertically, in a padded vise. You want padding, like a shop cloth, to prevent marring the housing. In addition to using the cloth for vise padding, drape it under the vise to catch the small parts falling off in disassembly.

First, take a steel punch smaller than the plunger, and with one hand, compress the plunger used to drive the hammer strut. With a smaller punch, press the retaining pin out from the grooved side toward the smooth side. It will fall free, and the shop cloth will catch it. (If you don't lay a cloth under the pistol, the pin will fall to the floor, roll out of sight, and require a weeks-long search and rescue mission to locate it.)

Ease the first plunger up and relax the spring. You can now unclamp the mainspring housing and shake the parts out of the housing. The top cup will push on the hammer strut, the spring, and the retaining plunger that bears on the groove in the retaining pin. That's it.

***The spring and its cap drive the hammer in the cutaway mainspring housing.***

The original M-S was steel, flat, and smooth. For the 1911A1, it was changed to arched and grooved for a non-slip grip. For a long time, people have assumed that the change was made to make the 1911 "more pointable" since point-shooting was supposed to be *the* combat-shooting method. Nope. The reasons were simple. It allowed a better fit to the hands of a wider array of soldiers and other users—the arched grip was a better fit for hand sizes from small to large. And, it provided more recoil control, of which the .45 provided plenty.

Today, you'll see flat and arched, steel and plastic. I don't recall ever seeing an aluminum M-S, which might have been a nice thing on a lightweight commander. The plastic ones weren't developed for weight, but cost. Colt came up with them as a cost-cutting measure since it could produce injection-molded mainsprings for pennies, compared to machined steel. While they offend my aesthetic sensibility, they get the job done.

*The mainspring housing can be flat or arched, smooth or non-slip, steel or plastic, but you've got to have one.*

To reassemble, clamp the M-S in the padded vise. Insert the spring and plunger array into the M-S, pointed end of the retaining plunger down. Use your steel punch to compress the array, and while it's compressed, insert the retaining pin into the M-S from the flat side of the M-S. Once in and holding the plunger array, you can relax. Remove the M-S from the vise and tap the retaining pin flush with the M-S surface with a small hammer.

There isn't much need to do this—you might never have to—but knowing how will save you significant hassle and perhaps lost parts if needed.

## INSTALLING IN THE FRAME

This is easy, but it takes a small amount of fussing. Once you've slid the M-S up into the frame most of the way, you'll see that the hammer strut is in the way. You must center the hammer strut on the plunger cup (and the hammer must be down against the slide as if it has been dry-fired for this to work). Then, you can compress the M-S the short distance it takes to insert the retaining pin.

## REPLACING A MAINSPRING HOUSING

You might want to replace the mainspring housing because yours is arched, and you want a flat one or one with a different checkering pattern. Or you want the black plastic replaced by a blued or stainless one to match the steel of your 1911. No problem. First, remove the old one and remove

The mag funnel speeds reloads. However, you also need to practice. Practice puts all kinds of dings and gouges on the funnel. If you see a pristine mag funnel, you know the owner doesn't practice, at least not with that pistol.

the spring and plungers. Check the fit of the new M-S to your frame.

OK, you may notice that the new M-S fits loosely in your frame. The machined recess and slots can be a loose fit, and the M-S housing will work fine. If it offends your sensibilities, you can do a few things. One is to keep swapping M-S housings until you find one that is a tight fit. Of course, to do this, you'll need a bin full of them, and that won't be easy unless you're an assembler at the factory. The other is to stake it. Use a flat-faced punch and strike the external flange of the M-S housing to compress the rail, widening it slightly. This is a "hit and fit" process. Hit too lightly, it will remain loose; hit too hard, and it won't slide on, and you'll have to carefully stone the edge until it fits. Stake once on each side to remove the slop.

With a fitting M-S, check the plungers' fit in the M-S bore. You can, if you wish, take a bit of time and use a slotted dowel and a power drill to polish things. Put some abrasive cloth (fine grit works best) in the slot, insert it into the M-S bore, and then turn it on. This method polishes the tool marks and whatever else might be in there. You can also polish the hammer plunger. Chuck the thin end in your power drill, and hold some polishing cloth against the side of the head with a hard backer as you pulse the power drill. Again, this won't take long.

Blow the grit out of the bore, put a drop of lubricant on the plungers and the spring, and reassemble the M-S. Then, install it in the frame.

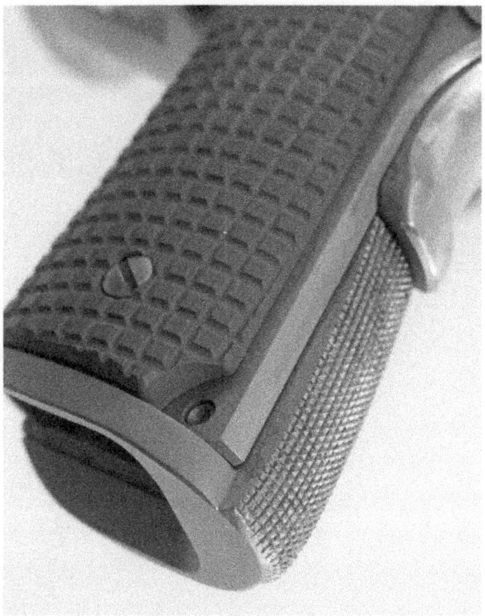

The integral mainspring housing and mag funnel, here in stainless, arched and checkered, with the red Dykem showing that a last bit of touchup is needed.

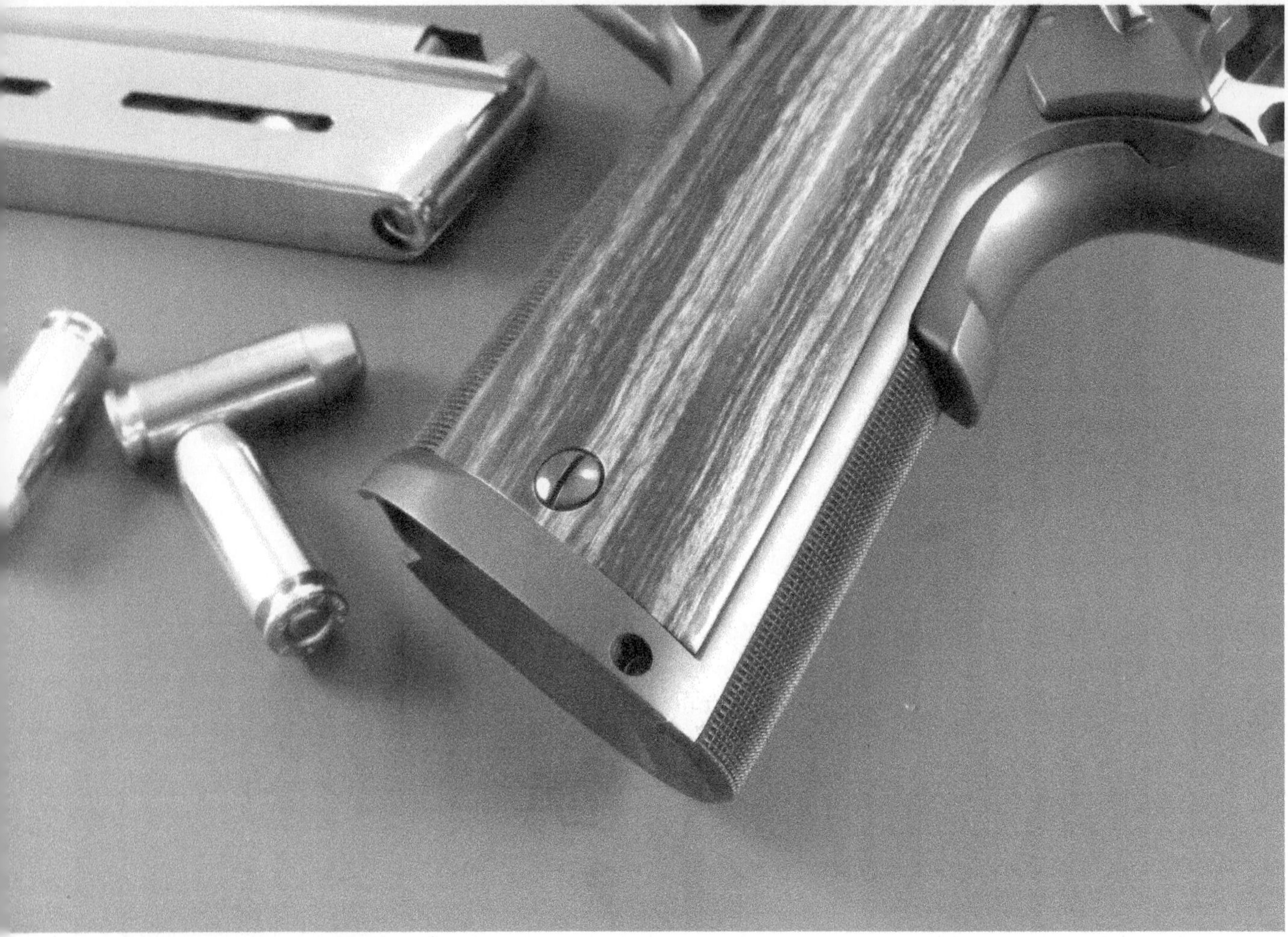

***This beautifully silver-soldered mag funnel by Ted Yost on a 10mm is blended to match the contour of the grips. Photo: Ted Yost***

## MAGAZINE FUNNEL

To make reloads against the clock faster and more assured, IPSC shooters developed the magazine funnel. It started as an accessory attached to the frame, with a portion extending below it, wider than the mag opening, to provide a funnel. Bill Wilson made the earliest one I recall, and it is an exemplar of the American Way. It was a simple piece of molded plastic with two tabs hooked over the grips' bottom bushings. Take the grips off, snap the tabs over the bushing, and put the grips back on—you have a magazine funnel.

One maker of special grips (I don't recall the name) produced them longer and thicker at the bottom, and the grips were the magazine funnel—an interesting, if not entirely aesthetic, approach.

The big jump came from Smith & Alexander, aka S&A, who used investment-cast mainspring housings. Two slats extended forward, forming a funnel on either side of the magazine opening. You could smoothen the transition and speed up reloads with careful sanding and polishing. This also accelerated the market for magazine base-plate extensions since the mag funnel made the frame longer by the length of the slats. You can now get them not just from S&A, but others, like Stan Chen.

Custom pistolsmiths took two other approaches. One was to weld or silver-solder steel to the frame sides. I used gauge stock, soldered them on, then ground and polished until the outside matched the curve of the grips, and the inside was a smooth and deep funnel for reloads. This approach did not make the frame longer.

The other approach was to clamp the frame upside down in a special fixture, heat the bottom red-hot, and drive a wedge into the opening to flare the frame sides into a mag funnel. Both of these approaches took a lot of time and effort and added a couple of hundred dollars to the cost of a custom build.

Today, there are better ways. One is by Stan Chen, who machines off the bottom of the frame, and welds in its place a funnel, complete

*In fitting a Stan Chen mainspring housing and mag well, you have to properly locate the parts to drill the hole for the retaining pin. Here, Jason Burton shows how it's done. Photo: Jason Burton*

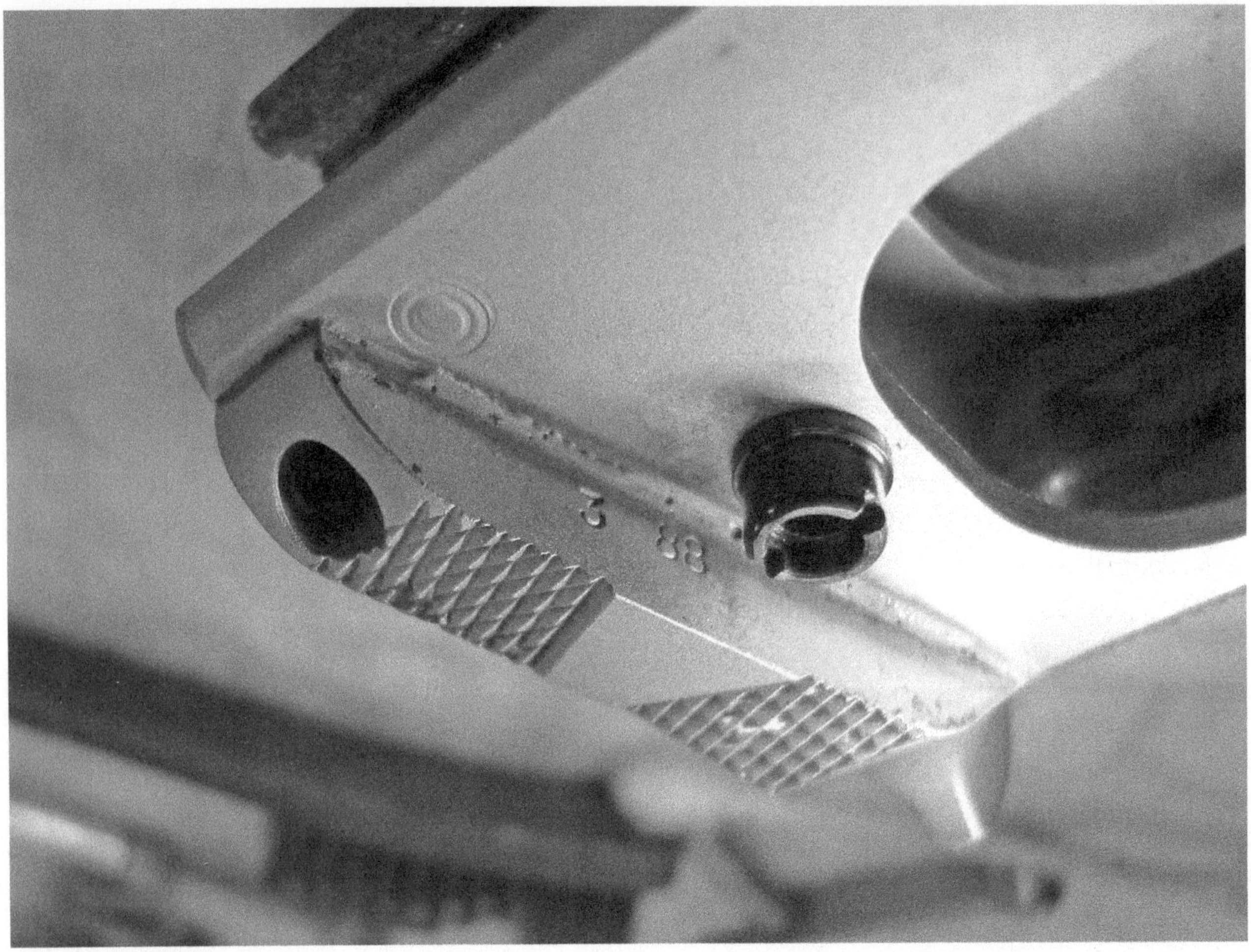

*A mag funnel with steel stock welded to the frame, then sculpted and matched to the grips. It has lasted now for 35+ years of use.*

with mainspring housing pin location (the fussy detail we had to account for in the previous two methods), which does not make the frame longer than original once added. And welded, it is strong, an integral part of the frame. The silver-solder and wedge methods both added stresses to the frame. That they held up was more a testament to John Moses Browning than our handiwork.

Today, most 1911s come with a slight bevel in the mag well to aid reloads. If you want to do this, your options are much like ours. A replacement mainspring housing is a relatively simple fit; the hard part is making it work as a funnel.

## FIT A NEW S&A

The first half is the same as fitting a new mainspring housing. Once you have it polished inside the spring tunnel, assembled and installed, look at the alignment of the two bars on each side of the magazine well opening. The work after this will likely remove the finish on your 1911 in obvious ways, so you'll have to decide if you can live with that. Of course, reloading at speed a few hundred times will wear the finish off of a blued gun anyway, so who cares?

Note: If working on a 1911 with a hard-chromed frame (and you will probably be installing a stainless M-S mag funnel in that case), fit and blend the M-S funnel—and the funnel alone—not the frame. First, the hard chrome will resist your files. Second, once you grind the hard chrome off, the frame won't be rust-proof where you ground it.

Ideally, the M-S funnel's edges should smoothly match the bevel inside the frame opening. The hard chrome fit will involve blending to the M-S only, with no extra bevel work on the frame. But you can carry the blending right on into the frame's metal on a blued gun that will be re-blued or a stainless gun.

A custom pistolsmith who is fitting an S&A or other mag funnel to your frame will either match the S&A to the frame or (at high cost) widen the S&A funnel and the bevel into the metal of the frame, creating a wider and deeper target for your reloads.

***This mainspring housing, installed by Stan Chen, has his texturing pattern machined into it.***

***The Chen mag funnel is a funnel and replacement mainspring housing requiring proper installation. But once done, it is beautiful.***

## MAG FUNNEL WRAP-UP

Oh, and Bill Wilson? He made the same plastic snap-on funnel in steel, so you can easily attach one. For a professional installation, blend it once it's attached and carefully relieve the back of the grips so they don't protrude at an angle at the bottom due to the attachment tabs.

Stan Chen's mag funnel comes in two types: the weld-on (which you either have to send to Stan, or have another custom pistolsmith attach, because of the welding) and the bolt-on. The bolt-on comes in two types: an integral mainspring housing and a clip-on. Both are solid because that's the way Stan designs things. Solid? No investment castings for Stan. He CNC machines them from billet steel.

The original S&A? They came out in the 1980s, were copied almost immediately, and have been since. It might just be me, but when someone comes up with a great new idea, I'm loathe to go with a copy. I'd rather the originator got my money. There was one variant

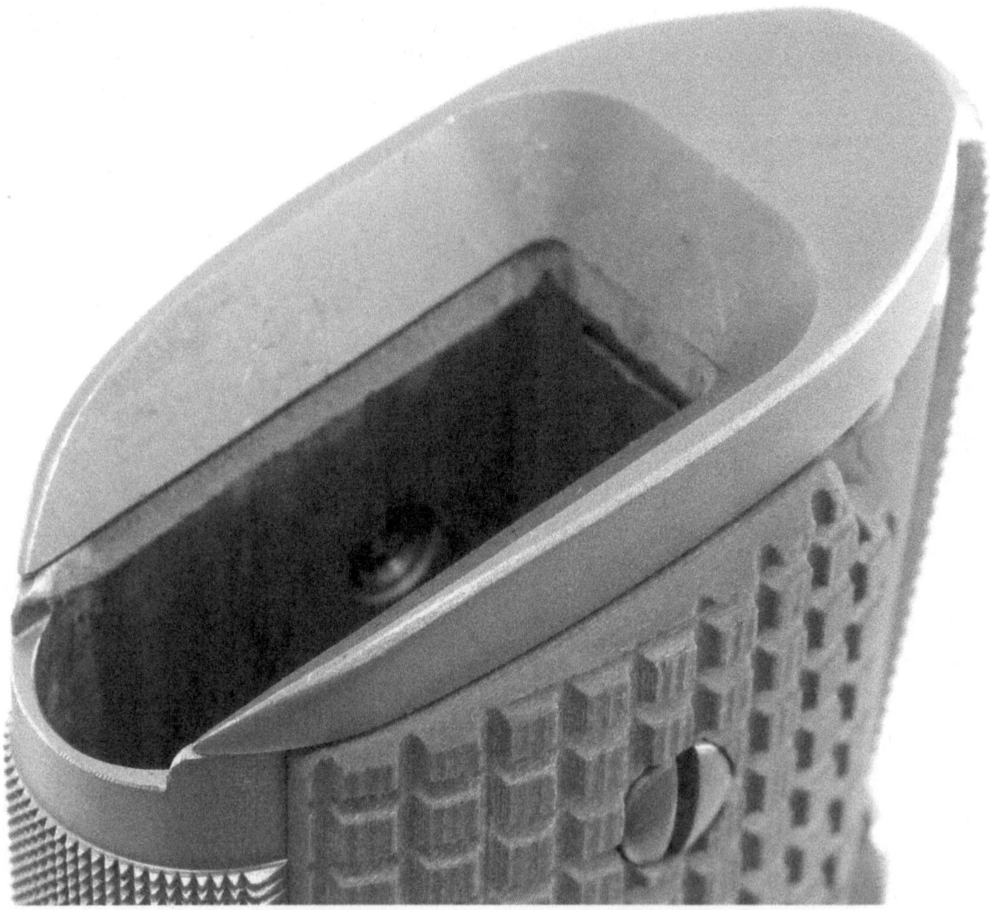

*Once the S&A is fitted to the frame, you will have to (or not, your choice) blend the ramp of the funnel to the frame. Files, grinding wheels, milling machines, the options are many, and the task is the same: a smooth transition with no edges on which a magazine can catch.*

of the S&A where the funnel wasn't an integral part but was bolted to the bottom of a special mainspring housing. It's an interesting approach, but I'm unsure what advantage it gave the maker or owner.

*The mag funnel makes reloads faster. This is what it looks like new. After you've done a few thousand practice and range reloads, it will get pretty scarred up.*

The old idea of extended grips to create a mag funnel had been updated to aluminum grips and much more durable synthetics than those available in the 1980s.

It's your choice. If you're like the rest of us, you'll go through two or three different funnels before you find what works best for you and your needs. ●

*A welded-on mag funnel, as a no-extra-length installation, does not have a gap between the funnel and the frame since the funnel* is *the frame.*

CHAPTER

# 16

# RECOIL SPRINGS

The name "recoil spring" is a misnomer. The spring is the feeding system of the pistol. A few gunsmiths have done some limited testing (the risk of damage is understandable) of firing a 1911 without a recoil spring installed. Basically, the slide slams back to the frame and stops. To check the results, with a milling machine, cut a small flat along the length of the slide. Set it up in a table vise on the mill and use an indicator to show the flat is straight to less than .001 inch. (Even flatter, depending on operator skills and mill accuracy.)

*Note how the recoil spring guide rod sits in the frame, with the spring wrapped around it.*

Fire the 1911 without a recoil spring as often as you dare, and then use the indicator to see if the slide flat has changed. So far, limited testing shows no change. The real test is to do a magnetic particle inspection of the slide before you fire it and then, after the testing, see if there has been any change in the slide at the recoil spring tunnel. I wouldn't be surprised to find that deep in the records room of Colt—or some government warehouse—there's a report on precisely this test. Someday, I might find it.

So, recoil springs.

The originals were made of "music wire" spring steel with a wire diameter of .043 inch, 30 coils, and a free length of 6.55 inches. The ends are not wound the same. The end that slips over the guide is crimped to a smaller diameter than the wind diameter, so it is a frictional fit. The other end is left at coil diameter and open. The open end is meant to be twisted into the recoil spring plug until it catches into and locks to the tab in the plug. The intent was simple: when a GI took the 1911/1911A1 apart, the guide, spring, and plug would all remain more or less together as a unit. They could be wrestled apart, but when cleaning in the field, they'd stay together as a unit, making it less likely they'd be lost.

Springs are simple in use and concept and incredibly complex in manufacture, design, intent, and service life. Let's get one thing out of the way right away: springs wear out. They wear out very slowly and last a long time, but they do wear out. *You cannot "restore" their strength by stretching them back to their original length.* This uses up most of the remaining service life they would have had at that point. How long is a useful service life? That depends on how cheap you are and how much abuse you will put your 1911 through.

Spring and pistol makers generally agree that you should replace springs every 5,000 to 10,000 rounds as a maximum. Checking with manu-

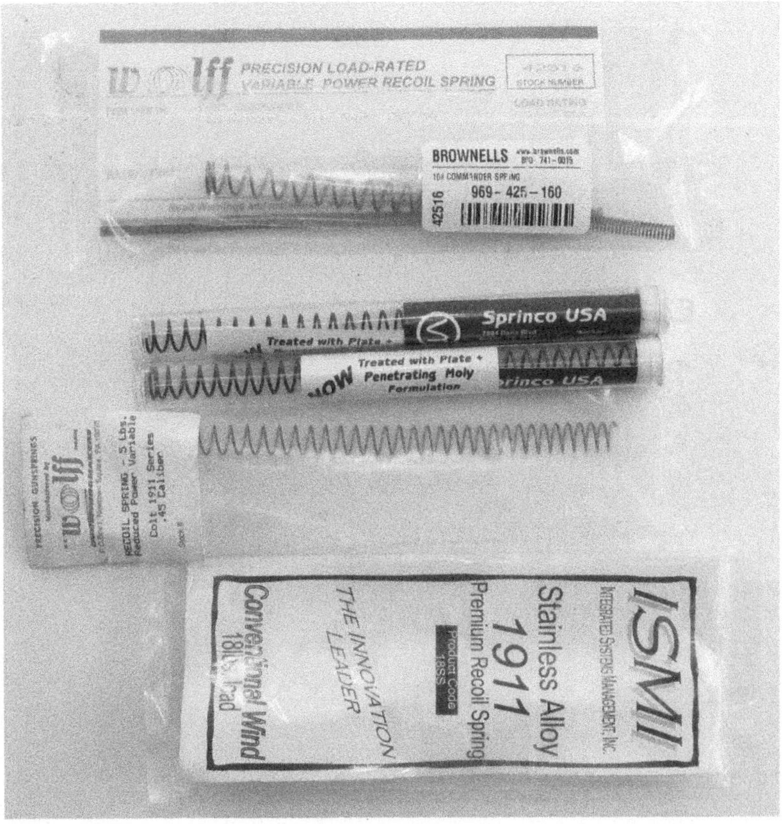


***Springs are common, inexpensive, and easily replaced. So don't be cheap. Spend nine bucks on a new one every 5,000 rounds, and do right by your 1911.***

facturers, you'll see suggestions of much less, as low as 800 rounds in some models. OK, let's dig in.

Starting with the original, the baseline: a Government Model with a 230-grain JRN. This pistol uses an 18-pound spring at the above 6.55-inch length and has a 5,000-round service life. Why change sooner? Timing. (An arcane subject we'll go into in a bit, just to tease you.)

## SHOCK BUFFS

You will see a product called a Shock Buff—or some variant of that spelling, such as Shok Buff—for use in your 1911. The intended use varies, from softening recoil to reducing wear, speeding up the slide, and reducing hair loss. (OK, so I made that last one up. Tell me you haven't seen claims as outrageous on other accessories.)

They are made out of one or another synthetic, although I can imagine someone carefully cutting them out of leather back in the Dark Ages. They are simple: Disassemble the pistol and pull the recoil spring off the spring guide. Slide the buff down the guide, put the spring back on, and reassemble. When you fire, the slide cycles back and impacts the shock buff sandwiched between the slide and the guide flange. The question is: do they work?

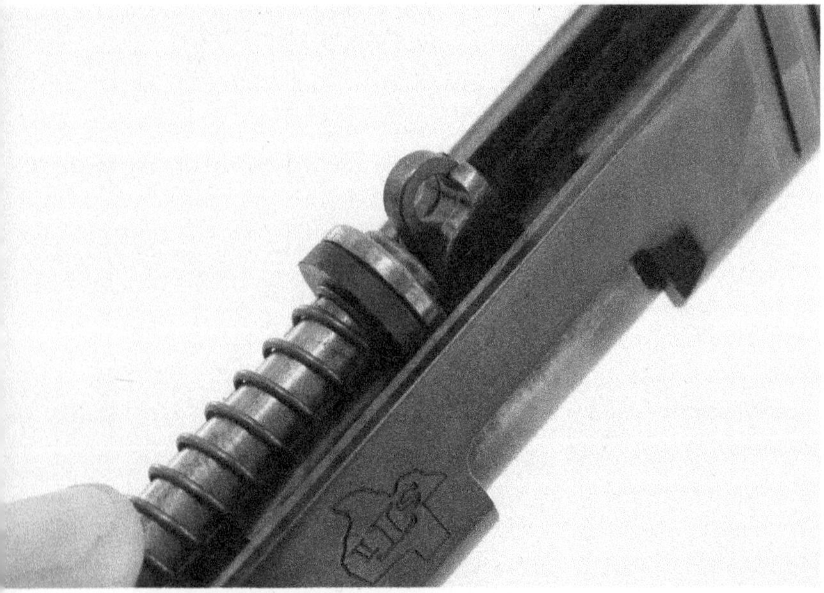

*This pin gun used in the 9mm event has a shock buff in it because, at warp speeds, anything that helps ... helps.*

That depends on what your definition of "work" is.

Yes, they soften the felt recoil and reduce the force of impact of the slide on the flange. Is the reduction in felt recoil enough to matter? Maybe, mostly not. Most shooters, even up to the Grandmaster level, if handed two otherwise identical 1911s, could not tell you which has the shock buff and which does not. For most shooters, as far as felt recoil is concerned, the shock buff falls in the "any advantage, real or imagined" category. If you think it helps, it probably does, *somewhat*.

Reduce wear and damage? Hmm. Let's take a Les Baer as a test case with 100,000 rounds through it, showing a slight dropoff in accuracy. When Les gets it back, what will he find, and what will he fix? He will likely find that the wear on the slide and frame rails has caused enough slop that the slide, barrel and frame don't always lock up precisely as they had when they left the shop. So, that sloppiness will be corrected by one of several methods. Occasionally, the barrel will show enough wear in the throat that it might be the cause. Once the slide and frame have been refitted and the barrel lockup corrected (if needed), it will get test-fired for accuracy. The task is done if the throat wear is within limits and the accuracy is proper. If accuracy still isn't there—even if the throat is within limits—or the throat is worn, it'll get a new barrel.

***The recoil spring guide rod head needs its center boss filed to an angle, providing clearance for the barrel lugs as it links down.***

And the slide at the recoil spring tunnel? The 'smith doing the inspection and rebuilding will examine it to see if someone dropped the slide or made some home-gunsmithing "adjustments"; otherwise, there's nothing to see there. He will also look at the recoil spring guide. The flange may or may not show some peening. A shock buff might have saved it from needing replacement if it shows peening. Here's the thing: the costs of new shock buffs fall at suggested intervals of 1,000 rounds per. At a dollar each, you will have spent $100 in shock buffs. A replacement recoil spring guide runs you $9. If your slide is peening your guide rod flange, you must look into the problem more deeply than a shock buff.

That said, I use them in some guns. My bowling pin 9x12 gun has one because the extra dampening can make a difference at the super-soft recoil level of the 9mm load (115-gr. at about 1,000 fps). That, and you can win or lose the event by a tenth of a second.

Still, for some shooters, the shock buff, in all its colors, thicknesses, makers, and uses, has almost a religious-level adherence. If you like using one, then knock yourself out. Except ...

If you find that your shock buff is mangled, torn, chopped, shredded or otherwise abused each time you swap it out, you have a bigger problem. Typically, this is one of two causes or a combination of them. One is sharp edges at the rear of your slide's recoil spring tunnel. These sharp edges are not just impacting but cutting the shock buff. Use a medium or fine Arkansas stone to knock off the corner edge around the tunnel. The other is you're using a recoil spring that is too light, meaning it is time to discuss the correct spring weight.

But which spring weight? Gather 'round and hear the tale.

Before going any further, go to Wollf springs (gunsprings.com) and see what weight spring you'll need for any application. If you're running a Government Model in .45, you'll need a spring weight different than that needed for a Lightweight Commander in 9mm, the Officer's Model, and so on. But we'll go with the Government Model as the baseline and proceed from there.

The standard is a spring weight of 16 pounds. The free length, as per government specs, is 6.55 inches, and when compressed inside the slide (with the slide closed), it has 3.75 inches to fit into, and when the slide is complete to the rear, it has 1.80 inches of room. Oh, and as an important note, but one you will be hard-pressed to manage, you cannot allow the recoil spring space to be crowded to the point that the spring "fully stacks" or is compressed so all the coils are in complete contact. Some overboard ham-handed pistolsmithing would be to blame, at least on the Government Model, of using four or five shock buffs and putting some sort of filler in the recoil spring retainer. The problem with full compression is that the slide no longer stops by hitting the guide rod flange but by having the fully compressed spring bang against the recoil spring retainer and bushing. That breaks things. It can become a problem in compact guns, so be aware.

*This guide rod and recoil ring system is a bull barrel and a reverse retainer setup. To begin disassembly, unscrew the two-piece guide rod (that's what the slot is for).*

With a 16-pound spring, your 1911 will cycle as Browning designed it. It will have a good, long life with replacement springs every 10,000 rounds (if you're cheap) or 5,000 if you are not cheap; hey, they are only $9, and it will last essentially forever.

So why do you read about Master and Grandmaster shooters running lighter springs? The answer is timing.

When you fire a round, the recoil causes the muzzle to rise. When the slide goes forward, the impact of the slide closing and your push to get it back on target can cause the muzzle to dip below the target—you must lift it to get your sights back on target. This timing is influenced by the recoil spring, pistol weight, grip strength, cartridge power, and how much practice you have put into getting the sights back on target. Despite what you may have read, no muzzle brake or comp "shoots flat" and keeps the muzzle from rising. They bring them down faster and keep them from rising as much, but muzzles still rise. Part of your "split" time is spent getting the muzzle back on target.

*This bushing setup has a one-piece guide rod, but it is shorter than flush, so you can use a bushing wrench to disassemble it.*

Changing the recoil spring changes the equation and where the muzzle stops once the recoil settles. The Master and Grandmaster shooters use lighter springs to get their muzzle on target without extra time.

Here's the thing to remember: a lighter spring does not let you shoot faster. That's backward. A faster shooter can use the advantage, but if you aren't fast, you can't. And more importantly, you have to be consistent. A fast, consistent shooter can take advantage of a lighter spring.

Let's do an Einsteinian thought experiment. You fire a round, and once the recoil ends, your muzzle stops at a certain angle to the target. If, on every single shot, your muzzle stops at that exact angle, you can then change the recoil spring and adjust the angle to be on-target at return. Now, let's change that. Instead of the same angle, your return point is a different angle. Let's put a number to it and say you come to return, and your angle off target varies by 15 degrees from shot to shot. And that a change in weight makes a difference in the angle of 5 degrees. OK, what weight change do you make? Should you try to split the difference? How about taking the average, as it were? Or change the max and adjust to that? Until you are more consistent, changing recoil springs won't make a noticeable difference. It may even make things worse.

It can also change reliability. Mostly, going too heavy does that, but ultra-light can do it, too. When the slide bottoms out on the flange, it bounces. Steel-on-steel collisions are among the most elastic collisions, and the timing of that collision is built into the system by Saint Browning. If you go too heavy, the slide stalls short and comes back too soon, and the top round in the magazine may not have "settled down" against the feed lips and may not be properly positioned. If the round is still rattling around, it might not be pointed properly to feed well. Conversely, if the recoil spring is too light, the slide may hit so hard when it bottoms out that it rattles the cartridge stack, again improperly orienting the top round.

So, stick in the middle with the standard weights.

You may read old advice from the prehistoric days of increased recoil spring weights to "improve reliability." Nope. Going from an 18- to a 20-pound spring won't make a recalcitrant pistol feed better. Finding the source of the actual problem and correcting it will, however.

You can also run into issues by going heavier if your grip isn't up to snuff. The action of any self-loading pistol depends on you being a sufficiently strong backstop to keep the recoil from moving both the frame and the slide/barrel assembly. If your grip isn't firm enough, you will encounter a malfunction known as a "limp wrist." Typically, this is caused by an empty case trapped in the ejection port, not having had time or energy to escape before the slide closed again. Designers and engineers will use a strong spring to keep the parts from battering, but weak enough that it will function even if you hold the pistol limply. They recognize that not all shots can be fired with a fully gripped, fully braced pistol. The test here is to hold the pistol with only one finger wrapped around the frame, and not very firmly at that. Relax your grip to almost dropping the pistol when it goes off, and fire a round. How far does the empty go? It should land at least a couple of feet away from you. Well, if you swapped out that spring for a stronger one, the case would not go as far or as fast. Oh, and if you do this at the range with others watching, someone will offer to show you how to hold your pistol correctly. Politely decline the offer, say you were testing it. (True.)

The .45 Commander takes an 18-pound spring. There's less slide mass, and the slide travels a shorter distance, so it needs more spring to handle the cartridge and feed properly. With an even shorter slide, the Officers Model requires a 22-pound spring. Also, changing cartridges can require a spring change. Going down in power, a standard .38 Super or 9mm calls for a 14-pound spring, as does the .38 Wadcutter. Curiously, the .40 S&W (should there be any call for that) needs a 19-pound spring. Why? Generally, the .40 has a higher bullet velocity even when it has the same power as a .45. While most calculations depend on momentum, kinetic energy weighs in once it reaches a high enough level.

Jumping up to the 10mm, you'll want a 23-pound spring to handle the factory ammo.

There's another potential problem to over-springing your 1911, and that is the returning mass and velocity. All that energy has to be stopped, and the stopping is done by the barrel feet, riding up on and stopping against the slide stop pin. You can cause peening on the slide stop pin and perhaps even over-stress the barrel feet. I've even heard of (although never seen) frame slide stop holes being hammered egg-shaped from over-springing.

The two-piece guide rod has an Allen wrench opening, and you unscrew the rod before using a bushing wrench on the bushing.

When to change springs?

I wish there were a formula. You know, "The standard length is X, and when it gets down to Y, it is time to change." But there isn't. However, back when the 1911 was a common item in armories, I'd bet the supply people there had their own rule of thumb. Then again, they were getting recoil springs by the foot-locker, which all came from the same place and would have been the same length, give or take half an inch or so. And then, being fed only 230-grain hardball, they could track round counts and spring lengths and work out a time to swap springs.

Springs can differ in length. They will be made of different materials. The only reliable method we have is round count. If this means tossing a recoil spring with a few thousand or ten thousand rounds of service life left in it, that's OK.

## VARIABLE SPRINGS

You'll hear about "variable" springs. OK, a bit of engineering-speak. The cross-sectional area of the wire determines the spring rate of any spring, the material's tensile strength, the wind's diameter, and the number of coils. The regular spring, also called a constant-rate spring, has everything the same on the spring, and thus, the force needed to compress it (or the force it generates while un-compressing) is equal, regardless of where it is in the compression cycle.

So, if we assign a theoretical spring a theoretical rate, called the deflection rate, and say it is a "one pound/inch" spring, the initial inch of compression requires a pound of force. The second requires a pound, the third a pound, and so on. Of course, that is additive, so when you compress from the third to the fourth inch, you are going up from three pounds to four pounds of force applied.

OK, how do we vary the force as the length changes? Well, we could change the cross-sectional area of the wire. No, I don't think so. How about tensile strength? What, by heat treatment or a different alloy? Again, nope. Diameter of wind? How is it going to fit in the space allowed? All we're left with is the number of coils. So, add coils (wind them tighter) at the end of the cycle stroke.

This allows your 1911 to operate at the beginning of the slide cycle as usual, with the slide unlocking and starting to move back, then encountering greater compression force as it moves to the rear. Do you need a variable-force spring in your 1911? For most applications, no. A .45 or 9mm, even a .38 Super, probably doesn't benefit from it, and you might not notice any difference. I'd be tempted to run a 10mm with a variable spring just because we're asking a lot of the 1911 in that application, and anything that helps will help! I'd add in the .40 Super, .45 Super, and .460 Rowland to that as well. And I'd be changing that spring at 5,000-round intervals, not 10,000 rounds, like in a .45 or 9mm.

## RECOIL SPRING GUIDE IN POUNDS

| Chambering | Government | Commander | Officers |
|---|---|---|---|
| .45 ACP | 16 | 18 | 22 |
| .38 Super/9mm | 14 | 16 | 20 |
| 10mm | 20 | 22 | 24* |
| .40 S&W** | 20 | 22 | 24 |

* *For the 10mm, factory ammo calls for the weight listed. However, if using heavy hunting loads, heavy bullets, or top-end velocities, try the next step up in spring weight.*

***In the .40 S&W, if shooting factory-power level ammunition, use the full spring weight. If downloading your ammo (making it, in essence, a fat 9mm), then use the 9mm spring weights.*

## EXTRA-SPRING SPRINGS

You will see ads and read glowing testimonials for guide rod assemblies that "eliminate recoil" and make shooting easier. Basically, they are some variant of an additional spring that only works when the slide and recoil spring assembly hit it at the end of the slide travel.

Well, this brings to mind the summation of the Three Laws of

Thermodynamics, as explained to me on the first day of class. (At 7 AM, on a bitterly cold January day, I might add.) "You can't win, you can't break even, and you can't get out of the game."

The additional spring slows the slide impact and spreads the impact out over a longer period. But. That extra force is usually borne by the bushing, the recoil spring retainer bearing on the bushing, and the slide impact hitting the additional spring and slamming the bushing. You'll be fine if it is hardened and thicker to withstand the impact. If not, then you won't be. When these were new, I saw a few bushings with the bottom skirt bent out from the impact.

Use one if you want to. It isn't magic. It might cause a problem. Indeed, don't put one into your daily carry 1911 until you've put a few thousand rounds through it just to be sure it works and survives the effort. ●

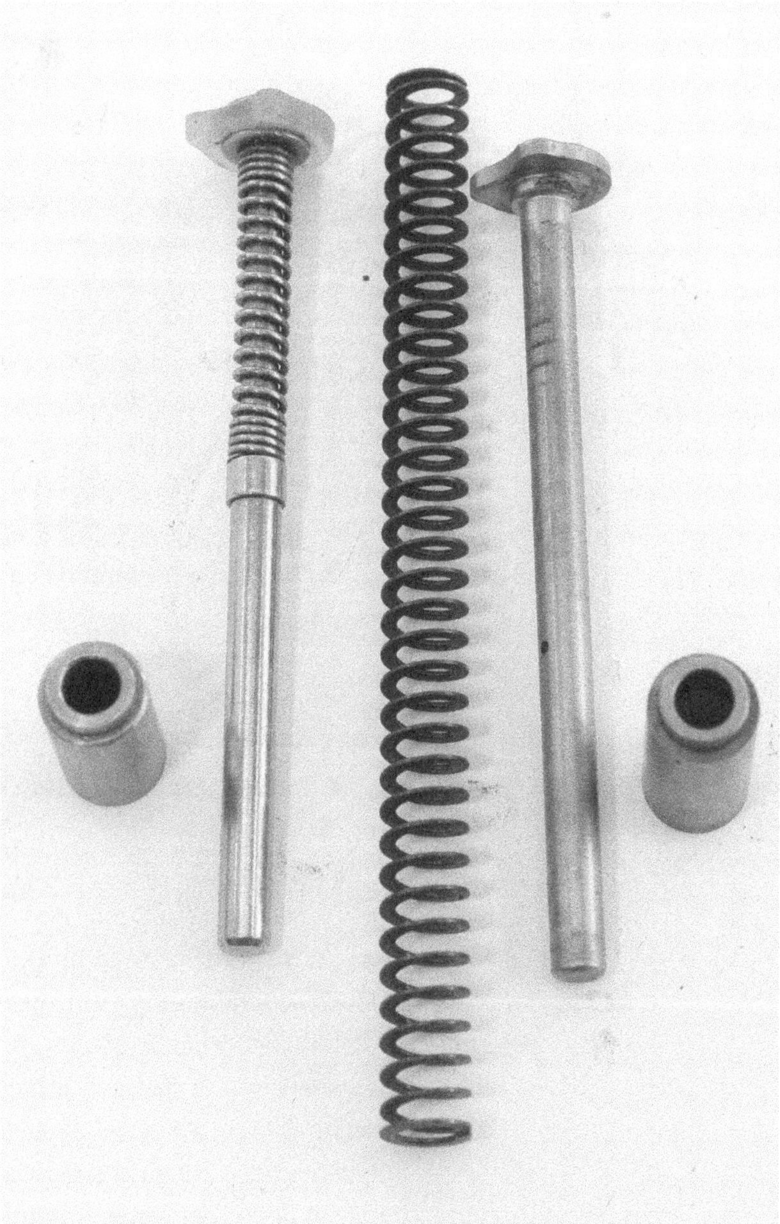

***On the right is a regular full-length guide rod with its spring retainer. On the left is a recoil-reducing one, with the extra spring to take up impact. That spring gets hit by the spring retainer, which is held in by the bushing. The bushing gets worked a lot harder on each shot. Test thoroughly before you use it in a daily carry gun.***

CHAPTER

# 17

# SIGHTS

Not to steal a line from Caesar, but iron sights are divided into four types: Original, BoMar, Novak, and LPA. We'll go over optical sights after we cover the irons because, if there's a pistol today associated with iron sights, it is the 1911.

## ORIGINAL

The first sights appearing on the 1911 are barely discernable to the modern eye. When the 1911 was adopted, pistols were still seen as "point-shooting" instruments. A cavalry trooper riding through an enemy position or group of infantry pointed his arm and the pistol straight at them and fired shots as he galloped through. Then, he'd wheel around, return, and do it again. The cavalry's job wasn't to get involved in pitched battles and dig into a fight at a given location. Once

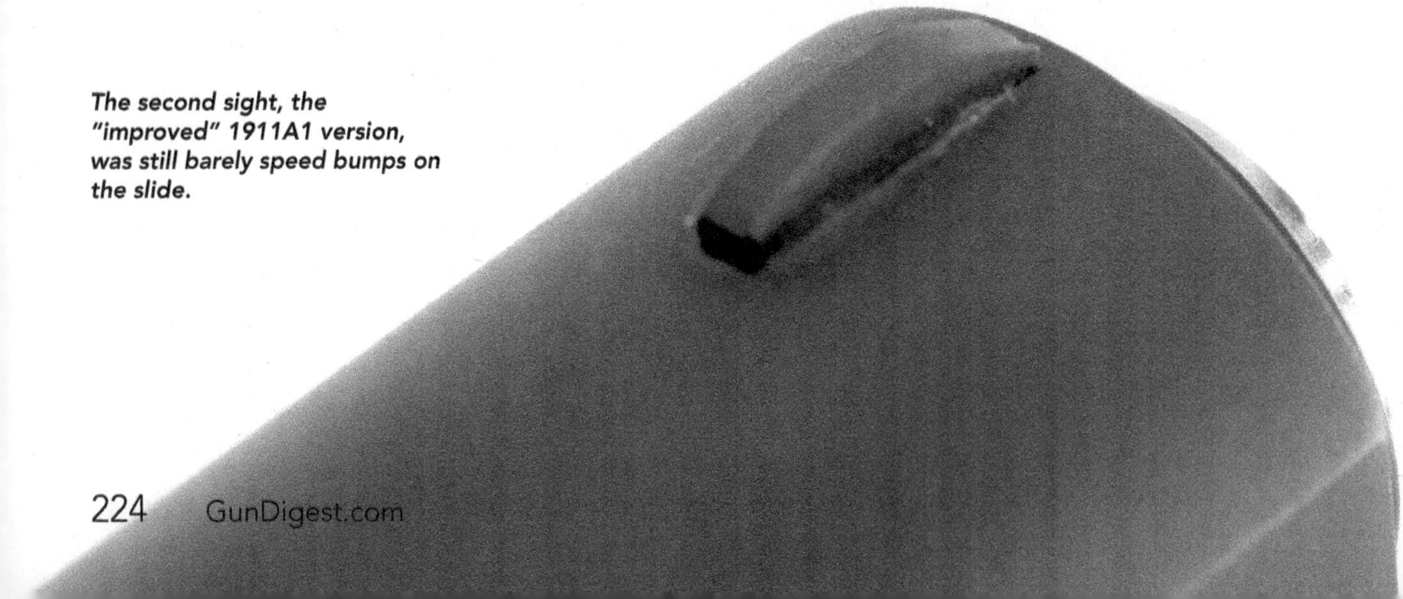

*The second sight, the "improved" 1911A1 version, was still barely speed bumps on the slide.*

the job of scouting, harassing, and reporting was completed, they were there to create chaos and confusion, disrupt organization, and muddle attempts at advancing or building defensive positions. Ride over, shoot, and keep going. The pointing approach was seen as the customary and fastest method. Since most pistol fights were conducted at short, even conversational distances, pointing worked, more or less.

*The 1911A1's rear sight was better than the 1911's, but barely by today's standards. Back then, it was a revelation.*

Point-shooting's shortcomings were well-known, and when the 1911 was updated to the 1911A1, it received larger sights. Well, they were larger compared to the originals. If you inspect an unaltered 1911A1, you'll be amazed at how small the sights are. How small? On a modern 1911 with iron sights, you're looking at a front blade that will be something like .125-inch wide and as much as .250-inch tall. (No, I won't measure a dozen pistols and take the average.) The blueprints for the 1911A1 show the front sight to be a nominal .102-inch tall and .080-inch wide. The rear notch is a similar .080-inch wide. These were not Bullseye sights, but they were improvements over the originals.

The original and A1 sights, being so small, were simple to install. The rear is a press-fit into a dovetail milled across the slide. For some curious reason, the GI rear sight's dimension is a 65-degree angle. A standard machinist's dovetail cutter is 60 degrees, but for reasons lost to the mists of history, 65 degrees was used. The rear sight is a press fit that stays put once correctly installed. You can adjust the windage (side-to-side) of the bullet impact by using a hammer and a brass drift and tapping the sight for the correct amount. (We'll delve into sight adjustments later.)

The front sight is another matter. The customary method is known as staking. Here, the slide has a small rectangular hole broached down from the top with a half-moon recess on the top. The sight blade has a rectangular stub machined on its foot (called a tenon) that matches the hole and half-moon. The stub is smaller than the width of the sight blade, which rides on top of the slide, and the foot passes through it.

To install, the front sight slides into the slide opening, and the end of the sight foot is staked, or swaged, to lock it in place. When the 1911 or 1911A1 sight is installed—which are not unlike fingernail clippings in size but made of steel—this works fine. However, when Colt went to larger sights, they were too heavy for the original method. Colt increased the size of the front sight foot, the tenon, to the full width of the sight and enlarged the opening in the slide.

This meant the new Colt sights could not be used on a USGI slide. That was a double benefit for Colt, as its sights stayed put and could not be installed on a GI slide. If you wanted the new sights, you had to buy a new gun—or slide. The new rear sights used the same dovetail size as the old ones.

One trick I used when installing a new wide sight in a slide was to use a ball-end grinding tip or carbide cutter in a Dremel tool. On the inside of the slide, I'd dish out the edges of the sight opening slightly. This gave the bottom of the sight foot more room to expand into, a mushroom if you will, and provided a better "lock" of the sight to the slide. However, this workaround was a relatively short-term situation as the change to the Novak sight system made all the previous work obsolete.

*The S&W rear sight, installed on a 1911 slide, was* de-rigueur *in the 1970s. When the BoMar got installed in a low-mount machined setup, the S&W dropped out of favor.*

The "new" sights were a bane to combat shooters and their pistolsmiths. In Bullseye competition, a "Softball" gun (the only 1911 that would have target sights, the "Hardball" gun had to be USGI) was fed a diet of 185-grain bullets at about 700 fps. IPSC shooters, on the other hand, fed their 1911s 200-grain bullets at 900 fps—almost 40 percent more recoil. Front sights flew off. It happened to me. Frank Paris, a well-known and experienced Bullseye pistolsmith, built an IPSC pistol for me, and the front sight came off. "You combat shooters and your hot loads" was his comment about attaching a new one.

Some, like Armand Swensen, went so far as to silver-braze the blade in place.

We now almost universally use the Novak system to attach front sights, except those built as deliberate "GI" guns.

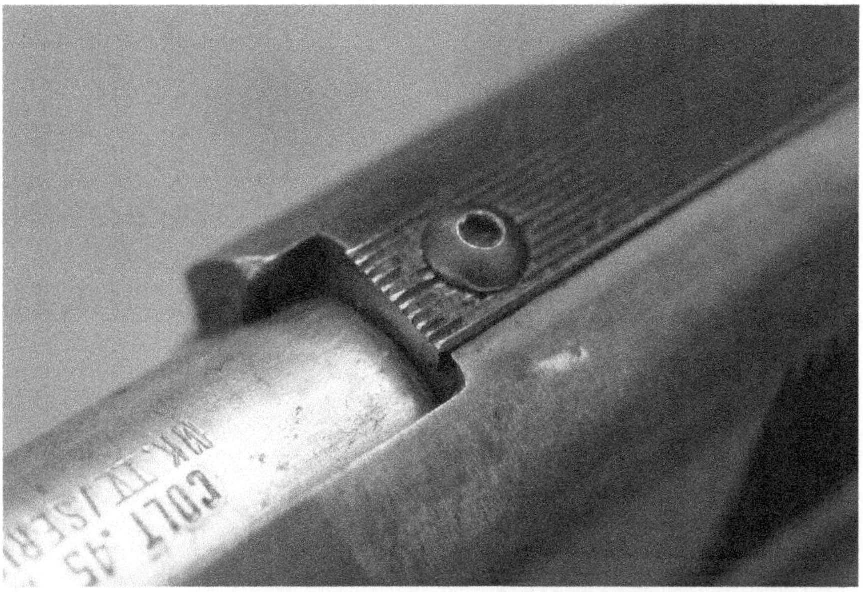

One problem the S&W sight had was the single anchor: a screw at the front that was meant to hold it onto the slide. The sight would leave the slide if it were not a strong fastener.

## CLASSIC FIRST STEP

Technically, there aren't four but five sight types, but the fifth was a high-tech fad for the time, now an anachronistic add-on that is done only if you want to re-create a classic (like building a Ford Model T hot rod today from a kit). That would be a S&W revolver sight added to the 1911 slide. It was the sort of thing Armand Swensen did, and you can tell his work by his use of the reinforcing rivet, with the original owner's last name initial stamped into it.

The job went like this. You often had to fill the old dovetail by silver-soldering the original sight into place and dressing it down. (The slide would be stippled on top and hard-chromed, so it wouldn't show much anyway.) Then, use a milling machine to mill a sight-wide slot down the center and drill the anchor hole for a rivet or screw. Next, cut cross-ways to provide clearance for the sight body. The tricky part was milling the undercut of the anchor plate for the rear sight vertical adjustment screw. That was a delicate cut and required a special-sized cutter.

All that, and you had an adjustable sight that wasn't as durable as required. If dropped, the sight blade bent or broke. With a lot of hard use, the rear sight might (more often than desired, it did) fly off. If you are doing a 1970s IPSC homage pistol, add a S&W rear sight. Otherwise, leave it in the past.

## BOMAR

Target shooters hate fixed sights. Yes, once zeroed, they are sturdy and reliable, but if you need a small change, it can be a hassle to tap one way, then back again, as you try to wring the last thousandth of correction out of the sight position to get your group centered on the target. A screw-adjustable, or better yet, click-adjustable sight, is what they wanted.

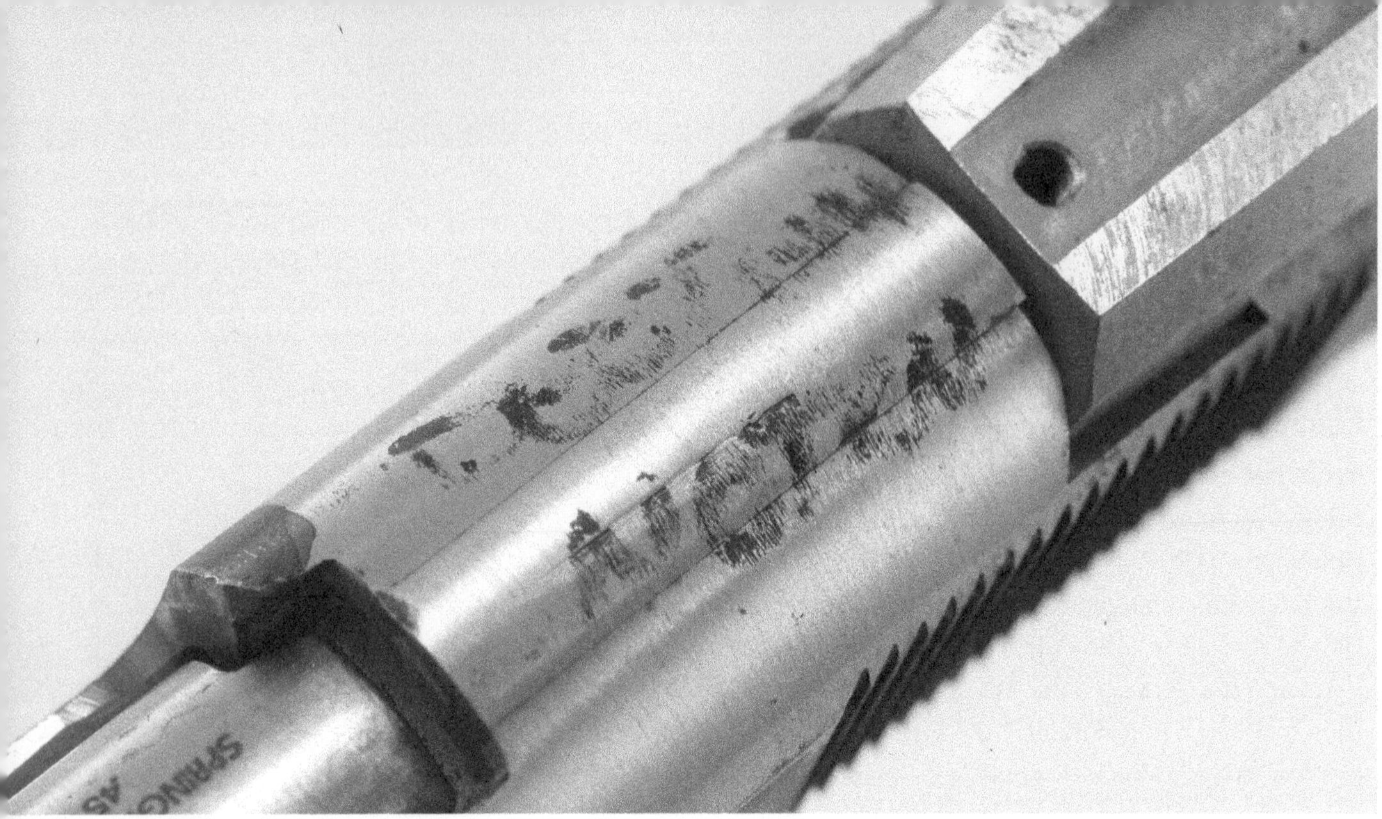

*How adaptable and buildable is the 1911? This USGI slide once had a S&W K-frame sight on it. It got filled (note the lines of the solder job) and milled for one of the early Novaks. If things keep going, it will get milled again for a red-dot sight. Top that, Glock.*

This they got in the late 1950s with the BoMar sight. As the story goes, George Elliason (yes, of the Elliason sight fame on Colt Gold Cups and Pythons) designed it, but he wasn't a manufacturer. So he teamed up with Robert Korzeniewski in Michigan to make them in Korzeniewski's machine shop. (As a legacy of WWII production, much work that we'd now consider "firearms manufacturing" was done in small, one- to two-man machine shops.) Well, they went their separate ways, and the machine shop moved to Texas, where Bob combined his name with his wife's (Mary) to make the BoMar sight.

Originally the BoMar was mounted by driving out the old sight, drilling and tapping the slide to accept the adjustment screw, and installing a taller—much taller—front sight to match the height of the rear sight. This worked just fine for Bullseye shooters, who were the primary buyers of the sight early on. It didn't require much machine work, and if you properly staked in the filing-card-sized front sight, everyone was happy. But the new "combat" shooters weren't happy. The front sight was too tall, would get hung up on holsters, and flew off when using real .45 ammunition.

Custom pistolsmiths developed the "melted" BoMar. Instead of using the factory rear dovetail, they milled a pocket on the slide for the BoMar to ride in a more protected location. And it meant the front sight could now be a standard height. That required a proper endmill and the skills to measure and machine correctly. The real show-offs did a "fenced" installation, where the rear of the pocket retained the sides of the back half of the sight assembly, and the right side of the fence was artfully dished to permit access for the windage adjustment screwdriver.

A "melted and fenced" BoMar signified a high-end custom IPSC gun. That was before optics took over. Also, as soon as pistolsmiths became familiar with the machine work to "melt" a BoMar into a slide, the S&W sight installation dropped out of favor. Dropped like a rock, it did.

The BoMar sight and company lasted until Elliason died in 2007, with no one buying the business or name. But you can find replacement sights, dimensionally identical, just not named BoMar, today.

## HARRISON DESIGN & CONSULTING

There are a lot of 1911 slides set up for the BoMar, but not all users want an adjustable sight. So, John Harrison makes a fixed sight that fits the BoMar slot. It bolts in place with a pair of set screws, and it is solid. He also makes numerous other 1911 parts.

## NOVAK

Wayne Novak wasn't interested in adjustable sights, but he was interested in durable ones. So, he designed a line of sights for the S&W pistols (S&W was on a tear to make pistols for all needs) that were easy to install, swap, and durable. The secret was that both front and rear sights used transverse dovetails. If you wanted something other than what was there (plain, three-dot, night sights, taller or shorter), you drove them out with a hammer and brass drift and press-fit the replacements in. No staking or swaging, and no extra machining needed.

*You need a milling machine to install a BoMar or other sight in a low-mount way. There's no way around it unless you're a British gun maker and used to filing for hours a day.*

The front dovetail was new, but the rear was not the same dimension as the original. If you wanted a Novak rear, you had to machine the slide. But the machining problem was much easier than the one for a BoMar installation. It was a quick dimension change, adjusting the sights to fit a 1911 instead of a S&W slide. Wayne has manufactured over four

*The BoMar sight, in a low-mount milled-in set. Also, notice that the machinist/pistolsmith has left the right-hand "fence" in place and provided clearance for the adjustment screw.*

million of them in the ensuing four-plus decades.

Now, the dovetail front sight isn't new. The original Luger pistol had such a thing. The later HK P7 had it. But on a 1911, you can credit Wayne Novak.

The rear sight grew from the S&W Third Generation pistols that Novak consulted on and the IPSC Model 745 sight. The Novak sight is a perfect embodiment of what we all desired. It is as solid as a ball peen hammer, and it is slick. It's so slick that you can't count on it to leverage against to rack the slide. That had to wait until almost the second decade of the 21st century, when designers started with the Novak as the base, chopped the front, and sloped the face, creating a ledge. That ledge gives you enough purchase that if you need to do a one-handed slide rack, you can push the rear sight against an edge, corner, or rigid holster and work the slide.

*If you have a milling machine and know how to use it, you can dispense with the BoMar base and attach it to the slide using the slide as the base.*

The Novak front has been universally adopted as the new front sight, not just for the 1911 but all pistols. It is the best way to do things (except for Glock, which can't conceive of someone else being better or having done it better). So, while some pistols might have a dovetail that isn't the same size as a 1911's, they are all the same design. That makes life for aftermarket sight manufacturers a lot easier, as they can count on just a few standard dovetail sizes and keep their SKU count down to a reasonable number.

***Brownells did a run of classic 1980s IPSC 1911s, and this has all the details: note that the sights are low-mount BoMars.***

## A WEEKEND IN THE SUN

While the Novak rear was being adopted, S&W offered an adjustable sight for its pistols. It was not only adjustable but designed to be set in and came with a heavy-gauge steel protective "U" that acted like a set of side wings. The neat trick here was that it was a dead-simple machine task. Mill a lateral slot across the top of the slide large enough for the sight assembly to a known depth, and drill and tap the anchor screw holes. Compared to the machine work to mill in a BoMar, you could teach your Labrador retriever to cut a slide for the S&W adjustable. The only problem was that it was just too utilitarian-looking. No one paying the price of a custom 1911 wanted it. I think I did two of them in total.

## LPA

At first glance, the LPA looks like another BoMar. There are slight differences in the locations and proportions of the dovetail and pocket that must be machined. But the big difference is the elevation screw. On the BoMar, it is behind the dovetail cut in the beefy part of the slide (not down through the original GI dovetail cut). The location was selected at a time when the BoMar was customarily installed in the existing dovetail, and locating the adjustment screw outside of the dovetail made sense. On the LPA, the elevation screw is in the dovetail boss of the sight.

Despite the similar appearance, you cannot fit (and have it look good, anyway) one of these in the other machined pocket. While at first glance, the BoMar and LPA look the same, the elevation screw location will tell you which is which if you don't see the markings first.

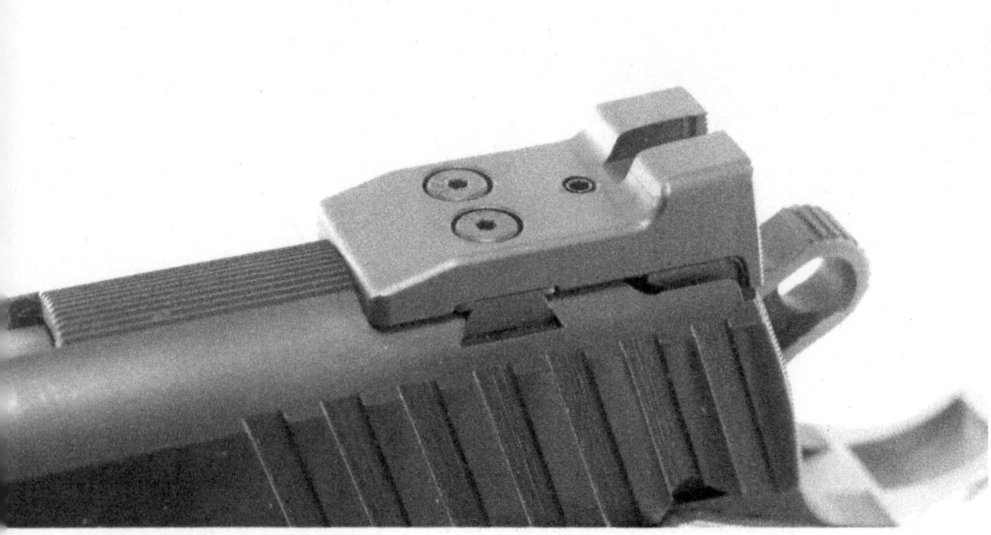

*The Harrison fixed sight replaced the BoMar. How good is it? The author has it on one of his main competition guns.*

## SIGHT ADJUSTMENTS

Adjusting fixed sights is easy. Well, straightforward in concept, not easy to do. Before we get into how, we need to determine how much.

The basic geometry to keep in mind is the Law of Equal Triangles. Look at the sights on your 1911. If you were to move the rear sight by some amount, then the old and new positions and the distance to the front sight would form a triangle. In a fixed ratio, the triangle of the old point of impact, the new point of impact, and the distance to the target is also altered. Since the lengths of each sight radius and the target distance have not changed, the rear sight movement is that fixed ratio to the bullet impact change.

The equation is:

SC/SR + DC/DR

SC is the sight correction, SR is the sight radius, DC is the distance correction, and DR is the distance radius.

The only unknown is the sight correction. Multiply both sides of the equation by sight radius, SR, and you get:

SC = DC x SR/DR

That is, the target correction needed, multiplied by the sight radius, divided by the distance to the target, gets you the amount your sight must be moved.

*A properly machined and installed Novak front sight using the transverse dovetail. The sight is solid, elegant, and easily changed if damaged.*

Ensure everything is marked or calculated in inches (3 feet or 36 inches to the yard), and you're good to go. Well, almost. The standard distance to a target of 25 yards is an odd number of inches (900), which makes the arithmetic awkward. As a result, Ned Christiansen used a tape measure to run his target frame to 28 yards. That's 1,000 inches. Actually, it's 1,008 inches, but the last 8 inches represent less than 1 percent of an "error." That makes the arithmetic so very easy with a Government Model.

Your sight adjustment directions on the rear will be the same direction you want the group to go. Moving the rear sight to the right shoves the group to the right, and vice-versa. Lifting the rear sight (on an adjustable sight) moves the group up. Changes to the front sight are the reverse of that. *Lowering* the front sight *raises* the group, and making it taller lowers it.

The LPA, despite looking like the BoMar, isn't one. Note the elevation screw in the sight body dovetail. It is a good sight and is becoming standard on many factory 1911s with adjustable sights.

## MAKING ADJUSTMENTS

Adjusting windage is relatively easy. Once you've determined the amount of change, you need to establish a zero. For this, you'll need a flat surface. (The top of the shooting bench at your gun club might or might not be flat enough.) One way to ensure a flat surface is to bring a steel rule or a spirit level. With your 1911 unloaded, place the slide flat against the spirit level, and with a dial or digital calipers, measure from the flat surface to a reliable spot on the sight. This could be a flat spot or an edge of the rear notch, but it should be something you can get a consistent measurement on, a consistent .001-inch location. No guessing is involved.

Now, lock the slide in a padded vise (I hope your gun club has a vise you can use) and give the sight a whack in the correct direction with the brass punch and a hammer. Having made your whack, measure again. Has it changed? If so, how much? If the change is close to, or right at, the change you want, reassemble, get to the firing line and shoot another group. You may have to do this a few times before you get it dialed in.

With adjustable sights, change it "X" number of clicks, and shoot another group. Compare the change from those clicks to how much you need, and recalculate.

You'll need a milling machine, knowledge, and experience to properly melt a BoMar or LPA sight into a slide.

## WHERE TO ZERO

In rifles, there are a great many arguments about the appropriate zero distance. You can break up friendships by starting an argument in a group of AR-15 shooters about "25- versus 50-yard zero" and which is best. This is because rifles are, or can be, used over much longer distances than pistols. A rifle might be used on a target from just out of arm's reach to 400 yards. And with the AR-15, where the sights are 2.6 inches above the bore, the trajectory, and knowing it, matters.

With the 1911, not so much. Let's put the outside practical distance at 100 yards. If you zero at 25 yards, your 9mm 115-grain FMJ bullet will be 9 inches low at 100 yards. A .45 230-grain bullet will be a foot low. Since the average shooter can't shoot a group smaller than a foot at 100 yards with a handgun, holding a foot high still means a 50/50 chance of a hit at 100 yards.

At the most likely distances, from hard off the muzzle to maybe 30 yards, the difference between the point of aim and the point of impact will be an inch or less.

So, the standard distance is 25 yards, where a decent shooter can still post a group of 4 inches or so. With a good group, you'll be able to see if the sights are off by an inch or more. If you're shooting a 4-inch group at 25 yards, and it looks like your group is off-center by half an inch, don't change it. It could just as well be you or the random fluctuation of bullet dispersion. You can make a change if you've shot four or five groups and they all show a half-inch off-center in the same direction. Otherwise, don't.

*A clever way to achieve a close setup of iron sights is to use a milling machine and extra tooling to indicate the sight height and center. The rest of us go to the range and test and adjust. Photo: Jason Burton*

## OPTICS

Rifles used to all come with iron sights attached. And a "scope" was a new thing that might or might not be trusted. Today, it is a rare rifle (other than lever guns) that comes with iron sights. Nearly all rifles are drilled and tapped for scope mounts, and you are expected to mount an optic on top.

The evolution of optics on the 1911, and pistols in general, is interesting. The first use of optics in practical competition came when Jerry Barnhart showed up at the 1990 USPSA Nationals with a red-dot on his pistol. The initial reaction from all was, "Well, that's stupid." When he was done blowing the doors off the competition, handily winning the match, everyone else got busy putting a "dot" on their pistols. Later that year, at the IPSC World Shoot, Doug Koenig had a red-dot on his pistol and won that match, with Jerry a close second.

By the 1991 Nationals, everyone who was a contender had a red-dot sight of one kind or another on their pistol, and the ones who had practiced had two or three pistols set up that way.

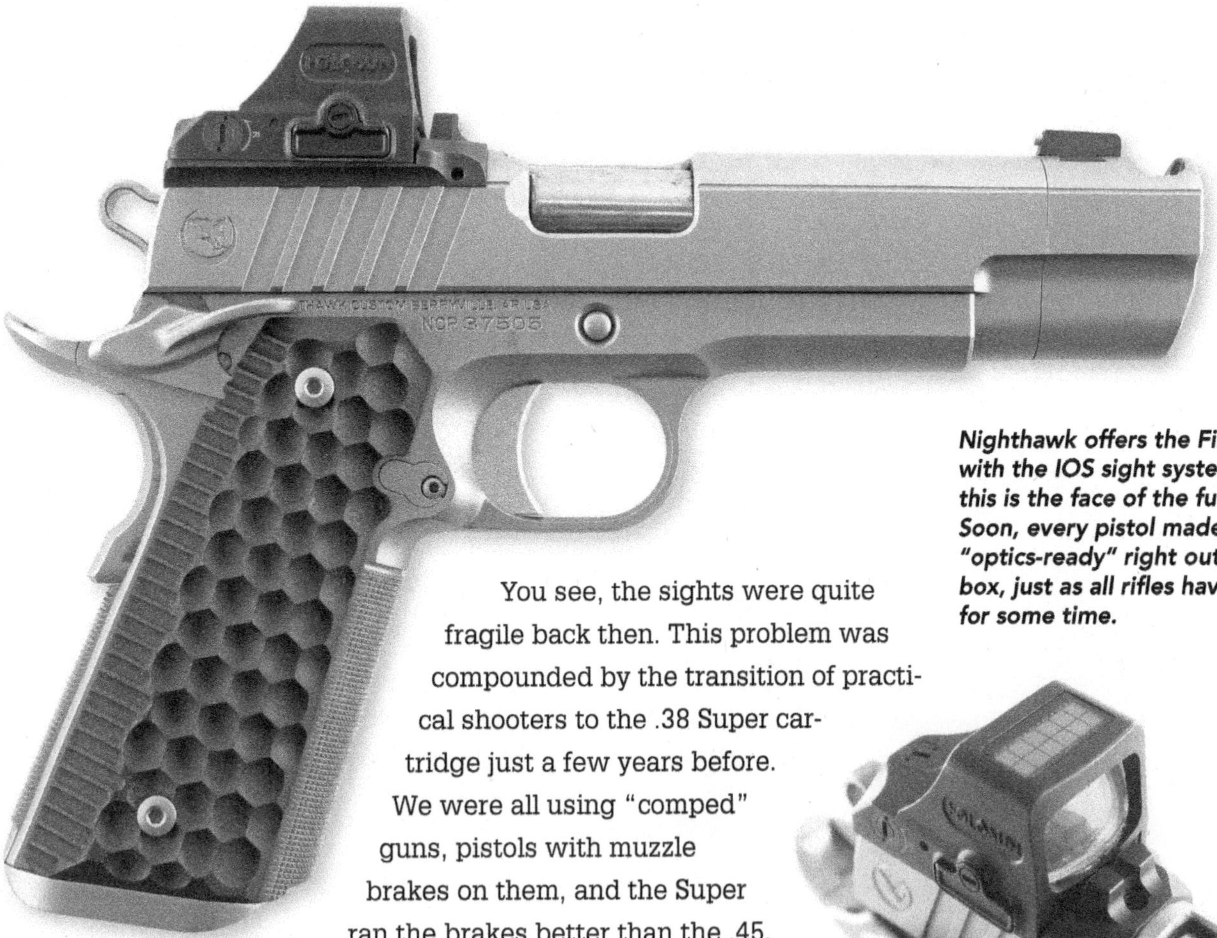

Nighthawk offers the Firehawk with the IOS sight system, and this is the face of the future. Soon, every pistol made will be "optics-ready" right out of the box, just as all rifles have been for some time.

You see, the sights were quite fragile back then. This problem was compounded by the transition of practical shooters to the .38 Super cartridge just a few years before. We were all using "comped" guns, pistols with muzzle brakes on them, and the Super ran the brakes better than the .45. So we were shooting 125-grain bullets at 1,400 fps, and while that was hard on the guns, it was epic on the sights.

The sights were so big they could not ride on the slide. Their weight would have stalled the pistol. And, the sights would have died even faster. So, we used frame-attached scope mounts. Koenig even went so far as to have his frame-mounted scope rings welded to the scope base because the vibrations from .38 Super at Major were so fierce. Within a few years, the sights got smaller and

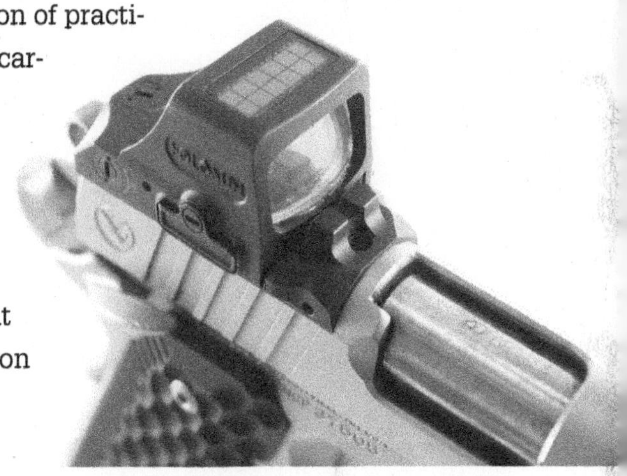

The Nighthawk IOS also has backup iron sights; the rear is mounted in front of the optic, so it's out of the way.

As an elegant bit of pistolsmithing, the Nighthawk IOS is two plates. One has the optic and irons, and the other irons are located by pins in the slide for a consistent return to zero.

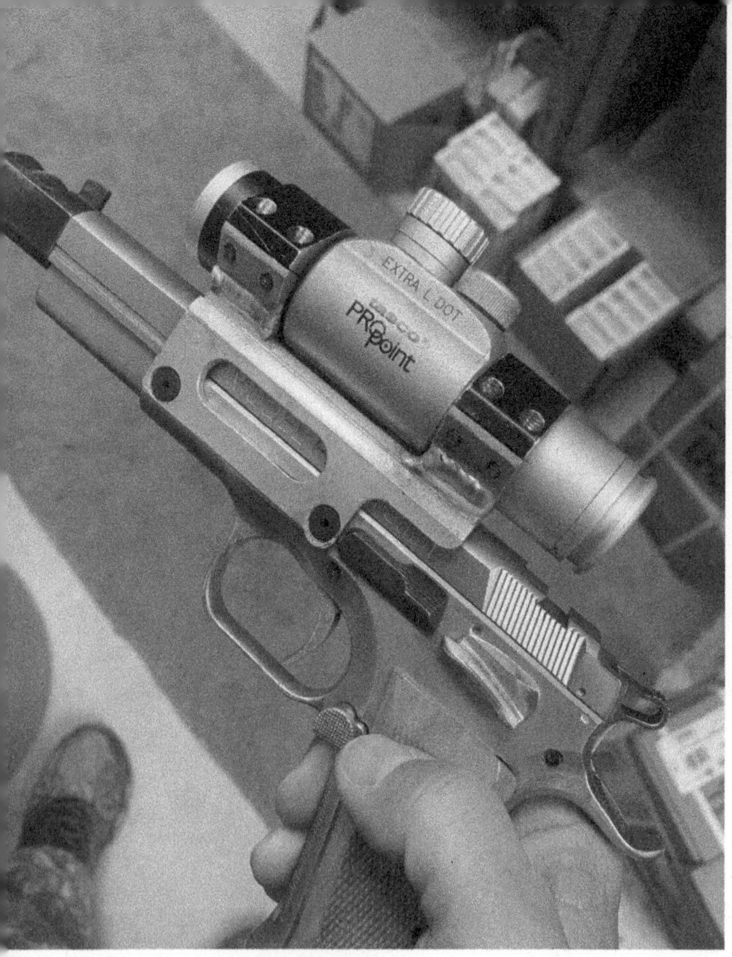


*Doug Koenig's 1990 IPSC World Shoot-winning pistol. Note that the rings have been welded to the base; otherwise, things would shake apart. Major loads are harsh now, and they were ferocious back then.*

had larger apertures. A fellow Open Division competitor on my squad mentioned he had a "box of sights." He had them pre-zeroed with batteries installed. If one died, he would use his screwdriver to unbolt it and replace it with one still working—that's how fragile they were. And a few months later, imagine my surprise at seeing his name listed in Mogadishu: Randy Shugart.

By the 21st century, it was possible to mount the sight on the slide. I did this in 1998 for my first IPSC World Shoot trip to Cebu, Philippines. And then again, for my trip to South Africa for the 2002 World Shoot. I was shooting in Modified Division both times, an equipment class that lasted only through the 2011 World Shoot. The sight survived those two IPSC shoots and a couple of USPSA Nationals. The matches were fun, but it became clear that I could not spend my time both as a writer and a competitor and do my best in both. I had to pick one and opted for writing.

Today, optical sights are so compact they can readily ride on the slide and survive the experience, and it's typical to see them coming from the factory so equipped. They weigh so little that they are not a hindrance. But, installing them can be a problem with the 1911. Various current hi-cap 9mm pistols with model variations ready to accept a red-dot optic can be found. But the 1911 is not so much, in part, because the slide is narrower. With a .900 to .910-inch slide, the 1911 is narrower than the Glock G17 (the typical 9mm hi-cap standard). But red-dot makers produce models narrow enough not to hang over the sides of a 1911 slide. It is possible, and many of those who mount red-dots on a 1911 do it, to use a mounting plate with a scallop or angled base to bring the width of the 1911 slide up to the width of the red-dot base. When done right, this can look good.

If 1911 makers in the production pistol marketplace are not yet commonly on board with the mods (that will change as they adapt their CNC cutting programs and

*The optical sight mounted on Sweeney's IPSC Modified Division gun for the 1999 & 2002 World Shoots.*

see the market demand), other makers have really jumped in. One is Nighthawk, with its IOS mod. It involves machining the slide to accept a replaceable plate. One plate has an iron sight; the other is machined for a red-dot optic and has a backup iron sight. This is cool, but there's a catch: Nighthawk won't install it on your 1911 unless it is a Nighthawk 1911.

***Another way to mount the optic is to leave space behind for backup irons.***

You could use an adapter plate that fits the rear sight dovetail onto which you mount a red-dot. But that puts the dot high over the slide and is also somewhat fragile. Ideally, you want a slide already machined for a red-dot or a pistolsmith who can machine the slide for you. You have some choices as far as optics-ready right out of the box are concerned, such as the Dan Wesson Specialist Black Optics Ready, Springfield DS Prodigy, several Kimbers, Ed Brown FX1, Wilson Combat CQB Elite, and much of the Staccato line.

If you have a 1911 that is not optics-ready, you'll have to find a pistolsmith with a milling machine and the skills and experience to mill the slide.

In perusing the offerings, you may see many 1911s ready to go with red-dots where the dot mount is curiously bolted to the frame. These are USPSA/IPSC competition guns meant for the Open Division. The slide-to-frame fit will be exacting, and the barrel will be comped. The durability it presents, being a frame-mount, is much superior to a slide-mount setup. "Well, I want the superior one," you say. It is superior in two ways: the frame mount will stand up to a season's firing of 50,000 rounds or more, and it's heavier, softening the felt recoil.

But will you shoot 50,000 rounds a year? Maybe, but that, at current prices, represents about $20,000 to $25,000 in ammo. I thought not. And as far as the weight is concerned, do you want to be holstering a pistol that weighs in at close to or over three pounds? No, a frame-mount RDS is not in the daily carry ensemble for a reason.

***The iron sights on this Springfield TRP can be used if the battery dies in the optic.***

But putting a red-dot optic on a 1911 is not something outré, unlike it used to be. ●

CHAPTER

# 18

# MAGAZINES

There was a time when magazines were a sore spot on the 1911 landscape. The first mags were designed and produced in the earliest era of pressed-metal technology. Yes, steel stamping as a technology had to be invented, and the details worked out in the first decade of the 20th century. It wouldn't be until the auto industry got onto the job in the 1920s that the technology moved into high gear.

The first 1911 magazines are now collectibles of the first order. The manufacturing process was involved: the sheet steel (of a particular alloy and in an annealed state) was fed into the blanking machine, where a cookie cutter-type mechanism stamped it out. Then, it went into another machine to be folded into a tube and the lips formed. In the next step, it got welded down the back, and the weld bead was cleaned up to create a smooth surface.

*The original taper-lip hardball or GI magazine. It worked fine, but it has been long since any were produced under government contracts. If you have any, retire them as historical objects and get new ones of modern design.*

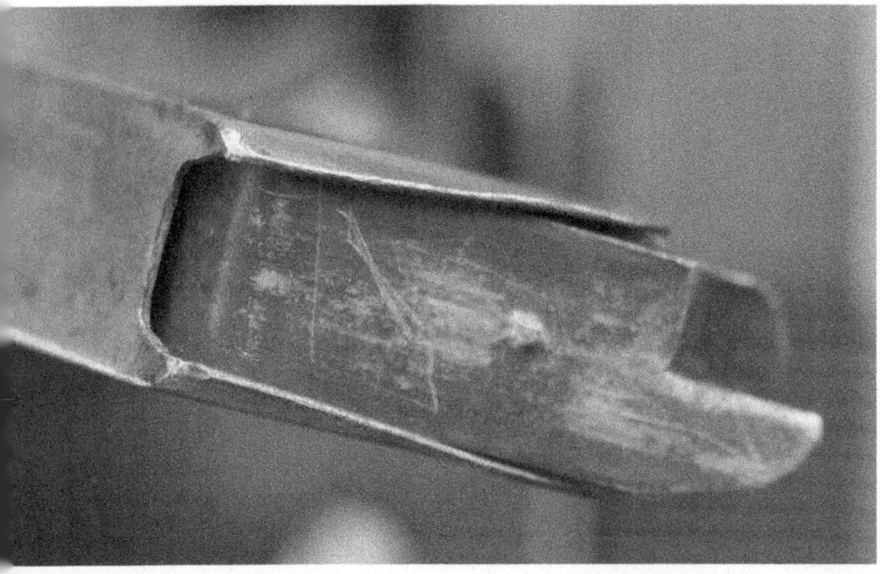

Meanwhile, the machine line was cutting small-sized bars of steel into baseplates, complete with tabs that would nestle inside the magazine tube. The next machine was a drilling station, and an operator placed the tube in a fixture that held each magazine tube and its baseplate while the machine drilled two holes through the tube sides and the baseplate and its flanges at the bottom and all the way through. Then, the baseplate was pinned to the tube with a pair of steel pins.

The next-to-last step was the most important: treatment. Steel stamping and alloy selection weren't advanced enough to make the magazine hardened and remain "springy" (technical term), so the feed lips had to be strong and durable. This involved dipping the finished mag into a cyanide solution, which hardened it. To make it springy, they fabricated the cutting head to create a keyhole-shaped slot on the top rear of the tube in the stamped plate or blank. This keyhole allowed the magazine to flex enough to feed and be hard enough not to deform while strong enough to last.

The cyanide treatment made the steel so hard that the last blueing step didn't take on the treated section. The top half of the magazine, where it had been cyanide-treated, would not take the bluing solution. So it stayed in the white but was so hard it would not rust. Those

***The first magazines used machined steel baseplates with cross pins to hold them on. They had to do this because steel pressings were a new technology, and the welding process was unestablished.***

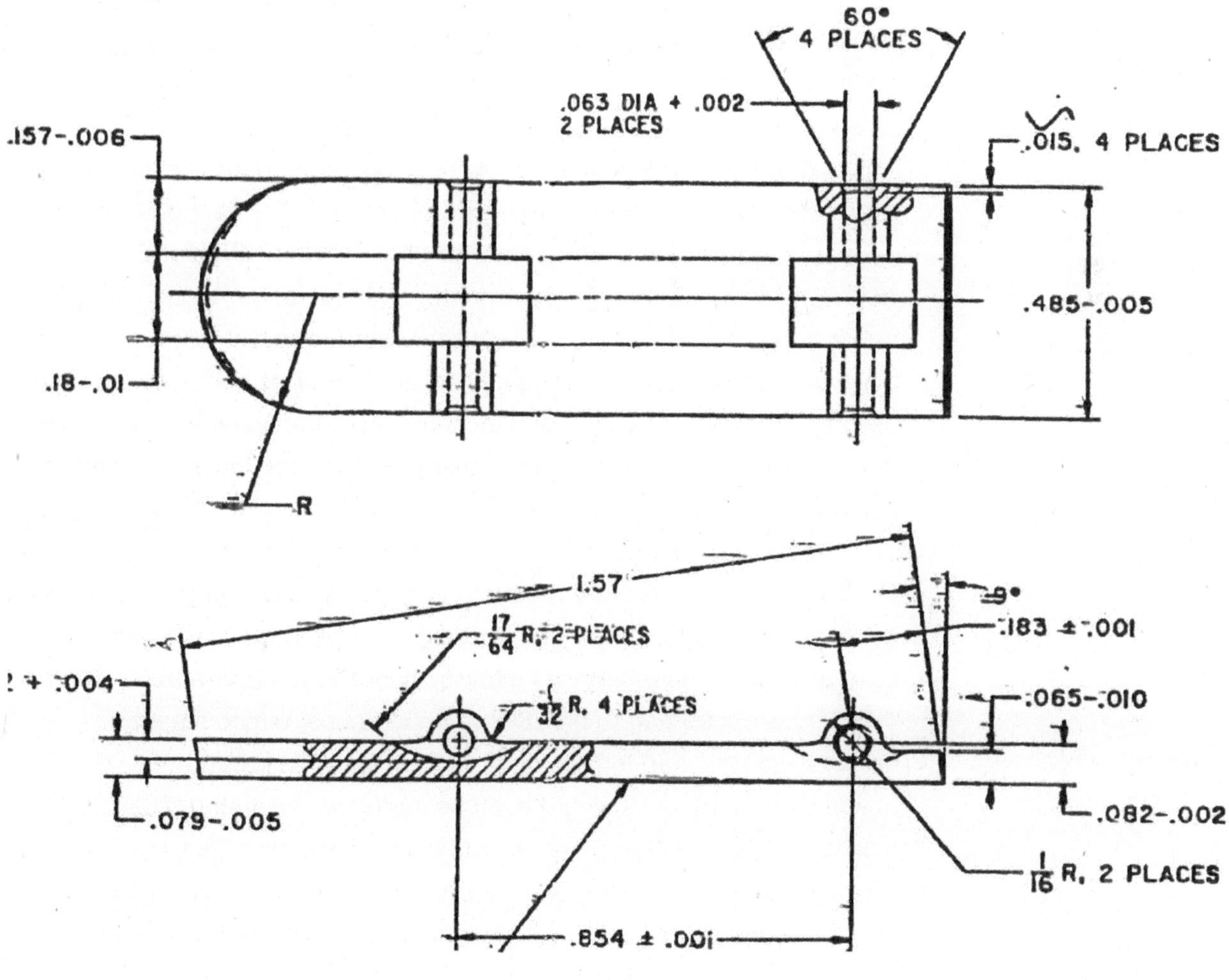

"keyhole" magazines were only made for a few years, and they are now so rare that they are fabulously expensive, as magazines go.

The next step was to change the alloy and heat treatment so that the keyhole wasn't needed, but they still got the cyanide treatment. Then, the alloying and heat treatment were improved even more, and the cyanide treatment was dropped, and they were fully blued. The machined baseplate got ditched for a stamped sheet metal plate welded to the tube's bottom.

Through all of that, the feed lips remained the same shape: a gradual taper to the front to control the path of the cartridge up to and through the extractor taking control. From this process came the shape of USGI magazines, from the beginning in 1911 through the last government contract for magazines, sometime in the 1960s. 1960s? Yes, while the last 1911A1 for government acquisition was made in 1945, magazines were consumable. As they wore out, were lost, "went missing," and were abused, the 1911A1 kept going and needed new mags. As the last of the 1945-era magazines became scarce, the government, still using the 1911, ordered more. And the specifications for those mags did not change, even as technology advanced. So, government contracts for magazines up to the Vietnam War were like those in WWII.

At the same time, magazine makers who were not government contractors were making them because the same forces were at work in the rest of the world. You might, in 1975, buy a USGI "surplus" 1911A1 (surplus in that the government was no longer using it, but not surplus because it would come as a surprise to the government to discover that that particular pistol had not been lost in combat outside of some small town in Germany in 1945, but came home in a GI's duffle bag) and the one magazine that it came with. But if you wanted more, you had to buy them.

So how and why did that change? Remember that the primary competition was Bullseye until the advent of practical shooting or IPSC. In Bullseye, you needed a .22 LR handgun, an Any Centerfire handgun, a .45 handgun, and a Service Pistol to shoot the full four-gun course. The Service Pistol had to be USGI in appearance, which meant no external change, and fed Hardball or 230-grain FMJ round-nose ammo. In many early matches, you'd even be supplied the ammo. The .22 LR was whatever met the rulebook, and that left the Any Centerfire and .45. We've covered this in the calibers section, but we're now looking at it from the perspective of magazines. For these two categories,

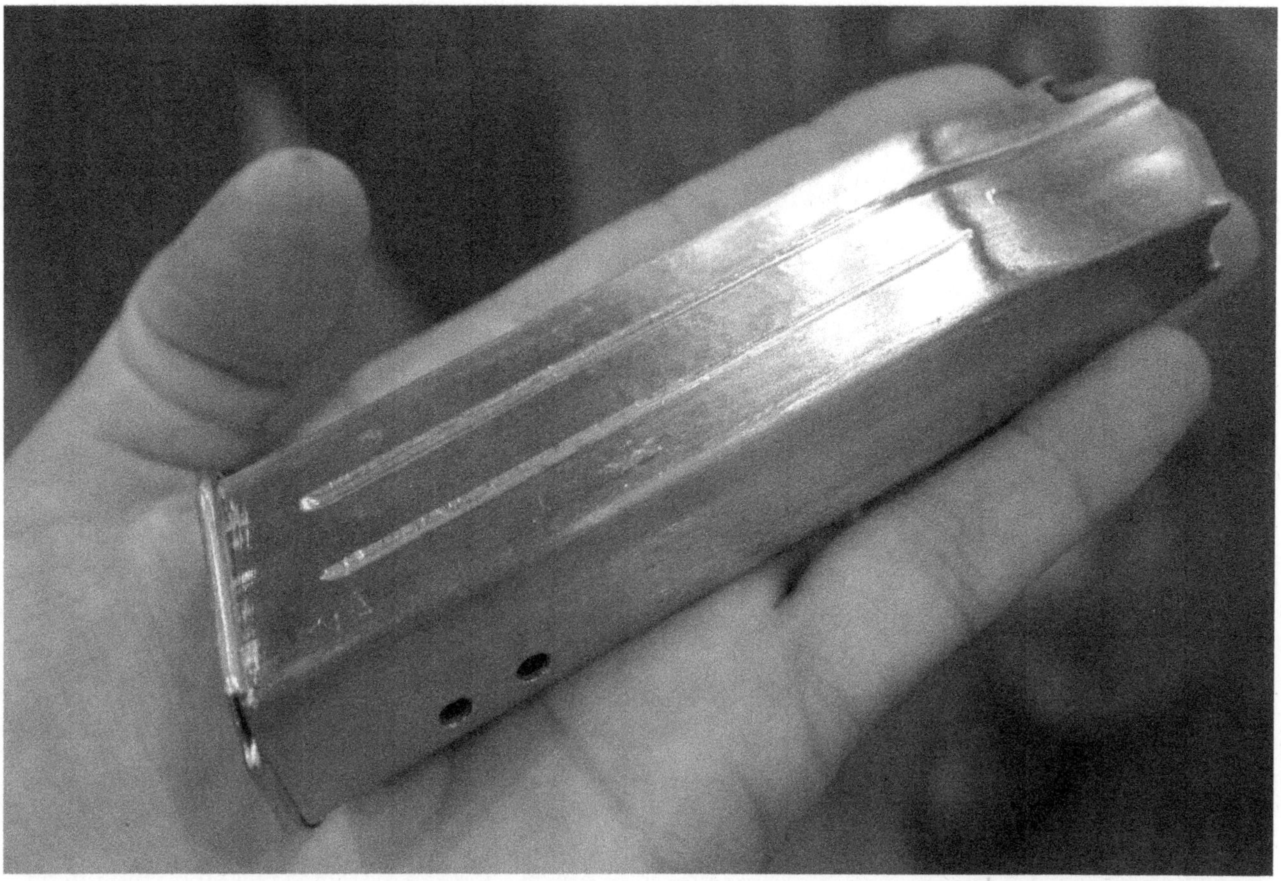

you did not have to use 230 hardball. So, serious competition shooters built "softball" guns, 1911s that would work with lighter bullets and softer loads. The common early—for a long time, factory—load was a 185-grain semi-wadcutter. Yes, it was softer in felt recoil but problematic in feeding; why? Because the nose of the 185-grain bullet was so much shorter than that of the 230-grain round nose. Why? I have no idea. I have suspicions and surmised reasons, but only the historical fact of the short-nosed bullet.

***An older-generation competition magazine made for the .40 S&W hand-fitted, adjusted, tuned, sweated over, and holds one more round than a standard mag.***

This meant that the bullet went forward for a longer distance on feeding, nosing downward before it struck the frame ramp to be forced upward. This changed the leverage angle and created problems. Also, traveling a longer distance forward contacted the extractor for a more extended period (in microseconds of travel) before camming upward. This also changed the leverage. The result was the bullet could be cranky in feeding. While Bullseye competitors could get "alibis" in the course (you could reshoot a string because your pistol jammed), it was disconcerting, threw off the shooter's concentration, and caused an annoying delay.

So, shooters altered the magazines. The shooting scene was awash in 1911 mags. Making them was easy; manufacturers filled contracts faster than the pistol makers during the war. This wasn't an issue during the war, as magazines were consumables, and you couldn't have too many. When the war suddenly ended, the government had warehouses full of them. So, there wasn't much of a market for new ones for some time, which meant you had to modify existing ones to have something different.

I'm sure the first experimenters were brutal and used pliers, grinders and who-knows-what to alter feed lips. Where it ended up was a special tool, the "lip-forming die," which you used to modify GI mags. The die was a hardened steel set of swaging dies. You'd put the magazine (no spring or follower) in the die, blocked or braced, and place the other on it, hit it with a hammer. Brownells offered it with complete instructions.

*The late Chip McCormick led the way, first with an eight-round follower for regular 1911 magazines, then better mags.*

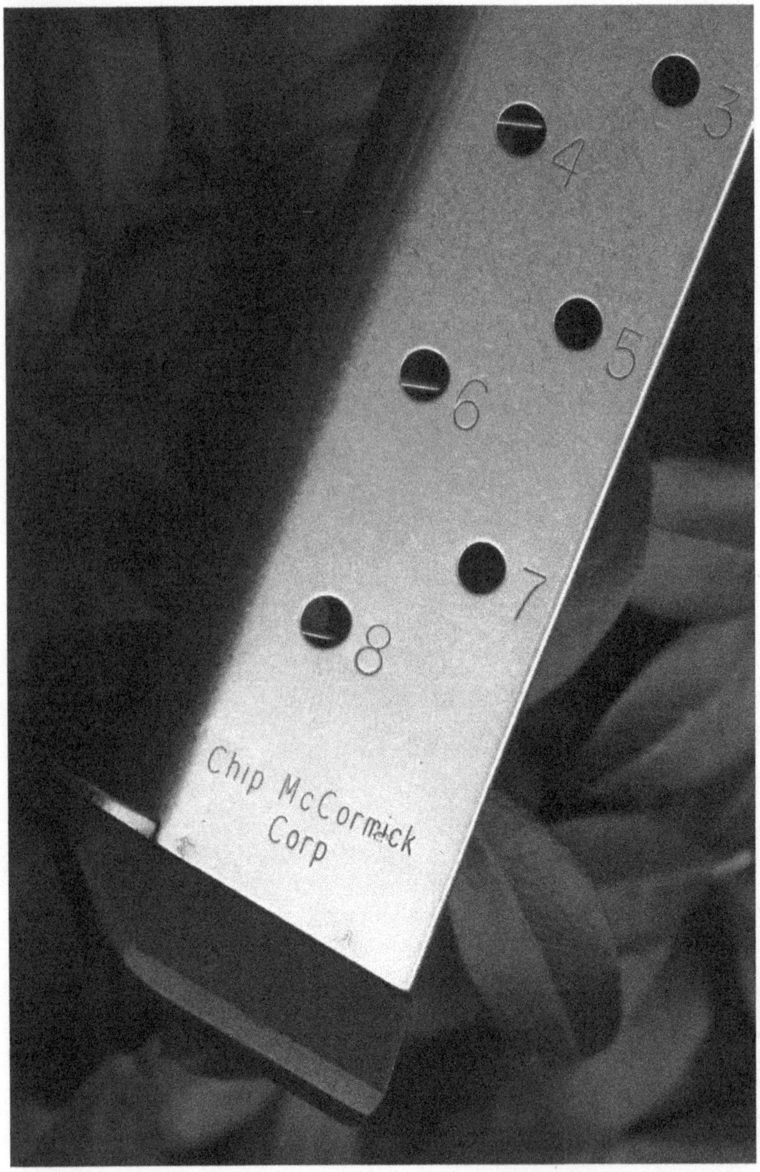


What good did it do? It reformed the feed lips so they released the cartridge sooner, keeping it from binding on the frame ramp from nose-diving; it also took the 1911 out of the controlled-feed status. The case rim was released, and the extractor picked up the rim on the fly. Magazines that were so modified were referred to as "wadcutter mags."

Colt, stocked with ample GI mags from wartime production, kept shipping pistols with them for many years after 1945. It wasn't until the supply started falling that it went to a modified wadcutter design. During that time, a new bullet began to make a much larger appearance—the H&G 68.

Designed in the 1940s, the H&G 68 bullet (the company was Hensley & Gibbs, now out of business) was a 200-grain semi-wadcutter with one significant difference from the short-nosed 185-grain semi-wadcutter: This rim of the nose was coincidental with the radius of the 230 bullet, and this

coincidental point was right where the round-nosed bullet struck the frame ramp. Superbly accurate, easy to stuff into a case in the reloading process (the base has a bevel, making insertion and alignment easier), and reliable in feeding, it became the default bullet of the new IPSC competition.

*If the baseplate on your "bolt-on" basepads does not come tapped, don't believe the "self-tapping" screws will work. Get a proper tap and cut the threads yourself.*

However, magazines were a problem. Since the H&G 68 fed like a 230 RN, it would have been fine in USGI mags. But the magazine supply was not uniform. If you were buying magazines in the late 1970s and early 1980s, you found everything: genuine USGI, reliable GI clones, craptastic copies that bent if dropped, altered GI to wadcutter lips, Colt-modified wadcutter, and newly made wadcutter mags of every dimension. And the mags' steel hardness was also all over the map.

One of the first articles I ever wrote was about selecting, testing, and *not ever loaning* your 1911 magazines. Back then, magazines that worked 100 percent of the time were so rare and precious that you never let anyone else use them.

Two things changed that. One was Shooting Star magazines,

which Chip McCormick and Bill Wilson, growing tired of crappy mags, endorsed. Chip, as was Bill Wilson, was a top competitor in the early 1980s. They were friends and also had another thing in common: they were businessmen. Most business people running gun companies, then and now, are not shooters. (In most businesses, the top people are not product people. Car companies are not run by "car guys," gun companies are not run by "gun guys," etc. One exception is software, only because the subject is so arcane, programmers must run things from the start, but as soon as a company grows, the money guys move in, and then MBAs run the software company. Someone with an MBA can run any company. Just ask them.)

Shooting Star produced new mags out of proper steel, with correctly shaped lips to feed even the H&G 68, and also added one extra: a special follower that increased capacity from 7 to 8 rounds. This feature was beyond fabulous, giving you a potential leg up in the competition. Chip parlayed his endorsement contract of the magazines into ownership of the company and used his business sense to improve it even more and add products.

Bill Wilson shifted his focus from being a top competitor to becoming a top businessman who made or sourced the improved products that shooters desired. His big foray was to unveil the 47D magazine, which was different in several regards. First, instead of making magazines by folding sheet metal, he extruded them—in stainless steel. To make an extruded magazine, you take a section of seamless steel tubing and force it into a die that squeezes it like toothpaste. That shapes it into a magazine and forms the feed lips. By selecting the correct alloy and introducing it into the die at the proper hardness level, you work-harden it to the correct hardness and springiness. Wilson used slots on the sides instead of holes to show capacity, which shed debris better. The bottoms of the mags did not have a welded-on baseplate. Instead, the tube had the bottom edges folded inward. A baseplate would slide onto the rails this fold formed. Inside, a bottom plate on the spring had a raised bump that

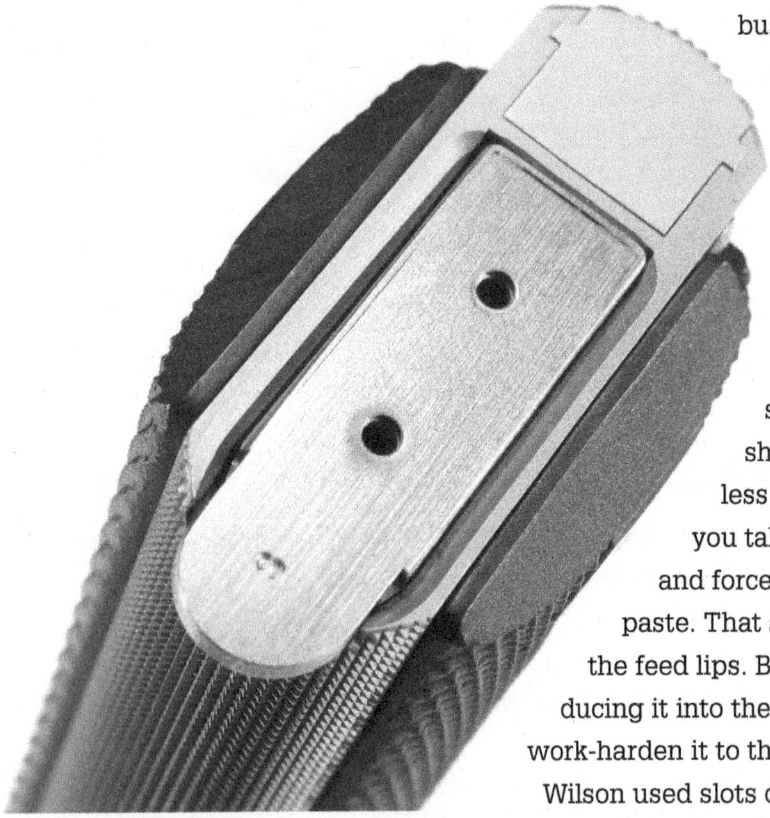

*The task is almost done. The mag well is slightly beveled, but the basepad isn't installed. Tap those holes, screw on the pads, and be ready.*

1911 magazines are incredibly tough. Sweeney has stepped on (and skidded on) them. This rusty one, found at the range, still works fine.

fits into a hole in the baseplate. It all interlocked. You could take your magazines apart to clean them and swap out the baseplate for something else. And we did. Oversized plastic and even brass baseplates became the norm in IPSC competition.

## EXTENDED BASEPLATES

A quick overview of extended baseplates. You may think they were meant to soften the impact on the ground. Well, maybe. If they hit that way, OK, but mostly, they enhanced magazine insertion and locking. With the magazine flush, it wasn't always a sure thing to get the magazine locked in place in the middle of a stage. And if you had used a bolt-on magazine funnel, the magazine had to go higher than the bottom of the mag funnel. So, we added length to the magazine as an extended baseplate.

Meanwhile, the older designs tried to keep up. You'd have to drill the baseplate and bolt on an extension to add an extended baseplate. Many magazine makers used the holes, and the baseplate makers provided their extensions with "self-tapping" screws. As if. After the first one, I measured the screws, used a tap to cut threads, and bolted on the extension. If you have one of these magazines, you'd be wise to spend a few dollars to buy a tap (most of the ones I installed were 4-40 thread pitch) and save the hassle of "self-tapping" the screw.

*Recon Marines are doing raid practice and packing M45A1 pistols. They are also using 10-round Wilson mags because more is better.*

I have Wilson 47D magazines from that era with brass baseplates on them. The length made them easier to reload during a stage, and the weight ensured they'd fall free quickly. Others are extended plastic or aluminum, held on with screws. And I have some that worked (so I used them) that weren't drilled or tapped. Instead, I used contact cement and crepe neoprene, shoe soles material. I glued and sanded them flush to the tube sides with a belt sander. They worked great. Imagine my surprise to pull them out of the magazine drawer a decade-plus later to find that the neoprene had hardened like concrete. Bye-bye soft reloads, and welcome to "just like metal" baseplates.

*The hi-cap mags are double-stack and thus will not fit into an original single-stack frame.*

Once it was evident that the 1911 could be a reliable feeder with proper magazines, and there was a market for them due to the increased IPSC competitions, sales and competition took off.

Fast-forward to the Clinton administration. With the passage of the Assault Weapons Ban of 1994 (AWB/94), magazines over 10 rounds in capacity could no longer be made. No problem. In the case of the 47D, a bit longer tubes were fed into the magazine machine, and it spits out 10-round mags. Called the "Bureaucrat," it was as reliable as the eight-shot original (oh yes, Bill Wilson figured out a way to make his seven-shot magazines into eight-shot), making the 1911 up-to-date. Yes, the magazine was slightly longer, but your 1911 in .45 held just as many rounds as a G17, and it had 10-shot magazines and bigger bullets at that.

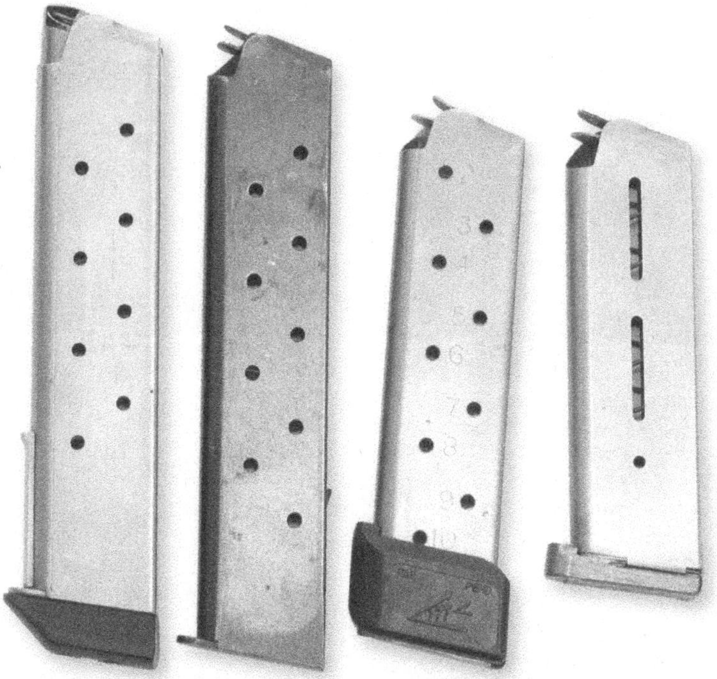

*Some big mags, next to a not-so-big one. Left is an Ed Brown, then one of the Italian magazines, a Wilson Combat, and one of the author's Wilson 47s with a brass baseplate.*

This magazine was so popular and of such utility that I saw USMC Recon web gear setups in photos of 10-round mag pouches for their issue 1911s. When the government gets on board, you know it's good. One detail about the 10-shot magazines: they were longer. Oh, it is obvious, you say? Well, a too-long magazine, shoved rudely into the frame in a speedy reload, can go past the mag catch, hit the ejector, and bind in place. It won't feed, and it won't fall out. Wilson solved that by using a larger plastic basepad that came up the sides of the magazine and stopped upward travel. Ed Brown riveted a stop block to the front of his tubes.

Today, the source of reliable 1911 magazines is legion. While some might be better made, last longer, or be better-looking, you'd be hard-pressed to find bad or unreliable ones. Bad magazine makers would soon go out of business.

## HI-CAPACITY AND CALIBER

Or standard capacity, depending on how obstinate you want to be. One variant is length. On the short side, a magazine for the Officers Model is shorter and won't lock into place in a Government Model. But, the Government will lock into an Officer's Model. Caution: You can over-insert a Government Model magazine into an Officers frame and wedge the top against the ejector if the ejector is extended. Wilson Combat makes a baseplate with a raised front lip, so you can use a government-sized magazine in an officers-sized frame and not have that problem.

*Before you stock up on magazines for competition, make sure you know what the rules allow. Some events might not approve the magazine capacity-increasing baseplate on the left.*

One of the earliest hi-cap mags was an import; we all called it the "Italian magazine." After all this time, I can't remember exactly why, but they held 11 rounds of .45 ACP. For IPSC—this was before the USPSA was founded—they were great. They were even better for the Second Chance match in the nine-pin event. That involved nine bowling pins set at the back of the table. A 9mm load would readily tip them off. A good 9mm load, a 124-grain at 1,075 fps, has a Power Factor of 135. Now, if you didn't have a 9mm, but only a .45, and wanted to shoot the nine-pin, shooting 230-grain hardball would suck. Your score is the time it took to knock them off the table, and recoil is not your friend here. Hardball PF is 178 for even a relatively mild load.

The crease or groove on the magazine on the right controls the bullet tip location. It is on magazines for 9mm, .38 Super, .40 S&W, and 10mm.

But, if you reload your ammo and use 185-grain lead semiwadcutters to 750 fps, your Power Factor is 139. You're in the ballpark. So, nine bowling pins, starting with 12 shots in the gun, means you are as good as anyone at the start.

We all had a fistful of those mags. Where they all are now, I have no idea.

Today, the event (there is still a bowling pin match, and it is still fun, called The Pin Shoot) is called the 9x12, and it involves 12 pins. Well, 12 shots for 12 pins is doable, but you'd have to be very sure of yourself. So we all use 9mms now. However, if you had literal buckets of .40 brass and a 1911 chambered for it—or a 10mm you could re-barrel—you'd be ready (.40-cal. 180s at 775 fps do the same thing).

The USPSA imposed length limits but not capacity limits on most divisions. You can buy magazines or tubes of the correct length or add a baseplate that increases capacity. The rules are the rules, so know them before you show up with equipment that will get your score docked.

Oh, and the grooves you see on the sides of magazines? Bullet control. The 9mm or .38 Super 1911 tube must be the same as that of a .45. The groove keeps the cartridge nose centered in the feed path. The base will square up when the stripper rail hits it, but the nose needs guidance or won't feed properly.

## BRAND-SPECIFIC

The hi-cap 1911 magazine world is split into STI and Para Ordnance. *They are not interchangeable.* You can tell the difference by looking at the tube from the back. The Para has a much sharper angle to the double-to-single transition. Know which your pistol is, and know what type you are buying.

## 9MM THEN AND NOW

The original 9mm magazines came from Colt (although Colt did not make them), and to address the shorter 9mm overall length, a sheet metal spacer was installed at the rear of the magazine. Until the early 21st century, 9mm 1911s were not considered reliable. That one now and then was, or that a pistolsmith could make them so, was a minor miracle. And we ascribed the unreliability primarily to the magazines. "Why can't Colt make a proper 9mm mag?" was the lament.

Well, things are different today. And the problem wasn't the magazine, but the pistols, which have been corrected so no one looks at a 9mm 1911 and thinks, "Jam-a-matic." There has been one significant change in magazines, however. While a bunch are still made with the sheet metal insert, there are also ones with the front of the tube creased in. This feature restricts the internal length, so it is proper for the 9mm. It also allows the makers to build a short feed ramp into the magazine. The big problem with the 9mm was that it was short. When the stripper rail hit the rim, the round nose-dived. The .45 impacts the feed ramp *before* it has dove too far and then feeds upward. The 9mm could keep diving and end up with the bullet nose wedged into the frame below the ramp.

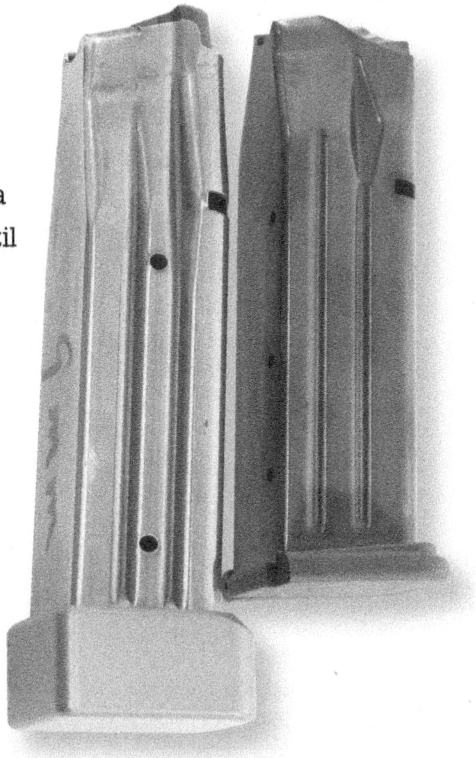

*The hi-cap 1911 world is split in two: on the left is an STI pattern, and on the right is a Para pattern.*

The magazine with the insert at the rear starts the 9mm farther forward, and it doesn't have time to wedge. The mags with the crease in the front and the internal feed ramp use that magazine ramp to pitch the 9mm round upward and feed properly.

In other words, 9mm 1911s now feed properly and are popular. The cost of ammo and the lessened recoil make it much more so than the .45, I'm afraid.

## MAGAZINE CARE

Keeping your magazines in good condition will make shooting a lot more fun. We've covered the Wilson 47D construction method, so let's start there. With an empty magazine, use a punch to push into the hole in the bottom of the baseplate and push the internal plate away from contact. Slide the baseplate forward off the rails. As you do this, restrain the interior plate and spring from launching themselves. Then, pull the spring and follower out of the tube. Wipe the follower, spring plate and baseplate

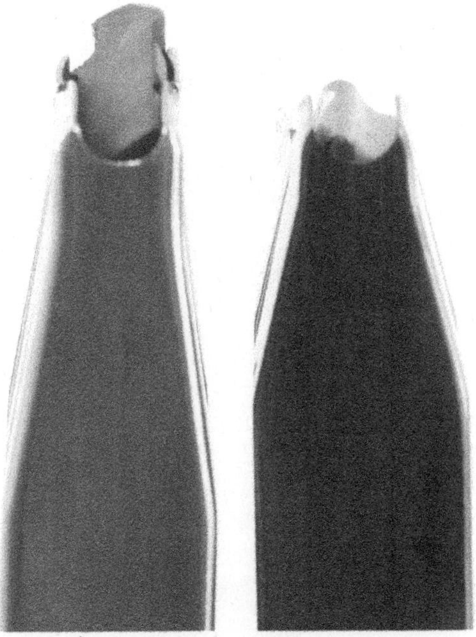

*Note the difference from the back: the Para (on the right) has a much sharper taper that starts higher on the tube.*

This 9mm magazine has a sheet metal insert at the rear of the tube.

clean. Use a dry brush to scrub grit out of the tube. Note the orientation of the spring and its angles to the follower and the interior plate.

*Never lubricate the interior of the magazine or its parts*. Never. All that will do is encourage the magazine to collect dirt, dust, lint, debris and god-knows-what, none of which belong on the inside.

Fit the follower on top of the spring, shove it back into the tube, and compress it with the interior plate. Slide the baseplate onto the rails and depress the interior plate enough to clear the retaining bump. Once it clicks together, you are done.

Magazines with baseplates that don't come off are different. Use a pencil to push the follower down a few rounds distance. Insert a punch through the tube holes to trap the spring in place. Turn the magazine over, tap the feed lips onto a padded surface, and let the follower drop. Pull it out the front of the tube, rotating it to clear the lips. Hold the feed lips against the padded surface and pull the punch out, letting the spring snap to the pad. Grab the spring and pull it out of the tube. Again, note the orientation of the spring to the tube and follower.

The sheet metal insert is part of the tube. It does not move down with the follower.

Scrub, don't lube, and reassemble. Reassembly is simple, if requiring some dexterity. Push the spring in until it is entirely under the feed lips. Next, take the follower, insert the bottom back side under the feed lips, and push it back over the spring. Rotate it to bring the lifter side to the top as you push and insert it into the tube. Once in place, ensure the spring is fully under it. If it isn't, tap the back of the magazine against your padded surface to snap the spring into place.

## MAGAZINE SPRINGS

Springs wear out and should be replaced if you get failures to lock open after the last round. I ran into this when I switched to the .38 Super for IPSC/USPSA competition. I was shooting PPC, Steel Challenge, USPSA, and bowling pins for a few years, all with a .38 Super. I was at the range two or three times a week in matches, running buckets of ammo through various Supers, plus regular practice, all with the same magazines. It took about two years for the magazine springs to take a set, and I replaced them.

***Putting a 9mm into the 1911 was a hassle, at least until reliable magazines came along. These have the crease in the front to take up space and create a slight feed ramp.***

As mentioned, it bears repeating: If your local gun club expert tells you to pull the spring out and stretch it back to its original length, *ignore him*. Ignore any other advice he might have. Springs don't work that way, and if you follow his advice, you are just making the problem worse. Springs are not expensive; if yours are worn out, replace them.

## LEAVING THEM LOADED

Some people will advise you to regularly rotate the ammunition in your mags if you carry daily. They'll claim this is to "let the springs rest." While I admire their concern for your safety, they are wrong. Properly designed springs are worked across perhaps 80 percent of their potential flexion movement. A spring properly made and worked within limits has 100,000 flexes to its service life. The best ones (like those used in racing engines) will withstand a million flexes with no change. Rest is not needed.

However, you should rotate the ammo. The top round is exposed to sweat, lint, dust and other stuff riding in the magazine. You are, or should be, concerned for the ammunition, not the spring.

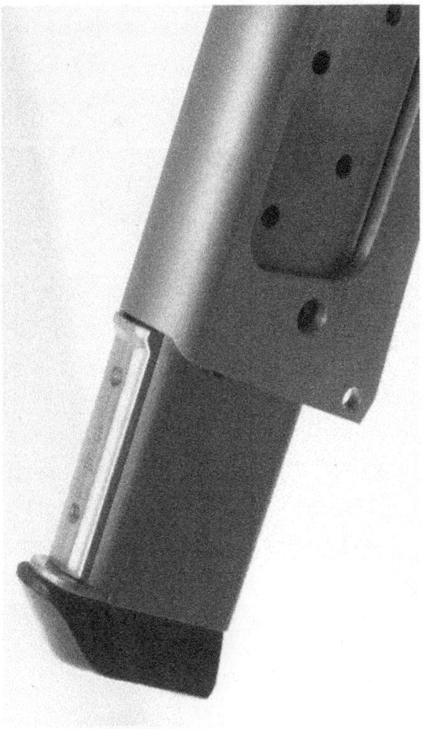

***The Ed Brown mag, with its stop plate that prevents over-insertion.***

As far as "how long?" I have an example from personal experience. A customer at our gunshop was a retired Marine NCO. She and her husband had both been Marine NCOs, and he had collected an enormous pile of gear. He had died 17 years before she arrived at our gunshop, and she had gotten tired of tripping over all the gear. So, the literal truckload of stuff arrived at the shop. There were ammo cans full of loaded magazines. The three ammo cans concerning this book had: one can full of 15-round M1 carbine magazines, one can full of 13-round Browning Hi Power mags, and one can full of 7-round GI-clone 1911 mags. (I wish I had written down the headstamp dates of the .45 ammo in those magazines.)

We took them to the range and shot them, and they all worked. Every. Single. One. So, we can use that as a benchmark: You can count on proper ammo in the correct magazines to work just fine 17 years later.

## MAGAZINE MODS

What modifications can you make to your magazines to improve them? Not much. For the most part, either they work 100 percent, or you swap/trade/ditch them for reliable ones. One minor modification you can consider, if your mag or mags need it, is to use a fine-cut file to knock off the right angle of the sheet metal at the point the magazine

***Rock Island uses Para Ordnance-pattern magazines for its hi-cap guns. This one is marked .22 TCM, but it will work fine with 9mm ammo once you swap the barrel and recoil spring.***

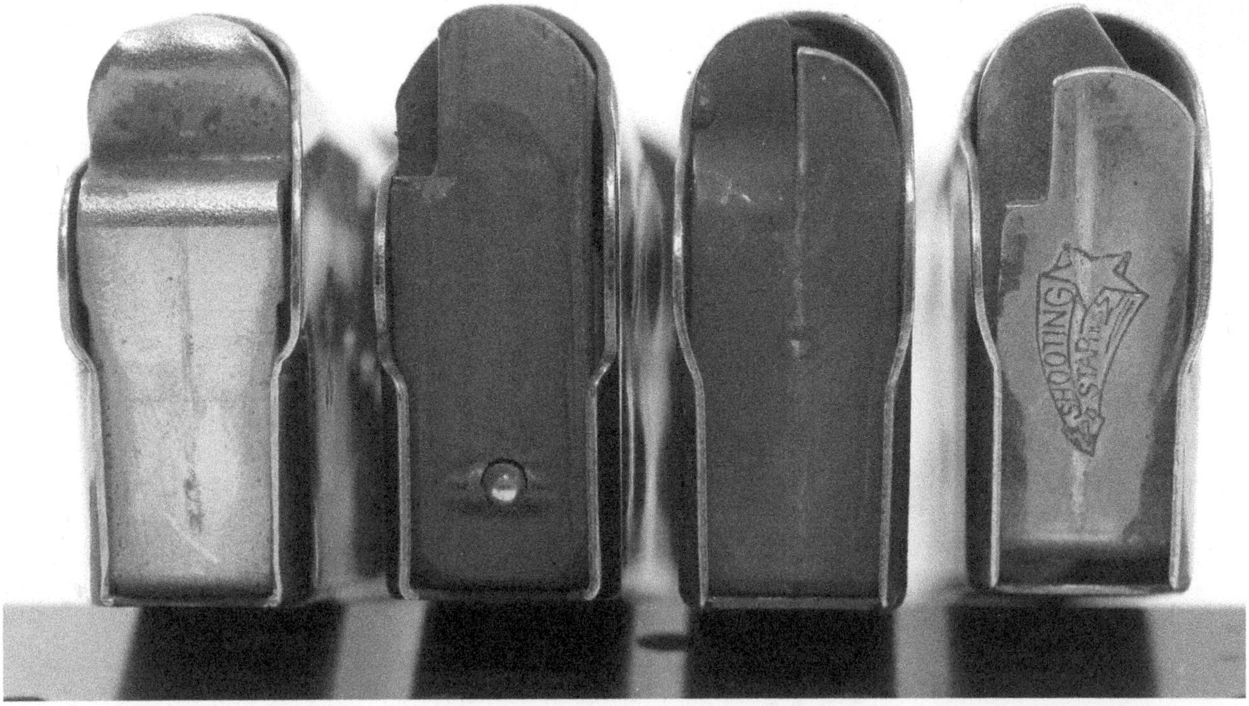


These are all versions of the modern feed lip geometry, each with minor variations. The modern marketplace has spoken: no one makes bad magazines anymore, so you have an easier job stocking up than in bygone years.

catch cams up over it. You don't want to do more than break the edge (don't turn it into a knife's edge), and only do this on mags that show a slight hesitation at that point of insertion.

The way to test it is simple: lock the slide back. Insert a test magazine and push it up with the tip of one finger. You'll feel it engage the magazine catch. If it takes slightly more effort to push the mag catch to cam over, no problem. However, it might need attention if it hangs up and takes significantly more than a continual push. You can also look at the magazine catch itself and see if some judicious polishing on the cam-up angle would help.

That and installing extended baseplates is about all you'll ever need to do. ●

CHAPTER

# 19

# SERVICE LIFE

Many shooters spend time obsessing over barrel life, and while there were times when that was needed, it was overdone even then. I have a reliable report from a historian and subject matter expert on 1911 testing the Navy conducted in the late 1960s. This testing would have been done with rebuilt wartime 1911A1s, which would not have been made of the hardest steel available. The full details aren't known (or are buried in the Navy's archives, never to be uncovered) and could have been done to a pistol with a hard commercial slide, but the barrel, even if it were a match barrel of the period, would not be up to the hardness and quality of the today's—close, but not as good as a BarSto or Kart. Still, it is informative, and it gives us some information.

The Navy built a softball gun (185-grain semi-wadcutter at 700 fps) for Bullseye and put it in a machine rest to check accuracy. Out of the machine rest, with factory wadcutter ammo, it shot a 20-shot group at 50 yards of 2.5 inches. Let that sink in: 20 shots, not five, into 2.5 inches. The 50-yard slow-fire Bullseye target has an X ring of 1.7 inches in diameter. That meant almost all shots fired would clip or touch the X-ring. The 10-ring is 3.4 inches in diameter so all shots would be inside its border. Woo-hoo indeed.

Then the Navy proceeded to test-fire it and, at regular intervals, put it back into the machine rest for an accuracy check. Up to 25,000 rounds, it maintained group sizes. By 30,000 rounds, it had opened up to 3.5 inches (still 10-ring accuracy), and at 35,000 rounds, the groups

This Les Baer delivered a 2-inch group at 25 yards. It can probably do better, and it will be long before you see it shooting worse than this.

were 4.5 inches. The conclusion was that barrels lasted only that long, at least for Bullseye use. Me? I suspect that if the Navy had taken the same gun and done all the usual tightening of slide-to-frame work covered in this book, it would have restored most, if not all, of that "lost" accuracy. Similar work with the hardball guns (230s at 800–850 fps) had shown a drop-off at about 15,000 rounds.

We can shrug off that accuracy loss, but for the High Master, that would be too much of a disadvantage. However, consider it from the defense perspective: a shot at 50 yards is a long way for a pistol. (Difficult technically, but also as a legally defensible shot.) The freshly built gun might hit an inch and a quarter from your aiming spot. The "shot-out" one in the same situation might throw it 2 inches from that spot. Can you *see* something three-quarters of an inch in size at 50 yards? For real-life needs, the accuracy difference is inconsequential.

Let's scale that down. Assuming that most defensive encounters are at 10 yards or less means the fresh gun will shoot a group—the Law of Equal Triangles makes this an easy calculation—of half an inch, center to center. The "shot-out" gun will deliver a group that is just under an inch in size, and at 10 yards, there is no practical difference between the two.

Meanwhile, IPSC shooters were putting 35,000 rounds or more through a .45 gun annually and not complaining about loss of accuracy. How do I explain that?

You may have heard the tale: Gun writer Ross Seyfried, talking to some other shooters about the chewed-up web of his hand, asked what he could do about it. Another shooter, passing by, called out, "Shoot more!" and kept walking. I was there. (No, I wasn't the smart aleck.) I was hanging around the small group of shooters at the 1982 IPSC Nationals at the Moline Rifle Club in Illinois. The group included Bill Wilson, Chip McCormick, and other name shooters. Ross turned to us and remarked, "I guess fifty-thousand rounds a year isn't enough, then." The top shooters were using uncomped .45 ACP 1911s and were not rebuilding their guns halfway through the season. Guns lasted several seasons at least before needing work, including things such as a busted thumb safety, replacement grips, new sights, or an improved trigger job. Not a complete overhaul.

So, what was up with the Navy? The comparison from then to now is like apples to oranges. The Navy was building on USGI 1911A1 frames and slides from WWII production. While solidly built, they had not been manufactured with the idea that they'd still be used decades later. The steel was good, but it was only as hard as it needed to be to serve during the war. They were hardened—when they were hardened—by "induction" hardening, which involved a coil of heating elements large enough to slip a slide into—a coil just like that found on an old-fashioned electric stovetop. The slide would be placed inside the loop, and the loop would have a huge electrical charge pumped through it. Just like your toaster or stovetop, the coil would heat up. The slide would be left there just long enough to heat up to the hardening temperature; then, the coil would be turned off, and the slide pulled out and replaced with the next one.

I suspect that during wartime, the coil was never turned off. Some unlucky production worker was assigned the hellish task of slipping slides into the fixture, counting to the desired time, and then pulling them out, working through rack after rack of slides with the coil always on. I could even see a metronome set up to tick off the time. "OK, insert the slide, count off five clicks on the ticker, then haul it out. Repeat."

The Navy guns were tightened by hammering, lapping frame rails, and squeezing slides. Most IPSC guns weren't, but some were. However, the top 'smiths did more than just peening and lapping.

Skeeter Skelton decided to test accuracy and talked Colt into sending him a brand new Gold Cup and various ammunition manufacturers (back then, his choices would have been Winchester, Remington, and Federal, realistically) into shipping ammunition. He ended up with some 15,000 rounds, a considerable amount then, but soon after

IPSC, competitors would shoot more than double or triple that annually. I suspect that in the late 1960s and into the 1970s, the Southwest Combat Pistol League top shooters, the original masters, were doing well over 15,000 rounds a year. After shooting "all that ammo," Skeeter found no change in accuracy.

At the same time, Bar-Sto sent new .45 barrels to the USMC Bullseye teams each year. A Bullseye shooter would have maxed out at about 5,000 rounds annually for practice and competition. There were 5,000 rounds in each gun, so 20,000 rounds each, but 5k was .22 LR, and 5k was a softball load. No gun got more than 5,000 rounds a year. They were getting new barrels each year, and the rumor started (and was hard to quash) that .45 barrels were only good for 5,000 rounds. No, the Corps was being clever and cheap. It had the budgetary authority to use new barrels for each season, so it did. The "old" barrels got plugged into rebuilt Recon 1911s to replace ancient WWII-era barrels. There weren't many Bullseye barrels to go around for rebuilds, but *some* was more than *none*.

This 1911 was fished out of a swampy drainage area, and once someone gets up enough nerve to test-fire it, it will work just fine. Yes, that's duct tape over the muzzle. We aren't barbarians or idiots.

So, how long will your modern production 1911 remain accurate? That depends. For most people, the answer is for the rest of their lives. And even through their kids' and grandkids' lives. Take the U.S. Navy softball gun as an example of low-end service life. It was capable of shooting 2.5-inch groups at 50 yards. Now, not to be a [fill in the blank] here, but how well can you shoot? For most people, shooting a group one foot in diameter at 50 yards is a good day. Hey, don't feel bad. With a 12-inch group, you've kept every shot on a USPSA target at 50 yards. That's pretty fine shooting for all but the pros. Anyway, 35,000 rounds later, that softball gun had groups that had grown from 2.5 to 4.5 inches. What does that mean for your accuracy? Your 12-inch group is now 13 or 14 inches at 50 yards. For most shooters, even those with some practice, those two guns still shoot the same—you won't be able to tell the difference. And, even if they don't start at the 2.5 inches at 50 yards level, modern guns will last much longer in accuracy than that Navy gun did, so you'll have that level of precision for a greater number of rounds. How much greater?

I have a Wilson Combat CQB that I have abused. It not only has had something on the order of 50,000 rounds through it, but it's also been buried, dug up and fired, shot underwater, tested with talcum powder, sand, and many other adverse-condition tests. When I last visited the Wilson Combat custom shop, I took it along, and the test shooter shot a newly built passing test-fire group with it. It shot well enough that had it just been built, it would pass the accuracy test. (The appearance test, not so much.)

A final note on accuracy. I once asked Les Baer why he didn't build lightweight 1911s. You know, aluminum-framed 1911s. "Because they won't hold their accuracy to 100,000 rounds," he replied. How many rounds a year do you shoot? Divide that into 100,000, and that's the minimum time you've got for a Les Baer to retain the accuracy Les expects from it. The current price of .45 ammo ($415 per 1,000 rounds) comes to $41,500 in ammunition costs alone. Suddenly, $3,000 for a primo 1911 doesn't seem like all that much. And at 5,000 rounds a year, you're looking at 20 years of shooting.

You may notice discoloration on the slide if you look at a USGI (a collectible 1911/1911A1). The slide would be induction-hardened at the front for the bushing slot or just ahead of the ejection port for the locking lugs. Nowhere else. After the war, Colt came out with "hard" slides. (Colt had probably been making hard slides pre-war, but since it wanted to sell guns post-war, it touted the "new" hard slides.) The hard slide was fully heat-treated. We were building IPSC guns with them. Well, some of us. My first IPSC pistol was a wartime Ithaca, and the slide was soft. We'll get into that shortly.

So, the soft slides would wear, and the slide rails spread or wore. The soft frames (no frame heat treatment on GI gun frames) would also wear. Even one-thousandth of an inch of wear (.001) between the slide and frame would grow that 2.5-inch group past 3 inches. Add in a thousandth of an inch of wear/peening on the barrel hood, lugs, and lockup surfaces, and suddenly, "accuracy goes to hell" with too much shooting—by Bullseye standards, anyway.

So why did IPSC shooters not have this problem? Heat treatment and chrome. By the early 1980s, building on a USGI gun was a thing of the past, except for new shooters. Top shooters were all building on heat-treated, hard-slide Colts. They also had the frames hard chrome plated, meaning the frame rails did not wear. And finally, the barrels were all Bar-Sto, which were (and still are) heat-treated to be as hard as the slides. Compared to the Navy guns, ours didn't peen or wear. We did not lose accuracy because of wear.

*Tight does not mean unreliable. This Wilson Combat CQB has been pulled out of the muddy gravel it rested in and fired. Yes, it worked.*

And then, there were the bullets used in each case. The Navy (and all the service teams plus many civilian competitors) were shooting 185-grain wadcutter bullets, or 230-grain round-nose bullets, factory-loaded and full metal jacketed. We IPSC shooters were almost to a man (and woman) shooting lead bullets, in particular the H&G 68 200-grain semi-wadcutter. Lead has a lower coefficient of friction than the gilding metal jackets of the ammo the Navy and everyone else used. The Navy's bullets wore the bore and the leade faster than the ones we used. Is this something I can put a number to? It's not a hard-and-fast one, but one of reports and experience. I have talked to 1911A1-era armorers who ran fleets of pistols for use by the regular troops, not Bullseye teams.

With the regular replacement of recoil springs (springs bought in the Army volume had a reputed cost of five cents each, so replacing them regularly was not a big deal) and round counts logged, they reported having hundreds of thousands of rounds through pistols and still being capable of producing "clean" scores (all hits) on the combat or qualification course. Not Bullseye, of course, but still keeping all the shots on a silhouette at the "combat" distance used. We IPSC shooters, using lead bullets, even at Major Power Factor, sent 100,000 to 200,000 or more rounds through a pistol, which did not need more than routine maintenance and spring replacements.

Oh, and my Ithaca? It was built by the late Frank Paris, a Bullseye pistolsmith who switched to building IPSC guns. The locking lugs on the soft WWII slide (mine was made in 1943) started peening and setting back and "ate" the barrel lugs. When it started to malfunction, I installed a drop-in Bar-Sto barrel. The harder Bar-Sto accelerated slide lug peening, and once that got bad enough, the slide also "ate" the Bar-Sto barrel and then quit. I replaced the slide with one from Caspian and fitted a gunsmith barrel from Bar-Sto, which has worked to this day.

This is highly unlikely to be the fate of your modern 1911. Unless you have found, used, or been gifted a USGI slide, your modern slide will be fully heat-treated and won't experience lug peening unless you do a fabulously bad job of fitting a new barrel to your new slide, which could do it. As I keep repeating, if you score a USGI slide, don't build it as an IPSC or competition gun. That slide is worth more to a collector than a new Caspian slide will cost you, and the Caspian will be fully heat-treated.

## BARREL FITTING

Before describing how to fit a new barrel, you must know how it fits into the slide/frame ensemble. At the front, the barrel rides in the bushing, and they should be snug but not compressed. You can press a fingertip against the muzzle and see if you can move the barrel within the bushing. If you can, you could increase accuracy slightly by properly fitting a new bushing to your slide/barrel combo. If the bushing itself moves, you can gain another slight increase in accuracy by precisely fitting a replacement bushing to the barrel.

***Service life can depend on things beyond your control. This bottom lug broke off for reasons unknown. Once in a hundred thousand barrels, this will happen to any pistol.***

On the chamber end, the barrel is locked into the slide by fitting between the back end of the hood, bearing on the breechface, and the locking lugs on top of the barrel. The Government Model has three lugs. It is not uncommon for a new gun to bear on just one lug. This is not a cause for concern. If the steel is hard enough, one lug is enough. If the steel is a bit soft (we're talking about relative softness here), the bearing lug will upset until the second lug begins to bear. With the second lug now taking up some of the load, the setback stops.

A custom pistolsmith will routinely measure and machine on a match barrel installation so the barrel starts out bearing on two lugs. Two lugs is a "forever" barrel, limited in service life to how much the bore wears with firing and cleaning. Getting it to bear on all three evenly is tricky and sometimes impossible. However, here's one way: make the slides and barrels yourself. Les Baer does just that, and since he controls all the dimensions on his CNC machines (other custom gun makers do the same), he can ensure maximum lug engagement. That's how he guarantees 3 inches and can build to 1.5 inches. That's also how you get accuracy to 100,000 rounds.

*This comped 1911 cracked and still worked. It had the occasional malfunction, but really? Sure, the coned comp held it together, but that is still one impressive pistol. Photo: Ned Christiansen*

The back end of the barrel, the hood, bears against the breechface. A quick note: the hood does not, nor should it, fit entirely in the sides. It should have a couple of thousandths of clearance on either side. "But how can I keep my barrel centered?" you might ask. Simple: it is centered every time it rises into the locking lugs on the slide. That, and the barrel feet, do a much better job centering it than the paltry hood sides could do.

On the bottom, the just-mentioned barrel feet ride on the slide stop pin. So, the barrel is positioned by its contact at four locations: the bushing, the top lugs, the hood rear, and the barrel feet. This sounds complicated, but these are the exact four locations that determine the positioning of the barrel in your Glock, Sig, or fill-in-the-blank pistol.

Remember, a pistol's accuracy is largely determined by the ammunition's accuracy (feed your pistol inaccurate ammo, and you will get, well, you know the rest) and the repeatability of the barrel positioning vis-à-vis the sights. Back in the days of surplus GI guns, accuracy was pretty good. And some were superb. How could that be, with the guns rattling audibly when shaken? Because every time the barrel locked up, the various loose parts came together consistently and repeatably. It didn't have to be tight to be accurate, just consistent. And even if the slide assembly was loose on the frame, if the barrel locked up to the slide consistently, the sights were attached to the slide, not the frame.

Which, as a short diversion, became a problem in the early days of optical sights on IPSC guns. All the scope mounts were fastened to the frame back then. (No optics, ca. the early 1990s, were compact enough to mount on a slide. Nor would they have survived the first magazine as they were too fragile.) Slide-to-frame fit became paramount.

Therefore, a tight fit is important only because it ensures consistency, not because it's desirable in and of itself. In fact, too tight means increased sensitivity to dirt, lack of maintenance, and a loose grip. ●

CHAPTER

# 20

# TRIGGER AND ACCURACY WORK

The 1911's most significant advantage over other pistols is its superior trigger pull. A clean, crisp, relatively light trigger pull is conducive to good shooting. However, it is entirely possible (and not uncommon) for 1911 owners and shooters to become trigger snobs—especially those who have spent time in practical competition, where a nice trigger can boost your scores. As I've often pointed out, things were different in the old days. Today, it's challenging to find a 1911 with a genuinely crappy trigger, and even finding one with a marginally good one can be tough. Most come with excellent or superb triggers simply because with CNC manufacturing, it isn't difficult to make a trigger good, and customers demand it.

*The author, having fired an LE patrol rifle qual course with a 9mm 1911 and three hits down from passing. Later that day, he shot a passing score on a course out to 65 yards. Yes, 1911s are accurate.*

First things first: installing a trigger is not a "trigger job." It can be part of one, but a trigger job is an improvement of the trigger pull and installing a trigger is, well, installing a trigger. But since doing the whole shebang usually includes a new trigger, we'll start there.

## TRIGGER SELECTION

So, you want a new trigger. Before you do that, look at

the installed one because it may have everything you need. What does a new trigger have that your old one might not? It could be a different length. Shorter is better for most people, but those with long fingers/hands can find a longer trigger more useful. A lighter-weight trigger allows you to tune the trigger pull a bit lighter, but that isn't always assured, and you can get a fine trigger pull without going light in weight/mass of the trigger.

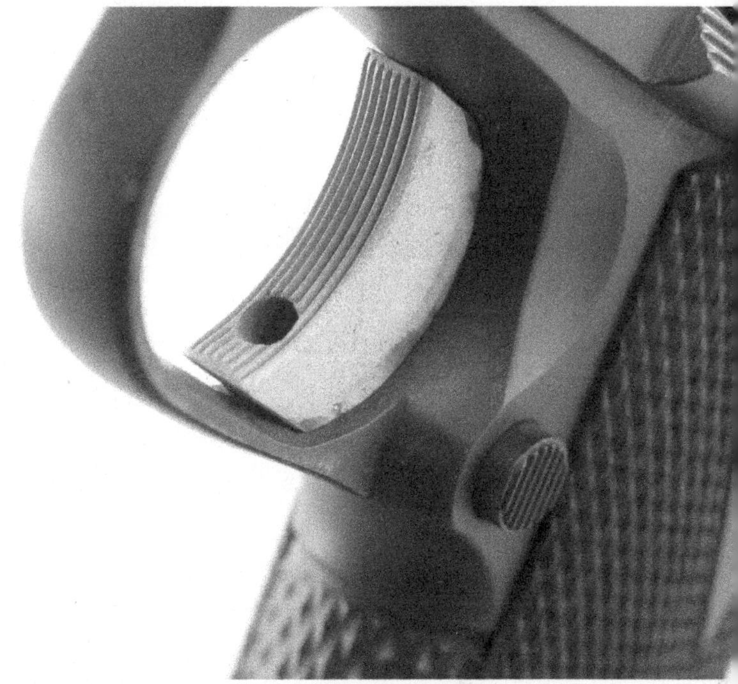

*If you see this on the front of your trigger, you have an overtravel adjustment screw. Lacking this, you probably don't have any way to control overtravel, but that isn't always a problem.*

The new trigger could have an overtravel stop, which, if you check, you might find that your current trigger already has and is doing precisely what it's supposed to do. First, does it have one, and how do you tell? Look at the front face of the trigger, below the centerline, and see if there's a threaded hole. If so, then yep, you've got one.

Overtravel? Pressing the trigger levers the sear, which pivots out of engagement with the hammer hooks. One of the exquisite details the Bullseye shooters discovered was that the trigger, any trigger, moves the sear to release the hammer, then abruptly stops when it runs out of space in which to move. That stop disturbs the alignment of the pistol to the target. Too much overtravel can be a hindrance to accuracy. How much? Enough to cost points, which is to be avoided. That said, most of the out-of-the-box trigger pulls these days on 1911s would have caused excited cries of envy from Bullseye shooters even a generation ago. Too much overtravel is a relative term, and I would be remiss if I didn't point out that too little is also a problem.

You can adjust your overtravel to the point where there isn't any. And what you will find is that when you try to pick up speed, you won't be able to go any faster and may tie the gun up. That is, you've just tried to shoot a very, very fast pair, and the second shot didn't happen. You have the trigger pinned back hard, and the hammer hasn't fallen. You let go, and when you press again, it fires. What happened? Simple: you speed up shooting by pressing more quickly with less time between presses and also by limiting the distance your trigger finger moves to release and return. With the absolute minimum overtravel, your trigger finger "learns" the shorter distance, but the shorter distance is also within the limits of your finger travel. You have, in essence, short-stroked your trigger.

You need a certain amount of overtravel to let your finger and the trigger play well together. Trying to remove all of it is a recipe for un-fun shooting.

Let's consider trigger release and its methods. You will be taught by some people that you must learn to "catch" the sear. That is, to manage the trigger by slowly releasing it after each shot until you hear or feel the click of the sear re-engaging with the hammer hooks and then stopping the release before pressing again. As far as I can tell, this is something the military teaches to keep recruits from learning to slap the trigger (which is curious because some of the best shooters have won National and World Championships by slapping the trigger).

My trigger finger, at speed, comes off the trigger so much that it nearly hits the inside front of the triggerguard before returning. One of the best, Robbie Leatham, does the same. Yes, we're old and old-school, but it works. The trick is not to disturb your sight alignment while slapping the trigger. Many excellent shooters started by catching the sear and not slapping. Either way works once you've practiced enough, but taking too much of the overtravel out of the system will cause problems.

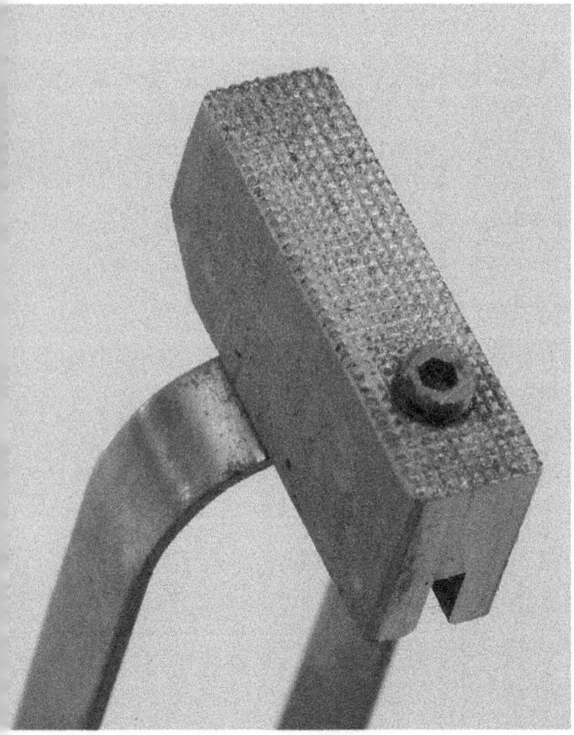

*The overtravel is easier to see on this aluminum trigger that has been converted into a flat one. And checkered because, well, why not?*

## TRIGGER INSTALLATION

To install a new trigger, first detail strip the frame, including the grips. Take everything but the ejector, plunger tube, and grip screw bushings off the frame. Attempt to push your new trigger into the frame backward. Yes, backward. This checks that the trigger bow fits into the frame slots without binding or catching. It's a quick and easy test; if it passes, it passes. If it doesn't, then you may have some serious problems on your hands. If it doesn't, the original trigger or frame (maybe both) is out of spec. Your new, in-spec trigger doesn't fit, and you must make it fit. Or, if the frame is out of spec (and the factory trigger is too, to fit into it), assemble everything, call it good, and vow not to buy the brand again. Either sell off your pistol or keep it as a "just as it is" gun and don't build on it. I mean, if the trigger slots and trigger are out of spec, what are the chances something else is as well?

Now that I've startled you, that sort of thing was not uncommon in the old days, but today, I'd be surprised, stunned even, at a name-brand 1911 that was that far out of spec.

So, the trigger fit. Pull it out, turn it around, and start it correctly. It will probably stop once the trigger body gets past the magazine shaft, which is why you have removed everything. You want to see where it is binding, top or bottom. Once you see which side (probably both), pull the trigger out and take a couple of passes with your pillar file. Two passes, then turn the file 45 degrees, knock the sharp edge off of each side, and try the fit again. Be patient and sneak up on the fit. You'll get to the point where you can start to force the trigger into the slot leading to the triggerguard. When you pull the trigger out, closely inspect the top and bottom. Note where it is rubbing and binding. File only there.

File to the point where the trigger fits smoothly into the slot and does not have up and down wobble but still slides out of its own weight when you turn the frame muzzle up—a smooth sliding fit with no wobble.

*The sear tip (the pointed part inside the circle) has to clear the safety notch or half-cock notch on the hammer, or parts will break quickly.*

## SETTING OVERTRAVEL

If installing a new trigger, now is the time to adjust overtravel. Before we dive into this, here's a heads-up. Overtravel is the subject of much more discussion and fussing than it warrants. For most shooters, as long as there is enough for the pistol to function correctly, it will not matter to your marksmanship or shooting pace. In fact, you will probably have to be a Master-class USPSA shooter working towards Grandmaster for it to make any difference. Yes, yes, yes, there will be those who will tell you that you need Grandmaster-level equipment if you expect to shoot your best. But in the scheme of things, overtravel is not even on the first page of priorities to make it anywhere near the top.

I'm giving this information so you understand what goes into it and that it is a minor, if sharply argued, detail that is most likely set at a "just fine" amount at the factory. If building a 1911 from a parts kit or installing a new trigger, you will have to do some overtravel setting, but it shouldn't involve hours of work, let alone days of work, testing, and refining. This is one of those areas where "good enough" truly is good enough.

The trigger and its adjustment screw came with a tiny Allen wrench to adjust overtravel. You might remember the mnemonic for right-hand threads; "righty-tighty, lefty-loosy." Well, here, righty means less overtravel, and lefty means more. Adjusting overtravel is a delicate, time-consuming task that will require concentration. First, take the unloaded 1911, and cock the hammer. Now, dry-fire it by pressing the trigger as slowly as you can. When the hammer falls, stop pressing, but don't lift off the trigger. Press some more and see how far the trigger travels.

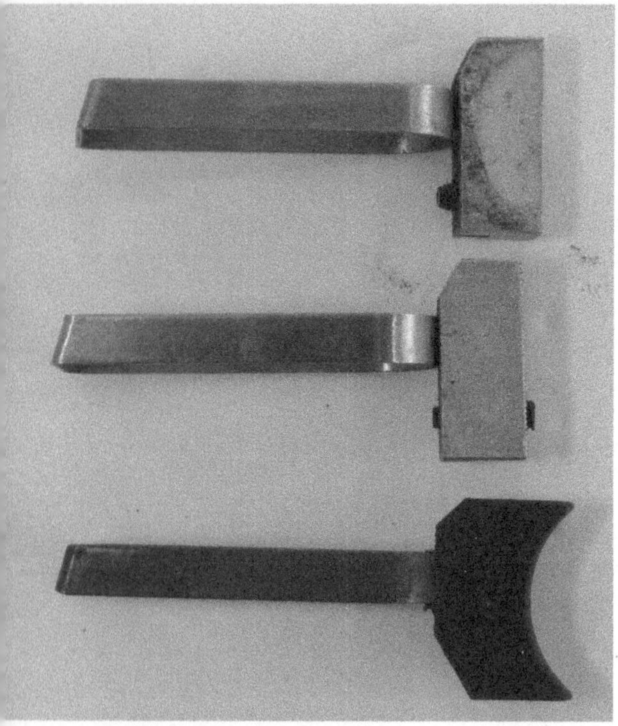

*Flat triggers are not new. They've been used in various competitions for years.*

The overtravel screw bottoms out against the magazine catch. Therefore, don't adjust the overtravel until *after* all work to the magazine catch is complete. Swapping in a replacement magazine catch can alter the overtravel setting.

If the trigger has too much overtravel (and this, while a personal thing, is also something that can become an obsession, so be careful), then give the overtravel adjustment screw one-quarter turn.

Now, before you dry-fire again, you must perform a test: Thumb-cock the hammer and hold it back with one thumb. Next, press the trigger fully back and ease the hammer forward until it is down. If there has been no contact, you have successfully adjusted. Now try dry-firing your 1911. If you can't feel any difference, then there is no difference. As I mentioned at the start, this is an esoteric subject, and it really doesn't matter much for the vast majority of shooters.

There are two ways to tell whether you have removed too much overtravel (which will cause problems). The first and most important one is mechanical. Let's go back to the thumb-lowering test. If, as you lower the hammer, you feel the hammer hooks kiss, bump, or push the sear nose out of the way, you have taken too much out of the overtravel. If you don't back it out, the hammer hooks will hit the sear every time you fire or dry-fire it. This will eventually (or quickly) chip one or both of them, destroying your nice trigger pull. It will probably fail to stay cocked. The best case is the hammer rides the slide down and won't stay cocked. Worst case, it chips the sear or hammer hooks enough that the jolt of closing causes the almost-securely-cocked hammer to fall, and you have a runaway magazine. That's unsafe and guaranteed to draw unwanted attention.

So, add more overtravel.

The second issue is where the hammer hooks don't touch the sear, but the overtravel is minimal. This condition will prevent you from shooting fast. Here, your trigger finger "learns" the short reset and overtravel and moves less and less on each trigger pull. This culminates in you having the trigger "pinned back;" that is, you didn't release it enough to let it reset. If you are trying to shoot fast and find you can't and the trigger is crushed back, stop. If you have adjusted overtravel, it may seem counter-intuitive, but you need to put some back so your trigger finger "learns" and get back to shooting fast.

Also, ensure the sear tip clears the safety notch, and the half-cock notch on the hammer, or bad things will happen.

## TRIGGER LENGTHS AND SHAPES

The original had what we now call a long trigger. Back then, the average man in the U.S. was about 5'8", and as it turned out, experience in The Great War proved the trigger was too long. That's how the A1 came about; one of the changes was to have a shorter trigger. And that's one of the bonuses of the 1911: you can swap triggers by length. You can also change the shape. The flat trigger is nothing new. When I was learning gunsmithing from Dan McDonald, he was experimenting with flat triggers. He had a bar of aluminum from which he'd lop a piece and fit it to a trigger bow before fitting the whole thing into a pistol. I don't recall if he figured that out himself or heard it from someone else, or it was some super-secret Bullseye trick that got adapted to IPSC.

Holes in triggers were a way to lighten them so any bouncing in the slot would have less of an impact on the sear and preserve the 'smith's trigger job.

Once fitted to a particular gun, a trigger can be pulled out and replaced with another fitted one. I have such a setup in one of my 1911s. I use it at The Pin Shoot, and when one of the other guys in our group wants to use it, I swap triggers. I have big hands and long fingers; he does not. The long trigger I use is not comfortable for him. Swapping prefitted triggers is easy during disassembly and reassembly as part of cleaning.

## TRIGGER JOBS

OK, you have concluded that your trigger pull is just too heavy. But how much is "light enough," and what should you expect?

Again, I'll caution you against "Grandmaster Fever." The top shooters do, indeed, run light triggers. I've heard of some running triggers in the pound-and-a-half region. Before we go any further, let me tell you this: those are their competition guns. Their daily carry guns have triggers in the more appropriate 4-pound range. When I wrote the book *1911: The First Century,* I handled many un-molested Great War guns. These were unaltered from the factory 1911s made before 1920. (Yes, they were actual 1911s, not 1911A1s, because the A1 wasn't developed until 1926.) They all had triggers we'd consider "too heavy" today—typically, 6 pounds. But stick with me here: they were excellent 6-pound triggers. You'd take up the slack, then press, and the trigger would not move until it reached the 6-pound mark, then the hammer would fall, and the pistol would cycle. They had slight overtravel, and I can well imagine that a lot of bad guys were put into the ground with triggers like that.

So, a carry gun, even a competition pistol of 4 to 4 ½ pounds, is ideal. Does your trigger do that? Then your job here is done, and the rest is educational. However, before we get too deep into this, let's consider trigger quality. You can have a trigger with a pull weight of only 2 pounds but gritty, and you can feel the sear dragging across the hammer hooks as things move, leaving you never really knowing when it will go off. That, despite being a light trigger, is a bad one. If, on the other hand, you have a trigger that works like the Great War 1911s I described— take-up, then no movement until the trigger "breaks" and releases the hammer—you have a good one. And, you might find that you and most everyone who dry-fires it "call" the weight a pound or more lighter than it is.

***A sear being stoned. If you have the fixture, the skills, and the time, this method can produce a superb trigger pull.***

More than once on a custom pistol, I'd dry-fired it and thought, "Oh, that's a nice 3-pound trigger," then, when I weighed it, it held 4 pounds and a few ounces. A clean trigger "feels" lighter than it is.

OK, how it is done and the recognition that most 1911s right out of the box these days don't need trigger work.

## TRIGGER JOBS OF YESTERYEAR

Historically, the way to improve trigger feel was to make the sear flat and even across its tip and ensure both hammer hooks were bearing evenly on the sear tip. Then, the hook height was adjusted so there would be just enough sliding friction of the sear nose camming out of the hooks to require the correct trigger pressure to fire.

How did early 1911 pistolsmiths do it? With mechanical fixtures and stones. Yes, stones. With a flat surface on a grinding or polishing stone, you could, in essence, "sand" the tip of the sear to be even, flat, and smooth. It required a heavy-duty but precise fixture to hold the sear and guide the stone while you worked. It also required a flat stone and entailed repolishing the face of the stone to keep it flat. And you had to know the correct angles to apply the stone to the sear.

*With a new trigger job, you'll probably want a new thumb safety. Even if you don't, the old thumb safety has to be checked for proper function with the new or modified parts. Don't assume it will work—check, test, and inspect.*

And if all that wasn't enough, you had to do the same thing to the hammer hooks, with an even more excruciating detail: stone edges. The hammer hooks had to be square and flat, but they also had to be sharp-edged in the bottom corner. If not, the rounded corner would push the sear nose out of the hooks enough to make the trigger pull lighter than desired.

The fixture was not cheap; the stones were delicate and required regular prep to make sure they were flat and square, and the whole thing was just an incredible hassle. Of course, it was the only way back then, so the hassle was worth it. Mostly.

All this stoning required skill and practice, and those who could do it well commanded higher prices for their work. That's why I developed a new method requiring more equipment but less continuous practice: a milling machine.

The mill could not do anything to the sear, but that wasn't a problem. I kept a selection of sears on hand, swapping them in and out with the prepped hammer until I got the trigger I wanted. The trigger work was easy to describe. I'd lock the hammer into the milling machine vise with the flat below the hooks dead level. Then, I'd insert a new, sharp carbide end mill into the chuck. (That tool was only ever used for this task, kept separate, and labeled "hammers only.") I'd get the cutter up to rpm and bring it down to the flat until it had just "kissed" the flat enough to indicate I had made contact. I might have only been taking a thousandth of an inch off, just hitting the high spots from when the factory had milled it.

Next, I'd bring it into contact with the hooks and barely touch them enough to cut a clean face along them. (The hammer would have been coated with Dykem, so I could see where I was cutting and had cut.) OK, the hooks were now flat and square, one last cut to take. I'd drop the table .018 inch and nick the tops of the hooks. They were now flat, square and .018-inch high.

With the hammer hooks perfect, I'd assemble the 1911 with the old sear. If it was as good as desired, the task was done. If not, set the original sear aside and swap others in and out until it was good. Later, when better aftermarket sears were available—if the original sear wasn't up to snuff—I'd drop in a Wilson, Ed Brown, or other. That almost always made it perfect.

This is not the course for you unless you own a milling machine (and one good enough to do the job properly, not a hobby tabletop one) and the skill or experience. There had to be a better way, and there is.

## THE NEW WAY

I described the previous two methods not because I expect you to undertake either but to let you know what it took to get a good trigger pull in the past. Now? The process is simple, and you can do it one of two ways. One is to order a matched hammer and sear set from one of the current makers and install it. Modern parts are far better than the old ones, partly because they are cut by wire EDM or machined by CNC machines that are far more precise than the traditional methods.

*Machining a 1911 barrel's bottom lug for an exact fit on the slide stop pin.*

Wire EDM uses a plate of hardened steel, and a wire stretched through a holder, much like a cheese cutter. If you electrically ground the plate and pump a huge electrical current into the wire, the electricity will jump the gap, erode, or cut the steel when the wire gets close. The distance it will jump is a known quantity. Movement can be controlled to a ten-thousandth of an inch. The part is precise.

A CNC machine measures and cuts, and tracks how many cuts a particular cutting tool has taken. It, too, can be controlled to "a tenth" (.0001 inch) as well.

Precision hammer/sear sets first came to market in the late 1980s or early 1990s when the late Chip McCormick offered them. He even sold a hammer made of titanium, and when I dropped it and a Chip sear into my USPSA Open gun, the trigger pull was a clean, crisp pound and a half. I loved it. I told him so at the following U.S. Nationals. "I'll be happy to swap that hammer out for one of our tool steel ones," he said. I wasn't too keen on that. "Well, they go full auto at around the 30,000-round figure, so call me then." Almost as if there had been a shooting equivalent of an odometer, mine did so, and I swapped hammers. So that's why you won't see titanium hammers, but lots of tool steel because those won't break or wear.

*If you or your pistolsmith have a lathe, this is a convenient way to adjust the hood length and tighten the lock-up.*

## ANOTHER NEW WAY

Or, you can ring up Nighthawk and get its drop-in trigger pack. This fully assembled hammer/sear/disconnector is a drop-in part. It requires its own leaf spring, which comes with it, and you simply remove those parts from your 1911, install the Nighthawk, and that's it. One of the problems with the 1911 is that the pin holes for the hammer and sear must be precisely positioned and parallel to each other. Any variance can alter the relationship between the hammer and sear and change the trigger pull. As a result, the same hammer-sear combo installed in a row of 1911s can cause variations in the trigger pull. Custom pistolsmiths prevent this by ensuring proper engagement and tuning it with the three-leaf spring.

The hammer and sear rotate on hollow tubes in the Nighthawk Drop-In assembly, and the two frame pins secure it. The orientation of the hammer to sear never changes, regardless of how many different 1911s you drop it into. AR owners reading this will be familiar with it since it has been used in the AR-15 (also introduced by Chip

McCormick in the wire EDM parts) for years.

## ACCURACY IMPROVEMENTS

Improving accuracy in the 1911 is something everyone turns their mind to, sooner or later. Accuracy is a matter not necessarily of precision but of consistency. As mentioned before, a rack-grade 1911 or 1911A1 can be superbly accurate if every time the "loose" parts slam back into battery, they do so in precisely the same way. The problem is that—short of an ultra-precise custom—you can't build it in; it's a matter of luck. Out of a rack of one thousand 1911s, one will be *that* accurate.

***This barrel will have the hood sides trimmed for clearance.***

Like I said, to build it in, you have to be precise. That means a precision barrel and a slide-to-frame fit with no slop or play. The barrel part is easy and delivers a good deal of the accuracy you seek. If you use a top-grade drop-in or Kart XACT-fit barrel and install it properly, you will have a 1911 that will be more accurate than you are until your skills rise to its accuracy.

Installing a new barrel is not difficult and is covered elsewhere, so here we'll go over the much more involved work that a custom pistolsmith will do to your 1911. It also gives you an idea of why it takes such a long time and costs so much and why you likely won't be doing it yourself.

***Note the barrel swelling at the muzzle to lock up tight to the bushing (not to fit the slide without a bushing).***

In the beginning, there was blacksmithery. The process began with measuring the bottom edge of the slide, the portion that rode inside the frame slots (the slide "rails" were smaller than the slot they rode in). Insert tool steel plates of the thickness of the slide rails into the frame slots, and use a great big hammer to pound the frame down onto the plates. This is "peening," and it works after a fashion. The problem is there's no way to make it even, so the outsides of the frame rails have high and low spots (or wide and narrow spots, depending on your mental 3D perspective). Also, a lot of the work involves not hammering the rails down but bending them down, so the bearing surface on the outside isn't the flat but the edge of the rail.

*This frame's rails were peened and filed, which looks like random abuse. And yet, it was the work of a "name" 'smith.*

That means the surfaces wear quickly. And when they wear, accuracy degrades to the previous "not accurate enough" level. To prolong the service life of such a fitting, yesterday's pistolsmith would do it several times. He'd peen the rails down, clean the high spots, lap the slide, and peen again, creating as much contact area as possible.

A more involved method was to use a fixture and an even larger hammer to "swage" the frame rails down. The fixture was an inverted "U" that only touched the frame at the rails and drove the hammered portions directly down. This meant more surface contact and longer wear, but they still wore. The waging would be done to an inch or so of the rails at the front and rear "corners" of the frame rail sections.

*While there are fixtures to locate the barrel for fitting, some 'smiths make their own. That way, they know every dimension and how it works because they made it. Photo: Jason Burton*

The problem with all this hammering was that to get the maximum surface contact for the most extended service life, you had to overdo it, swage down past the measured slide fit, and use lapping compound to make things work smoothly. In other words, peen it down tighter than the slide, then lap the slide onto the frame. You could do all this because frames are soft, which was also why they wore down. Again, this might have been done two or three times before the final fitting.

There was also the "squeeze" method. It involved using an X-shaped tool in the vise to squeeze the rear portions of the slide until they were the same width as the frame rails. This worked with soft USGI slides (which also wore quickly) but risked cracking the harder Colt commercial slides.

It was possible to do all this work, produce a superbly accurate pistol, and see it used up in a season or two of competition. IPSC shooters could make it last longer by hard-chroming the parts once fitted, but those shooting in Service matches could not. What they did, at least those who wanted results and were willing to work for it, was to shoot and accuracy test everything in the armory or sort them. This would entail tasking a PFC with measuring every frame rail set in the racks and sorting them by size. Then, measure every slide rail set. The Master Sergeant would assemble some 'rack-grade' pistols using the best-fitting parts and set them aside for those who warranted it. Unfortunately, few of us have a hundred 1911s we can sort through.

Power tools make work faster, but you must know what you're doing. Otherwise, a surface grinder can eat up your frame or slide in seconds.

What do custom pistolsmiths do? They weld. Actually, they have welders who can do precise work, and then the pistolsmith works on the welded frames. The first step is to measure every aspect of the frame and slide precisely. It isn't uncommon for rails and slots to "wander" or vary in width, depth, or thickness from one end of the frame to the other. Some aren't even parallel. This must be measured, plotted, and calculated to be corrected. It may entail welding to the frame rails' sides or the sides and top. And, as with all things, the welder can't do "just enough," so they weld past the needed steel.

So, the welder does their work, and the custom pistolsmith uses sharp cutters and a well-maintained milling machine to cut the frame rails to the exact size. It is still lapped afterward, just to be exacting. As a bonus, the welder, knowing what steel alloys are used in 1911s, can use the proper "stick" to ensure no warpage. (TIG and laser welding are good for that.) He can also make the metal harder if need be. There are limits, of course. He can't weld on extra steel that is so different that it causes problems with the frame (it is always steel;

you cannot do this to an aluminum-framed Commander). He can't weld on steel that is so unlike the frame alloy that it won't stay attached. But he can make the added stuff better. And, since the pistolsmith is machining, hand-filing and lapping it to a perfect fit, there won't be high spots to wear down.

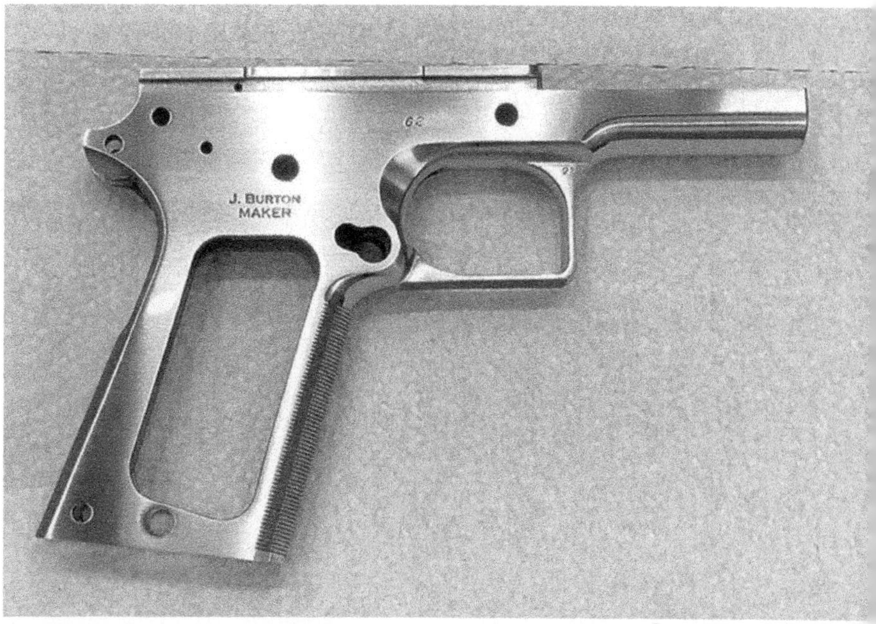


*Once the details have been worked out and things like a squared triggerguard have been added, the custom 'smith is ready for assembly and testing. Photo: Jason Burton*

## EXTRAS

OK, you have your 1911. It works well and accurately, but you want to increase its service life. One of the hard platings will do that. Good ol' hard chrome has worked wonders for decades. Electroless nickel works well. One thing to keep in mind is that hard chrome and electroless are "last step" processes. You can't do anything else once the frame or slide is plated. A hard-chromed slide could have the top machined for replacement sights, but that removes the hard chrome where the steel has been machined.

So, things like checkering, stippling, and fitting a new grip safety will remove hard chrome and break the rust-resistant integrity of the plating. Have your 1911 hard-chromed *after* everything else has been done. Any fitting, checkering, cosmetic metal work, sights, etc., get done first, and the hard chrome goes on last.

*The "carbidizing" that is, alas, no longer offered. It is welding a super-hard layer onto a softer one (in this case, titanium) so it will not gall and last a long time.*

The various baked-on surface coatings won't do the job of adding service life to the fit. They are good, but not what we're looking for here. They add thickness but are not hard enough. A proper application of Cerakote is one mil, or about one-thousandth of an inch. If your slide-to-frame fit is more than a thousandth, adding a Cerakote layer might not help. And if it's that or less, the Cerakote will make them not fit together. If you need the thousandth and then some, the slide and frame will scrub the high spots,

*Part of fitting a new barrel, as done by a pistolsmith and not as a drop-in, involves creating clearance on the barrel for the bushing behind its lockup area to slide smoothly and without binding.*

wear down the Cerakote, and be back where you were, plus the cost of the coating. It is the toughest coating, but it isn't hard chrome tough.

One plating or treatment that was particularly effective, but as far as I can tell is no longer available, was "carbidizing." It involved sputter-welding carbide directly onto the surface of the steel plate. The welding was not a smooth layer, so it required multiple passes. It also required that the two surfaces be lapped between each application to knock off the high spots. The carbide would only weld to be base steel, not to itself, so after enough passes, you had a continuous plating and a smooth enough surface that would never wear.

I had the titanium frame of my custom 1911 carbidized by Tripp Research, which no longer does it. I have not found anyone else who does, although it seems to be used in knifesmithing circles.

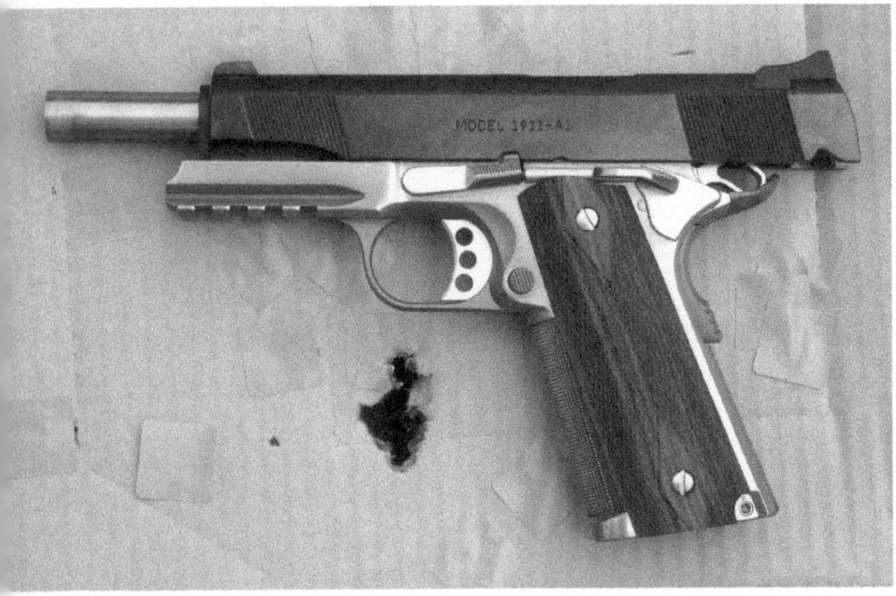

*One of the 1911's advantages is that you can get an accurate one right out of the box, which isn't because you got lucky. This Rock River delivered this group in testing.*

You may think, "Well, there's got to be someone who does a treatment like the Tenifer of Glock, right?" Yes, there is. Smith & Wesson calls it Melonite, and others use other names. The problem is that it is alloy-specific. Not that the chemicals used have to be adjusted—although they may well have to be, depending on the alloy—but the problem is this: your slide isn't theirs. Knowing the alloy, you can tune the process, in time, temperature, etc., for the alloy you use and the slides you make. If you do the process wrong, you could end up with slides that are no harder than when they arrived or so hard that they are brittle.

So, no one does an a la carte Tenifer/Melonite process.

That leaves hard chrome and the other processes, but if you want a non-silver 1911, you'll need to have the work done and then get it coated with a bake-on or Cerakote finish.

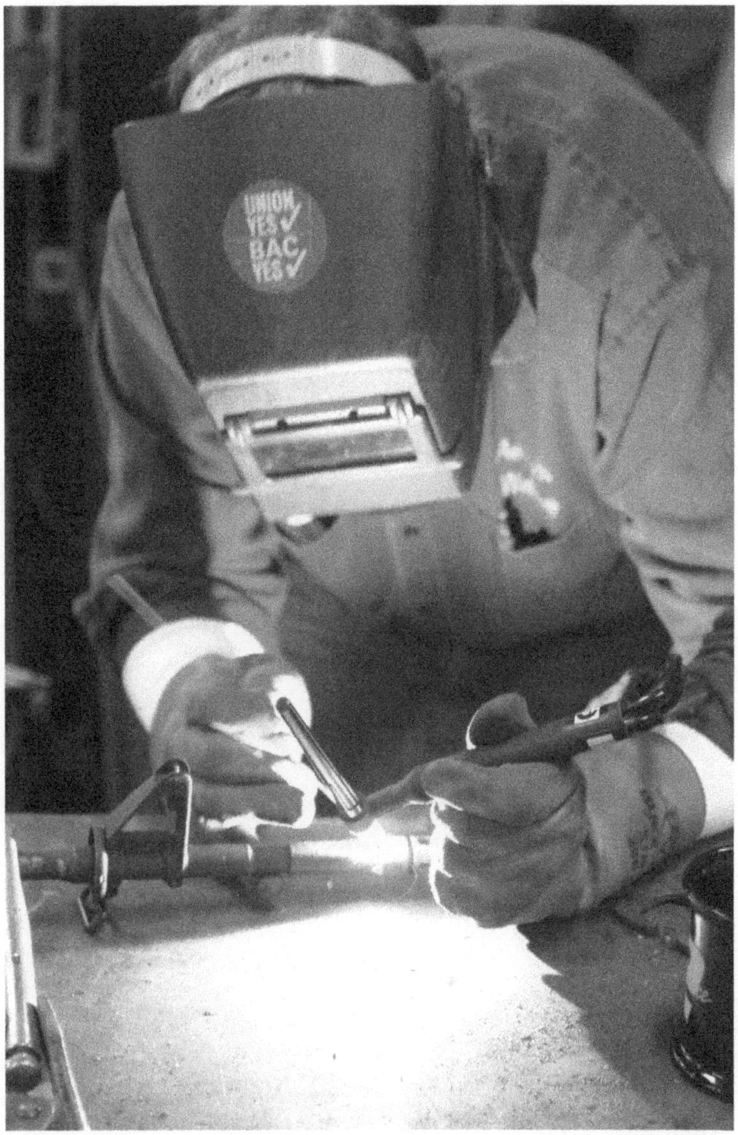


*Welding the rails of a frame is the first step to "blueprinting" a 1911, making it accurate and lasting a lifetime.*

## SOMETHING NOT TO DO

You may hear from a fellow gun club member about ways to improve accuracy. One is to install a "taller" barrel link. The link has holes drilled through it, connecting it to the slide-stop pin and barrel feet. The idea is that if you use a taller link, you can wedge the barrel up tight into the slide and also use it to lever the slide up and tight to the frame rails. The problem: that's a lot to ask of a little link. It wasn't designed for that, and it will wear or break. There's also the problem of fit. A taller link with the holes farther apart will change the timing of the unlocking and the distance the barrel travels back as it unlocks. An excessively tall link could bind the barrel, and the locking lugs of the slide and barrel, on their tops, may grind against each other.

It is a "solution" that won't last long.

## SUMMARY

If you want more accuracy (which is not as common a need these days as many people think it is), the only option you, as the home pistolsmith, have is to replace the barrel with a better one. The other accuracy-improving options involve some pretty heavy lifting, be it peening, swaging, or welding.

One way to get a precise fit is to order a frame and slide from Caspian. You can ask for a set (you will specify the features on each, so this is just one more set of specs) that will not fit and then carefully file, measure, fit, lap and ensure a smooth, sliding fit with no play.

You're back to heavy lifting and building your 1911 from parts, a noble and worthy goal. ●

CHAPTER 21

# HIGH-END CUSTOM

I've mentioned the custom pistolsmith repeatedly, so here's a peek at some of their work. Of course, you can see many examples online, but if you ever get a chance to handle or shoot a high-end custom pistol, do not pass up the chance.

I don't mean to be condescending, but if you're thinking Kimber, Dan Wesson, or Colt in any model other than basic, you aren't there yet. Not even close. Those are the guns custom pistolsmiths *start* with. Heck, I was just looking at photos of a custom pistol that the pistolsmith started work on, and he *began* with a Les Baer. Custom makers like Stan Chen produce their own slides and frames from billet so that the dimensions will be exact.

The closest you can come to a custom bespoke 1911 is to get one from Nighthawk, which offers many models, each with a list of add-ons, accessories, changes and upgrades you can order. Just go down the list, check off what you want, and place your order.

None of this comes cheap or fast. You could place an order with one of the name 'smiths, and they won't even ask for the gun you want to be built on for two, three, four or more years. And yes, it is not uncommon for them to not ask for the gun until it is time. Hey, if you were doing a dozen guns a year, would you want 40 or 50 pistols sitting in your safe, just waiting their turn? A dozen guns a year is not unusual. It is a steady pace when you're doing full-house custom guns that bill for $5,000 to $10,000 each.

**_It takes a lot of practice, skill, and dedication to turn out custom 1911s. Here, Jason Burton machines a welded-up set of rails. Photo: Jason Burton_**

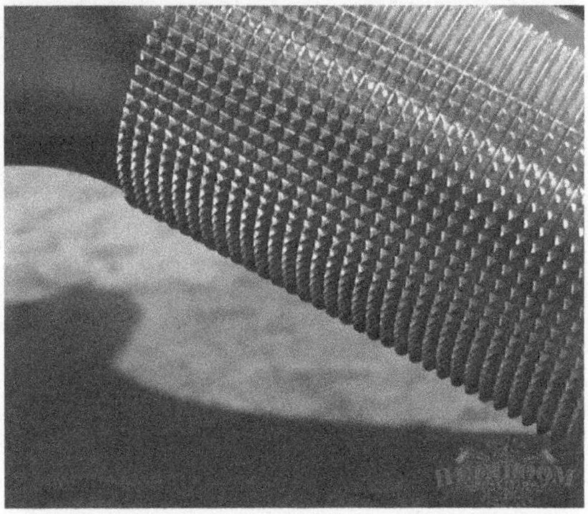

**_Modern checkering is perfect. In this case, Jason Burton did the hand checkering. Photo: Jason Burton_**

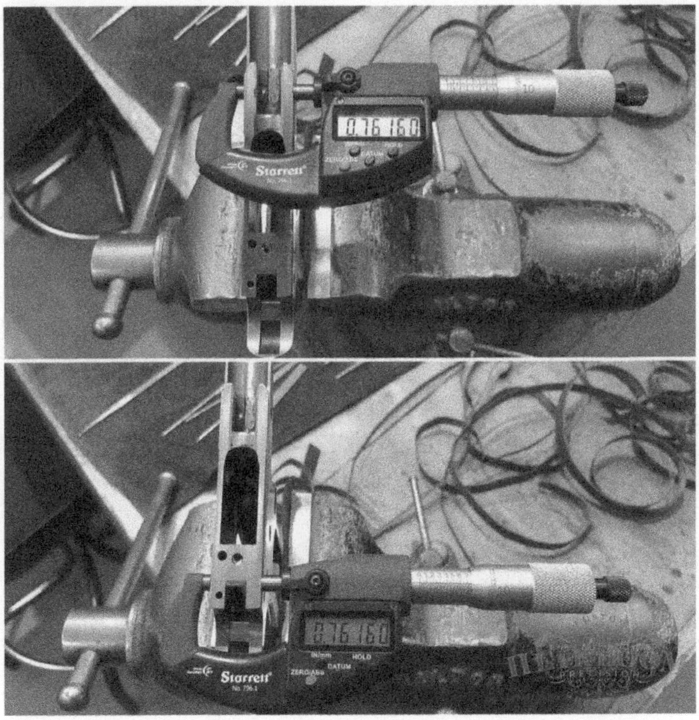


**_How close do top-end pistolsmiths make their subjects? How about this? The same to five decimal points. Photo: Jason Burton_**

*A custom builder will match the thumb safety, frame, and grip safety curves.*

*To achieve precise dimensions, you need power tools and the knowledge to use them. Ned Christiansen uses a surface grinder to make the rails dead-straight on this frame. Photo: Ned Christiansen*

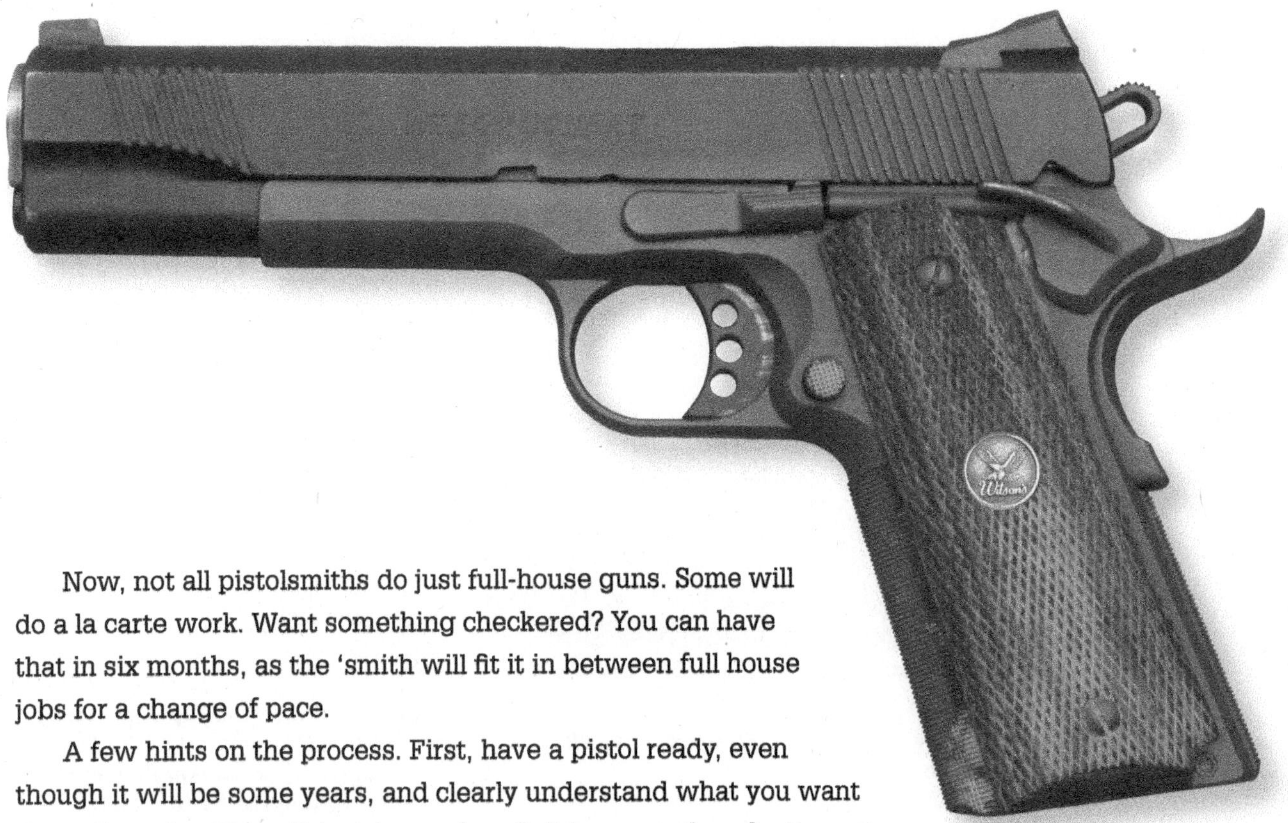

Now, not all pistolsmiths do just full-house guns. Some will do a la carte work. Want something checkered? You can have that in six months, as the 'smith will fit it in between full house jobs for a change of pace.

A few hints on the process. First, have a pistol ready, even though it will be some years, and clearly understand what you want done. Some 'smiths will insist on only a Colt because they don't want to spend their time on other brands. Some will be more liberal, but you must have an agreed-upon gun. And have a backup. When it comes time to ship yours, send it, and the 'smith will inspect it and tell you if it's suitable. If the rails are too far off, the slide is wonky in some way, or the pin holes are not parallel, he'll kick it back, saying, "Too much work," "Too much cost," or "Can't be fixed." So, send the backup.

*A custom gun is an art object and a tool. This Wilson Combat CQB has been tested, abused, run through classes, used in matches, and carried daily.*

What constitutes a "suitable" 1911? Right up front, most Colts. As I said, some will be out of spec because that's what Colt did more often than anyone would like to admit. The new ones, not so much, but there were periods when the Colts were awful.

I've told the tale before, but it is illustrative if you haven't heard it. I went to the 1981 Targetworld Nationals to compete. It was an indoor range in the winter, and we were all there to win. Due to some gaming, I won a brand new, in-the-box Colt Series 70, blued, in .45 ACP. Woo-hoo! However, that brand-new pistol could not go a magazine without malfunctioning. And it would malfunction differently each time. Looking back, I probably should thank Colt for that pistol because I had to learn gunsmithing to make my prize gun work. (I still have it, and it has run 100 percent for the 40 years since.) From gunsmithing to writing to here. If Colt QC hadn't sucked in 1981, you wouldn't be

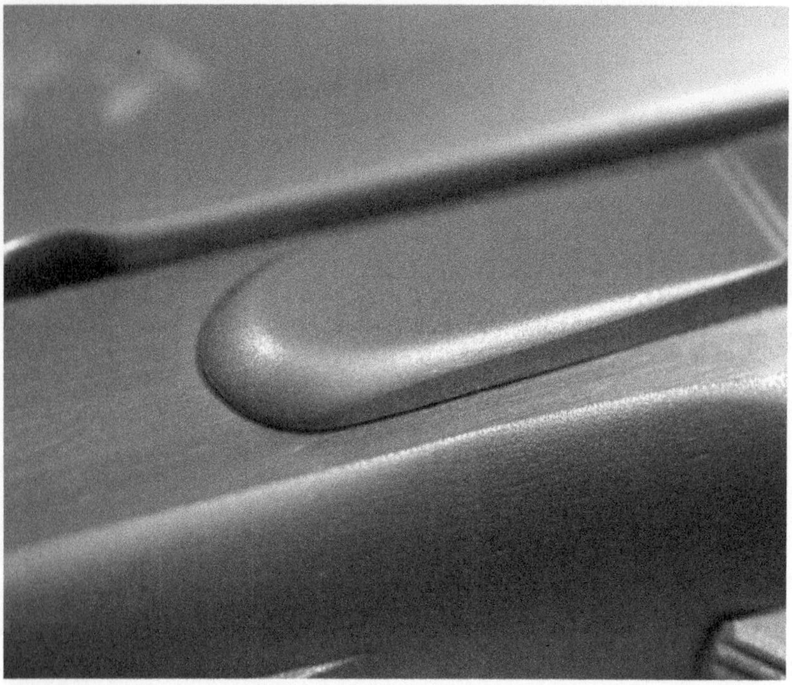

*Details like the radiused front edge of the slide stop lever so it won't abrade your hands or holster are what a top-end 'smith looks after. This one, by Ted Yost, shows how it is done.*

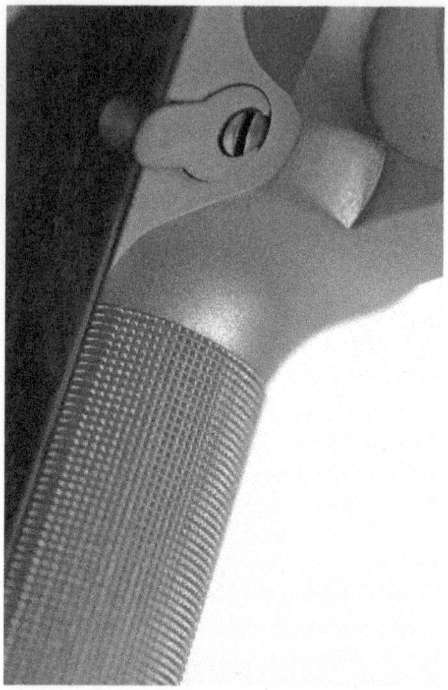

*Ted Yost "lifted" the top end of this frontstrap. He enlarged the radius so you can get your hand higher. He then checkered it perfectly to 30 lpi.*

*The best-built customs sport cosmetic touches like this "frenched" border Ted Yost put on this 1911.*

reading this. And a couple of generations of custom pistolsmiths would not have had to perform such Herculean labors to make Colts work.

The names of what would be accepted are much more numerous than not. While I can see a 'smith saying "Colts only," I can't see the majority of them turning down Dan Wesson, Springfield Armory, Les Baer (although you have to be *really* particular to say a Les Baer "needs work"), Ed Brown, the list goes on.

You won't see the top 'smiths working on the new crop of basic 1911s, the ones that work right out of the box but don't have the cachet to attract the eye. The Tisas 1911s from Turkey and the Rock Island Armory pistols work 100 percent, but you'll be hard-pressed to find a name gunsmith who will work on them. They are booked for years doing Colts whose owners found one built the year they were born. Yes, that's a thing: To find one made in the year you were born and have it built to your specs. But, there are new pistolsmiths, those making their name, who would take on such a project.

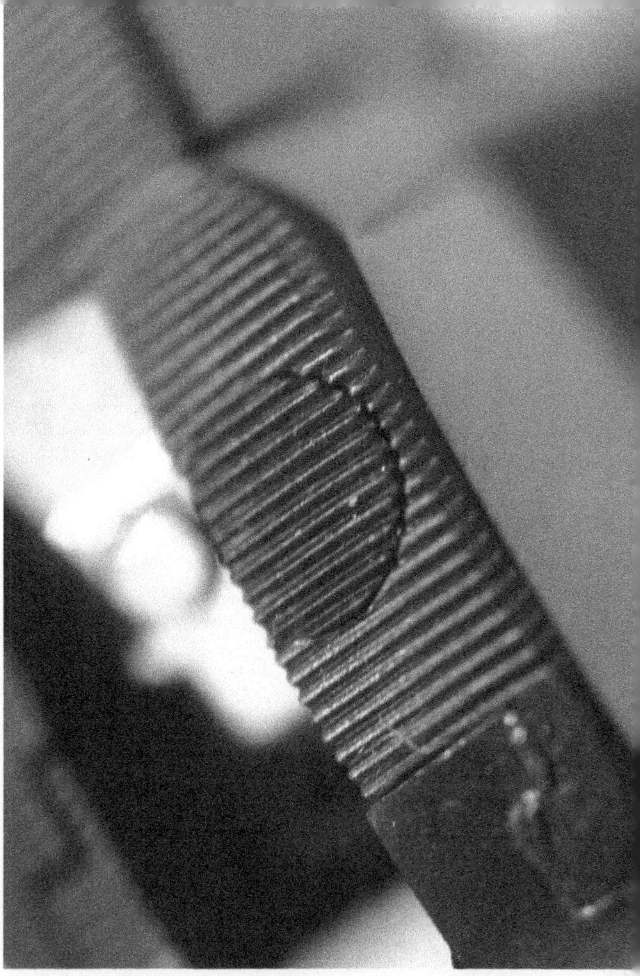

***When a custom maker fits your extractor, he will also cosmetically match it to the rear face of the slide. And some will do that to two of them, so you have a matching spare.***

One I suspect none of them would work on would be a clean USGI 1911A1 or 1911. One look at the rollmarking on the slide and the military proofs, and they'd tell you it's a collectible as-is, to leave it alone, and to send them a vanilla-plain Colt or something else.

Once you send your build gun in, be patient. Things happen, problems come up, and life goes on. If he promised it in six months, but it takes eight, that's life.

Once it comes back, look it over carefully. And compare it to the written agreement on the work to be done. If you sent it in for 30 lpi checkering, and it comes back

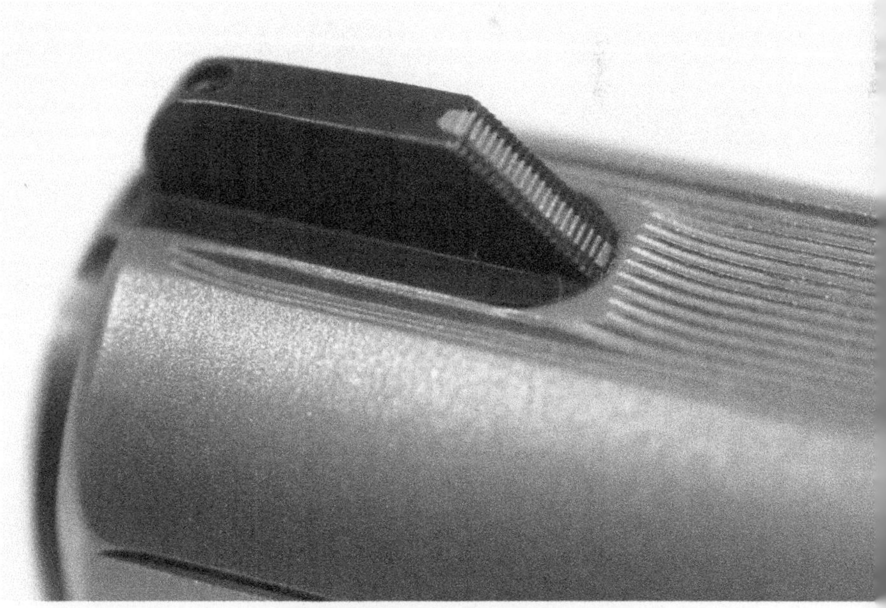

***An inlaid line of gold in the front sight is the no-radiation method of making a low-light sight. And it looks good, too.***

Stan Chen makes his frames because he wants them to be perfect. Note that the rails have been recessed in the non-bearing area to reduce friction and provide "gunk" room.

*Stan Chen's Progressive Traction Checkering (ProTrac) on the frontstrap.*

*The Chen ProTrac checkering seamlessly transitions from the mainspring housing to the frame. It also extends down onto the welded-on magazine well funnel.*

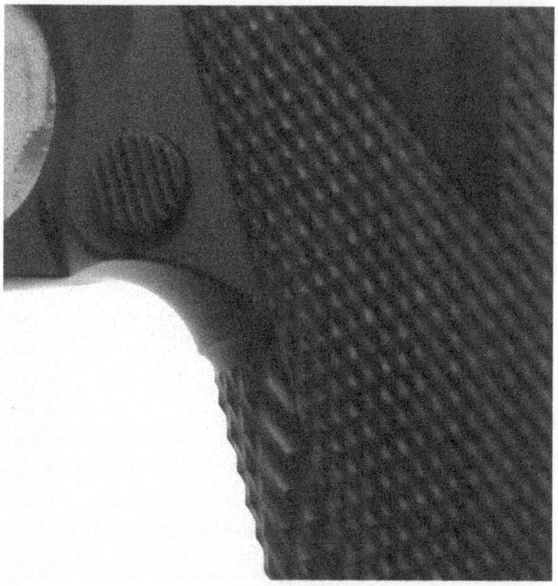

*When Stan Chen worked on this one, he lifted the frontstrap to allow the shooter's hand to grip higher on the frame.*

*A Nighthawk Thunder Ranch, which its owner uses daily to teach SpecOps people how to shoot.*

*This custom project has several high-end features, such as dehorning and a non-slip texture applied underneath the slide stop lever.*

with 20, you've got a legitimate gripe and probably a new pistol coming your way. If all the details are correct, then you're good to go. Let the 'smith know you've looked it over and are happy, and you can get on to the next project.

Finally, take it out and shoot it. It's a tool designed to be used, and what you have is an exemplar of perfection, so enjoy it. ●